D0154321

N

American River College Library
4700 College Oak Drive
Sacramento, California  95841

3 3204 01424 0583

AMERICAN RIVER COLLEGE

# Race, Ethnicity, and Gender in Early Twentieth-Century American Socialism

LABOR IN AMERICA
VOLUME I
GARLAND REFERENCE LIBRARY OF SOCIAL SCIENCE
VOLUME 880

# LABOR IN AMERICA

DAN GEORGAKAS, *Series Editor*

RACE, ETHNICITY, AND GENDER
IN EARLY TWENTIETH-CENTURY
AMERICAN SOCIALISM
edited by Sally M. Miller

WORK, RECREATION, AND CULTURE
*Essays in American Labor History*
edited by Martin Henry Blatt
and Martha K. Norkunas

# Race, Ethnicity, and Gender in Early Twentieth-Century American Socialism

Edited by
Sally M. Miller

Garland Publishing, Inc.
New York and London
1996

Copyright © 1996 by Sally M. Miller
All rights reserved

Library of Congress Cataloging-in-Publication Data

Race, ethnicity, and gender in early twentieth-century American socialism /
    edited by Sally M. Miller.
            p.    cm. — (Garland reference library of social science ; vol. 880.
Labor in America ; v. 1)
    Includes bibliographical references and index.
    ISBN 0-8153-1163-X (acid-free paper)
    1. Socialism—United States—History—20th century.    2. Women and
socialism—United States—History—20th century.    3. United States—Ethnic
relations—History—20th century.    4. United States—Race relations—History—20th century.    I. Miller, Sally M., 1937– .    II. Series: Garland reference library of social science ; v. 880.    III. Series: Garland reference library
of social science. Labor in America ; v. 1.
HX83.R33    1996
335.5'09730904—dc20                                          95–40447
                                                             CIP

*Cover illustration:* Milwaukee, Wisconsin, 1930s May Day rally. Mass meeting
of workers (strikers). Photograph WHi (X3) 47137 CF 663  courtesy of State
Historical Society of Wisconsin.

Printed on acid-free, 250-year-life paper
Manufactured in the United States of America

To the memory of my parents,
immigrant supporters of Franklin Roosevelt
and the New Deal, who never understood
my choice of research topics

# Contents

xi    Series Editor's Introduction

xv    Acknowledgments

Part I: Introduction

Chapter 1
3    In the Shadow of Giants: American Socialists
and Policies of the Second International
on Race, Ethnicity, and Gender

Part II: Race

Chapter 2
33    Red and Black: The Socialist Party
and the Negro, 1901–1920

Part III: Ethnicity and Immigration

Chapter 3
47    The Socialist Party and "Old" Immigrants:
The Milwaukee Movement to 1920

Chapter 4
73    Germans on the Mississippi:
The Socialist Party of St. Louis

PART IV: GENDER

CHAPTER 5
97  WOMEN IN THE PARTY BUREAUCRACY:
SUBSERVIENT FUNCTIONARIES

CHAPTER 6
119  A VOICE OF THE PARTY LEFT:
THE INTELLECTUAL ODYSSEY OF MARY E. MARCY

PART V: DOCUMENTS

CHAPTER 7
153  THE SOCIALIST PARTY AND THE AFRICAN-AMERICAN

PARTY DEBATES
153      "THE NEGRO RESOLUTION" OF THE
SOCIALIST PARTY
154      "THE NEGRO PROBLEM" BY A.M. SIMONS
158      "THE NEGRO PROBLEM" BY CHARLES H. VAIL
164      "MANIFESTO CONDEMNING THE LYNCHING OF
BLACK AMERICANS" OF THE INTERNATIONAL
SOCIALIST BUREAU
165      "THE NEGRO IN THE CLASS STRUGGLE"
BY EUGENE V. DEBS
168      "NEGRO LOCALS" BY ERASTE VIDRINE
172      "SOCIALISM AND THE NEGRO" BY E.F. ANDREWS

AFRICAN-AMERICAN SOCIALIST VIEWS
175      "SOCIALIST OF THE PATH" BY W.E.B. DU BOIS
176      "NEGRO AND SOCIALISM" BY W.E.B. DU BOIS
176      "HOW AND WHY I BECAME A SOCIALIST"
BY REV. GEO. W. SLATER, JR.
178      "THE NEW EMANCIPATION" BY G.W. WOODBEY
181      "SOCIALISM AND THE NEGRO PROBLEM"
BY W.E. BURGHARDT DU BOIS
184      "THE NEGRO PARTY," THE CRISIS

AN AFRICAN-AMERICAN SOCIALIST NEWSPAPER:
THE MESSENGER

185     "SOME REASONS WHY NEGROES SHOULD VOTE
        THE SOCIALIST TICKET"
187     "WHO SHALL PAY FOR THE WAR"
187     "WORKMEN'S COUNCIL"
188     "THE SOCIALIST VICTORY"
188     "SOCIALISM THE NEGROES' HOPE"
        BY W.A. DOMINGO
190     "NEGRO WORKERS: THE A.F. OF L OR I.W.W."
194     "WHY NEGROES SHOULD JOIN THE I.W.W."
195     "PSYCHOLOGY WILL WIN THIS WAR"
        BY CHANDLER OWEN
196     "WHY NEGROES SHOULD BE SOCIALISTS:
        THE NEGROES AND LABOR"
197     "WHY NEGROES SHOULD BE SOCIALISTS:
        EDUCATION AND THE NEGRO"


CHAPTER 8
199  THE SOCIALIST PARTY AND
ETHNICITY AND IMMIGRATION


PARTY DEBATES
199     "IMMIGRATION IN THE UNITED STATES"
        BY MORRIS HILLQUIT
209     "IMMIGRATION AT STUTTGART" BY LOUIS B. BOUDIN
212     "ASIATIC EXCLUSION" BY CAMERON H. KING, JR.
220     SOCIALIST PARTY, *Proceedings* OF THE 1908
        NATIONAL CONVENTION (EXCERPTS)
232     "A LETTER FROM DEBS ON IMMIGRATION"
        BY EUGENE V. DEBS
234     SOCIALIST PARTY, *Proceedings* OF THE 1912
        NATIONAL CONVENTION, APPENDIX J
239     "OUR ASIATIC FELLOWS" BY BRUCE ROGERS


CHAPTER 9
241  THE SOCIALIST PARTY AND GENDER ISSUES


WRITINGS ON WOMEN AND SOCIETY
241     "100 YEARS AGO" BY MARY E. MARCY

248 "True Homes Under Socialism" by May Walden
249 "The Law and the White Slaver" [excerpt]
      by Kate Richards O'Hare

      PARTY DEBATES
253 "The National Convention and the Woman's
      Movement" by Jessie Molle
255 Proceedings [excerpts] of the 1908 Socialist
      Party Convention, "The Woman Suffrage
      Question"
258 "Aims and Purposes of Women [SIC] Committee"
      by May Wood Simons
259 "Do You Help Or Do You Hinder?"
      by Anna A. Maley
260 "Separate Organizations"
      by Josephine Conger-Kaneko
262 "Woman and Socialism" by Luella R. Krehbiel
264 "Where Do We Stand on the
      Woman Question?"
      by Theresa Malkiel
267 "The Socialist Movement And Woman Suf-
      frage"
      by Ida Crouch Hazlett
269 "Enfranchisement of Womanhood,"
      by Eugene V. Debs
271 "Report of the Woman's Department,"
      Appendix I, Proceedings of the 1912 National
      Convention of the Socialist Party
282 "Socialism and the Feminist Movement"
      by Mary White Ovington

      CHAPTER 10
287 Bibliographic Essay: Further Readings
297 Name Index

# Series Editor's Introduction

With this volume, Garland Publishing inaugurates a new labor history series that will reflect the massive changes that have occurred in the field during the past three decades. Pioneering labor historians generally equated labor history with the history of trade unions. Within that perspective, there was a decided tendency to focus on the careers of individual labor leaders to determine the movement's spirit and rationale. This approach inevitably led to a concentration on English-speaking males of European ancestry.

Contemporary labor historians, while highly appreciative of the groundwork laid down by their predecessors, have found that their paradigms did not accurately define the full scope of the labor movement and did not satisfactorily account for either its successes or failures. The major break with those paradigms has been to look beyond trade unions to the broader social and political contexts in which they were formed. Understanding the everyday life of workers has proven vital to determining what was happening within trade unions and society at large. This work has revealed previously hidden or undervalued labor histories.

Among the social forces now more fully understood is the impact of foreign-born workers as seen through their ethnic organizations and native language media rather than as reflected through English-language sources. This research has proved especially fruitful regarding groups of relatively small numbers usually passed over as "and other immigrant workers." How such populations functioned in locales where they happened to make up a large percentage of the work force and how they interacted with larger ethnic groups and English-speaking workers have been essential in understanding the broad dynamics of the American labor movement. The role of numerically larger immigrant groups such as Germans and Italians and of ethnic groups such as Jews and Finns that played a central role in specific labor organizations has also been enhanced as more non-English language press and organizational documents have been analyzed.

More publicized areas of new research have involved women and ethnic groups defined as racial minorities. This interest was catalyzed by the civil rights and feminist movements of the 1960s, and many researchers have done their work under the aegis of women's studies or black studies rather than labor studies. Whatever the formal academic discipline, this new work has demonstrated that from at least the time of the antislavery crusade and the women's suffrage movement, formal links and interactions with the labor movement were far more substantial than previously projected.

One of the immediate consequences of the growth of black studies has been a parallel development in the study of Spanish-speaking minorities such as Mexicans and Puerto Ricans. More recently, similar attention has begun to be directed to Filipino, Chinese, Indian, Korean, Japanese, and other Asian immigrant workers. All these groups have proven to have internal political structures and ideological divisions similar to those of the more fully studied European immigrants. And like their European counterparts, the Spanish-speaking and Asian immigrants have also always maintained a transnational link to the homeland with leaders and ideas flowing in two directions.

Yet another large area that is being reevaluated is the role of movements based on radical ideology. Treatment of specific individuals and groups, often amounting to little more than their outright dismissal as irrelevant or subversive, has usually reflected the personal ideological bias of the historian rather than workplace realities. The passage of time has begun to soften some of this passion. American radicals associated with the First International have been written of with more objectivity; and increasingly, the anarcho-syndicalist Industrial Workers of the World is seen as the key link between the industrial unions of the nineteenth century and the Congress of Industrial Organizations. Socialists have been allowed their place in American labor history, and with the fall of the Soviet Union, Communists may finally be judged by other than the devil/angel alternative prevailing in most of the existing literature. Exorcising the Communist demon would also make it easier to appraise other radical movements in their own right.

Greatly abetting the development of this expanded concept of labor history has been the growing body of oral histories, memoirs, and autobiographies of labor veterans, particularly those active from the turn of the century to the great labor upsurge of the late 1930s. Labor archives located in major academic institutions have also been successful in gathering impressive collections of personal papers, organizational records, ephemeral literature, and other primary materials. Facsimile editions and microfilms of the labor press have further built the academic arsenal. This reservoir of data has made it possible to examine how immigrants, women, racial minorities, and radicals created organizations that were parallel to, fused with, or hostile to mainstream labor organizations.

Sally Miller's *Race, Ethnicity, and Gender in Early Twentieth-Century American Socialism* embraces many of the themes that will characterize the series. She discusses in artful detail and offers substantial documentation on how women, racially defined groups, and language minorities interacted with the Socialist Party at a time when the Socialist Party was a central force in American labor. Future volumes will deal with other eras and other movements, some closer to the mainstream, some further. Rather than having an organization as a point of reference, they may have a regional, chronological, or occupational focus. In all instances, our aim is to see labor history in its full dimensions and to contribute to the multifaceted scholarly effort now engaged in defining labor's role in the history of the United States.

Dan Georgakas

# Acknowledgments

It is always a pleasure when reaching the end of the substantive work on a book to remember those who assisted the author along the way to its completion. I am very grateful to the individuals and institutions named below, all of whom were generous with their time and resources. While research and writing by their nature are isolated activities, those who pursue such work see their projects come to fruition only thanks to the support of others.

My greatest debt is to the Newberry Library in Chicago for a Fellowship which allowed me a term in residence to enjoy the camaraderie and wonderful research facilities beloved to all scholars who have the opportunity to visit the Newberry. I am pleased to acknowledge the help of the staffs of a number of other institutions, which include the Missouri Historical Society, the University of Missouri-St. Louis, the University of Missouri-Columbia, and the International Institute of Social History. For help in locating materials, I wish to thank a number of rare book dealers, especially my friend, John Durham, of Bolerium Books in San Francisco; Don Stewart of MacLeod's Books in Vancouver, British Columbia, Canada; and Franklin Rosemont of Charles H. Kerr Publishing Company, Chicago. For encouragement and suggestions related to the substantive work itself, I am grateful to Dr. James R. Grossman of the Newberry Library; Dr. Laura Edwards of the University of South Florida; Dr. Allen M. Ruff of Madison, Wisconsin; Dr. Arturo Giraldez and Dr. George P. Blum of the University of the Pacific; Dr. Sally Roesch Wagner of Aberdeen, South Dakota; Dr. Gary M. Fink of Georgia State University; and to Professor Emeritus Robert Reinders of the University of Nottingham; and, again, Franklin Rosemont, with whom I had a number of helpful conversations about Kerr and Company. I am happy to acknowledge the hospitality of Leona Zelener of Chicago during my stay there.

I wish to thank Kathelen Johnson of Stockton, California, for help with the translations of a few of the documents. I am also grateful to Coralee Pauls of St. Louis for assisting me with research at archives in that city, which I did not have time to complete. For indispensable assistance in the area of word processing skills, I am happy to acknowledge Tamarin Janssen, a former student, and Pamela Altree and Kathleen Cooper of the support staff of my department at the University of the Pacific. The university's support over the years has been instrumental in my publications. I am especially grateful to Dean Robert R. Benedetti, who enabled me to obtain a 3M Faculty Development Grant. I am also indebted to the university for a semester-long leave during which some of the research was conducted. It is also a pleasure to acknowledge once again the University of the Pacific's Faculty Research Committee for awarding me a small grant for incidental expenses, and the staff of the Interlibrary Loan Department of the University's Libraries for always being so resourceful and tenacious in seeking needed materials.

I am happy to thank three publishers for generously permitting me to reprint three of my articles: the Association for the Study of Afro-American Life and History and its *Journal of Negro History* for "The Socialist Party and the Negro, 1901–1920," which was published in volume 56 (July 1971): 220–29; the University of Notre Dame Press for "Casting a Wide Net: The Milwaukee Movement to 1920," which appeared in Donald T. Critchlow, ed., *Socialism in the Heartland*, published in 1986; and the Greenwood Publishing Group, Inc., for the article "Women in the Party Bureaucracy: Subservient Functionaries," which appeared in its imprint, Sally M. Miller, editor, *Flawed Liberation: Socialism and Feminism,* published in 1981. The use of the dated word "negro" and the occasional non-gender neutral wording are evidence of the fact that the three articles were written earlier.

Finally, this volume would never have been developed but for the role of two individuals. Kennie Lyman, a former editor at Garland Publishing, engaged me in a lively conversation at a convention of the Organization of American Historians in 1991, which led to my interest in working with Garland. A year later, in an unrelated event, Dan Georgakas, the editor of this series, invited me to develop a volume for Garland. I am grateful to the two of them as I have very much enjoyed this work. I hope that the book fills one of the proverbial gaps in the literature, and I trust that any problems or errors in it are viewed as my responsibility alone.

# PART I
## INTRODUCTION

# 1 IN THE SHADOW OF GIANTS

## AMERICAN SOCIALISTS AND POLICIES

## OF THE SECOND INTERNATIONAL

## ON RACE, ETHNICITY, AND GENDER

The organized social democratic movement that flourished on the eve of World War One shaped socialist parties throughout the world. The Second International through its organizational structure—its Congresses held in various European capital cities between its inception in 1889 and 1912, and its executive body headquartered in Brussels—passed resolutions and established principles that individual parties were expected to treat as guidelines. By the early twentieth century the Second International epitomized revisionist Marxism while nevertheless enunciating orthodox Marxist positions, and its Congresses were often battlegrounds between the two positions. Over the years debates on a variety of subjects dominated every Congress. In 1900, in Paris, a Congress debated the question of socialist participation in bourgeois governments; this debate resulted in a policy that allowed for membership in non-socialist cabinets as a temporary tactic but condemned formal alliances. Four years later, in Amsterdam, the next Congress formally rejected revisionism, following the path of the German Social Democratic Party (SPD), the major force in international Congresses. The SPD in 1903 had condemned any emphasis on immediate demands and social reforms—despite its own policies—for their possible undermining of the increasing social tensions inherent to the capitalist system and, therefore, slowing its demise. At Stuttgart in 1907 a major debate occurred on the subject of colonialism, which was roundly denounced despite some delegates' concerns in regard to their own nations' policies. The issues that dominated the final Congresses of the Second International, at Copenhagen in 1910 and Basle in 1912, were militarism and war. Some of the delegates, led by Jean Jaurès of the French Socialists, pledged to oppose war under all circumstances and by all means, including even the general strike, while others argued that war might become the means to bring down capitalism and initiate a social transformation.[1]

Whatever policies delegates favored, they sought to place their positions within the context of the class struggle. All matters were measured against the so-called Social Question, that is, the need to transform the economic system from capitalism to collectivism. That change would solve all existing inequities including those suffered by minorities (the so-called Negro Question in the United States) and by women (the Woman Question). Topics that were seen as irrelevant to the class struggle were not deemed worthy of significant attention, and a great many matters were judged to be transitory problems that would be resolved automatically when the cooperative commonwealth replaced the capitalist order. Accordingly, issues of race, ethnicity and immigration, and gender were not central concerns of the international socialist movement. Where individual parties, because of their particular national or geographic contexts, were obliged to deal with these or indeed any other issues that might be considered of little importance by the Second International, they found it useful to establish policies that were in accord with the general direction of the International, did not appear to violate its spirit of international solidarity, and were in tandem with the central goal of promoting the achievement of socialism.

The Socialist Party of America, which represented the great majority of American socialists, was an enthusiastic if relatively minor player in the international socialist arena. Organized in 1901 and rapidly developing a dynamic if minor movement across the United States, it participated in virtually all of the Congresses of the Second International and even occasionally sent its representatives to meetings of the executive body, the International Socialist Bureau. The American party, handicapped by the nation's two-party system set in a non-parliamentary structure and lacking a close connection to the trade union movement, admired the stronger European parties, especially the German and even the disunited and fragmented French and British. Operating in the shadow of those parties that enjoyed greater membership in proportion to population and more success at the polls, the Americans seemed to revere many of the leading figures of international socialism. To work in proximity to August Bebel, Victor Adler, Rosa Luxemburg, Keir Hardie, and others might endow them with the stature that their modest success as a political party denied them. In specific matters, the party's participation in the workings of the International might help it in its competition for members and support with the Socialist Labor Party and the Industrial Workers of the World, and might even convince the American Federation of Labor of the party's significance because of its ties to organized labor internationally. In less concrete terms, the American socialists derived from their participation in the Second International a sense of involvement with a critical mass of political activists who were believed to be achieving a historic mission on the world stage. That connection could not help but bolster the Americans in the face of their relatively minor achievements.[2]

Issues the Congresses focused on were not always of crucial importance to American socialists, nor were issues that mattered to the Americans necessarily significant to their international comrades. As an example of the former, in the major debates cited above, such as on policy toward participation in non-socialist governments or on calling for a general strike to preclude military conscription and national war, the issues were so far removed from the political world in which the American socialists functioned that their positions in the debates could be argued to be entirely theoretical. Conversely, matters which Americans sought unsuccessfully to bring before the International included issues such as anarchosyndicalism, which the Europeans no longer faced.[3]

The Socialist Party as a political movement based in the United States confronted issues of race, ethnicity and immigration, as well as gender, matters which were often either of limited interest to their comrades overseas or were perceived in a different context. The party was sometimes placed in the difficult position of applying principles to matters or situations which were clearly distinct from those e.:perienced by the leading European parties. The Americans, thus, were faced with various choices—following, ignoring, or resisting the leadership of the International.[4]

## RACE

The Congresses of the Second International did not deal directly with issues of race, other than implicitly when delegates discussed colonialism. As a result the International's guidance on this matter was minimal. The Americans, however, were forced by circumstances to confront the variable of race owing to the demographics of the United States and to the anomalous position in which African Americans were placed within society. The party took the view that Blacks as a working-class population were participants in the class struggle and, therefore, were welcome to join the party, as were all workers. Thus at its founding convention in 1901 the delegates declared that capitalism "seeks to preserve the peculiar condition [of Blacks] . . . and to foster and increase color prejudice and race hatred between the white worker and the black . . . " in order to more easily exploit all workers. The party extended its fellowship as well as its sympathy to African Americans, and assured them that workers everywhere suffered from the very same treatment that capitalism imposed. The resolution was fully in accord with the most basic tenets of international socialism, inviting all workers of the world to join together in a common struggle against their capitalist foes. (See Documents, pp. 153–54.) An article by Eugene V. Debs commented that no Negro Question existed outside working class issues. He wrote: "The Class Struggle is colorless. As Marx said, 'Workingmen of all countries unite.'" This position, in and of itself, placed the Socialist Party in a distinctive position in the United States, where the overwhelming majority of social and political institutions at the time excluded black membership. It must be noted, however, that it was one of the three Black delegates who had introduced the resolution welcoming African-American members. Had no African Americans been present, it is entirely plausible that no mention of black Americans would have been made.[5]

The membership of the Socialist Party of America was not entirely comfortable with this open-ended welcome. A little over one year later the Louisiana State Party was organized, and it immediately set about instituting a system of segregation, for which the National Committee denied its charter until it rewrote its platform. In fact, southern members argued back and forth over the place, if any, of African Americans in the movement. They debated the legitimacy of social segregation, with some members arguing that the party could serve as a force to defuse racism. When the party surveyed its members on the question of segregated locals ten years later, in 1913, the National Office found that African Americans in the northern states enjoyed membership in mixed locals. In the ten southern states that responded, and in the District of Columbia, it was clear that the southern socialists were split on the issue of opening their locals to Blacks. In at least three states of the Deep South—Florida, Georgia, and Mississippi—a Black was not enrolled in a "white" local. Others, including Louisiana and Arkansas, reported that mixed locals were allowed, but some also noted that they had no black members. Elsewhere, in the North and the West, Blacks were sometimes nominated for office. For example, in Los Angeles in 1911 an African American was nominated for City Council. But meanwhile some southern socialists theorized that, assuming unequal evolutionary progress by the different races, locals ought to be able to decide on establishing at least sub-locals for black members, a practice which some thought might be applied to Caucasian subgroups too, so that Italians, Jews, and others might have their separate organizations within the party.[6]

However, George W. Woodbey, an African-American Baptist pastor in California, served on the State Executive Committee and was nominated for party vice president in 1908 (receiving, however, only one vote at the convention); he was a general organizer for the party. The National Executive Committee in 1910, at the suggestion of Lena Morrow Lewis, one of the party's most seasoned organizers, discussed specifically routing at least one black organizer to African-American populations in states where black males were still enfranchised. The next year the Committee received a resolution from New York to investigate the issue of locals excluding Blacks, which no doubt inspired the survey of the party on its practices by the National Office. In 1912 the NEC invited W.E.B. Du Bois to prepare a leaflet on the situation of Blacks for purposes of outreach, although it is not clear whether or not he responded. George W. Slater, Jr., another socialist black pastor, wrote a column for the *Chicago Daily Socialist*. (See Documents, 176–78.) In 1913 he requested that the party establish a permanent office with responsibility to represent black socialists, as it had in previous years established machinery for foreign-speaking socialists and for women. While the NEC ended up tabling his request, at least one member was troubled by what was clearly inattention to black Americans. Kate Richards O'Hare suggested that the party demonstrate "at least . . . some willingness to co-operate in the propaganda among the colored people, or work out a plan . . . . It is a problem we have to meet."[7]

O'Hare's remarks were quite suggestive of the ambivalence of the Socialist Party toward black Americans. O'Hare herself believed Blacks to be less evolved than Caucasians, and she warned against social integration, even drawing on popular culture to imply that black men were potential rapists. But simultaneously she favored political and civil rights for African Americans. Her close comrade Gene Debs, who acknowledged that socialists were infected by American racism, continued to speak for full black equality and rights, and refused to appear before segregated audiences when he toured the South or Southwest. But he hoped that the "Negro Resolution" would be repealed because separate appeals to specific groups of workers were inappropriate. (See Documents, pp. 165–68.) He also regretted that so many trotted out the issue of social equality, which he called a "mask" for the real issue of economic freedom, but he commented that the party position did not promise social equality. Oscar Ameringer, a Bavarian-born organizer and journalist, led efforts by some of his fellow socialists to defeat the introduction of segregation in Oklahoma and campaigned against the grandfather clause. But other German immigrant party leaders and intellectuals held disparate positions from Ameringer's, as seen when Victor Berger and Ernest Untermann in convention debates denounced African Americans in virulent and racist terms. Untermann even admonished his fellow delegates that not only should party locals in the South be segregated but westerners, too, ought to be careful to avoid inviting Asians into their locals. Yet still other socialists were among the handful of Caucasians and African Americans who joined together in 1909 to found the National Association for the Advancement of Colored People.[8]

The International directed only minimum attention to the plight of African Americans. In 1903 it requested information from the Socialist Party on working conditions in the South. More pointedly, the International Socialist Bureau at the behest of its French and Argentine sections took up and condemned the practice of lynching of Blacks, an event all too common then in the United States. The ISB invited worldwide demonstrations against that barbaric phenomenon. (See Documents, pp. 164–65.) George Herron, a former minister and the representative to the Socialist Bureau from the Socialist Party, was concerned, however, that the Bureau's accompanying statement of solidarity with all peoples of color was too "extreme," and he advised his American comrades that he "declined personal responsibilities" for the scope of the resolution in his report to the party (see note 9). The executive committee of the party advised the Bureau that lynchers as well as "lynchable[s]" and kleptomaniacs and other "offensive . . . human degenerates" would not be "produced" in a socialist system, as quoted by Ira Kipnis. These minimal indicators of any interest in and support of African-American workers and their particular plight were certainly insufficient to prod the Socialist Party to champion their cause; the disclaimer by Herron, plus the party executive committee's negative comment, further diluted any impact the International's initiative might have had. So the party never interested itself in African Americans beyond its original absentminded resolution, as has been noted by more than one author.[9]

As for African Americans themselves, in the prewar period there may have been two or three hundred in the Socialist Party sprinkled among the general membership or housed in two or three segregated locals. The most prominent Black in the Socialist Party was W.E.B. Du Bois, who in 1912 decided to cast his ballot for Woodrow Wilson in the general election, a decision he soon regretted as the new president moved immediately to intensify segregation throughout the federal bureaucracy. But Du Bois also had become quite skeptical of the Socialist Party and its apparent indifference toward African Americans. He remarked poignantly that while the socialists seemed so indifferent, at least the party had not rescinded its 1901 resolution on Blacks.

By the next presidential election, while pronouncing a vote for the socialist candidate, Allen Benson, as thrown away, Du Bois nevertheless described the party as "excellent." But his enthusiasm remained less than that of comrades such as A. Philip Randolph, Owen Chandler, and W.A. Domingo, who believed that the socialist movement in the United States and throughout the world was the central force that would raise the status of black people. The latter reminded his readers in *The Messenger* that socialists were "characterized by the broadness of their vision towards all oppressed humanity." He called their attention to the fact that socialist leaders had protested atrocities in the Congo, British rule in Egypt, and segregation in the American South. (See Documents, pp. 188–90.) When during World War One more African Americans were attracted to the Socialist Party, they supported it perhaps over wartime issues and questions of colonialism that had relatively little to do with the party itself.[10]

That the Socialist Party never seriously implemented its outreach to African Americans is not surprising. It never really embraced its original resolution, and over the years its policymakers refrained from initiating any real programs to convert black Americans to socialism or to alleviate the problems that were peculiar to their situation. Any suggestions aimed at reaching out to African Americans were not implemented. The party might have been propelled to action only if the Second International had emphasized it. Other than a condemnation of the atrocity of lynching, which the Americans also condemned (even if some were careful not to do so expansively), the Second International was too far removed from the issue and too preoccupied with its own priorities to monitor the policies of the American section on a matter it perceived to be minor. So the socialists continued on their ambivalent path toward African Americans. By the time the Socialist Party had a larger black presence during the war era, the Second International had collapsed. African Americans, particularly in Harlem, began to mark their ballots for socialists, 25 percent casting such votes in an election in 1917. The Socialist Party, possibly impressed that numbers of African Americans were evidently susceptible to the party's propaganda, even planned to send organizers into their neighborhoods. Both the Comintern, which arose after the war, and its American section, the Communist Party of America, took a much more pronounced interest in African Americans, although for them, too, blacks were seen purely in their identity as workers.[11]

## ETHNICITY

While clearly the Second International did not assign much of its attention to the American issue of race, it did take seriously the matter of ethnic divisions within nation-states and, following from that, within the international socialist movement itself. Starting as early as 1900 the problem of representation in the International of specific groups from heterogenous nations loomed as a significant matter. Whether the socialists in question represented a specific nationality bloc within a nation—Italians in Argentina or Poles in the United States—or a manifestly unique group based on ideological views, the International could not sidestep taking a stand on the issue of separate representation. As Victor Adler told the International Congress meeting in Paris in 1900, "We in Austria have a little International ourselves . . . " and had found it necessary to establish national sections within their party (which, however, did not solve the exacerbating problem of one ethnic group dominating the whole).[12]

The American Secretary to the Bureau in 1908, Morris Hillquit, opposed the International's intervention to try to sort out divisions among socialist groups within a section of the International. His predecessor, George Herron, in 1903 had had to deal with an ultimately unsuccessful request of the Italian Socialist Federation of the United States for direct affiliation with the International. Hillquit argued that a danger existed of unending divisions, particularly if the International initiated a policy of representation for not only nationality groups but even ideological divisions within one section. Specifically, Hillquit rejected the suggestion of representation for Zionist groups, whether in the Russian Pale or New York City. While Hillquit's key goal was no doubt that of limiting or even eliminating the role of the Socialist Party's chief rival in the United States, the Socialist Labor Party in the International, nevertheless he was sufficiently dismayed by the issue of sectional fragmentation that he opposed further steps in the direction of ethnic recognition.[13]

In 1910 the eighth Congress of the International, meeting in Copenhagen, faced the same issue of diviseveness in a different guise. Czech socialists favored the expansion of the principle of nationality representation in ethnic socialist parties within a nation to labor unions. The Americans opposed this move, as did the majority of the delegations present, wishing to minimize divisions if possible. That very year, however, the Socialist Party of America took a different approach. The party had failed throughout its history to come to grips with the phenomenon of non-English speaking socialists who wished to have full representation in the party and also the ability to interact in their own languages. It had not put much more energy into organizing these groups than it had into reaching out to African Americans. The reasons for this myopia were not only the view that all workers could be reached by the same propaganda, but also the fact that the leadership of the Socialist Party was dominated in the pre-war years by English-speaking socialists of immigrant background and by native-born Americans who were not sympathetic toward Eastern Europeans then arriving in the United States by the millions.

Finally beginning to face the issue of the changing composition of the American work force, party delegates agonized during a National Congress in 1910 as to the appropriate means of representation for non-English speaking members. The National Secretary, J. Mahlon Barnes, argued for the need at least to establish a proper relationship between such immigrants who were self-identified socialists and the party. The delegates decided that it was necessary to acquiesce to the requests for foreign-language federation affiliation with the party. By World War One, seven federations—Finnish, Italian, Lettish, South Slavic, Scandinavian, Hungarian, and Bohemian—were officially associated with it. However, some non-English speakers chose not to join these federations and instead remained members of foreign-speaking locals of the party; thus only a minority of the non-English speaking were somewhat integrated into the Socialist Party. The federations themselves operated autonomously, and the National Executive Committee of the Socialist Party sent fraternal delegates to their conventions as they might to a totally separate organization—for example, sending party organizer George Gobel to the Lithuanian Socialist Federation meeting in Philadelphia in 1913. Hillquit himself ended up praising the soundness of the policy of allowing the foreign-language federations autonomous status. He alluded to the fact that non-English speaking socialists in the United States worked under different conditions than most party members, and that they needed full freedom to deal with what he referred to as not only different conditions but different psyches. This surprising statement from him in contradiction to his earlier position reflected the party's having been influenced by the International's recognition of the need for ethnic sections.[14]

Of the major debates which occurred in the Congresses of the International, the one that had the greatest ramifications for its American section was on the subject of immigration. While international socialism in accord with its principle of worker solidarity could not easily favor barriers preventing workers from immigrating from one country to another, nevertheless the differing positions of nations which were either sending countries or host countries, as well as racist attitudes toward various racial and ethnic groups, tended to undermine the all-embracing ideological framework. From the perspective of the Americans, immigration was a more vital issue than it was to all other sections of the International—minimizing, as they did, the fact that immigration to a number of countries in the southern hemisphere was impacting their population composition also. Moreover, as pointed out by the leading authority on the Second International, Georges Haupt, the Socialist Party of America, unlike many other non-European Socialist parties, had not been organized by those groups dominating the immigration rolls at the turn of the century. As already suggested, long-settled individuals of German or Russian background, and Anglo-Saxons, made up the bulk of the American party and its leadership, and such groups did not necessarily confront the question of immigration without biases.[15]

The International Congress of 1907 at Stuttgart was the scene of a full-scale debate on immigration, but even earlier a number of efforts had been made to deal with that topic. At the previous Congress in 1904 at Amsterdam, the delegation from Argentina had moved that emigration and immigration be scheduled as a joint agenda item. Argentina proposed that the International condemn propaganda encouraging immigration as contrary to the interests of workers of receiving countries, and that it oppose legislation that allowed naturalized citizens to reclaim their original citizenship. One of its delegates, A.S. Lorenzo, also emphasized that "young countries" were opposed to all artificial immigration and that European nations should control agencies that promoted it. A year earlier an Interparliamentary Commission of socialists serving in their national legislatures had been set up; it included representatives from England, Belgium, France, Holland, Sweden, Germany, and Austria—all sending countries—who met and discussed the issue of foreign workers. Notably absent were any representatives from countries such as the United States who were receiving nations.[16]

At Stuttgart, Morris Hillquit and Louis Boudin of the Socialist Party, as well as Frank Bohn of the Socialist Labor Party, served on the committee charged with recommending a policy on immigration to the Congress, with Hillquit serving as vice-president of the commission. Two competing resolutions were initially debated; one, sponsored by the majority on the commission, favored unrestricted immigration while another, offered by Dutch and Australian representatives as well as Hillquit, stressed the opposition of organized labor in their various countries to the "importation" of "backward" peoples. In the course of the debate, both resolutions were withdrawn as delegates tried to forge a policy that a majority could support. Hillquit argued that there were distinct types of immigration. A contemporary natural flow included Italians, Belgians, and others who were capable of being educated to the class struggle, he said. Conversely, the artificial type was engineered by capitalists in order to import additional workers, and he cited Chinese, Japanese, and other unnamed Asians as representative of the latter strain. While he insisted that he harbored no prejudices, he maintained that such workers were not organizable and might be excluded. Denying that his remarks violated the fraternal principles of socialism, he introduced a resolution on behalf of the Socialist Party of America which, he stated, was based on a revolutionary position assuring the unfettered development of the workers' movement. The resolution opposed induced immigration and proposed combating the importation of peoples who would destroy workers' organizations, lower standards of living, and retard the triumph of socialism. (See Documents, pp. 199–209, 209–12.) An amendment by Algernon Lee, a Hillquit comrade in New York, agreed with the resolution, and went on to put a positive patina on Hillquit's position by declaring that socialists were obligated to protect all workers' rights, promote their organization into unions and their assimilation into societies, and encourage good will between alien and native-born workers. A Belgian delegate, in response, took exception to the Hillquit-Lee measures, and commented that any resolution which dared to decide who was a bonafide immigrant was inappropriate. Instead, he argued that socialists serving in their respective parliaments must insure equitable social legislation for immigrant workers and that unions must give equal rights to incoming workers.[17]

The Hillquit-Lee position was defeated soundly, receiving support only from delegates of two of the other twenty-two nations represented, Australia and South Africa. The Congress eventually passed a resolution condemning the exclusion by a government of any people. For the protection of all workers, it recommended opposition to contract labor, promotion of protective legislation, and that unions be open to workers of all nationalities, including automatic admission of those who were members of unions in their home countries.[18]

Following the conclusion of the Congress, debate over a party position on immigration in the face of the International's resolution raged within the Socialist Party of America at its next three national meetings, held between 1908 and 1912, and in the pages of socialist newspapers. Apologists for the majority of the Socialist Party delegation to Stuttgart argued that while the movement must not seek the exclusion of groups, it must be aware of the adamant views of organized labor and must discourage artificially induced immigration while simultaneously promoting the organization of immigrant workers residing in the United States. Their critics maintained that the party must abandon forever "the principle of dividing immigrants along racial lines into "organizable" and "unorganizable." Nor could the party ever consider favoring the exclusion of those assigned the latter label, irrespective of the misguided position of organized labor. Such an effort represented an unsocialistic "snare and [a] delusion." (See Documents, pp. 209–12, 220–32.) [19]

Exemplifying the party split on the issue, an article entitled "Asiatic Exclusion" by a rank-and-file party member from the West Coast, Cameron H. King, Jr., charged that the position of the International amounted to an open shop resolution. (See Documents, pp. 212–20.) The writer insisted that solidarity with the American labor movement required that the party cast aside idealisim and, instead, favor a policy of Japanese exclusion. But another rank and filer, Bruce Rogers, spoke of "Our Asiatic Fellows" and argued that such individuals were "no peril to white labor." (See Documents, pp. 239–40.) Although full of stereotypes, the latter article asked "Has the national soil become so sacred to the Socialists" that they join with the capitalist state against Asian workers? Finally Gene Debs weighed in with his pen. (See Documents, pp. 232–33.) Never participating in party conventions in order to avoid distasteful combat with his own comrades, Debs wrote that exclusionary talk had no place in socialist debates, and he dismissed any tactic which required "the exclusion of the oppressed and suffering slaves . . ." He announced that those trying to enter the United States had as much right to do so as those arguing against them. He maintained:

> In this attitude there is nothing of maudlin sentimentality, but simply a rigid adherence to the fundamental principles of the International proletarian movement. If Socialism, international, revolutionary Socialism, does not stand staunchly, unflinchingly, and uncompromisingly for the working class and for the exploited and oppressed masses of all lands, then it stands for none . . .[20]

Despite those views expressed by Debs, at various national gatherings delegates such as Max S. Hayes of the Cleveland Central Labor Council, known for his strong advocacy of the policy of boring from within the American Federation of Labor, displayed bald racism, denouncing "unrestricted Coolie immigration." Victor Berger, a founder of the party and perhaps the most influential force in its reformist wing, stated: "We are the party of the working men, only we don't want to stand for the things that will help them. . . . If we admit the Chinese, the Japanese and the Korean." But others such as Ester Nieminen of Minnesota argued that Chinese came to the United States simply to seek work, and "we good, honest Americans, and even some Socialists, want to starve them. And then we say all men are equal, of whatever color. Soon we will be saying all men are equal but Chinamen." She and her fellow Finnish Minnesotan, Esther Laukki, argued that the barring of one race of workers could lead to the exclusion of others in turn. Reverend Woodbey announced that:

> There are no foreigners, and cannot be unless some person came down from Mars, Jupiter, or some place. I stand on the declaration of Tho-

mas Paine when he said, "The world is my country." It would be a curious state of affairs for immigrants or the descendants of immigrants from Europe themselves to get control of affairs in this country, and then say to the Oriental immigrants that they should not come here. So far as making this a mere matter of race, I disagree decidedly with the committee. . . . [21]

At the 1908 convention no consensus could be reached on an immigration policy other than that Stuttgart was not specifically binding on the American party. (See Documents, pp. 220–32.) A committee was appointed to study the issue and to draft a resolution. In shaping its charge to the committee, the delegates defeated a measure to instruct it to explicitly condemn Asian immigrants. The racism voiced in the debates was sufficiently evident that the Secretary of the International Socialist Bureau in Brussels directed a letter to Hillquit to remind the Socialist Party of the International's position. Two years later at the next national gathering, the committee, which included the racist exclusionists Berger and Ernest Untermann (both immigrants from Central Europe), recommended that Asians be barred from the United States. They were to be prohibited entrance not as races but because their backgrounds in undeveloped nations meant that they were psychologically and economically backward and, thus, obstacles to the progress of the working class. The delegates wrangled over the resolution and ultimately rejected the majority report. Instead they endorsed a resolution pressed forward by the indefatigable Hillquit, which again referred to the need to prevent immigration of contract laborers and strikebreakers who would inevitably lower the standard of living of American workers, after which it repeated that the party opposed the exclusion of specific racial groups. Thus the resolution seemed not to reject the principle of worker solidarity yet simultaneously endorsed the idea that there were differences within the working class.[22]

The American party's next convention in 1912 was the last one at which the issue of immigration was considered. Delegates once again endlessly repeated the same points, with a majority report arguing that exclusion of some groups was necessary on economic and political grounds, while noting that their European comrades did not have an "army of aliens" to educate. A minority report opposed restrictions, and one delegate predicted that Asians in the United States would "grow into the class struggle." It noted that, indeed, there had not yet been a serious effort to organize them. Amazingly, both reports were accepted, suggesting party exhaustion over the subject. (See Documents, pp. 234–39.) The party position remained within the framework that Morris Hillquit had sketched when the discussion began several years earlier. A recommendation for the exclusion of specific groups had been sidestepped, but that such exclusion was endorsed by many delegates was obvious to party members and to the organized American labor movement, to which the party sought to appeal. On this issue the Second International had made its position abundantly clear, and many in the Socialist Party of America had expended energy over the years in finding ways to resist the spirit of its resolution.[23]

## GENDER

The final issue to be considered in these pages is the Woman Question in the context of the Second International. In this case the various sections appeared to share a consensus that the solution of the Social Question would also resolve the Woman Question. When individuals or groups differed over whether or not specific struggles on behalf of women were necessary, the existence of a woman's movement within a particular party and its stage of development was an influential factor. A view held within international socialism was that not only were working women, like men, victims of capitalistic exploitation but that, as Engels had argued, women were additionally victimized by the institution of the family as currently constituted. Those adhering to this position believed that programs and strategies were mandatory to reach out to women in order to convert them to socialism.

As has been stated, the German Social Democratic Party formed the most influential component of the international socialist movement, and thus, German women became the leaders of socialist women's international activities. They were the pioneers in raising a variety of issues concerning dimensions of women's liberation, placing some of them before the Second International at its founding Congress in 1889. At that Congress the delegates went on record as insisting that women would be accorded equal rank with their male comrades, and they endorsed the concept of equal pay for equal work. But socialist men tended to see the female proletariat as what writers have termed "carbon copies" of the male, and therefore they disregarded the more complex facets of the situation of women. Those women—and some men—who were cognizant of gender-related barriers to women's full freedom and independence were confronted with the need to find an appropriate strategy of liberation within the socialist context. Problems of priorities and uncertainties dogged their efforts.[24]

Clara Zetkin of the German Social Democratic party became the leading figure in the international socialist woman's movement. She served as editor of *Die Gleichheit* (Equality), the most important socialist woman's newspaper in the world, with a circulation of more than 125,000. Unlike her comrade Rosa Luxemburg, she viewed gender as a relevant variable that had to be confronted by socialists if women were to be fully emancipated. At the same time Zetkin endorsed only strategies and goals for women's liberation that seemed to her to promote the class struggle. For example, she originally opposed the concept of protective legislation for women on the grounds that it would be counterproductive to separate the struggle of working women from that of men. Her rejection of special demands for women, however, was short-lived, and within a few years she endorsed protective legislation on the basis of women's political, economic, and social vulnerability, as well as the fact of their responsibilities as mothers. In the meantime she and other German Socialist women held a series of conferences, starting in 1900, which became the model for international socialist women's conferences.[25]

In the Socialist Party of America, as at the Congresses of the Second International, it was left essentially to a number of feminist party members to demand a full embrace of a socialist woman's liberation policy. At its founding convention in 1901 the party endorsed equal civil and political rights for men and women. However, that pledge—possibly a gesture toward the Second International—was not pursued, and no programs were established that in any way promoted women's equality. Clearly, the Socialist Party by its actions demonstrated its belief that the solution of the Social Question was its one concern. As a result, some American women, imitating their German sisters, promoted serious party recognition of the specific plight of the female proletariat. To ensure that the situation of women would be addressed, they demanded that a special bureaucracy be organized with responsibility in that area. Despite some opposition from both men and women, the national convention of 1908 established the Woman's National Committee as a focus for the activities of socialist women. (See Documents, pp. 255–58.) A not unrelated fact in the formation of the WNC was that autonomous women's socialist groups were mushrooming in the country, and their appeal to potential women activists was apparently not lost on some socialists.[26]

The key figure in the formation and functioning of the Woman's National Committee was Wisconsin-born May Wood Simons, a social worker, teacher and journalist, and the wife of party intellectual and editor A.M. Simons. A well-respected party leader, she served on a variety of committees, was nominated for a number of its high offices, such as the National Executive Committee and as a candidate for the vice-presidency, ran for public office on the Socialist ticket, and was a delegate to socialist conventions in the United States and abroad. She was active in establishing the party's Socialist Sunday Schools and its placement bureau for teachers in the public schools. As the major figure in the WNC, serving on it throughout its seven years of existence, Wood Simons's views were not easily discounted. She believed that the woman's sector was an integral element in the work of the party rather than a separatist institution, as its opponents charged. She viewed its tasks as inculcating a socialist perspective in American women, insuring that women members were integrated into party offices and activities and prodding the party to work on behalf of women's suffrage. (See Documents, pp. 258–59.)[27]

An important goal of the WNC was to develop routine interaction with European socialist women. It sent reports on its activities and copies of its own publications to Zetkin's *Die Gleichheit* in Berlin and to the London-based women's newspaper, *Justice*, edited by Dora B. Montefiore. By the time that the WNC was established both of these newspapers had become clearinghouses of information for socialist women. The WNC subscribed to these and other socialist women's papers and supported the effort of the autonomous American paper, *Socialist Woman*, to become a parallel clearinghouse of information. Immigrant women within the party were encouraged to secure reports of European women's programs and to translate them into English. One year, one of the WNC's major interests was socialist women's activities abroad, which its members studied and publicized. After a few years, in 1912, the WNC moved to further institutionalize interactions with European comrades, and appointed an "international correspondent," Meta Stern Lilienthal, to translate news of interest for the committee. Finally, as one of its last initiatives, in 1914 the committee elected her to attend a planned international conference of socialist women in order to insure even more direct communication with comrades abroad.[28]

*Socialist Woman* was a monthly newspaper published in Girard, Kansas and in Chicago from 1907 to 1913. It experienced two name changes, becoming *Progressive Woman* after two years and then *Coming Nation*, and its subscription list grew to 3,000. Its editor, Josephine Conger-Kaneko, was a niece of J.A. Wayland, publisher of *The Appeal to Reason*, and wife of a Japanese socialist, a fact which perhaps endowed her with an expansive view of the socialist world. Under her auspices the paper needed no prodding to embrace the responsibility of alerting its readers to overseas socialist activities. Features and reports regularly described the agitational campaigns of German women, some being reprints of reports by Zetkin herself. Readers were informed of a Dutch socialist woman's newspaper, of Danish women's activities as voters and as candidates for public office, and of Finnish social democratic women's programs. They learned of the campaigns of English socialist women as well as activities of Austrian, Bohemian, Hungarian, and other women in Central Europe. Further, owing to the presence on the staff of Kiichi Kaneko until his untimely death in 1909, articles appeared on the life of women in Japan.[29]

Overall, the more the lines of communication were opened, the more the Americans were impressed by some of the Europeans' propaganda efforts. For example, a Finnish-American Women's Agitation Committee asked the WNC to adopt some European women's methods of accumulating data on the working and living conditions of women workers. Some of the American socialists also sought to emulate the European women's campaign tactics to achieve women's suffrage, and were especially interested in such activities in Prussia.[30]

In 1907 at the International Congress at Stuttgart, for the first time since the founding Congress eighteen years earlier, an agenda item directly pertained to women. The final item on the crowded agenda was the issue of women's suffrage, placed there at the urging of German and Austrian women. Clara Zetkin again addressed a Congress on behalf of women workers as she had in 1889. She was the major speaker on the suffrage item, and she argued that where socialist parties waged campaigns for the right to vote, it must be on behalf of universal adult suffrage, and it must be "advocated in [the] agitation as well as in parliament." She called suffrage a necessary "social right" for women. Careful as usual to place her remarks in the context of working women's need to be armed in the class struggle, and to separate her position from that of bourgeois suffragists, she criticized Austrian comrades who had recently held back on women's suffrage so as not to weaken the campaign for universal male suffrage. The delegates to the Congress turned out to be receptive to Zetkin's words and passed a general resolution in support of women's political and legal equality; it specifically advised member parties:

> . . . to fight energetically for the introduction of the universal suffrage for women. Their battles waged on behalf of the proletariat's suffrage leading to the democratization of the legislative state and county governing codes must be simultaneously waged as battles for women's suffrage.[31]

As usual, such resolutions were only guidelines, however strongly they might be worded, and socialists responded as individuals as well as parties. In contrast, one woman writing in *Socialist Woman* referred cynically to the "escape hatch" the International provided to member parties. She concluded that if the parties could not be dictated to by the Congresses, neither could individual members, and for herself, she reserved the freedom to promote female suffrage even in collaboration with bourgeois suffrage forces.[32]

One woman delegate from the Socialist Party of America served on the women's suffrage committee that had recommended such an endorsement to the convention. She was Vera Levene Hillquit, wife of Morris Hillquit. A cousin of her husband's, she had become a lawyer also but did not practice. She joined in party activities in New York where the couple resided but was not active on the national scene; she had accompanied her husband to Stuttgart, and was able to obtain official credentials in order to fill out the Socialist Party's delegation. Another American woman present at Stuttgart was Corinne S. Brown. She had been one of eight women delegates at the founding convention of the Socialist Party of America six years earlier. Brown, whose conversion to radicalism had occurred as a result of the Haymarket Affair, had been active in the women's club movement, had been an avid Bellamyite, and was a leader in the earlier autonomous socialist women's movement. But no woman present at Stuttgart was a major leader in the national party.[33]

Clearly, whether or not individual parties would proceed "energetically" to implement the resolution remained to be seen. But the main focus of activity during the Stuttgart Congress for those committed to advancing the cause of working women took place not at the Congress but at the separate International Socialist Women's Conference that met that same week in Stuttgart. International conferences of women had a long history by the time the socialists gathered at Stuttgart. As recent work by Ulla Wikander of the University of Uppsala has pointed out, since 1878 women's international gatherings on behalf of various issues had convened in major cities in Europe and North America. Thus, when the socialist women held their first international conference, they had as a model an institution pioneered by bourgeois women. However, in the German Empire women who were legally prohibited from participating in political parties until 1908 had already held separate social democratic women's conferences, the first in Mainz in 1900. At a conference in Mannheim in 1906 it was agreed to issue a call for an international women's conference to coincide with the International Congress in Stuttgart.[34]

Fifty-eight delegates from more than a dozen countries were present during the deliberations. The conference passed a number of measures, including an endorsement of an eight-hour day for women workers and a six-hour day for workers under the age of eighteen, as well as at least a thirty-six hour interruption of work per week; a prohibition on women's employment in industries dangerous to their health; a recommendation for maternity leaves of six weeks; and an endorsement of factory inspection legislation where women worked. Most significantly, it also established an International Women's Bureau as a parallel institution to the executive body of the International. Zetkin was elected as Secretary and *Die Gleichheit* at this time became the official newspaper of the international socialist women's movement. The institutionalization of international socialist women's activities had begun and, from all indications, would develop further.[35]

In the following years international ties among socialist women became more and more routine. In 1909 the Woman's National Committee, attempting to initiate direct interactions, tried to win official endorsement from the Socialist Party for routing a visiting British socialist, Daisy Halling, on an American speaking tour. But even though the party's executive was on record as willing to route any socialist speaker from abroad, it told the WNC that it could not see its way to do so. It apparently preferred bigger names, such as Karl Kautsky and Victor Adler, to whom it wrote to encourage them to undertake American speaking tours. The next year, however, Dora B. Montefiore came to the United States from London and addressed socialist women's gatherings, including one held in conjunction with the party's National Congress in May in Chicago (see below).[36]

The next time the International held a Congress, in 1910 in Copenhagen, three women leaders of the Socialist Party were elected as delegates. The three women of a party delegation of eight were May Wood Simons, Lena Morrow Lewis, and Luella Twining; elected as an alternate was Elizabeth Thomas. Lewis was one of the most prominent national organizers in the party and had been the first woman to be elected to its National Executive Committee in 1909. A native of Illinois, she initially was involved in the temperance and the woman's suffrage movements. After joining the Socialist Party in 1902, she separated herself from women-focused activities. In fact she was one of the prominent women leaders in the party who was opposed to special programs for women, fearful that women members would then ensure their own consignment to an auxiliary position. Twining was a journalist from Colorado who was in the second tier of leading female socialists. She had been one of her party's candidates for the United States House of Representatives in 1906, worked as a party organizer, managed Big Bill Haywood's speaking tours, and was a staff member of the Western Federation of Miners. On the national level, she served on the Woman's National Committee. The alternate, Thomas, was the long-time mainstay of the Milwaukee Social-Democratic party, serving as the right-hand staffer for Victor Berger for decades. She had converted to socialism from a background of Quaker activism.[37]

The delegates sailed on the *Lusitania* from New York to London, and traveled by train from there to Copenhagen. At the International Congress, Wood Simons was elected by her comrades as secretary of the Socialist Party delegation. She served on the Committee on Worker Legislation and Unemployment, Lewis served on the Committee on Cooperatives, and Twining served on the Committee on Resolutions. None were major committees, since the attention of the Congress focused on issues of war and militarism. In the various votes during the proceedings, the three women supported the majority in reaffirming the Stuttgart resolution endorsing socialist unity with the worldwide labor movement. They also voted with the majority and a unanimous American delegation in favor of tabling a Keir Hardie measure calling for a general strike in case war was imminent.[38]

Wood Simons, Lewis, and Twining also participated in the Second Conference of Socialist Women, scheduled to coincide with the Congress. Thus, at this second such international gathering, leading American socialist women played a role. The agenda for the conference included measures enabling women to work for peace, further systematizing interactions between socialist women of all countries; strategies toward achieving universal suffrage; and social protective legislation particularly focused on women and children. The conference endorsed a general measure in favor of antimilitarist propaganda, not allowing itself to be hindered by specifics with which the Congress itself struggled. It embedded its support for women's suffrage within overall campaigns for universal suffrage, thereby continuing to deflect any charges of undue preoccupation with female suffrage. But the delegates nevertheless insisted that women's political emancipation was important for the pursuit of the class struggle, and demanded that May Day demonstrations emphasize the achievement of full political equality for all. They also demanded that an annual Woman's Day be held by all socialist parties, the first goal of which would be suffrage for women.[39]

The delegates endorsed a variety of measures in the area of social legislation, expanding on their work at Stuttgart. These included an end to the stigmatizing of children born out of wedlock, maternity leaves of sixteen weeks at half-pay, obstetric care at home, and the establishment of lying-in hospitals and homes for pregnant women. They also demanded state instruction on maternal duties, day care centers and kindergartens, free meals and medical and dental services at schools, and other provisions for orphaned children. They recommended that school attendance be mandatory until the age of eighteen. In addition, they suggested programs of national health care and state insurance for widows, and demanded support of unwed mothers and children by the fathers. The delegates voted down a resolution to establish a special international socialist woman's newspaper in favor of relying on *Die Gleichheit*, which was charged with publishing an internationally-oriented issue every three months.[40]

A major controversy erupted among the delegates over the issue of limited female suffrage. All the American delegates supported a measure introduced by German women to condemn a bill in favor of granting limited women's suffrage, which was then before the House of Commons. Some of the English delegates favored partial suffrage as a step forward but their position was not endorsed. Twining was one of the strongest speakers against the measure, arguing that experience in Colorado where women had been fully enfranchised for over a decade proved that women would vote along class lines.[41]

Twining also introduced a resolution which opposed autonomous socialist groups. This was a curious measure in that socialist women party members over the years had cooperated with such groups, trying to draw them into the party. The socialist woman's conference itself was open to women unionists and other interested individuals who were not party members.[42]

The conference sessions were enhanced by festive banquets and supplementary events. Altogether, it was an exhilarating time for the Americans. It was a foregone conclusion that the conference delegates would decide to hold a third conference to coincide with the next International Congress, scheduled for August, 1914. The agenda that was eventually drawn up for the Vienna conference included female suffrage, protective legislation for women and children, and the high cost of living. But with the outbreak of World War I that very month, neither the International Congress nor the Socialist Woman's conference was held.[43]

The American socialist women had every right to be invigorated and impressed by the Copenhagen conference. Those committed to enhancing working and living conditions for women knew that they could not easily assume serious support from their male comrades but, at the socialist woman's conference, they had experienced an environment where such issues were considered very significant. The American political environment made the programs they debated abroad, such as maternity leaves and national health care, unrealistic, and indeed Wood Simons's proposal to investigate the idea of a mother's pension did not even receive support within the WNC, for that very reason, some months later. Still it had to be deeply satisfying for those few American women to have worked in an environment where such measures seemed feasible and their significance valid. Not long after their return from the conference, Wood Simons proposed to the Woman's National Committee that it sponsor a national conference along the lines of the international socialist women's conference and those held regularly by German and Austrian women. She suggested that it be held two days before the party's national convention scheduled for Chicago in 1912, and that it be open not only to party members but also to other socialist and trade union women. It would be valuable, she argued, as a time of give-and-take regarding policies, the results of which could be presented at least in an ad hoc fashion by those women who were official delegates to the national convention. Dissenting views were voiced, however, by Lewis and others who basically were opposed to separate events for women. A conference was held, nevertheless, in May 1912, at the time of the National Convention, and four hundred women attended.[44]

In another example of the influence of their European exposure, the WNC held discussions on moving the major women's suffrage demonstrations from the recently established annual Woman's Day to May Day. In Prussia the time scheduled for suffrage demonstrations was May Day, and because the Socialist Party of America paid more attention to that date than it did to Woman's Day—indeed, most locals did not hold any events that day—May Day would make more sense for the promotion of women's suffrage. Woman's Day itself, initiated by American socialist women in 1908, indicates mutual influence between the European and the American women. Woman's Day began to be adopted by various European socialist parties at the urging of some of their women members. Zetkin promoted the notion of an International Woman's Day at Copenhagen, and the Americans proposed it during preliminary planning for the Vienna conference. Counter-arguments were pressed that national movements must be free to choose their own dates and programs so that they would be compatible with conditions of the individual socialist movements.[45]

In other areas, evidence suggests that European and American socialist women marched on parallel courses. Issues such as family planning and modification of the very institution of the family, for example, were fraught with both significance and risk to those socialists who explored them, and so most but not all socialist women avoided them. Kate Richards O'Hare who in 1912–1913 was the Socialist Party's representative to the International Socialist Bureau, the only woman to serve in that capacity other than Rosa Luxemburg, occasionally promoted, if circumspectly, the need for birth control and the option of abortion. Clara Zetkin opposed such issues as inappropriate and misguidedly bourgeois solutions to women's emancipation. But the organized women's sectors of their respective parties tended to ignore these subjects. In the meantime, the fundamental question of redesigning the family so that women would not bear full responsibilities for home and childrearing was not really confronted by organized socialist women or their parties. Not only was that issue too volatile but most socialists were unable themselves to question critically the current family structure. Two American socialists took up those issues directly and envisioned a variety of community institutions to ease women's caregiving responsibilities. The more well known who did so was not a party activist but a writer, Charlotte Perkins Gilman. She discussed these issues in her *Women and Economics*, published in 1898. The other was Meta Stern Lilienthal, whose booklet *Women of the Future* argued that a socialist society would uproot the existing institutions of the home and the family, which were based on women's economic dependency, and would institute a situation of individual freedom for all adults.[46]

In a not surprising juxtaposition, both the German socialist woman's movement—the largest expression of organized socialist women's activities—and the American WNC were snuffed out by their respective parties within a few years of each other. In the case of the former, the German Social Democratic Party eviscerated its woman's movement after the German government granted women the right to organize politically with men in 1908. Separate women's organizations were phased out over the next few years so that no autonomous voice of socialist women could be heard. The Socialist Party of America, which that very year first permitted the organization of a woman's sector, was apparently as uncomfortable with its existence as were their German comrades, and abolished the Woman's National Committee in 1915 amid great controversy.[47]

In the course of those few years, however, the international socialist woman's movement had given American women socialists a sense of integration into a large, seemingly world-wide woman's movement within a socialist framework. That fact inevitably emboldened, pushed and encouraged them to promote issues of importance to them in a more sustained and fullsome manner than would have been possible had there not been an international socialist woman's movement. Thus, as the fact of involvement in the International in and of itself strengthened the Socialist Party, the existence of the international woman's movement played the same role for the socialist feminists. However, while the Socialist Party at times found it useful to ignore or to resist guidelines of the International, American socialist women did not have those same needs. The international socialist woman's movement, the offspring of the German Socialist woman's sector, served to enhance the activities of the feminists of the Socialist Party of America. The destruction of both at the hands of unsympathetic party comrades was a not unexpected shared fate.

NOTES

1. An excellent overview of this history is found in Julius Braanthal, *History of the International 1864–1914* (New York: Frederick A. Praeger, 1967).

2. For a fuller treatment of the role of the Socialist Party of America in the Second International, see Sally M. Miller, "Americans and the Second International," *Proceedings of the American Philosophical Society* 120 (October 1976), 372–87.

3. Ibid., pp. 377–78.

4. This same suggestion of exceptionalism might also apply to the Japanese section of the International and other non-European sections, since the focus of the International was on the European experience. More research on a variety of sections would be welcome, as Georges Haupt observed over a generation ago.

5. The resolution may be found in *International Socialist Review* 5 (January 1905), 392–93. It can also be found in *Proceedings of the 1901 National Convention of the Socialist Party of America*, Socialist Party of America Collection, Reel 140, microfilm edition; the quotation from Marx is in Eugene V. Debs, "The Negro in the Class Struggle," *International Socialist Review* 4 (November 1903), 259.

6. Carl D. Thompson to State Secretaries, and replies, May 1913, Information Department, Socialist Party of America Collection, Perkins Library, Duke University, Durham, NC; James Weinstein, *The Decline of the Socialist Party of America, 1912–1925* (New York: Monthly Review Press, 1967), 69.

7. Philip S. Foner, "Revered George Washington Woodbey: Early Twentieth Century California Black Socialist," paper read to the Southwest Labor Studies Conference, April 25, 1975, Stockton, CA; Philip S. Foner, *American Socialism and Black Americans: From the Age of Jackson to World War II* (Westport, CT: Greenwood Press, 1977), 140, 147, 164–67, 155; Socialist Party, *Official Bulletin* 7 (December 1910), 3; ibid., 8 (November 1911), 6; source of quotation: see O'Hare comments in Socialist Party, *Party Builder*, No. 29 (May 21, 1913), 3.

8. See, for example, O'Hare's "'Nigger' Equality" in Philip S. Foner and Sally M. Miller, *Kate Richards O'Hare: Selected Writings and Speeches* (Baton Rouge, LA: Louisiana University Press, 1982), 44–49; Debs, "The Negro in the Class Struggle," 257–60; Eugene V. Debs, "The Negro and his Nemesis," *International Socialist Review* 4 (January 1903), 391–97; Weinstein, 69–70; Socialist Party, *Proceedings of the 1908 National Convention* (Chicago: Socialist Party of America, 1908), 110–12.

9. This report includes the International request on working conditions in the South: Congrès socialiste international d'Amsterdam des 14–20 août 1904, *Rapport and Projet de Resolutions sur les questions de l'ordre du jour par le Secretariat Socialiste International* (Brussels, 1904), 25; these documents include the statement in condemnation of lynching: Georges Haupt, *Bureau Socialiste International, I, 1900–1907, Comptes rendus des réunions manifestes et circulaires* (Paris: Mouton, 1969), 90–93; Herron's concerns are found in George Herron, "Report of the International Bureau by the Secretary for the United States," *International Socialist Review* 4 (1904), 743–44; the party executive spoke of "degenerates" as inherent to the capitalist system as quoted in Ira Kipnis, *The American Socialist Movement, 1897–1912* (New York: Columbia University Press, 1952), 132.

10. Foner, *American Socialism . . .*, 252; W.E.B. Du Bois, "Socialism and the Negro Problem," *The New Review* 1 (February 1, 1913), 138–41; "The Presidential Campaign," *The Crisis* 12 (1916), 268–69; W.A. Domingo, "Socialism: The Negroes'

Hope," *The Messenger* (July 1919), 22. On Du Bois, see David Levering Lewis, *W.E.B. Du Bois: Biography of a Race, 1868–1919* (New York: Henry Holt, 1993), I, 420–21; see on Randolph, Jervis Anderson, *A. Philip Randolph: A Biographical Portrait* (New York: Harcourt Bruce Jovanovich, 1972).

11. Sally M. Miller, "The Socialist Party and the Negro, 1901–1920," *Journal of Negro History 56* (July 1971), 227–28; See Socialist Party, *Congressional Program*, 1918 (Chicago: Socialist Party, 1918).

12. James Joll, *The Second International, 1889–1914* (New York: Harper and Row, 1966), 117–19.

13. Miller, "Americans and the Second International," 377; *Compte-Rendu Officiel*, Bureau Socialiste International (1908), 35.

14. Charles Leinenweber, "The American Socialist Party and 'New' Immigrants," *Science and Society* 21 (Winter 1968): 17, 22; *Party Builder*, No. 29 (May 21, 1913), p. 3; J. Mahlon Barnes, "Report of the National Secretary to the National Congress, May 15, 1910," typescript, International Institute of Social History, Amsterdam; Morris Hillquit, "The Propaganda of Socialism," Report to the National Congress of the Socialist Party (May 15, 1910), 9.

15. Georges Haupt, *La Deuxième Internationale, 1889–1914: Étude critique des sources; Essai bibliographique* (Paris: Mouton, 1964), 68–69.

16. VIIe Congrès Socialiste International tenu à Stuttgart du 16 au 24 août 1907, *Compte rendu analytique*, 229–30; Congrés Socialiste International d'Amsterdam des 14–20 août 1904, *Rapports and Projets de Resolutions sur les questions de l'ordre du jour . . .*, 24.

17. Morris Hillquit, "Immigration in the United States," *International Socialist Review* 8 (August 1907), 65–75; VIIe Congrès Socialiste International . . ., 237–38; *Proposals and Drafts of resolutions with explanatory reports submitted to the International Socialist Congress of Stuttgart*, 558–61.

18. VIIe Congrés Socialiste International . . ., 254.

19. Louis B. Boudin, "Immigration at Stuttgart," *International Socialist Review* 8 (February 1908): 489–92. Boudin of the left wing had been Hillquit's most vociferous critic within the party's delegation to Stuttgart.

20. Cameron H. King, Jr., "Asiatic Exclusion," *International Socialist Review* 8 (May 1908), 661–69; Bruce Rogers, "Our Asiatic Fellows," *International Socialist Review* 15 (April 1915), 626; Eugene V. Debs, "A Letter from Debs on Immigration," *International Socialist Review* 11 (July 1910), 16–17.

21. Socialist Party, *Proceedings of the 1908 National Convention*, 106–21; editorial, "The Socialist Congress and the Immigration Question," *International Socialist Review* 10 (June 1910), 1124. The final quotation is found on p. 21, *Proceedings, 1908*.

22. Editorial, "The Socialist Congress and the Immigration Question," 1124–125; Morris Hillquit to Camille Huysmans, September 21, 1908, New York, *Compte Rendu Officiel*, Bureau Socialiste International, 35.

23. Appendix J, "Reports of the Majority and Minority Committees on Immigration," Socialist Party, *Proceedings of the 1912 National Convention* (Chicago: Socialist Party, 1912), 209–13.

24. Philip S. Foner, *Clara Zetkin: Selected Writings* (New York: International Publishers, 1984), 24; Marilyn J. Boxer and Jean H. Quataert, "The Class and Sex Connection: An Introduction," in Marilyn J. Boxer and Jean H. Quataert, *Socialist Women: European Socialist Feminism in the Nineteenth and Early Twentieth Centures* (New York: Elsevier, 1978), 3, 15–16.

25. Jean H. Quataert, "Unequal Partners in an Uneasy Alliance: Women and the Working Class in Imperial Germany," in Boxer and Quataert, 124; Karen Honeycut, "Clara Zetkin: A Socialist Approach to the Problem of Women's Oppression," in Jane Slaughter and Robert Kern, eds., *European Women on the Left: Socialism, Feminism, and the Problems Faced by Political Women, 1880 to the Present* (Westport,

CT: Greenwood Press, 1981), 33–40; Josephine Conger-Kaneko, "Socialist Woman's Movement in Germany," *Socialist Woman*, No. 2 (July 1907), 4; Josephine Conger-Kaneko, "Socialist Woman's Movement in Germany," *Socialist Woman*, No. 13 (June 1908), 10. Conger-Kaneko in reporting enthusiastically on the social democratic movement among German women observed wistfully that American socialist women did not yet have the consciousness or the numbers to organize themselves and make demands on their male comrades; however, she thought that the time might be imminent when they would.

26. Mari Jo Buhle, *Women and American Socialism, 1870–1920* (Urbana: University of Illinois Press, 1981), 135–40.

27. May Wood Simons, "Aims and Purposes of Women Committee," *Progressive Woman*, No. 29 (October 1909), 2; "May Wood Simons," No. 1 (June 1907), 1; Gretchen and Kent Kreuter, "May Wood Simons: Party Theorist," in Sally M. Miller, ed., *Flawed Liberation: Socialism and Feminism* (Westport, CT: Greenwood Press, 1981), 37–60. See also Chapter 3 for Wood Simons.

28. Socialist Party, *Official Bulletin* 7 (August 1911), 5; ibid., 8 (November 1911), 2. Meta Stern Lilienthal translated various classics of international socialism from German to English, including August Bebel's *Women Under Socialism*. See also "The International Socialist Bureau," *Progressive Woman*, No. 33 (February 1910), 3–4.

29. Editorial, "Why 'The Socialist Woman' Comes into Existence," *Socialist Woman* No. 1 (June 1907): 4; Mari Jo Buhle, "Socialist Woman, Progressive Woman, Coming Nation," in Joseph R. Conlin, *The American Radical Press, 1880–1960*, II, 442–49. (Westport, CT: Greenwood Press, 1974). Conger-Kaneko, who also wrote occasionally for *The Masses*, was the first woman to be nominated for Chicago's city council.

30. A perusal of issues of the *Socialist Woman* is the best way to glean insights into the American women's reaction to their European comrades.

31. The resolution was reproduced in Socialist Party, *Official Bulletin* 4 (October 1907): 6, and also in *Socialist Woman* No. 5 (October 1907): 2; it is also found in Foner, *Clara Zetkin*, 29–31, 98–107; see also Honeycut in Slaughter and Kern, 40; Susan Groag Bell and Karen M. Offen, *Women, the Family, and Freedom: The Debate in Documents* (Stanford, CA: Stanford University Press, 1983), II, 228.

32. Josephine R. Cole, "The International and Woman Suffrage," *Socialist Woman*, No. 6 (November 1907), 3. The husband of May Wood Simons, Algie M. Simons, who was frequently a member of the National Executive Committee of the Socialist Party, was one of the official delegates to the Stuttgart Congress. When he reported on the Congress in the pages of *Chicago Daily Socialist*, he omitted any mention of the women's suffrage resolution.

33. Little information exists on Vera Hillquit, but see Norma Fain Pratt, *Morris Hillquit: A Political History of an American Jewish Socialist* (Westport, CT: Greenwood Press, 1979), 28. Aspects of Corinne Stubbs Brown's career can be traced in issues of *Socialist Woman*: a biographical sketch of her appears in *Socialist Woman*, No. 9 (February 1908): 1. See also Buhle, 71–72, 77, 105, 138.

34. Ulla Wikander, "International Women's Congresses, 1878–1914: The Controversy over Equality and Special Labour Legislation," in Maul L. Eduards, Inga Elgquist-Saltzman et al., *Rethinking Change: Current Swedish Feminist Research* (no place: Humanistisksamhallsvetenskapliga forskningsradet, 1992), 11–36; Foner, *Clara Zetkin*, 26; "Conférences Internationales des Femmes Socialists," in Haupt, *La Deuxième Internationale . . .*, 346–47.

35. *Rapports pour la Première Conferénce Internationale des Femmes Socialistes tenu à Stuttgart le samedi 17 août 1907 à 9 heures du matin dan la salle de la Liederhalle* (no pp.); Foner, *Clara Zetkin*, 26. The Conference's endorsement of protective legislation helped to encourage a secondary labor market for women, which of course was not the intention of the various organized movements which promoted

female protective legislation.

36. Socialist Party, *Official Bulletin* 5 (April 1909), 2; ibid., 6 (December 1909): 3; ibid., 6 (April 1910).

37. "Lena Morrow Lewis," *Socialist Woman* No. 4 (September 1907), 2; Mari Jo Buhle, "Lena Morrow Lewis: Her Rise and Fall," in Miller, *Flawed Liberation*, 61–86; "Luella Twining," *Socialist Woman* No. 7 (December 1907), 2; Weinstein, p. 59; John D. Buenker, "The Politics of Mutual Frustration: Socialists and Suffragists in New York and Wisconsin," in Miller, *Flawed Liberation*, 129. All three of the official delegates were featured in an article in *Socialist Woman*. See No. 39 (August 1910), 10.

38. "From the International Congress," *Socialist Woman* No. 41 (October 1910), 2–3.

39. "Conférences Internationales des Femmes Socialistes," in Haupt, *La Deuxième Internationale . . .*, 348; Second International Conference of Socialist Women, 1910, *Program*, Copenhagen, 20–22.

40. Second International Conference of Socialist Women, 1910, *Program*, Copenhagen, 22–23; "From the International Congress," *Socialist Woman*: 2–3.

41. "From the International Congress," *Socialist Woman*: 2–3.

42. Lida Parce, "The Examiner's Glass," *Socialist Woman* No. 40 (September 1910), 8.

43. *Party Builder*, No. 62 (January 10, 1914), 5. In March 1915, Clara Zetkin was instrumental in the convening of an International Socialist Woman's Conference at Berne, Switzerland, which drew up peace resolutions. See G.D.H. Cole, *A History of Socialist Thought III*, Pt. 1, *The Second International* (London: Macmillan, 1967), 101.

44. Socialist Party, *Official Bulletin* 8 (February 1912), 5; ibid., 8 (November 1911), 3; ibid., 8 (June 1912), 3, 5; Josephine Conger-Kaneko, "Women at the National Socialist Convention," *Socialist Woman* No. 61 (July 1912), 3. American precedents existed for the holding of such a conference. Informal conferences had occurred prior to the party's national meetings in 1908 and 1910, and in at least three states—Kansas, Massachusetts and New York—socialist women had held statewide conferences.

45. *Party Builder*, No. 63 (January 17, 1914), 2–3; ibid., No. 83 (June 6, 1914), 5; Foner, *Clara Zetkin*, 31, 108; Honeycut, 40.

46. Foner and Miller, 110–14; Honeycut, 16–17; Meta Stern Lilienthal, *Women of the Future* (New York: Rand School, n.d.), 8–10. It should be noted, however, that individual women of the SPD, as shown by Quataert, explored the possibility of municipal programs of laundry, dining, and childcare services, among others, which would liberate women within the existing system of some of their burdens. See Quataert in Boxer and Quataert, 126–29, and see also Jean H. Quataert, *Reluctant Feminists in German Social Democracy, 1885–1917* (Princeton, NJ: Princeton University Press, 1979), 84–106.

47. Honeycut, 40–41; Foner, *Clara Zetkin*, 33

# PART II
# RACE

# 2  RED AND BLACK

The Socialist Party of America, a minor party of considerable note for the twenty years after its founding in 1901, holds an anomalous position in the history of American radicalism. The socialists obtained the greatest number of votes of any party of the left in a Presidential election, organized locals in all regions of the nation, and elected a Congressman regularly, but nevertheless the party has received much less attention than its controversial and seemingly more threatening offspring, the American Communist Party. The Communist Party, following its organization in 1919 as the Socialists split into three groups, has been studied by scholars of the various disciplines and scrutinized by the press and public; its attitudes have been explored and distorted, but most especially publicized. Thus, whether or not accurate, judgments on its positions and activities are felt to be common knowledge, while by comparison its predecessor, the Socialist Party, remains in the dimly perceived background.[1]

The Communist focus on the status of the Negro in America in the 1930s is well known, but in contrast the attitude and program of the Socialist Party toward the black American has not been assessed by scholars in terms other than generalities, and the public, as in all matters relating to this once prominent party, remains unaware of the party's early notoriety and its specific programs. Among historians of the Socialist Party, there has been a tendency to impose sweeping statements on the organization despite its constant divisions into separate factions, and this has served to distort understanding of the party in its relationship with the Negro as well as in other matters. It is unenlightening to learn from Ira Kipnis in 1952, a time when the Negro's subordinate position was coming to attract attention, that the old Socialist Party was increasingly racist; it is no more edifying to be informed by James Weinstein in 1967, a year in which New Leftist historians attempted to find their own past, that the party grew to recognize the Negro's plight.[2] Each of these historians has allowed the concerns of the present to shape his writing of history to the extent that the subject becomes disfigured rather than clarified. Both men, molded by their intellectual environment, have manipulated the Socialist Party of the early twentieth century in accord with their own visions formed in the latter half of the century.

It should be noted, however, that both historians, as products of the American mind, share the position of the Socialist Party. It, too, was shaped and formed by the attitudes of the nation despite its generally critical posture. And, thus, the Socialist Party in the Progressive Era failed, as did the country at large, to view the Negro as an individual, as a distinct human being in a unique dilemma. The Socialist, concerned as he might be with the downtrodden, the impoverished, the under-represented, nevertheless did not see the Negro. The American Negro for the Socialist Party was, as aptly described by Ralph Ellison, "the invisible man." The party did not reject Negro membership—it stood for Negro suffrage when the issue arose—yet with the exception of a vocal minority, it doubted Negro equality and undertook no meaningful struggles against second-class citizenship. The Negro might be noticed by the party in his economic role as a worker, but he was not seen to be a worker with peculiar difficulties imposed by the existing semi-caste system. Marxist ideology, instead of leading Socialists to seek out the Negro as the worker with absolutely nothing to lose but his chains, reinforced the existing national tendency to overlook his comprehensive exploitation. In an era dominated by distorted Darwinist views of competing species and nations with different degrees of adaptability, even a socialist party based on international brotherhood and anti-colonialism—in theory at least—endorsed the consensus on the Negro. The reform movements of the times rested, among other elements, on a comfortable assumption of Anglo-Saxon superiority. A paternalism toward the non-Anglo-Saxon, reflected in an imperialist phrase such as "the little brown brother," and supported by the uncertain social sciences of the day, pervaded the general climate. Rare was the organization opposed to the prevailing ethos.

The Socialist Party was never a monolithic organization imposing decrees upon its membership. Moreover, its genuine fragmentation meant that always there were at least three opinions on any subject, that of the Marxist or revolutionist left, the revisionist or reformist right, and the amorphous middle or center which might agree with one of the extremes or hold to a distinctive view. The party's view of the Negro must be examined in the light of this division.

The dominant reformist wing of the party was closely tied to conservative organized labor. Some reformist leaders were trade unionists themselves and all of them were anxious to cement a firm alliance with the American Federation of Labor which might lead to its ideological capture. Courting the federation as they did, it was logical for reformists to support increasingly segregationist labor's contention that the Negro was unorganizable and to be ignored except for condemnation as scab. Therefore, the reformist orientation to the trade union movement reinforced whatever racist tendencies were present.[3]

As an example, reformist leader Victor L. Berger was a trade unionist as well as the dominant voice in the dynamic socialist movement in German Milwaukee. All contemporary strains leading toward racism coalesced in the European-born Berger. As a unionist he saw the Negro as unorganizable, as a Socialist he thought him irrelevant, and as a German he believed the Negro, and indeed all others, to be inferior. In a debate before the party's National Congress in 1910, Berger acknowledged that the recent electoral success of the Milwaukee Socialists was due to trade unionist support and insisted that support must be rewarded. "If we are a party of workingmen," he told the Congress, "we must stand for what will help them." He referred to the existence of a race problem but one which was to be shunned rather than rectified: inferior races ought to be kept out of the United States for, with the Negro presence, ". . . we have troubles enough. . . ." The Negro was a burden whose weight the party, in partnership with labor, must wear as lightly as possible. To Berger's mind a Negro problem existed rather than a dilemma created by the inequities of American life. Berger held a pronounced vision of a natural inequality of peoples. In almost a pyramidal view he spelled out distinctly superior and inferior racial and ethnic classes. White was at the top of the color pyramid, yellow below, and black at the bottom, and potential for education, unionization and even morality progressively declined. When dealing with numbers of yellows or blacks, this Socialist Party leader was capable of telling his comrades in convention that ". . . this is a question of civilization mainly. I believe that our civilization, the European or Caucasian or whatever name you choose to call it, I believe that our civilization is in question."[4] He was not able to transcend the existing contrast in standards of living or life styles to analyze the forces extant.

Such blatant racism, however, was voiced publicly by few of the party's leaders. Some, unlike Berger, were so appalled by the inequities, jim crowism, and violence to which the Negro was subjected, that they welcomed the first moves in the Negro community away from Booker T. Washington's Atlanta Exposition philosophy, enunciated in 1895, of narrow economic advancement at the price of social inequality, limited vocational education, and subordinate political status. They applauded and cooperated with the

Niagara Movement of W.E.B. Du Bois and others after 1905, and helped to organize the National Association for the Advancement of Colored People at the end of the decade.

Mary White Ovington, a young settlement house worker descended from Massachusetts abolitionists, had immersed herself in the social problems of the northern Negro after the turn of the century. As a Socialist, she was convinced that the major problem facing civilization was economic. While her life's work was that of helping the Negro to obtain his constitutional rights, it was her hope that subsequently he might choose to join with white workers in the promotion of the collective ownership of the means of production and distribution. But she did not think her task should be prostelyzing the Negro; he must make his own decisions. [5]

Mary White Ovington's efforts, perhaps more than those of any other individual, provided the impetus for the formation of the NAACP. She, as other sympathetic Northerners, was aghast over the violence that swept Lincoln's Springfield, Illinois, for two days in August of 1908, resulting in lynchings and other less deadly but forceful pressures upon Negroes to flee the city. She read an analysis of the riots by a fellow Socialist, William English Walling, which concluded with an open-ended plea: ". . . what large and powerful body of citizens is ready to come to their aid?" Miss Ovington responded to his hope for an organization of black and white Americans which would secure the rights still remaining to the Negro and would reclaim those lost or never obtained.[6]

Walling was the son of a wealthy Kentucky family. He had moved beyond his narrow elitist background to embrace causes as diverse as factory inspection, settlement house social service, the National Women's Trade Union League, and the Socialist Party. While he did not become a member of the party until the next year, in 1908 he was a leading propagandist for the uncompromising, revolutionist wing. In that capacity he and Victor Berger became involved in a bitter quarrel over his assertion that the reformists who controlled party machinery were deflecting the movement toward progressivism. [7] The two men were as acrimonious in their charges over policy as they were distant in their assumptions about the Negro.

For Walling the trauma of race riots in Lincoln country was magnified by the fact that he had just returned from a visit to Czarist Russia with his wife, Anna Strunsky, and there the government at least had to stoke fires to create a pogrom. In Springfield, however, spontaneous violence had erupted and Walling clearly found that while mob action was frowned upon by the respectable, nonetheless public opinion in the North endorsed race hatred. In order that the "southification" of the country be countered, political democracy saved, and the Negro reach " . . . a plane of absolute political and social equality . . ." the next year Walling and Miss Ovington, along with Socialist friends such as the muckraker Charles Edward Russell and the non-Socialist, abolitionist-descended publisher, Oswald Garrison Villard, organized the National Negro Committee, soon to be known as the NAACP. While Villard in his personal correspondence could write that the ". . . most ardent workers who are really accomplishing something. . . are all Socialists . . ." none attempted to exploit the Negro for the advancement of the Socialist Party.[8] It is apparent that all of them held an underlying belief in the efficacy of a coalition of the downtrodden—workers both white and black, the unemancipated woman, defenseless consumers, etc.—but through the NAACP they simply began at the beginning and attempted to end legal barriers obstructing the Negro's path to where he might want to go.[9]

The Socialist Party, encompassing attitudes toward the Negro as different as Berger's was from Walling's, moved through its first two decades acknowledging the Negro in a rather absent-minded fashion. A few Negroes were present at the Unity Convention of 1901 in Indianapolis where some feuding factions came together to form a Socialist Party in which they could quarrel at closer range. The gathering put together a constitution which contained a clause pertinent to the Negro. Article II, Section 1 of the Socialist Party's constitution spoke out against discrimination in American life.[10] The party even went so far as to recognize the Negro's unique experience in the United States but nevertheless declared his position and his interests to be identical to that of the white worker.

In its daily functioning the party did not concern itself with the Negro's economic and political problems. Only when it became necessary to assume a formal posture, as above, did the party comment on the Negro directly. For example, the first Socialist Congressman supported Negro suffrage when the issue was before the House of Representatives. Ironically, this Congressman was the racist Berger, elected in 1910 by the voters of the Fifth Congressional District of Wisconsin, but nevertheless when a stand had to be taken, he endorsed a bill for federal supervision of primaries in the South. Berger's committee assignment was that of the District of Columbia and he introduced various measures for the benefit of District residents which, had they passed, would have aided the large Negro population of Washington. Berger sponsored home rule, a cooperative store for the civil servants of Washington, and limitations on women's hours of employment. In his various speeches to his colleagues he condemned what he called the starvation wages prevalent in the District. In all of these efforts, he was representing the interests of the Negro but that was beside the point for him. Berger, in this term and in his later service from 1922 to 1926, was not thinking particularly of the Negro's plight.[11] The only other Socialist ever elected to the House of Representatives was Meyer London of the Twelfth Congressional District of New York, the Jewish ghetto. He served from 1914 to 1918 and was elected again in 1920 and he, like Berger, attempted to represent the American worker without regard to the gradations of problems which color imposed.[12] Thus, the only representatives in Congress of the workers of the world were not representing those most oppressed.

In the South however, Socialist locals in some areas demonstrated direct interest in attracting the black man. While historians have generalized mistakenly on the racism of Southern Socialists, the party in the South offered a varied picture.[13] In 1913 the party, prodded by a request for membership information, circulated a questionnaire to determine the number of Negroes in the party and the number of integrated locals. The survey handled by the party's Information Department, revealed that Northern locals had no special provisions pertaining to race, while in the South a color curtain divided the party between integrated practices of locals in the Upper South and segregated procedures of those in the Deep South. South Carolina, Georgia, Mississippi, and Florida all were recorded as practicing segregation within locals. In cases where there were insufficient numbers of Negro members for a black local, Negroes were enrolled as members-at-large in the state organization. On the other hand, state secretaries from the Upper South, such as the District of Columbia, Maryland, Kentucky, and Tennessee, reported that Negroes were enrolled automatically in the local nearest to their home. The state secretary for Kentucky, Walter Lanfersiek, within a few months of assuming the role of Executive Secretary of the party, reported that an important factor in the easy relationship among white and black members was their mutual participation in the integrated United Mine Workers. The state secretary for Tennessee wrote simply, "If a negro (sic) signs our application cards (sic) . . . we give him a membership card." But he added sadly that most Negroes were stand-pat Republicans.[14] The survey thus demonstrated that regional ideology and habit tended to overwhelm Marxist colorblindness.

The National Office did not use the knowledge it gained from the survey to interfere with segregationist practices although had it chosen to do so, the party tradition of local autonomy would have prevented any such manipulation. The leadership refrained from initiating measures on behalf of its now formally recognized Negro membership or from seeking to alter the status quo in any way. The Socialist Party had been led to its inquiry but it had no interest in exploring the ramifications further.

During and immediately after World War One, the Socialist Party took a few tentative steps toward the Negro, but none of these efforts was either imaginatively conceived or vigorously implemented. That the party recognized the Negro to any extent may have been due to the simple fact of increasing migration of the Negro to the North where he became somewhat more visible to the public in general. In addition, during the war, as Harlem became the black mecca it began to contain different strains of cultural and political ferment, including a few radical notes.[15]

One of those who evinced interest in the Socialist Party was W.E.B. DuBois. As early as 1907, only four years after he broke with Washington's limiting vision, DuBois gravitated toward the party. Influenced by some of his colleagues in the NAACP, he joined the movement briefly to embrace its gospel of collectivist advancement and brotherhood. His commitment to socialism in the Progressive Era was not so much ideological as humanistic. While he called some Socialists fanatics, he nonetheless believed they promoted the public good and gave the Negro hope that was lacking elsewhere. Moreover, he wished to see a linking of various reform movements which would inevitably strengthen all forces for change. He left the Socialist Party to support Woodrow Wilson in 1912, although with considerable ambivalence; he felt impelled to contribute to the defeat of Theodore Roosevelt's blatantly lily-white Progressive Party while nevertheless harboring skepticism of the Democratic Party.[16]

A. Philip Randolph and Chandler Owen, both with backgrounds in organized labor, became members of the Socialist Party, and in 1917 transformed a black unionist monthly into the *Messenger*, whose masthead proudly proclaimed itself "the only radical Negro magazine in America." The *Messenger* advised its readers to vote socialist because the party represented all working men. It reproduced the usual arguments on the advantages of socialism over capitalism, but in most cases an emphasis was provided to appeal specifically to a Negro audience. One of Randolph's editorials offered the Marxist analogy of chattel-slavery and so-called wage-slavery with pointedness. The People's Council of America, which arouse [sic] in conjunction with the Socialist Party as a response to events in Russia, was held by the *Messenger* to be a force which would democratize labor and deprive the racist American Federation of Labor of its monolithic position. Negroes were also advised to join the Wobblies as "the labor organization which draws no race or color line.[17]

The *Messenger's* analysis of the war followed the usual socialist critique but here again a twist was given to certain points. It was emphasized that colonial rivalries and the exploitation of colored peoples was the real issue of the World War. The magazine proposed the establishment of an International Council on the Conditions of the Darker Races to administer, educate, and insure the self-determination of the oppressed. The League of Nations was dismissed with a reflection on white capitalist associations of governments.[18] The editors stressed that democracy and self-determination of peoples must become a reality within the United States. Since these conditions were absent, it was clear that Negroes had no taste for the war. When DuBois advised the closing of ranks behind the national war effort, the *Messenger* attacked him and compared his "disgraceful" position with the Atlanta Exposition philosophy of accommodation. It argued that no "subject race" ever improved its position by participating in the oppressors' wars.[19] For its stance, the *Messenger* found itself banned from the United States mails, as did other dissenting journals.

The *Messenger* supported Socialist Morris Hillquit in the mayoralty election in New York in November of 1917. The magazine exulted over his strong showing and most especially over the twenty-five percent of the Negro vote he had won. The hope was expressed that in the next election, fifty percent of Negro voters would cast ballots for Socialists. Six months later, the *Messenger* rejoiced again as a heavily Negro local was organized in New York's Twenty-First Assembly District. Randolph himself campaigned in 1920 for public office on a socialist ticket and while he won over 200,000 votes, the party by then had split and his performance was not a harbinger of future electoral successes by Socialists of any color.[20]

The *Messenger* not only advised its readers to turn to the Socialist Party, but also steered them toward the party-related Rand School of Social Science as one of the few institutions where Negroes might obtain an equal education. Some enrolled there, such as Lovett Fort-Whiteman, later to join the Communist Party and settle in Soviet Russia, and editors Randolph and Owen taught a course at the Rand School entitled "Economics and Sociology of the Negro Question."[21]

The magazine and its promotion of black radicalism suffered a blow in the postwar era as the Socialist Party divided. The *Messenger* shied away from the more revolutionary Communists and continued to support the reformist Socialists, but with the competition between the separate parties and the attraction for the dissatisfied of the Garvey movement, then peaking in Harlem, there was less chance than ever to create a radical movement among mass numbers of Negroes.[22]

The party's interest in the Negro as radical during the war was demonstrated by an invitation to Randolph and Owen to address the People's Council on the problems of the Negro. In 1918 it planned to send organizers into the black community, even into the South. The ramifications of its program implied conflict with the trade unions; they are indicative of the radicalization of the party as the war progressed and an increasing criticism of and distance from organized labor.[23]

More instructive, however, than announced intentions and formal gestures of reaching out to the Negro, is the performance and evidence of the Socialist Party to view the Negro traditionally. Following the split in 1919, the shrunken remnant of the Party issued a pamphlet entitled "Why Negroes Should be Socialists." They were advised to join the Party in their capacity as workers since the Party was the only representative one of the workingman. The pamphlet maintained that race was not the issue, and gave examples of white employers exploiting white workers.

> Were not the steel and coal strikers beaten down by white soldiers and policemen when they committed the crime of striking for a living wage? Both the strikers were white men and the employers were white men, yet their interests were opposed and they fought . . . Is not white Ireland oppressed by white England?[24]

Therefore, it was maintained, the oppression of the Negro was due to class rather than to race and the remedy was prescribed to be working class solidarity. That the Socialist Party could issue such a pamphlet in the aftermath of World War One, a time when the Negro was threatened with violence throughout the country on a level not seen in decades, must be taken as a comment on the nearsightedness of the party. It could not be denied that the Negro was of the working class, the most insecure element within that class, and in need of representation. But more fundamentally, the menaced position of the Negro—the violence meted out to returning black veterans, the race riots promoted against ghetto dwellers, the increased rate of lynchings, and the revival of the Ku Klux Klan—surpassed the economic exploitation cited.[25]

The Negro's position in America was far more complex than the Socialist Party seemed willing to realize. The party's belated appeal to the Negro in 1920 was couched in unrealistic terms which refused to recognize the dimensions of the inequities he faced. Socialists attempting to respond to the American environment had themselves been shaped by it, even members who were of alien backgrounds. Thus, they dealt with the issue of race, never of great interest to them, within the existing restrictive context. They lacked the desire, vision, and imagination to discern or to strive for a wholly equitable social, as well as political, situation. The Socialists, as many other

Americans of relative good will toward the Negro, were captives of the intellectual climate of their time.

However, had the Socialist Party as an organization in opposition to many existing injustices been able to reach out to the Negro in a more realistic fashion, it is unlikely that a fruitful relationship would have evolved. With American workers as a whole slow to respond to an ideology which appeared alien to them, there is no reason to think that Negroes would have reacted in mass numbers had a more pertinent argument been presented. They, too, despite the failure of the country to apportion to them a fair share of its goods and services, were shaped by the American mind.

In the first decades of this century the Negro demonstrated very little interest in the abolition of capitalism. What he wanted was his opportunity to prosper within that system. As much as other more favored Americans, he was taught the American mystique of individual initiative. Few of his leaders pointed to other vistas. And while his willingness to accept the legend of Horatio Alger and its various implications may appear improbable, no evidence indicates otherwise. The Negro, too, was shaped by the intellectual environment of his country and absorbed its teachings as did the American Socialists. As a result, the Socialist Party remained as invisible to the Negro as the Negro was invisible to the party.

NOTES

1. Manuscript sources for this paper are found in the Socialist Party Collection, Duke University, Durham, NC; the William English Walling Collection, Wisconsin State Historical Society, Madison, WI; the Victor Berger Collection, Milwaukee County Historical Society, Milwaukee, WI. In 1912 Debs captured 901,062 votes, almost six percent of the ballots cast in the U.S. presidential election, while the party occupied the office of mayor in seventy-four cities in states as disparate as Pennsylvania, North Dakota, Arkansas, and California. In addition, it elected a member to the House of Representatives in every election between 1910 and 1926 with the exception of 1912. Standard works on the Socialist Party are Daniel Bell, *Marxian Socialism in the United States* (Princeton University Press, Princeton; NJ: 1967); Ira Kipnis, *The American Socialist Movement* (New York: Monthly Review Press, 1952); David A. Shannon, *The Socialist Party of America* (New York: Quadrangles 1955); and, most recently, James Weinstein, *The Decline of Socialism in America*, 1912–1925 (New York: Monthly Review Press 1967).

2. Kipnis, 134; Weinstein, 67, 75. For a critique of the New Leftist historians and American socialism, see Irwin Unger, "The 'New Left' and American History: some recent trends in United States historiography," *American Historical Review*, LXXII (July 1967), 1250–51.

3. On labor and the Negro, see Gerald N. Grob, "Organized Labor and the Negro, 1865–1900," *Labor History*, I (Spring 1960), 174; Herbert Hill, "In the Age of Gompers and after—the racial practices of organized labor," *New Politics*, IV (Spring 1965), 39; August Meier and Elliott Rudwick, "Attitudes of Negro Leaders toward the American Labor Movement from the Civil War to World War I," in: *The Negro and the Labor Movement*, ed. Julius Jacobson (New York: Anchor 1968), 27.

4. Socialist Party, *Proceedings* of the National Congress, 1910, 119–21.

5. Mary White Ovington, *The Walls Came Tumbling Down* (New York: Harcourt, Brace 1947), 47–48; Gilbert Osofsky, "Progressivism and the Negro: New York, 1900–1915," *American Quarterly*, XVI, pt. I (Summer 1964), 159–61. Osofsky remarks that Ovington's optimism in the face of overwhelming obstacles marked her as a product of the confident era in which she lived.

6. William English Walling, "The Race War in the North," *Independent*, LXV (September 3, 1908), 534 [quotation]; as quoted in Walling, "The Founding of the NAACP," *Crisis*, XXXVI (July 1929), 226.

7. William English Walling to Eugene V. Debs, December 14, 1909, William English Walling Collection, Wisconsin State Historical Society; Walling, *Socialism as it is: a survey of the world-wide revolutionary movement* (New York: Macmillan 1912), 179–80; Victor Berger to Algie M. Simons, December 6, 1909, Socialist Party Collection, Duke University.

8. Villard as quoted from his papers in Charles Flint Kellogg, *National Association for the Advancement of Colored People*, Vol. I: 1909–1920 (Baltimore: Johns Hopkins University Press 1967), 45. Ovington, 102; Ovington, "William English Walling," *Crisis*, XLIII (November 1936), 335; Walling, *Independent, LXV*, September 3, 1908, 530.

9. Ibid., 534; *Negro Year Book, I* (1912), 134–135; Years later Walling maintained that he specifically wished the new organization to embrace people of all political persuasions and to avoid any descent to sectarianism. Walling, *Crisis, XXXVI*, 226. See also Charles Edward Russell, *Bare Hands and Stone Walls; some recollections of a side-line reformer* (New York: Charles Scribner's Sons 1933), 224–26; Oswald Garrison Villard, *Fighting Years: memoirs of a liberal editor* (New York: Harcourt, Brace 1939), 192–94.

10. The constitution of the Socialist Party is most readily found with its convention proceedings. See, for example, Socialist Party, *Proceedings* of the 1908 National Convention, 324–28. The measure, however, was introduced by a Negro delegate; see R. Laurence Moore, "Flawed Fraternity—American Socialist Response to the Negro, 1909–1912." *Historian, XXII* (November 1969), 17.

11. Victor Berger note of April 17, 1911, Victor Berger Collection, Milwaukee County Historical Society; Berger's record in the Sixty-second Congress is summarized in Milwaukee Social Democratic Party, *Campaign Manual*, 1912, 17–26.

12. Meyer London's congressional record is found in typescript in Box D50 of the Meyer London Collection, Tamiment Institute, New York City.

13. See, for example, Dewey W. Grantham, Jr., "The Progressive Movement and the Negro," *South Atlantic Quarterly*, LIV (October 1955), 461–77. Grantham holds that "the Socialists of the South proved no more tolerant on the race question than non-Socialists." He offers no distinctions among party practices in the different areas of the South (472). The same faulty overview characterizes Sterling D. Spero and Abram L. Harris, *The Black Worker* (New York: Atheneum 1968), 407. These historians echo mildly a contemporary charge levelled at the Party by one of its antagonists, the anarchist Emma Goldman. Her periodical claimed that Socialists treated blacks "like dogs" and that "the party consists chiefly of national and racial philistines, moral eunuchs, and religious soul savers." *Mother Earth*, VI (October 1911), 198.

14. Carl D. Thompson to State Secretaries, and replies, May 1913, Socialist Party Collection, Duke University. There are no extant figures on Negro membership in the party as a whole.

15. Harold Cruse, *The Crisis of the Negro Intellectual* (New York: William Morrow 1967), 11–63. Chapter two contains a comprehensive analysis of Harlem's cultural and political evolution at this time.

16. W.E.B. Du Bois, *The Autobiography of W.E.B. Du Bois* (New York: International Publishers 1968), 289; Du Bois, *Dusk of Dawn: an essay toward an auto-*

*biography of a race concept* (New York: Harcourt, Brace 1940), 234–35; Du Bois, "Socialist of the Path," Horizon, I (1907), 7: Du Bois, "Negro and Socialism," ibid.

17. The *Messenger*, November 1917, 19; March 1919, 12; July 1919, 8; Spero and Harris, 389–90. On the relationship to the I.W.W., see Philip S. Foner, "The Industrial Workers of the World and the Black Worker," *Journal of Negro History*, LV (July 1970).

18. The *Messenger* November 1917, 10; May–June 1919; 14.

19. Ibid., November 1917, 11; January 1918, 23; July 1918, 27.

20. Ibid., January 1918, 11; July 1918, 8; November 1920, 135.

21. Ibid., January 1918, 22; August 1919, 6; Cruse, 118.

22. Cruse, p. 40, 118. Christopher Lasch, echoing Du Bois, comments that had black radicals and the Socialist Party fully coalesced, each would have been immeasurably strengthened; the former inevitably would have weaned the party from its overdependence upon European political and economic frames of reference while the latter would have taught the need for self-determination for the ghetto within a collectivist orientation. Christopher Lasch, *The Agony of the American Left* (New York: Knopf 1969), 41.

23. The *Messenger*, November 1917, 10; *Eye Opener*, August 1918. This issue of the party newspaper contains the Socialists' congressional platform for the November elections and includes for the first time since the party's formative years fresh recognition of the Negro.

24. *Why Negroes should be Socialists* (Chicago: Socialist Party). Internal evidence suggests this publication appeared in 1920.

25. *See Negro Year Book*, V (1918–1919), especially pp. 67–71, for a record of the terror to which the minority was subject.

# Part III
## Ethnicity and Immigration

# 3 THE SOCIALIST PARTY AND "OLD" IMMIGRANTS

## THE MILWAUKEE MOVEMENT TO 1920

Milwaukee is marked by a relatively unique political history among larger metropolitan areas in the United States. For many decades of the twentieth century, Milwaukee was represented by Socialist public officials, a phenomenon that is, to say the least, rather exceptional in the politics of this essentially two-party political system. In a seemingly anomalous pattern, Milwaukee elected Socialists to its mayor's office, as its congressional representatives, to its city council, to its school board, and to other city and county positions. Beginning in the first years of the century, Milwaukee developed a three-party system; Socialists became familiar figures in public office, and from 1910 to 1940 seemed to be the rule rather than the exception, if at times superficially. Even as late as 1960, a generation after the Socialist movement nationally had dissipated, Milwaukee's third and last Socialist mayor completed a twelve-year period in office.

This essay will explore the Socialist phenomenon in Milwaukee and will consider the growth of the movement, its component parts, the policies and trends associated with Milwaukee socialism, and the meaning of any emergent patterns to the history of the Cream City and the United States. Milwaukee socialism evolved during the era of greatest Socialist activity in the country. After the turn of the century and throughout the era of the First World War, the United States experienced its most vibrant and politically successful Marxist movement, creating more of an image of respectability and acceptability among Americans than American Marxists were able to do in the 1930s when their presence seemed tainted by foreign ties. But at the start of the century, the Socialist Party of America, which organized in 1901, appeared to many to be a homegrown product and was in fact numerically dominated by a native-born membership. The Socialists organized locals in all regions of the United States, including the South. The party had followers in proportionately large numbers in Oklahoma and Kansas and had supporters in immigrant communities, too, in large urban enclaves in the East and the Midwest. On the eve of the Great War, it enjoyed its peak membership of 118,000, and it elected mayors and other public officials throughout the country, while simultaneously developing its own mass media that saw three-fourths of the states produce Socialist periodicals. The party's perennial candidate for the presidency, the charismatic Indianan Eugene V. Debs, made his most impressive campaign in 1912 when he garnered almost 6 percent of the ballots cast.[1]

It was against this background that the Socialists of Milwaukee, calling themselves locally the Social Democratic party, strode into the center of the political arena and brought their movement to fruition. First electing several aldermen, state assemblymen, and a state senator in 1904, in 1910 they experienced their greatest triumphs. In the 1910–12 term, the Milwaukee Socialists elected a mayor for the first time, sixteen of twenty-three aldermen, seven aldermen-at-large, two civil judges, eleven of sixteen supervisors, the city treasurer, city attorney, and comptroller as well as electing the first Socialist ever to the United States House of Representatives from the Fifth Congressional District and putting on a strong race in Wisconsin's Fourth as well. That period witnessed the Socialists' most sweeping victories. After a setback in 1912, the Socialists again captured the mayor's office in 1916 and held it uninterruptedly until 1940. They carried Milwaukee County three times and several times offered strong gubernatorial and senatorial candidacies. It was essentially a Milwaukee city and county phenomenon, however, and they never enjoyed again the political control they tasted in 1910–12. Even their recapturing of the mayor's office in 1916 after a four-year hiatus was marked by less meaning because they controlled only the executive branch and because issues of interventionism and war blurred and eventually modified party direction. Because of this pattern, this exploration of Milwaukee socialism will focus especially on the 1904–6 to 1916 period.[2]

The Milwaukee context at the beginning of this century was striking. In fact it seemed to suggest a caricature of what the American urban populace was becoming. Milwaukee was insistently non-English, it was increasingly Roman Catholic, and it was experiencing an influx—if not impressively large—of Central and Eastern Europeans. At the start of the century, first and second generation Milwaukeeans were three-fourths of the city's population. Yet in 1910, Milwaukee had the largest foreign population base of the largest U.S. cities. Of those of foreign birth 60 percent had been born in Germany. The German population had been the largest nationality bloc as early as 1850, the date of the first census after Wisconsin had earned its statehood, and over the subsequent decades Germans had shaped the city in accord with their culture, occupational pursuits, and institutions.[3]

German Milwaukee had its own foreign-language newspapers, recreational and cultural organizations, and fraternal orders. German was the commercial language of the city for most of the century. German neighborhoods, clustered especially on the northwest side (although individual Germans were dispersed throughout the metropolitan area), were marked by a high degree of home ownership. The German migration, as reported by Kathleen Neils Conzen, had been essentially a family migration. German families came in three waves, responding to economic and political impulses in the homeland, and established themselves in Milwaukee in one-and two-story frame houses. Germans worked in the city's tanneries, breweries, mills, tool factories, and processing industries. Germans, while heavily skilled and filling half the small shopkeeper ranks at the time of the Civil War could, in fact, be found in all occupations and socioeconomic groups. Their early numerical preponderance also meant that they were able to develop their own institutional network that led to a Germanic microcosm that eventually, as it grew and experienced some dilution, formed the cultural ambience of Milwaukee in general. Because of their numbers, skills, and capital, as well as the fact of their initial settlement in the city before it established a firm economic, political, or social framework, Germans were able to make an enormous imprint on the area.[4]

Poles were the other sizeable nationality group, composing 20 percent of the foreign-born element by 1910. But because their numbers were far less than the Germans and their entry into the area came essentially after 1880, a generation later, they had to fit into the overall environment which they found rather than shape it to their own needs. Indeed, they have been described as "defensive in their dealings with the German majority." They settled on the south side of the city, near heavy industry in which the Poles' unskilled majority tended to labor, while a smaller enclave of Poles established itself in a small industrial area to the north. But nevertheless the Poles did have some effect on the Milwaukee context. The southside ward in which they most heavily clustered, the Fourteenth, became the most congested area of the city. It featured small houses, a high degree of homeownership, as with the Germans, often involving sharing domiciles with renters who helped meet mortgage payments, and numbers of chickens and goats in the yards.[5]

The history of Polish Milwaukee is only now emerging. Hitherto, the Poles had been seen as simply a group bent on developing secure neighborhoods. Except for the degree to which their cohesiveness through their church led to occasional municipal influence, for example their success in 1909 in convincing the Milwaukee school board to agree to the teaching of Polish, they were seen as compliant. But *Polonia* in Milwaukee did succeed in playing a "salient role" locally. Milwaukee's Poles tended to come from German-controlled provinces, especially the area around Poznan, and they were thus more experienced with industry than were Poles from totally rural eastern European areas who settled in other Great Lakes cities. A handful of Milwaukee Poles established their first parish in 1866. By 1910 the approximately seventy thousand Poles developed a full institutional network of parishes (including parochial schools), banking associations, shops, fraternal societies, two newspapers, and they began to elect Poles to public offices. Community leadership tended to come from the clergy both because of the group's religious commitment and also its small numbers in the proprietary, professional, and clerical occupations. The Polish community divided on issues and politics and yet asserted itself in matters perceived to be significant.[6]

No other immigrant group was large enough to play an influential role in the city. Nearly a dozen other so-called New Immigrant nationalities were represented before World War I, but numbers were not impressive. Yet some were successful in creating a semblance of community. Slovenians, who settled after the 1870s just south of the central business district, arrived as unskilled workers, often having been miners in the Austrian Empire. Slovenians worked in Milwaukee's plants, especially in its tanneries, and they strove toward homeownership and toward becoming autonomous businessmen. Tavern ownership was the most common goal, with taverns eventually serving as quasi-social centers for the group. By the second decade of the twentieth century, the Slovenians had established a formal community center and organized fraternal societies, singing societies, parishes, and drama clubs.[8] The Greeks, another New Immigrant group, settled in Milwaukee in the first years of the twentieth century, especially after 1905. Numbering four to five thousand, they too worked in the tanneries and also in the city's iron and steel mills. They, as the Slovenians, quickly established fraternal and beneficial societies despite their small numbers. Czechs, who were one of the earliest groups in the area, their arrival coinciding with the early Germans, more often chose agrarian rather than urban places of settlement. Thus, their numbers in Milwaukee were limited among the Czech Wisconsin population and their potential influence was further reduced by the hostility and enmity between them and Slovak settlers. The two groups established separate institutional networks as a result. Hungarians, Italians, Jews, and the earlier-settled Irish were other Milwaukee groups. But as historian Bayrd Still long ago noted, these groups were "suspended" in the urban cul-

TABLE 1

Percentage Distribution of Foreign-Born by Country of Birth
City of Milwaukee, 1880–1920[7]

|  | 1880 | 1890 | 1900 | 1910 | 1920 |
|---|---|---|---|---|---|
| Germany | 27.0 | 27.0 | 19.0 | 17.0 | 8.7 |
| Poland | 1.5 | 4.5 | 6.0 | — | 5.0 |
| Britain | 2.0 | 1.7 | 1.0 | 0.7 | 0.6 |
| Ireland | 3.2 | 1.7 | 0.9 | 0.5 | 0.3 |
| Bohemia/Czech | 1.3 | 0.7 | 0.6 | — | 0.8 |
| Austria | 0.8 | 0.5 | 0.6 | 3.0 | 1.2 |
| Russia | — | — | 0.4 | 3.2 | 1.6 |
| Hungary | — | — | — | 1.4 | 1.0 |
| Italy | — | — | 0.3 | 0.9 | 0.9 |

ture rather than "integrated" into it, and were not prominent.[9]

Black Americans were only slightly represented in pre-war Milwaukee. While blacks in the second decade of the twentieth century migrated in increasing numbers to neighboring Chicago and Detroit, Milwaukee's percentage of the migration was so slim that blacks made up less than one percent of the population in 1920. Those two thousand individuals tended to work in manufacturing and mechanical occupations rather than personal services, and a tiny middle class began to emerge in these years on the near west side. Institutional developments were marked with the founding of a black newspaper, the establishment of branches of the National Urban League and Marcus Garvey's Universal Negro Improvement Association, and a growing number of black churches.[10]

In this environment, one of the most intriguing municipal histories developed. Marxists had first been active in Milwaukee in the 1870s and again in the 1880s, but it was not until the last decade of the nineteenth century that they were able to build a growing and lasting organization for a leftist political movement. The local scene, paralleling developments nationally, witnessed a number of impermanent socialist organizations, coalitions, and parties until the emergence of the Socialist Party of America in 1901. Handfuls of Milwaukeeans, often German, energized a Socialist Labor party presence which was followed by the appearance of a Populist group in the area. In 1897 Milwaukeeans were major proponents of the Social Democracy and the next year helped found its successor organization, the Social Democratic party which itself was replaced by the Socialist party. Preferring the Social Democratic label, the Milwaukee Socialists began to field tickets in municipal elections in 1898.[11]

This was an era of enormous ferment in American society and politics, a fact of fortuitous importance for the Milwaukee comrades. Citizens' leagues, journalists, and maverick politicians promoted reform across the country. A significant ingredient in Milwaukee that created an opening wedge for Socialist success was the revelation of a network of corruption which involved both Democrats and Republicans. By 1904, a half-dozen years after the party's electoral debut, public officials of both old parties began to face indictments on charges of bribery and graft. Mayor David S. Rose, a Democrat who held office with one interruption for a decade after 1898, came to be known as lax about his promises and disinterested in reform. LaFollette Progressives, for the most part active everywhere in Wisconsin except Milwaukee, left the city to find its own route to self-help. Mass meetings of civic indignation, the formation of additional voters' groups, and electoral reforms all geared toward clean and honest government crystallized in a search for a new repository of the public trust. Accordingly, the Socialists began to win elections.[12]

The Social Democrats of Milwaukee were revisionist Marxists and, thus, were representative of the thrust of the Second International and of the Socialist Party of America. Although in both cases—internationally and nationally—revisionism was challenged by orthodox Marxists as opportunistic, it nevertheless dominated party practices (if not policy statements), and this was certainly true in Milwaukee. The local comrades maintained the inevitability of the triumph of socialism but they simultaneously believed in pursuing political action en route to the expected social transformation of the economic system. Political action was viewed as significant for its propaganda value but also for the increasingly real prospect of electoral victories. The party's first platform, hammered together in 1898, emphasized the class struggle and the goal of the collective ownership of the means of production and distribution. Specific planks offered to the city's voters included municipal ownership of utilities, an equitable tax burden, public works projects, free legal, medical, and educational services, urban renewal programs, and cultural and recreational activities. These apparently attractive proposals, in tandem with the fact that the old parties were on the defensive, led to the election of nine Socialist aldermen in 1904 and the capturing of 25 percent of the ballots cast for mayor. In 1906 the Socialists elected twelve aldermen and won 27 percent of the mayoralty vote.[13]

Party growth was aided by, and in fact dependent upon, close ties to organized labor. Organized labor in Milwaukee meant German skilled workers who, because of their background in Bismarck's Germany with its large Social Democratic party, took for granted the existence of a political voice in the guise of a labor party. In 1887 the Milwaukee locals of the nascent American Federation of Labor created a central labor organization, the Federated Trades Council. As soon as the Social Democrats emerged, an intertwining of membership, offices, assumptions, policies, and goals occurred between the F.T.C. and the Social Democrats so that almost all historians write of an "interlocking" of the two. The autonomy of each organization was respected by the other, but the mutual goal of collectivization and the immediate demands of social and economic legislation to be achieved through political action meant that, in the phrase of the time, they were two arms of the same movement—one economic and one political. For the next two decades, until the stresses of the First World War, the relationship between organized labor and the party was fully harmonious and mutually advantageous.[14]

The leadership of the party came most especially from the dynamic Victor L. Berger, whose abilities led him easily to his role as the spokesman and even boss of Milwaukee socialism from the 1890s until his death three decades later. Berger (1860–1929), who immigrated to the United States in 1878 from the Nieder-Rehbach region of the Austro-Hungarian Empire, initially taught school. Simultaneously, he pursued third party politics, and became a founder of both the local and the national Socialist parties, built a number of German- and English-language Socialist newspapers—the *Vorwärts*, *Social-Democratic Herald*, and *Milwaukee Leader* especially—and was elected to both the Milwaukee common council and, six times, to the United States House of Representatives from the Fifth Congressional District of Wisconsin. He was also a member of the AFL's typographical union. Berger tried to "Americanize" the movement and, as a product of a Germanic background and as a unionist, was the perfect embodiment of the Milwaukee party. The other early important Milwaukee leader was Frederic F. Heath (1864–1954) whose local uniqueness lay in the fact that he was not German but a Yankee. He was, like Berger, a founder of the national party, and locally he frequently ran for office, serving as alderman, as county supervisor, and as a school board member.[15]

The Milwaukee party as it developed was much more in the image of European social democratic parties than reflective of American political organizations. While David Shannon argued the opposite some years ago, emphasizing that the Socialist Party of America was "a fairly loose alliance of regional political groups . . . unconsciously following the pattern of the major political parties", nevertheless, this was at best only part of the picture. The Milwaukee version of the Socialist party in structure and in functions resembled its European antecedent. Party discipline over its public office holders was maintained through the sixty branches in the county; the movement came to envelop its members and supporters. It provided leadership, solidarity and a sense of involvement through its hierarchical levels. With its programs and activities—its newspapers, bazaars, carnivals, picnics, singing societies, and Sunday schools, among other functions—the party provided a framework for the lives of its followers. Friendships were formed and shaped within the party environment, while members' leisure time and that of their children was enhanced by it. The Milwaukee Socialist organization was certainly not limited essentially to actions geared to bringing out the vote during election campaigns.[16]

The party's outreach programs, its pervasive presence in the city, as well as its stand on issues, resulted in the Socialists winning the support of others besides labor into their first decade. Among the ethnic voters of the city, the party's strongest support came from the German community. While German voters never gave a majority of their votes to the Socialists but rather to the two mainstream parties, nevertheless, their wards were the foundation of the party's electoral strength. Eighty-seven percent or twenty-six of the first thirty of the party's aldermanic victories came in the heavily Germanic northwest-side wards. In 1910 the German vote was the basis of the election of the first Socialist mayor who won 27,608 votes out of 59,484 cast in a three-way race. In 1912 when he was defeated for re-election against a fusion candidate, German wards gave him a high of 71 percent of their votes (Ward 20) to a low of 38 percent (Ward 19). In 1916, the year the second Socialist mayor was elected, he won 61 percent for a high in the Germans wards (in Ward 21) to a low of 48 percent in a German ward (Ward 22).[17]

Socialist support was not limited to German Milwaukeeans. Both party composition and voting patterns show that some Poles and less numerically strong other Central and Eastern European groups followed the red banner. Foreign-language branches existed in the various wards and neighborhoods, providing party representation for Italians, Hungarians, Russians, South Slavs, Slovenes, Jews, and Bohemians, as well as Poles and monolingual German-speakers, and there was also a general Austro-Hungarian branch. Polish wards, the Eleventh and Fourteenth, gave the Socialists 58 percent and 52 percent of their ballot in 1912 and 71 percent and 68 percent respectively in 1916. Wards in which the smaller New Immigrant groups were clustered, the Second, Sixth, Ninth, and Thirteenth, voted Socialist in 1912 in percentages varying from 36 to 46, and in 1916 three of these wards gave the Socialist candidate 50 to 56 percent of their votes.[18]

Clearly, heavy Socialist inroads were made in Polish areas, with Polish voters often giving Socialist candidates greater support than they averaged in the city as a whole. Thus, a trend can be shown of Polish voters moving away from the Democratic party for which they originally voted to the Socialist party, and to a lesser extent, to the LaFollette Republicans in the pre-war era. Polish workers, especially those who were trade unionists, joined the Social Democratic party, briefly enjoyed a Socialist paper of their own in 1910, *Naprzod*, and organized a Polish women's branch of the party. A Polish Socialist was elected as alderman-at-large in 1910; that same year another was elected to the State Assembly from Milwaukee's south side, and in fact, seven of the twenty-three Polish aldermen up to 1940 were Socialists. Therefore, in the not inconsiderable Polish political presence in Milwaukee, the Socialists fielded a strong contingent. The major Socialist leaders in the Polish community were Leo Krzycki (1881–1966) and Walter Polakowski (1888–1966). Krzycki, born in Milwaukee, was an officer of the Lithographic Press Feeders Union of the Amalgamated Clothing Workers Union, as well as a party official, and he was elected to public office on the Socialist ticket as an alderman and county undersheriff. Polakowski, who was also a skilled worker, was a representative to the Federated Trades Council and held office as a Socialist as both a state assemblyman and a state senator. Under the leadership of such individuals, influenced in part by Germanic political and economic traditions both in the Old World and in Milwaukee, and clearly distancing themselves from their church's preaching against the socialist menace, Poles in some numbers comfortably followed the party banner until 1918. Support then declined as a result of the party's disinterest in Polish nationalism during the postwar remaking of the map of Eastern Europe.[19]

Numbers of women also responded to the party's messages. The party nationally, in tandem with international socialism, committed itself to equal political rights for men and women, and the Milwaukee Social Democrats followed suit. Despite the general unpopularity of woman's suffrage among German-Americans, the Milwaukee comrades supported it through policy statements and, when in public office, legislative proposals. Nonetheless, they always demonstrated some ambivalence over the issue, and their most consistent ideological position, as was true of Socialists generally, held that the Woman Question, under which suffrage was subsumed, would be solved only after the Social Question. Fragmentary party membership statistics, both nationally and locally, make membership data in general and by gender suspect, but the Socialists throughout the country always had a visible number of women activists, organizers, and convention delegates, as well as a structure of women's committees for a half-dozen years. Milwaukee, accordingly, had it's own women's branch, female activists, and convention delegates. As an example, at the party's state convention of 1918 which was held in Milwaukee, four of the fifty-five delegates were women. Three of them represented women's branches and one attended as a regular ward representative.[20]

Suffrage campaigns in Wisconsin saw Milwaukee Socialist women in the forefront. They worked within the Wisconsin Woman Suffrage Association, despite the party's prohibition of collaboration with bourgeois organizations, and they were part of a coalition on behalf of woman's suffrage which included groups such as the State Teachers Association, the Women's Christian Temperance Union, and the Federation of Women's Clubs. These activists fought for the unsuccessful 1912 state referendum in favor of woman's suffrage, its reintroduction into the state legislature, and on behalf of the passage of the Nineteenth Amendment to the U.S. Constitution. The leading woman Socialist in Milwaukee and in these campaigns was Meta Schlichting Berger (1873–1944). She was the first Socialist elected to a school board in the country, serving there from 1909 to 1939, including election to its presidency; was a major figure in the Wisconsin Woman Suffrage Association; worked with the National Woman's Party; served on the Woman's National Committee of the Socialist party; and was active, along with her husband, on all levels of the local party.[21]

Some of the other leading women Socialists in Milwaukee were of non-German heritage. May Wood Simons (c. 1870–1947) was a leader of the party nationally and came to Milwaukee from Chicago before the war because of her husband's commitments as a party journalist. She herself was a journalist, a socialist theoretician, and the first woman to run seriously for the party's vice presidential nomination. She headed the party's Woman's National Committee, chaired its National Education Committee, helped establish a Socialist Sunday School network, and attended meetings of the Second International abroad and the Second International Conference of Socialist Women. Another American of English background, prominent locally if not nationally in the movement, was Elizabeth Howland Thomas (1870-c. 1930). She was New York-born to a long line of Quaker activists and had begun her career at Hull House in Chicago. She came to Milwaukee to work on Victor Berger's *Social-Democratic Herald*, held party positions, was elected to the school board, and spent three decades collaborating with Berger on his newspapers and in the movement. These several women, who often shared their commitment to the party with Socialist husbands, endowed the Milwaukee movement with visible female role models.[22]

One particular policy of the Social Democrats apparently opened friendly avenues for them among some women and also to the middle class, the civic-minded, the educationally aware, and others who were neither ethnic nor working class. The Socialists' broad support for public education enhanced the party image far beyond its obvious sphere of influence. In contrast to an interpretation historians of education usually offered of the public schools and elitist social control in this era, Milwaukee Socialists demonstrated how sympathizers of the workers and the poor could meet with some success in shaping the schools to their needs. It has been argued that the Social Democrats achieved a degree of "power in the schools and endeavored to use their influence along with other civic groups to reform Milwaukee education."[23]

From its origins, the party was interested in public education and the wider use of school facilities on behalf of the whole community, including programs of worker and adult education. Socialist leaders Victor Berger and Emil Seidel, among others, wrote and spoke of the significance of education in the expansion of democracy and the development of full human potential. In concert with voluntary associations such as parents' groups, women's clubs, and other civic-minded organizations, the Social Democrats successfully promoted school reforms on the basis of symbiotic relationships among otherwise distant entities. They endorsed each other's educational and social service programs in the schools. Socialists Meta Berger and Frederic Heath were elected to the school board in 1909, and the Socialists enjoyed domination of policy through control of as many as one-third of the seats and alliances with other members. The coalition attained direct election of school board members, expanded appropriations for education, promoted continuation schools for young workers, vacation schools, free lunches, medical and dental programs for children, use of the schools as community centers open to all neighborhood groups, and was able to establish additional social and recreational programs.[24]

Milwaukee Social Democrats had their movement reinforced by pockets of support outside their city and county. Locals were organized and appeared in northern and central Wisconsin and along the lakeshore winding north from Milwaukee. State conventions always saw representation from such outlying sites as Rhinelander, Two Rivers, Superior, Manitowoc, Racine, Fond du Lac, Sheboygan, Madison, Green Bay, Oshkosh, Kenosha, and LaCrosse. Socialists won election to public office from Wausau, Rhinelander, and Manitowoc County. The state party, headquartered in Milwaukee itself, routed organizers to rural areas, especially the ubiquitous Oscar Ameringer, a close colleague of Berger in the movement and, later, on his newspaper. As a native German-speaker and an organizer in rural Oklahoma, Ameringer was an ideal choice for party work in agrarian areas of Wisconsin. Berger, very much an urbanite, promoted working farmers' interests, such as cooperative marketing, state ownership of grain elevators, and agricultural education and insurance programs. A combination of factors throughout Wisconsin, such as German ethnicity, war dissent, as well as the basic effort the party exerted to interest ruralities, led to a degree of success in the second decade of the twentieth century as measured by membership and successful election campaigns in cities and counties outside Milwaukee.[25]

The gathering Socialist momentum was pronounced both nationally and locally. Socialists, well organized in Milwaukee, able to respond to voter interests, and aided by the disintegration of the two major parties, experienced a groundswell toward the election sweep of 1910. In 1904, reflective of growing numbers of supporters and new party locals, as well as increasing propaganda devices via a "bundle brigade" capable of delivering campaign literature in particular languages to appropriate households, the Social Democrats moved into several common council seats and county offices while Victor Berger won virtually one-fourth of the votes for mayor. In 1906, they added three seats to their nine on the common council and increased their mayoralty vote, while in 1908 they captured nine seats and 33.1 percent of the votes cast for mayor. Their decline in the council races directly resulted from an anti-Socialist measure passed by the state legislature based on an old party coalition which sought to minimize minor party strength by providing for the election of a dozen aldermen-at-large. This measure, the thrust of which was reinforced in 1912 when the state introduced nonpartisan city elections for cities "of the first class," i.e., over a certain size, which meant only Milwaukee, pointed toward both decentralization and depoliticization of the local scene after years of graft. But the point was not only insuring honest government but limiting the impact of a party with localized pockets of strength.[26]

The Social Democrats fought back with their only weapons: intensifying their propaganda efforts and widening their appeal. Recognizing that their base was German and working class, they began to reach more deeply into other ethnic communities with their newspapers and foreign-language branches, and they sought to utilize their solid connections with various civic reformers to actually win the vote of the middle-class concerned citizen. The Socialists backed off from their explicit hostility toward organized religion, particularly Roman Catholicism. They deleted a key platform plank prohibiting the granting of franchises to private utility corporations in favor of fully supervised franchises regulated in the public interest. In general, they came to emphasize honesty in government more than the class struggle, modernization of city services rather than collectivization, and home rule for the city. Complementing their overall efforts was the fact of the half-dozen years of office-holding which meant they were no longer unfamiliar to the voters. During these years of growth and modification, two figures came to the fore who together epitomized the Socialists' near monopolization of the mayor's office from 1910 to 1940. Emil Seidel (1864–1947) was the son of working-class German immigrants who himself was a skilled worker, a woodcarver and patternmaker. A self-effacing figure, he was elected several times to the common council, ran for other local and state offices, and for the vice presidency on the Socialist ticket in 1912. In 1910 he became the first Socialist to win the mayor's office in a large American city and, upon election, stressed "the sacredness of the trust" placed in the Socialists by Milwaukee voters. Daniel Webster Hoan (1881–1961) also hailed from a poor background as a second generation German-American born in Waukesha. He managed to attend law school and, at the age of twenty-nine in his first run for office, was elected on the Socialist ticket as Milwaukee's city attorney. Cases he pressed successfully against local public utilities made him a popular official. Moving to the mayor's office, he held that position until his defeat for an eighth consecutive term as mayor in 1940 when he was fifty-nine years old.[27]

By the time of the party's great 1910 victory, their representatives had sponsored common council measures that strictly regulated franchises and that promoted city services, labor reforms, and cultural and recreational programs for Milwaukee's citizens. In the wake of the 1910 spring and fall elections when they won 47 percent of the mayoralty votes for a plurality and won a majority of the common council and the County Board of Supervisors, two-thirds of the county's delegations to the state legislature, the office of city attorney, and other local positions as well as electing Berger to Congress, the party was able to move in a relatively unencumbered manner. Through its taxation policies and wider view of public service, as well as of the citizenry, a different spirit was markedly clear in city government. Perhaps most explicitly signaling a changed outlook, the city under Mayor Seidel initiated wide-ranging policies on behalf of local workers. Union wages and an eight-hour day were granted to city employees, with a free employment office established. Strike arbitration service was offered, while companies were offered not simply that assistance but also encouraged to unionize. Industry was regulated more energetically than earlier in the city's history, and required to comply with all existing ordinances and regulations. New factory and building regulations were passed, with fire prevention measures enforced. Long-term franchise holders, as anticipated, were required to respect scrupulously the condition of their franchises. The Milwaukee Electric Railway and Light Company, the local utility which came to epitomize the Progressive Era struggle against corporate control, was forced to reduce its rates, to implement safety ordinances, and to pave the roadways along its tracks. To finance some of their efforts, the party office holders were able to win a more equitable assessment of the wealthier wards.

Other efforts included crime prevention and anti-vice ordinances. Housing and fire commissions were established as well as public health and city planning programs. Free public concerts and lectures, and various programs in the parks were instituted to enhance the quality of life for Milwaukee's average resident. Local bureaucracies (such as within the school district), often having a life of their own, were encouraged by example, and where possible, forced by regulation to take a wider view of the public and its needs than had traditionally been common. Policies pursued without success usually were those which went beyond social and welfare measures toward basic measures of economic control: the Socialists were unable to implement direct purchasing or to establish municipal lodginghouses, ice houses, slaughterhouses, or markets, nor could they end the contract system.

Public administration practices were modernized by the Socialist administrations. A Bureau of Economy and Efficiency was established at Berger's initiative and was headed by the noted economist, John R. Commons of the University of Wisconsin, who mirrored the era's respect for government by technicians. His recommendations led to the introduction of cost accounting and centralized purchasing. In addition, deficit financing was terminated, the city's credit rating was improved, and the taint of corruption disappeared.[28]

Daniel Hoan, whose main thrust as city attorney from 1910 to 1916 had been anti-transit company measures on behalf of the public, entered the mayor's office in 1916 with the handicap of an anti-Socialist majority on the common council. In fact, the Socialists had less than one-third of the council seats. Nevertheless, Hoan attempted to build in the image of the Seidel administration of 1910–12, and to add measures suggestive even more of municipal ownership. He sought a municipal-owned lighting plant, harbor improvements, better sewage facilities, more municipal planning, a restoration of centralized purchasing, and a renewal of an energetic struggle for home rule, but these efforts were unsuccessful. Indeed, as symptomatic of his weakness, Mayor Hoan was not even able to win common council approval for one of his appointments to the directorship of a city department in his first six years in office. Both Seidel in his two years in office and Hoan in the 1916–20 period of his mayorality were limited by state and charter regulations, handicapped especially by the lack of home rule in the face of an antagonistic state legislature and weakened by the need of a three-fourths majority on the common council, required for the passage of procedural changes.[29]

Beyond the statutory limitations, the lack of sufficient majorities, and the specific anti-socialist structural reforms of the political system, the fact of the First World War affected Germanic-dominated Milwaukee so arbitrarily that early in Hoan's first term, the promise of the Seidel era in which anything seemed possible became merely a distant memory. In fact, the brief Seidel term which ushered in three decades of Socialist visibility was ironically the crest of Socialist achievement. Never thereafter was there both executive and legislative control or, most significantly, the momentum of a decade of national and local party growth.

Paralleling the city and county pattern, Socialists in the state legislature also enjoyed their pre-war peak strength during the Seidel years. Social Democrats were elected to the Wisconsin legislature for three decades, and sponsored measures such as state insurance, a public defender office in each county, and a reorganization of the judicial system. They found their greatest success in the 1911 session when fourteen Socialists sat in the legislature (all representing the Milwaukee area) and, coalescing with state progressives, they passed labor, health, and safety measures.[30]

The assessment of the Social Democratic record can be attempted by noting how uniquely they approached ongoing governmental responsibilities. As early as the first six months of the Seidel administration, a journalist in a national magazine described Socialists in office as distinct from reformers because they wanted to change the system. A recent author has explored that issue through a case study of the Milwaukee police, and has argued that the Socialists tried to reconceptualize police service so that it was working class in orientation. The Seidel and Hoan administrations were limited in the administering of the policing system because of the civil service-protected, lifetime tenure of Police Chief John Janssen, who held the position from 1888 to 1921. He was comfortable with the anti-strike and social control activities of the department which Seidel sought to undermine. Mayor Seidel unsuccessfully attempted to house the police and other major functions in an extended public service agency which would at least redirect activities if not control the police as an institution. The Socialists and their allies on the Board of Police Commissioners initiated reviews of department disciplinary actions, and the party opposed incidents of police brutality against striking workers and sought to improve conditions for House of Corrections inmates, for individuals under arrest, and for rank-and-file police officers themselves. Major Socialist measures tried to enhance workers' recreational hours by liberating saloons, which their platform always described as the proletarian's club house, from police-endorsed or tolerated vice, and by neutralizing police regulation of workers' dance halls. The Socialist record in this instance was clearly not simply that of professionalization of police services as reformers elsewhere but of restructuring the role of the police and mitigating existing class bias. Thus, the police issue demonstrates that Socialists brought a new perspective to urban government. Just as their effort, discussed above, to broaden the educational system to meet the needs of the community at large and give the workers of the city input and even control of the educational system, their parallel efforts in the area of the police function illustrate the fact that they tried to democratize public institutions to the extent of their ability. They viewed the working people of the city as not simply another interest group which merited a place in the public dialogue but, more, as the embodiment of the citizenry whose needs and interests must be the primary concern of the government.[31]

Milwaukee's Socialists wanted to go beyond new and improved public services and hoped to transform political, economic, and social institutions. While their platforms clearly displayed a reform-minded aura, as did many of the measures they were able to implement, nevertheless interest in radical social experiments and change was evident. They were without the necessary political power and were even more fundamentally constrained by the lack of municipal autonomy, as well as the party's own belief that socialism could not be implemented in one city alone. They were also limited by taxation rates which they did not seek to raise drastically. Legal limits on general fund taxes were retained, and Socialist state legislators did not even attempt to remove levy limitations. The Milwaukee Socialists depended instead on property reassessments, but increases here were minimal. No doubt the heavy proportion of homeowning workers among the party's German and Polish supporters and potential supporters dampened whatever enthusiasm the Socialists felt for property tax increases. Efficient management techniques seemed a wiser avenue. Various modest thrusts, such as utility regulation rather than municiplalization were certainly unimpressive to them, but the realities of franchises already awarded prevented an alternative course, and takeovers and drastic innovations were impossible. While proposals such as municipal lodging, mar-

TABLE 2

Socialist Percentages of Total Votes Cast in Mayoralty Elections
With Ethnically and Occupationally Identifiable Wards[32]

| Ward | Ethnicity | Occupations* | 1912 | 1914 | 1916 | 1918 | 1920 |
|------|-----------|-------------|------|------|------|------|------|
| 1 | | skilled, white collar | 18 | 19 | 31 | 20 | 21 |
| 2 | | skilled, white collar | 36 | 38 | 44 | 48 | 50 |
| 3 | | skilled, *unskilled* | 22 | 23 | 32 | 24 | 28 |
| 4 | | skilled, white collar | 25 | 22 | 28 | 22 | 23 |
| 5 | Slovenian | *unskilled*, skilled | 40 | 44 | 56 | 52 | 54 |
| 6 | | *skilled*, white collar | 42 | 44 | 50 | 60 | 61 |
| 7 | Italian, Slovenian | skilled, white collar | 51 | 54 | 58 | 75 | 71 |
| 8 | | *skilled*, white collar | 43 | 50 | 58 | 40 | 47 |
| 9 | German, East European | skilled | 46 | 49 | 56 | 64 | 64 |
| 10 | German | skilled | 52 | 51 | 60 | 69 | 71 |
| 11 | Polish | *unskilled*, skilled | 58 | 65 | 71 | 67 | 67 |
| 12 | | unskilled, skilled | 49 | 55 | 63 | 46 | 53 |
| 13 | | skilled | 39 | 42 | 50 | 51 | 51 |
| 14 | Polish | *unskilled*, skilled | 52 | 59 | 68 | 28 | 51 |
| 15 | | skilled, white collar | 26 | 25 | 32 | 43 | 39 |
| 16 | | skilled, white collar | 20 | 20 | 31 | 24 | 25 |
| 17 | | *unskilled*, skilled | 48 | 53 | 59 | 49 | 56 |
| 18 | | skilled, white collar | 21 | 17 | 25 | 23 | 20 |
| 19 | German | skilled, white collar | 38 | 41 | 49 | 56 | 51 |
| 20 | German | *unskilled*, skilled | 61 | 61 | 64 | 69 | 69 |
| 21 | German | *unskilled*, skilled | 51 | 53 | 61 | 68 | 65 |
| 22 | German | *skilled*, white collar | 41 | 42 | 48 | 57 | 53 |
| 23 | | skilled, white collar | 43 | 46 | 55 | 51 | 55 |
| 24 | | | 51 | 58 | 65 | 58 | 61 |
| 25 | | | 55 | 58 | 63 | 76 | 74 |

* These broad occupational categories of unskilled, skilled, and white collar are adapted from Simon, *Transactions* 68:22–23. Italics indicate that a particular category was heavily represented.

keting, slaughterhouses, and banking were never enacted, the Socialists' implementation of social and cultural measures on behalf of the population symbolized their commitment to promote the social good in the broadest sense.

Supporters who helped win public office for the Socialists and stayed with them from the earliest triumphs in 1904 until at least 1916 tended primarily to be workers and ethnic Germans. The Socialists' general momentum and their evolution as exemplified by their performance, alliances, and changing platform, were accompanied by a widening voter base. Although an empirically verifiable causal effect cannot be traced, the labor and Germanic roots of the party's political base deepened as each election saw greater percentages of the wards those groups dominated casting Socialist ballots, while simultaneously increasing numbers of the middle class and of non-German ethnics, such as Poles, also voted for the party's nominees. These new constituencies may have been engaged by the proliferation of planks offering better public services and honest government and, thus, planks which lacked a particular class dimension, as class consciousness became less of an obvious hallmark in each campaign. However, it may be argued that while the Socialists layered over their original message, the worker orientation of the party was still present. The central focus was yet apparent.

The state party's platform in 1916, Mayor Hoan's first year in office, repeated the general promise of ameliorative reforms, with touches that transcended that milieu. The party offered measures endorsing proportional representation, public control of vocational schools, adequate salaries for state legislators, and opposition to injunctions against unions, among other reforms, but it also endorsed the establishment of state municipal banks, including agricultural cooperative banks. The delegates resolved that:

> . . . state and municipal banks be provided whereby the savings of the people may be used to promote such public ownership utilities as will make for community welfare, such as elevators, storage warehouses, street railways, water power and all the state functions prescribed by our platform—thereby accumulating revenue-bearing property, for security and payment of interest for the people's savings and diverting the savings from the channels of exploitation which we condemn.

The 1918 platform, however, bore a new thrust. Issues of the right to dissent, the support of foreign-language institutions, the sanctity of First Amendment freedoms, and the party's own patriotism now dominated the platform. While it also endorsed collectivism (which in an aside was stated to have "proven its superiority and efficiency here and abroad during the war") the preoccupations of the delegates were far different from earlier. What had happened in those two years was the unravelling of the social fabric due to the stresses of the war in German-dominated Milwaukee.[33]

The loyalty issue was raised in this most foreign-appearing city as early as the November 1914 campaign. Much of the population was pro-German in 1914, while by early 1917 many individuals and institutions muted their position to that simply of anti-intervention by the United States. Different aspects of the war energized different components of the Milwaukee demographic scene. Poles and other Slavic groups began to look toward American participation in the war as a positive step toward the eventual independence of their homelands upon the destruction of the Austro-Hungarian Empire. Anglo-Saxon institutions and individuals seemed convinced of the need for the United States to become a full partner with the allies against the Central Powers. Indeed, party leaders of English heritage moved away from their former ties. A.M. Simons, May Wood Simons, and Winfield R. Gaylord, a popular party figure who had been elected to the state legislature, abandoned the party and campaigned against their former comrades. Through the Wisconsin Loyalty League and citizenship schools hastening the acculturation of immigrants, such individuals attacked the patriotism of German Milwaukeeans and party members alike.[34]

The local party tried to walk a fine line. It changed its name to the Socialist party to distance itself from Germany's Social Democrat party, but it joined the national party in its anti-interventionism and anti-preparedness. When the Socialist Party of America denounced the declaration of war in April 1917 in its St. Louis Proclamation, Victor Berger signed the document but Mayor Hoan sidestepped an endorsement of it. Hoan, who had transformed a pre-war preparedness parade into a civic celebration, distanced himself personally from issues of war support or opposition as much as he could. Under duress, he cooperated with a reaffirmation of the party's war stand but he also addressed patriotic meetings. His civil defense duties as required by his office were his primary wartime activities. He chaired the County Council of Defense and its Bureau of Food Control, prevented war profiteering by local business and industries, and promoted civil liberties in whatever ways his position permitted. He invited the convention of the People's Council for Democracy and Peace, a Socialist-dominated, American-style soviet promoting peace negotiations, to meet in Milwaukee, and he helped Berger's newspapers to continue to publish in the face of government censorship measures. By trodding such a careful path, he won re-election in April 1918, winning 51 percent of the vote as he had in his first run for office. His totals increased in every German ward while he lost support in Polish wards, losses which were offset by enlarging his base in other areas. The Socialist contingent in the common council grew to more than one-third, and that November Victor Berger was elected to the House of Representatives after three consecutive defeats. Undoubtedly, as scholars agree, war issues were involved in the vote. Distrust of Milwaukee's foreign population, mob actions against German-Americans, and indictments of some Socialist party candidates under the Espionage Act, all seemed to lead to a peace and civil libertarian vote on behalf of Socialists in the Milwaukee elections.[35]

When the postwar era began, the party and the city reflected their earlier images only dimly. A long decline lay ahead for the Milwaukee Socialists. Nationally the Socialist party had experienced a schism which resulted in a pro-Bolshevik Communist party and a Communist Labor party, with those Milwaukeeans who had retained membership during the war tending to remain with their shrunken party after the split. Membership across the country plummeted from the pre-schism figure of 104,822, the second highest totals in the party's history, to 26,766 in 1920. Locally, numbers also fell off, though lack of party records precludes an estimate. The party was perhaps mortally wounded by the evolution of its twin pillars, labor and the German community. The Federated Trades Council, after ambivalence initially in the war, had embraced patriotism and war bond drives. Slowly it moved away from its Socialist ties. Its membership, affected by the Americanization campaigns and the influence of the conservative American Federation of Labor, pulled away from the Socialist orbit. Simultaneously, the German population of Milwaukee felt the impact of the Americanization programs during and after its wartime defensiveness. German names were changed and culture minimized. Moreover, the Germans among Milwaukee's foreign-born population numbered only 8.7 percent in 1920 compared to 19 percent in 1900. Milwaukee would continue to be known as a Germanic city, but henceforth an amorphous ethos and a distant heritage rather than a firm domination existed.[36]

The Socialist effort in 1920, the first true postwar year, generally revolved around Mayor Hoan and party members on the common council and the school board. Numbers of Polish voters as well as middle-class voters came to join the German wards and endorsed each Hoan re-election effort. Often coalitions with non-Socialists were necessary to pass legislation. Hoan promoted party reform measures inherited from the previous Socialist mayoralties, including efficiency and honesty, the use of technicians and merit appointments, home-rule, and public welfare measures, such as a stone quarry, street lighting, sewage disposal, and water purification. His major innovation, if of brief duration, was municipal housing. The first low-cost housing project in any American city, the Garden Homes, was established in 1923.[37]

The party remained on the local scene as a fixture until midway in the Great Depression. Mayor Hoan stayed in office until 1940.[38] But the halcyon days were long in the past.[39] The Golden Age had amounted to a few fast-paced years. At the start of the century, the party found support mushrooming and momentum developing. The Socialists' positive image in the city, the tainting of the major local parties, and the support of the national party with its impressive growth, led to energy and vitality. Each election from 1904 onward saw the party move forward into public offices, and its great triumph of 1910 witnessed the takeover by Socialists of one of the largest cities in the country. In the 1910–12 term, they built their record and also their legacy. They were a party that stood for reform, for good government, for the public interest, and especially for the inclusion of working people in the city's power structure or, indeed, insuring that the workers and their representatives were its central ingredient. Socialists had built on the premise that the introduction of public ownership was necessary to the alteration of economic relationships among sectors of society and was in fact the key to transforming the system into one of worker control. But by 1910 they had begun to hedge and move away from that goal. They did so because of what they would term a realistic recognition that there were structural restraints on their abilities, and also no doubt because of an interest in garnering as much public support as they could. Thus, they continually sought to cast a wide net in their march to office.

In 1906, the Socialists had acknowledged that municipal efforts were small and insignificant parts of "the grand social and economic revolution" but that cities and towns had to be carried before the Socialists could win a national election. Victor Berger self-consciously promised a few days after the Seidel election that the party would "show the people of Milwaukee that the philosophy of international socialism can be applied and will be applied to the local situation and that it can be applied with advantage to any American city of the present day . . . we want to show . . . that our principles will lose nothing of their revolutionary energy by being applied to a local situation (though) the cooperative commonwealth will not appear now."[40]

Clearly, the socialists knew that class conscious policies were less feasible at the municipal level than the national. Capitalism and its attendant class structure provided the national framework, and therefore municipal governmental powers could hardly address basic structural issues. The Milwaukee Social Democrats would argue that they accomplished the most that local factors permitted.

1. On Milwaukee socialism, see Marvin Wachman, *History of the Social-Democratic Party of Milwaukee, 1897–1910* (Urbana: University of Illinois Press, 1945); Frederick I. Olson, "The Milwaukee Socialists, 1897–1941" (Ph.D. diss., Harvard University, 1952); Frederick I. Olson, "Milwaukee's First Socialist Administration, 1910–1912: A Political Evaluation," *Mid-America* 43 (July 1961), 197–207; Henry Pelling, "The Rise and Decline of Socialism in Milwaukee," *Bulletin of the International Institute of Social History* 10 (1955), 91–103; Sally M. Miller, "Milwaukee: Of Ethnicity and Labor," in Bruce M. Stave, ed., *Socialism and the Cities* (Port Washington, NY: Kennikat, 1975). For an overview of socialism in the United States, see David A. Shannon, *The Socialist Party of America: A History* (New York: Macmillan, 1955); James Weinstein, *The Decline of Socialism in America, 1912–1925* (New York: Monthly Review Press, 1967); Sally M. Miller, *Victor Berger and the Promise of Constructive Socialism, 1910–1920* (Westport, CT: Greenwood Press, 1973).

2. Voting records for Milwaukee are conveniently available in Sarah C. Ettenheim, ed., *How Milwaukee Voted, 1848–1969* (Milwaukee: Institute of Government Affairs, University of Wisconsin, 1970); George Allan England, "Milwaukee's Socialist Government," *American Review of Reviews* 42 (November 1910), 445–55.

3. Bayrd Still, *Milwaukee: The History of a City* (Madison: State Historical Society of Wisconsin, 1948), 574–75; H. Yuan Tien, ed., *Milwaukee Metropolitan Area Fact Book* (Madison: State Historical Society of Wisconsin, 1967), 23; Kathleen Neils Conzen, *Immigrant Milwaukee, 1836–1860: Accommodation and Community in a Frontier City* (Cambridge, MA: Harvard University Press, 1976), 1–7; Roger D. Simon, "The City-Building Process: Housing and Services in New Milwaukee Neighborhoods, 1880–1910," *Transactions of the American Philosophical Society* 68 (1978), 18–19.

4. Conzen, *Immigrant Milwaukee*, 5, 7, 50–51, 67–69, 84; Simon, "City Building," 18; Still, *Milwaukee*, 127, 258, 265–67; Gerd Korman, *Industrialization, Immigrants, and Americanization: The View from Milwaukee, 1866–1921* (Madison: State Historical Society of Wisconsin, 1967), 41–43. For comparison, see the South Bend experience where Germans settled early in that city's history, in Dean R. Esslinger, *Immigrants and the City: Ethnicity and Mobility in a Nineteenth Century Midwestern Community* (Port Washington, NY: Kennikat Press, 1975).

5. Donald Pienkos, "Politics, Religion, and Change in Polish Milwaukee, 1900–1930," *Wisconsin Magazine of History* 61 (Spring 1978), 181; Simon, "City-Building," 19–21; Roger D. Simon, "The Expansion of an Industrial City: Milwaukee, 1880–1910" (Ph.D. diss., University of Wisconsin, 1971), 81, 98–101. Thomas W. Gavett stresses the antagonism between Germans in organized labor and the Poles, beginning in 1876 with Pole scab activity. See Gavett, *The Development of the Labor Movement in Milwaukee* (Madison: University of Wisconsin Press 1965), 25, 115. Korman takes the same position; see Korman, *Industrialization*, 44.

6. Pienkos, "Politics," 179–83; Donald E. Pienkos, "The Polish Americans in Milwaukee Politics," in Angela T. Pienkos, ed., *Ethnic Politics in Urban America: The Polish Experience in Four Cities* (Chicago: Polish American Historical Association, 1978), 66–68, 70, 72, 90; Still, *Milwaukee*, 278, 464.

7. Figures are not available for all groups. The number of Polish-born present in 1910 in Milwaukee was integrated into the German and Russian figures. Sources for these figures are U.S. Census Department data for the years 1880–1920 as adapted from Still, *Milwaukee*, 574–75 and from Tien, *Milwaukee Fact Book*, 23.

8. Christine M. Ermenc, "Going Back: A Journey to Slovenian Milwaukee," *Historical Messenger* 32 (Autumn 1976), 88–100.

9. Theodore Soloutos, "The Greeks in Milwaukee," *Wisconsin Magazine of History* 53 (Spring 1970), 175–77, 185; Karel D. Bicha, "The Czechs in Wisconsin," ibid.: 194–99; Still, *Milwaukee*, 267–78.

10. See Joe William Trotter, "Race, Class, and Politics: The Milwaukee Experience, 1915–1932," paper read to the American Historical Association Pacific Coast Branch 1981 Convention, and his *Black Milwaukee, 1915–1945: The Making of an Industrial Proletariat* (Urbana: University of Illinois Press, 1985). Trotter demonstrates that some black leftist activity existed in the 1930s through the declining Socialists, the Communist presence, and a Garveyite group in Milwaukee.

11. Herbert N. Casson, "Socialism, its Growth and its Leader," *Muncy's Magazine 33* (June 1905), 296–97; Miller, "Milwaukee: Of Ethnicity and Labor," 45–46; Miller, *Victor Berger*, 35–36; Wachman, *History*, 9–19; Olson, "The Milwaukee Socialists," 1–40.

12. Frederick I. Olson, "The Socialist Party and the Unions in Milwaukee, 1900–1912," *Wisconsin Magazine of History* 44 (Winter 1960–61), 110–11; Olson, "Milwaukee's Socialist Administration," 199–200; Herbert F. Margulies, *The Decline of the Progressive Movement in Wisconsin, 1890–1920* (Madison: State Historical Society of Wisconsin, 1968), 152–53.

13. See *Social-Democratic Herald*, Aug. 14, 1909, and *Herald* editorials collected in Victor L. Berger, *Broadsides* (Milwaukee: Social-Democratic Publishing Co., 1912), such as "Real Social Democracy" (September 1906) and "Are Socialists Practical?" (March 1903). Party platforms are not extant for the first nine years of the party's existence, and hence the Socialist newspapers become the best source for the evolution of the platform before 1908. Platforms dating from 1908 onward are found in the State Party Conventions and Constitutions File in the Social Democratic Party Collection of the Milwaukee County Historical Society. Wachman is the most useful secondary source on the early platforms. See Wachman, *History*, p. 22, on 1898 and Miller, "Milwaukee: Of Ethnicity and Labor," 45–48. A pro-labor perspective was evident in the common council as soon as the Socialists began to win elections. See *Social-Democratic Herald* for council coverage and Gavett, *Development of the Labor Movement*, 121–31.

14. Gavett, *Development of the Labor Movement*, 27, 77–97; Korman, *Industrialization*, 58–59; Gerd Korman, "Political Loyalties, Immigrant Traditions and Reforms: the Wisconsin German-American Press and Progressivism, 1909–1911," *Wisconsin Magazine of History* 40 (Spring 1957), 165. Edwin Wittke maintained that "At no time were the Wisconsin trade unions a mere appendage to the Socialist Party" but trade unionists first and Socialists second. See Edwin Wittke, "Labor in Wisconsin History," *Wisconsin Magazine of History* 35 (Winter 1951), 139. Also see Olson, "Socialist Party and Unions," 112–13.

15. "Victor Berger: The Organizer of Socialist Victory in Milwaukee," *Current Literature* 49 (September 1910), 265–69; "Life and Labor of Victor L. Berger," *New Leader*, August 10, 1935; Miller, *Victor Berger*, see Chapter two; Miller, "Milwaukee: Of Ethnicity and Labor," 46; Frederic F. Heath, "How I Became a Socialist," *The Comrade* 2 (April 1903), 154–55. See their biographies in Frederic F. Heath, ed., *Social Democracy Red Book* (Terre Haute: Debs Publishing Co., 1900), 107, 113.

16. Shannon, *Socialist Party*, 7. Party activities can best be followed, as was indicated about platform and policy evolution, in the pages of the party press. See Berger's *Social-Democratic Herald* (1898–1913), the *Milwaukee Leader* (from 1911), *Political Action* (1910–11), *Voice of the People*, published during election campaigns, and a few other short-lived Milwaukee Socialist papers. See also convention proceedings, such as the Wisconsin Social Democratic Party, *Proceedings* [summary] of the 1910 State Convention, Milwaukee County Historical Society.

17. Ettenhein, *How Milwaukee Voted*, 124–25; Korman, *Industrialization*, 50.

18. See Wisconsin Social Democratic Party, *Proceedings* [Summary] of the 1910 State Convention, 5; the 1916 *Proceedings*, 2; and the 1918 *Proceedings*, 3, for listings of foreign-language branches. Foreign-language branches outside the county of Milwaukee included Danish, Finnish, and Lithuanian groups. Ettenheim, *How Milwaukee Voted*, 125.

19. This revisionist view of Polish political behavior in Milwaukee builds on the work of Donald Pienkos, who emphasizes precinct data as more precise than ward data; see Pienkos, "Polish Americans," 68, 70, and Pienkos, "Politics," 185–86, 188, 190–92, 206–8. His work challenges Still, *Milwaukee*, 468, and Shannon, *Socialist Party*, 23, on Polish political behavior in Milwaukee. On Krzycki, see Gary M. Fink, ed., *Biographic Dictionary of American Labor Leaders* (Westport, CT: Greenwood Press, 1974), 194, and on Polakowski, see Pienkos, "Politics," 193. A pamphlet by Krzycki entitled "The Unions and the Socialists" was published by the national party (no date).

20. Sally M. Miller, "Women in the Party Bureaucracy: Subservient Functionaries," in Sally M. Miller, ed., *Flawed Liberation: Socialism and Feminism* (Westport, CT: Greenwood Press, 1981), 13–15; Wisconsin Social Democratic Party, *Proceedings* [summary] of the 1918 State Convention, 2–3. The Milwaukee Public Library in its Social Democratic Party Collection has membership figures only for 1934 and 1935. A Branch Membership Report of January 1, 1935 lists 2339 members, of whom 586 were women. Obviously this indicates nothing definitive about pre-war membership.

21. See John D. Buenker, "The Politics of Mutual Frustration: Socialists and Suffragists in New York and Wisconsin," in Miller, *Flawed Liberation*, 128–40; Wisconsin Social Democratic Party, *Proceedings* [Summary] of the 1918 State Convention, 2–3; Meta Berger, "Unpublished Autobiography," n.p., State Historical Society of Wisconsin; William J. Reese, "'Partisans of the Proletariat': The Working Socialist Class and the Milwaukee Schools, 1890–1920," *History of Education Quarterly* 21 (Spring 1981), 23, 28–30.

22. Sally M. Miller, "Other Socialists: Native-Born and Immigrant Women in the Socialist Party of America, 1901–1917," *Labor History* 24 (Winter 1983), 90–91; Gretchen and Kent Kreuter, "May Wood Simons: Party Theorist," in Miller, *Flawed Liberation*, 37–60; Buenker, "Mutual Frustration," 129; "Elizabeth Howland Thomas," *Milwaukee Leader*, Dec. 7, 1929, Dec. 8, 1930.

23. Buenker, "Mutual Frustration," 135–36; Reese, "Partisans of the Proletariat," 6.

24. Socialists' campaigns always had an education component among their immediate demands; see Wachman, *History*, 22, for the 1898 platform. *Milwaukee Leader*, March 6, 1915, January 5, 1917, December 3, 1913; Meta Berger, "Unpublished Autobiography"; Reese, "Partisans of the Proletariat," 1–33; Buenker, "Mutual Frustration," 135.

25. Wisconsin Social Democratic Party, *Proceedings*, [summary] of the 1910 State Convention, 6; the 1916 *Proceedings*, 2; and the 1918 *Proceedings*, 1–2; James M. Lorence, "'Dynamite for the Brain': The Growth and Decline of Socialism in Central and Lakeshore Wisconsin, 1910–1920," *Wisconsin Magazine of History* 70 (Summer 1983), 251–254, 259–60, 262, 264, 268; also see James J. Lorence, "Socialism in Northern Wisconsin, 1910–1920: An Ethno-Cultural Analysis," *Mid-America* 64 (October 1982), 25–51. Lorence stresses a Polish Catholic component to the heavily German vote outside Milwaukee for Socialists in the war period. Ibid., p. 51, n33. On Oscar Ameringer, see his *If You Don't Weaken: The Autobiography of Oscar Ameringer* (New York: Henry Holt, 1940), 283–84, and James Green, *Grass-Roots Socialism: Radical Movements in the Southwest, 1895–1943* (Baton Rouge: Louisiana State University Press, 1978), 36–38, 44–45. The city of Sheboygan had German Socialists active as early as 1895 and elected two Socialists as aldermen in 1898. Heath, *Social Democracy Red Book*, 60; Works Projects Administration, Wisconsin, *A Guide to the Badger State* (New York: Duell, Sloan and Pearce, 1941), 287; "Berger," *Current Literature* 49: 265–69.

26. The *Social-Democratic Herald* on April 16, 1910, maintained that the bundle brigade blitz of the area for five Sundays prior to the election solidified the party's victory. See Carl D. Thompson, "How the Milwaukee Socialists Distribute Literature," Socialist Party of America, State and Local Collections, Wisconsin, 1898–

1920, Duke University Library. *Milwaukee Leader*, May 4, 1912; *Milwaukee Journal*, May 4, 1912; Wachman, *History*, 53, 60–66; Olson, "Milwaukee's Socialist Administration," 197–207.

27. Much of the national media coverage analyzed the electoral patterns in Milwaukee and emphasized that Socialist votes were simply a convenient form of protest rather than a sign of ideological conversion. See, for examples, "Tide of Socialism," *World's Work* 33 (January 1912), 252, and "Advance of Socialism in the United States," *Chatauquan* 44 (September 1911), 18–19. The Socialists, whatever softening they permitted ideologically, did introduce a measure to the common council in 1910 seeking power to take over public utilities; see *Political Action*, Dec. 17, 1910. Mayor Hoan wrote that regulation of private companies had always failed and that public ownership of utilities was mandatory; his position was ironic since much of his career success was based on his reputation as a regulator of the public utilities. See Daniel Webster Hoan, *City Government: The Record of the Milwaukee Experiment* (New York: Harcourt, Brace, 1936), 48–54. On Emil Seidel, see Seidel Inaugural Speech, April 19, 1910, Emil Seidel Collection, Box 3, Milwaukee County Historical Society; Olson "Milwaukee's Socialist Administration," 197. On Hoan, "Socialists Again Elect Milwaukee's Mayor," *Survey* 36 (April 15, 1916), 69–70; Joseph P. Harris, "Our American Mayors; Daniel Hoan of Milwaukee," *National Municipal Review* 18 (September 1929), 550; Frank P. Zeidler, "Dan Hoan, Successful Mayor," *Historical Messenger* 17 (March 1961), 23–24. Gilbert H. Poor, *Interesting Sketches: Blazing a Trail, The Story of a Pioneer Socialist Agitator* (n.p., 1911), 84; Olson, "The Milwaukee Socialists," 187–88; Wachman, *History*, 58–59; Miller, "Milwaukee: Of Ethnicity and Labor," 46. Indicative of a pattern over the years of muting the ideological thrust, in 1926 the party dropped the goal of collectivization from its platform.

28. Ettenheim, *How Milwaukee Voted*, 124. Seidel lost to a fusion ticket in 1912 but won 7 percent more votes than in 1910. Frederic C. Howe, *Wisconsin: An Experiment in Democracy* (New York: Charles Scribner's Sons, 1912), 48–49; John Collier, "Experiment in Milwaukee," *Harper's Weekly* 55 (Aug. 12, 1911): 11. David P. Thelen argues that the struggle over control of the street railway was the key issue in leading to a reform mood in Wisconsin; see David P. Thelen, *The New Citizenship: Origins of Progressivism in Wisconsin, 1885–1900* (Columbia, MO: University of Missouri Press, 1972), 252, 288. Olson emphasizes how limited the Socialists' power was in office; see Olson, "Milwaukee's Socialist Administration," 197–207. Gavett, *Development of the Labor Movement*, 111–12; Olson, "Socialist Party and Unions," 116; Miller, "Milwaukee: Of Ethnicity and Labor," 51–53, 55.

29. Mayor Seidel wrote about the limited self-government as hampering his efforts in office in his article "Milwaukee Achievements," *American Labor Year Book*, 1916 (1), 117. Home rule, which the Socialists always promoted, was attained in 1926; see *Political Action*, Feb. 18, 1911. Mayor Hoan, maintaining that the municipality was the key agent in improved social conditions, nevertheless wrote that the party's ultimate aim was always the cooperative commonwealth; that goal kept the party from deteriorating into selfish office-seekers. Hoan, *City Government*, 9–10, 70–71. Olson, "The Milwaukee Socialists," 319–32; Miller, "Milwaukee: Of Ethnicity and Labor," 58–59.

30. In the 1919 session of the legislature Socialists held twenty seats, but they were then on the defensive because of the issues raised by the war. Carl D. Thompson, "Social Democratic Progress in the Wisconsin Legislature," *American Political Science Review* 1 (1907), 457–65; Fred L. Holmes, "Socialist Legislators at Work," *Independent* 70 (March 23, 1911), 592–94; Ethelwyn Mills, *Legislative-Program of the Socialist Party: Record of the Work of the Socialist Representatives in the State Legislatures, 1899–1913* (Chicago: Socialist Party, 1914), 10–11; Socialist Party, *The Party Builder* (August 30, 1913); Olson, "The Milwaukee Socialists," 381; Gavett, *Development of the Labor Movement*, 107–11.

31. England, "Milwaukee's Socialist Government," 445–55; *Social-Democratic Herald*, July 2, 1906; Wachman, *History*, 80; Sidney L. Harring, "The Police Institution as a Class Question: Milwaukee Socialists and the Police, 1900–1915," *Science and Society* 46 (Summer 1982), 197–221. As early as 1898 the Socialist platform included a demand for the reorganization of police court for the benefit of the workers and the poor. The *Social-Democratic Herald* of March 19, 1910, contained a Berger column in which he wrote: "We admit that we will not give the laws that hateful and oppressive construction towards the working class which they usually receive under the capitalist administration and regimes. We also declare that we will *change* and *abolish* all the *oppressive* laws at the first opportunity we get."

32. Victor Berger maintained that workers were 95 percent of the Socialists of Milwaukee in his article "What is the Matter With Milwaukee?" *Independent*, (April 21, 1910), 841. Ettenheim, *How Milwaukee Voted*, 125–26, lists mayorality results by wards; Simon, "City-Building," 17–25.

33. Wisconsin Social Democratic Party, *Proceedings* [Summary] of the 1916 State Convention, 5–10; *Proceedings* [Summary] of the 1918 State Convention, 6–9.

34. Still, *Milwaukee*, 455–63; Kreuter, "May Wood Simons," 51–52; Miller, "Milwaukee: Of Ethnicity and Labor," 55–56.

35. Berger's *Milwaukee Leader* itself appealed for votes of "lovers of peace" in the March 9, 1918 column by John M. Work entitled "Berger for Senate." Charles D. Steward, "Prussianizing Wisconsin," *Atlantic Monthly* 123 (January 1919), 103–5; Robert C. Reinders, "Daniel W. Hoan and the Milwaukee Socialist Party during the First World War," *Wisconsin Magazine of History* 36 (Autumn 1952), 48–55; Gavett, *Development of the Labor Movement*, 129; Miller, "Milwaukee: Of Ethnicity and Labor," 56–57.

36. Socialist Party, Membership Reports, Socialist Party Collection, Duke University; Gavett, *Development of the Labor Movement*, 130, *Milwaukee*, 455–63; Kreuter, "May Wood Simons," 51–52; Korman, *Industrialization*, 167–72. Miller, "Milwaukee: Of Ethnicity and Labor," 55–56; Tien, *Milwaukee Fact Book*, 23.

37. Reidners, "Daniel W. Hoan," 48–55; Gavett, *Development of the Labor Movement*, 126–31, 146–51; Miller, "Milwaukee: Of Ethnicity and Labor," 59–60; after two years of a cooperative experiment, the tenants voted to receive individual titles to their units.

38. A 1929 article described Hoan as "no visionary" but a pragmatist; see Harris, "Our American Mayors," 553. Olson, "The Milwaukee Socialists," 416–34; Miller, "Milwaukee: Of Ethnicity and Labor," 62–63.

39. Years later Socialist Frank P. Zeidler occupied the mayor's office from 1948 to 1960 but without any movement to support him. See an early biographical profile of Zeidler in the *Milwaukee Journal*, March 17, 1948.

40. *Social-Democratic Herald*, Mar. 6, 1906: April 9, 1910.

# 4  GERMANS ON THE MISSISSIPPI

## THE SOCIALIST PARTY OF ST. LOUIS

In 1900 St. Louis, with a population of 575,238 was the the fourth largest city in the United States. It was one of a number of midwestern cities that developed a vibrant socialist movement early in the twentieth century.[1] However, unlike in Milwaukee, Minneapolis, Flint, and cities further removed, such as Schenectady, Butte, and Berkeley, the St. Louis socialists were never able to elect a mayor or city council members or to dominate municipal politics. But they were able to offer local residents alternative policies and candidates and to insert a distinctive point of view into the public dialogue. The socialists came to enjoy the support of men and women of a variety of backgrounds whose interests were apparently not served by either the Democrats or the Republicans during the Progressive Era. This chapter traces the history of the Socialist Party in St. Louis up to World War One.

The city's working class life had an ethnic foundation. Early in its history St. Louis claimed more of an immigrant population than any other city in the nation; in 1850 a majority of its residents had been born abroad. By 1910 the foreign-born had declined to only 18 percent of the local population, but the city was still visibly populated by a great number of different groups. Whereas earlier it was heavily German and Irish, groups who were labeled by historians as Old Immigrants, in the early twentieth century St. Louis attracted various groups which were termed New Immigrants. Living near the central business district and close to the Mississippi River were newcomers such as Italians, Eastern European Jews, Poles, Bohemians, and Greeks, as well as some Chinese, Syrians, Romanians, Hungarians, and handfuls of South Slavs such as Croatians and Serbs. Census figures demonstrate that while those of German background were 52.8 percent of the population and Irish 17.5 percent, Russians (no doubt mostly Eastern European Jews) were 4.3 percent, Poles 2.6 percent, and Bohemians 2.3 percent. While more than 20 percent of all religious services in the state of Missouri were conducted in languages other than English, thirty-four of St. Louis's eighty-nine Roman Catholic parishes officially used two languages. Dozens of parochial schools of a variety of religious persuasions offered their curricula in languages other than English. The international mosaic was so pronounced that one student of its history has termed St. Louis ". . . a hyphenated city in thought and fact" before World War One.[2]

Germans dominated the city's ambience, so much so that a German-American Republican mayor, Henry Kiel, in 1913 publicly regretted that he could not speak his ancestral tongue. The German presence was overwhelming in the city's early days, and, emblematic of their impact on the municipality, German was a required subject in the city's public schools until 1887. Residing throughout the north and south sides, the German-born and their offspring were 56 percent of the population in 1900. That critical mass was able to sustain an expansive cultural life; although less impressive after the days of the immigrant generations, it supported a rich institutional tapestry of hundreds of organizations, including German-language newspapers, *turnvereins*, singing societies, and a *Deutscher Schulverein*, which supplied German teachers and texts to the public school system. As additional testimony to the city's significance to German-Americans, a number of national German organizations were headquartered in St. Louis.[3]

The St. Louis Socialist Party was built on the city's ethnic base. The party enjoyed its strongest backing among first- and second-generation workers, and while Germans dominated the local hierarchy, as they did the city, ethnic workers of a variety of backgrounds voted the socialist ticket and held red membership cards. The St. Louis branch of the Socialist Party of America was one of the charter members of the national party when the latter was founded in 1901. The city was the site of the party's national headquarters for its first three years, and St. Louisans served on the first National Executive Committee and as National Secretary. Earlier, in the 1880s and 1890s, a branch of the Socialist Labor Party of the authoritarian Daniel De Leon had claimed the allegiance of most St. Louis socialists, but the majority of its members, as occurred nationally, began to abandon it in favor of organizing a new party by the end of the century. By that time the socialists already had established a weekly newspaper of their own, the *Arbeiter Zeitung* soon followed by an English-language version, *St. Louis Labor* (initially called *Missouri Socialist*), which they managed to publish for three decades. They had also played a role in helping to establish the Missouri State Federation of Labor as well as the central labor body of the city, the St. Louis Central Trades and Labor Union.[4]

The party's tie to the local labor movement was so close that one labor historian has argued that the St. Louis party was one of the most successful in the United States in cultivating a relationship to organized labor. While the Central Trades and Labor Union refused to take partisan stands in municipal elections or to affiliate with any political party, nevertheless the relationship between organized labor and the socialists grew. The Central nearly always supported the same municipal programs as the socialists. Historian Gary Fink argues that it engaged in "flirtations" with the socialists, and, after 1920, with others who supported pro-labor reforms. Some of its member unions owned stock in the socialist cooperative printing company that published the party newspapers. Furthermore, socialists routinely held high office in the CTLU, even though the membership was not overwhelmingly socialist. For example, socialist David Kreyling, a cigarmaker, occupied the positions of President or of Secretary-Organizer from at least 1896 to 1933, and had been the first President of the State Federation of Labor in 1891. Kreyling was scrupulously non-partisan in the execution of his duties, but his long-term presence in the CTLU affirmed the tie between the two organizations. Similarly, socialist Louis Phillipi was elected CTLU president in 1910, and socialist Reuben T. Wood, originally a cigarmaker from Springfield, Missouri, was in 1912 elected president of the State Federation of Labor, a position which he held until 1953.[5]

German workers like Kreyling dominated the leadership of the St. Louis party. The most significant individual was Gottlieb A. Hoehn of the Typographical Union, who was a socialist activist from the 1880s until the 1930s, after which he remained involved in union affairs and the Democratic party. Hoehn was born in 1865 in the German Empire, where he became a cobbler. In the 1880s he immigrated to Baltimore to join an uncle, and he quickly became involved in the eight-hour movement and drifted into writing for the labor press. He was a journalist in Chicago briefly, succeeding August Spies on the *Chicago Arbeiter Zeitung*, and settled in St. Louis in 1891, where he joined the Socialist Labor Party and became a founding member of the Socialist Party. Hoehn was the local voice of labor, and for a time edited both the English- and German-language editions of the party's newspaper, *St. Louis Labor*. He was the perennial head of the local party, ran for the city council, the U.S. Congress, and other public offices on the Socialist ticket, attended state and national Socialist Party conventions as well as Congresses of the Second International, served on the original National Executive Committee of the party, and participated avidly in every strike and issue that affected local unions over the decades.[6]

Second in importance to Hoehn was William M. Brandt, a second-generation German American. He was born in 1868 in Pennsylvania, where he apprenticed as a cigarmaker, and settled in St. Louis in 1893. He at once immersed himself in the labor scene, becoming active in the CTLU, which he would head during the 1930s, and served as a delegate to conventions of the American Federation of Labor. He often held the position of Secretary of the Central Committee of the St. Louis Socialist Party, was President of the Board of Directors of the Labor Publishing Company, and ran for public office frequently on the Socialist ticket, including races for the city council, for mayor in 1905, and for the U.S. Congress in 1914.[7]

Otto Kaemmerer, a garment worker, was another important party leader. He headed the United Garment Workers locally and was often a delegate to conventions of the state Federation of Labor, where he fought to promote usage of the union label and the boycott. Kaemmerer was a key figure in local strikes and made headlines in 1912 when he was arrested during a major upheaval. As a party member he ran on the Socialist ticket for public office, including for city council in 1911, and at least once held the position of Secretary of the Central Committee of the St. Louis party. While not active in the party nationally, he was a delegate to the International Socialist Congress in Stuttgart, Germany, in 1907.[8]

Otto Pauls, a cigarmaker, served as State Secretary of the Missouri State party as well as Secretary of the St. Louis branch. He wrote a regular feature of commentary for *St. Louis Labor* called "Life as It Is." He was a very energetic State Secretary, who was once put into the position of defending the St. Louis party leadership from charges by other socialists that they had nominated non-socialists as candidates for public office.[9]

Joseph Hauser of the Brewery workers was another leader whose career served to link the party and the CTLU. He ran for mayor as a Socialist and in 1914 was elected president of the Central Trades and Labor Union, after which he could not run for political office.[10]

Such men of a variety of trades monopolized the Socialist slate of nominees in every election campaign. In the municipal election of 1909, for example, the party nominated printers, cigarmakers, brewery workers, railway clerks, electricians, carpenters, foremen, tanners, molders, patternmakers, furniture makers, bottlers, tailors, blacksmiths, and unskilled laborers. A sprinkling of white collar professionals was also evident, such as nominees who were undertakers, dentists, merchants, insurance agents, journalists, lawyers, and physicians, but they were in the minority.[11]

A few of the top leaders were not of the working class. For example, Otto Vierling was another activist who held local party positions, ran for the city council, and also served as State Secretary. Vierling was a physician who as Secretary of the state party in 1913 and 1914 enthusiastically routed organizers throughout Missouri and pushed hard on fundraising. He prepared circulars pointing out instances where organizations in other states, such as Oklahoma, were much more comprehensive in organizing efforts in all districts of their states or that other cities with less population than St. Louis, such as Milwaukee, boasted larger socialist movements. Vierling was the pivotal figure in starting a State Organizing Fund and was able to get his own ward branch to lead the way in pledges.[12]

Leaders who were probably not of German heritage nor of the working class included L.G. Pope and E. Val Putnam. Pope, a lawyer, ran for the city council and Board of Education on the Socialist ticket and for state public offices as well, and Putnam, also a lawyer, ran for the city council and other positions.[13]

Led by the above individuals, the St. Louis party clearly bore a decided German cast. General meetings were often conducted in the German language and held at Turner Hall, which was also the normal site of meetings of the CTLU. But as English evolved into the language of discourse, German-speaking branches were organized. Of the twenty-five ward branches, a number had German-speaking sub-branches. A German-speaking women's group also existed. As late as spring, 1914, one branch officially became bilingual to satisfy the needs of its German membership. But the German socialists found themselves increasingly accompanied by comrades from a variety of other backgrounds. By 1914, ethnic branches of the local party included Jewish, South Slavic, Lettish, Polish, Bohemian, and Italian. Some of them even organized sub-branches across the Mississippi River in East St. Louis. Large general meetings would feature addresses in even a greater number of languages than represented by the branches, including in addition to English and German, Russian, Yiddish, Hungarian, Bohemian, Slovenian, Croatian, Roumanian, and Lettish. At least one mass meeting was reported to have been addressed by speakers in thirteen different languages. To further meet the interests and needs of the local socialist community, the national secretary-treasurer of the Italian Federation of the Socialist Party of America came to speak in St. Louis and to obtain subscriptions for *La Parola del Socialista*, published on the East Coast. The editors of Chicago's Polish socialist paper, *Dziennik Ludowy*, and of that city's Croatian socialist newspaper, M.G. Jurishitch of the *Rudnicka Strazag*, also spoke in St. Louis.

The party candidates for public office, however, did not tend to be representatives of the non-German ethnic branches. The party attitude toward these various recent immigrant groups might well be suggested by an editorial lament in the pages of *Labor* that "slum wards" where recent immigrants predominated represented a floating population that offered poor material for Socialist converts in contrast to the wards "composed of solid, earnest workingmen." It could be argued that the norm for a Socialist candidate for party and public office was taken to be a skilled worker of German heritage.[14]

The local membership included perhaps a few dozen women, the numbers of which are not extant, but a fragmentary national party survey in 1908 suggested that women were between 1 and 2 percent of the St. Louis party. Since in the next few years there were both an English-speaking and, as cited above, a German-speaking women's group, their percentage within the party no doubt grew. Their roles as party members, however, were limited to auxiliary ones; the image of the party office holder suggested above should include only the male gender. Women organized their locals' social functions and prepared the food; indeed, at annual summer all-city festivals, of the dozens of assignments for various activities women served only on meal committees. Party programs which related explicitly to women, such as publicizing the annual International Socialist Woman's Day each March, were always assigned to women members exclusively.

The St. Louis socialists, unlike those in some other areas, did not tap women as potential leaders. They registered surprise when a Kansas City woman filed as a Socialist candidate for State Superintendent of Schools in 1910. An issue of *St. Louis Labor* noted that, "So far as is known here, she is the first woman to seek a State office in Missouri." In contrast, Chicago socialists nominated several women as candidates for city council. The St. Louis comrades never ran a woman for public office in the city other than for school board, the most likely position for which a socialist woman might be nominated anywhere in the country. Several state socialist organizations responded when the Socialist Party of America established a Woman's National Committee (see Chapter 5) and issued a "Plan of Work for Women," but the Missouri State Secretary, unlike 40 percent of his peers, did not even report to the national party on any such local activities. Given the climate, neither in St. Louis nor Missouri did a woman leader emerge to build a dynamic woman's sector.

Unlike in neighboring Kansas, where a critical mass of women socialists resulted in a state-wide convention of women and women holding party positions, Missouri never even placed a woman on its State Executive Board or named a woman as a representative to the party's National Committee. Nor did it tend to select women as delegates to national conventions, although by 1910 about 10 percent of delegates nationally were usually women. Missouri did not specifically appoint a woman organizer, unlike

Kansas and Illinois. If anything, it seemed to depend on those organizers crossing state lines into the Show-Me State, or on women organizers on a national tour. For example, Caroline A. Lowe, an organizer in Kansas, probably came to Missouri as she was the vice president of the Joint Kansas-Missouri Teachers' Association. Also, Luella Krehbiel (also spelled Kraybill) was an organizer in 1907 in Kansas and might have visited St. Louis. Lena Morrow Lewis worked the Upper South on behalf of the national party in 1909 and spent several days in St. Louis at the end of that year. In the national party, where a woman was specifically appointed to organize among women in a particular area, she would schedule public meetings as well as talks in homes and would address women's groups and Young People's Socialist League chapters, but such a blitz may well not have happened in St. Louis or Missouri. The party newspaper, *St. Louis Labor*, devoted two columns to what were considered women's issues, one on female suffrage and one that focused on child labor and women's domestic responsibilities and similar topics. These were typically canned pieces from other socialist newspapers.[15]

In 1909, the Woman's National Committee directed locals to organize a women's sector. But it took Missouri four years to appoint someone to the key position of Woman's State Correspondent—Hope Berry of Joplin—by which time thirty-two state organizations already had done so. So St. Louis and Missouri clearly did not enthusiastically embrace the Socialist Party's program targeting women or mount campaigns to reach out to them.[16]

Ella Reeve "Mother" Bloor lived briefly in St. Louis, organizing for the United Cloth Hat and Cap Makers Union in 1916 and 1917, but the exact dates or the scope of her activities while in the Mound City are not clear. She was active in a seven-month-long Cap Makers strike, but whether she attended socialist meetings, which is possible, and worked directly for the party cannot be verified. Later when she resided in Kansas City, Missouri, in 1919, her commitment was to the communist movement, through which she earned her fame.[17]

One nationally known woman socialist, however, moved to St. Louis and thereby endowed the local party with a woman leader. When Kansas-born Kate Richards O'Hare arrived with her family in 1911, she was known throughout the Socialist Party as a speaker, journalist, and activist. For almost ten years O'Hare had crisscrossed the country on speaking tours to the party faithful; she was especially popular in the Plains States, the Midwest, and the Southwest. As a resident of Kansas she had run as a Socialist for the U.S. House of Representatives in 1910 and had participated in state-wide party activities. Once settled in St. Louis to join the staff of the monthly, *National Rip-Saw*, O'Hare immersed herself in local and state activities. She addressed branch and all-city meetings, she pinch-hit for major speakers when they were late for their talks, and she spoke to county audiences. She involved herself in St. Louis politics, ran for school board on the Socialist ticket, was the first woman candidate for the United States Senate in 1916, brought a socialist perspective to a municipal committee on unemployment through a mayoral appointment and to State Senate hearings on a minimum wage as an investigative reporter, and addressed local female suffrage groups. She was the only Missouri woman to sit on the party's National Executive Committee and Woman's National Committee and to participate in national conventions. She even represented the party to the international socialist movement through her election to the International Socialist Bureau in 1913, only the second woman to do so.

However, O'Hare's commitment to expanding the party's outreach to women was uneven. While she wrote party publications on issues of presumed concern to women, such as white slavery, and while she participated in the woman's sector for one term on the Woman's National Committee, she did not seek to organize women directly. Her writings demonstrated interest in and awareness of the variety of concerns which women held, and she may have touched on more issues to which women gave attention than any other party leader—problems of working women and intimate topics such as birth control, abortion, and divorce. A decade earlier, when she lived in Kansas City, Missouri, she and her husband, Frank, took the lead in organizing the first socialist club for women in that city, but in St. Louis Kate O'Hare did not assume responsibility for building up the woman's sector. And no one else did.[18]

African Americans were 43,960 or 6 percent of the city's population in 1910, but no extant records indicate how many may have belonged to the Socialist Party. Revisionist historians of American socialism have shown that blacks participated in the socialist movement in various states, and the Socialist Party went on record at its first convention as accepting them as members, although not without ambivalence (see Chapters 1 and 2). Many Caucasian socialists demonstrated reservations about that policy, and if blacks chose to join the party, they could find themselves facing racism within its ranks and also the possibility of segregation. In the North and in the Upper South, locals were integrated, unlike in the Deep South, so an African-American St. Louisan would have been automatically enrolled in the nearest local. St. Louis itself did not feature the full segregation and disenfranchisement characteristic of southern states at that time, although the Missouri constitution upheld segregation. African Americans had been able to play a role in the political process for most of the city's history so that they were positioned to defend themselves. The city, however, in 1916 was the site of the first segregationist housing ordinance passed anywhere in the United States by initiative petition. It also witnessed riots when middle-class African Americans purchased homes in lily-white neighborhoods. But, as in a struggle over the imposition of segregation in the state of Oklahoma, where some socialists filed suit against anti-black measures, St. Louis socialists opposed such trends. They condemned ongoing disenfranchisement of African-American voters elsewhere—in the states of Alabama and Maryland, for instance—and they loudly blasted lynchings near Charleston, Missouri, in 1901. Socialists went on record against the housing initiative favoring municipal segregation. While the measure passed in the city handily by 51,110 to 17,877, the votes in German workers' wards where socialists were strongest showed the greatest opposition to it. The initiative was never effected, since the U.S. Supreme Court struck down block segregation, but restrictive convenants became the norm.[19]

General meetings of the party, especially during the summer when large open-air events were held, often featured well-known socialist speakers from elsewhere. Regional, national, and even international figures addressed the St. Louis socialists. Regionally known speakers included John H. Walker, President of the Illinois Federation of Labor; Adolph Germer, Secretary-Treasurer of the United Mine Workers of Illinois; socialist mayors of Milwaukee, Emil Seidel and Daniel W. Hoan; Wisconsin State Senator Winfield R. Gaylord; German-born party organizer Oscar Ameringer; and Walter T. Mills, a quixotic if not eccentric lecturer, teacher, and author. The nationally known party leader who most regularly appeared was the charismatic Eugene V. Debs, the perennial U.S. presidential candidate who often opened and closed his campaigns in St. Louis. His summertime speeches drew audiences in the thousands, attracting enormous crowds by his personal magnetism amd human decency.

Other national socialist figures who spoke in St. Louis included muckraker Charles Edward Russell; Frank Bohn, who wrote for the *International Socialist Review*; and party organizer Arthur Morrow Lewis, among others, as well as O'Hare. Socialists from abroad also appeared in St. Louis from time to time during speaking trips across the United States. They included Keir Hardie, a Member of the British House of Commons; James Connelly, the Irish socialist and Wobbly; Karl Legien, head of the General Federation of Labor Union in the German Empire; and Dr. Franz Soukup, of Prague, a Social-Democrat known for an anti-Austrian brand of nationalism. Such an impressive roster of speakers demonstrated that the city was viewed as an important socialist center.[20]

The St. Louis Socialists enjoyed a full calendar of activities throughout the year. Local branches as well as the party as a whole sponsored picnics, dances, and other events on a regular basis, inviting each other to their suppers and bazaars and other programs. They gathered together in mass numbers to commemorate major events in socialist history, such as the Paris Commune and the anniversary of the death of Ferdinand Lassalle, as well as to celebrate the Fourth of July and Labor Day. They were entertained at these events by ethnic singing societies, other musical presentations, and programs of the Young People's Socialist League.

The St. Louis party claimed a membership in 1914 of about 1,200 in dozens of locals. By that time the party had developed and refined its detailed platform. For example, in its 1911 platform it stood for municipal ownership of the street railway system, public utilities, ice plants, and lodging houses, and opposed the awarding of franchises to private business. It espoused a public employment bureau, public works for the unemployed, hot meals and medical services in the public schools, a municipal loan office, free legal advice, and city-owned public markets for farmers. In addition the party demanded an eight-hour day for city employees, prohibition of anti-union discrimination, housing and food inspection measures, free public restrooms, additional public parks, railway smoke abatement programs and, finally, homerule. In constructing their platform the St. Louisans had virtually no guidance from their national party.

Although American socialists had been developing municipal programs across the country and nominating candidates for public office on the basis of party platforms even before the founding of the party in 1901, the Socialist Party of America had refrained from offering a model municipal program to its members. Finally, at its national convention in 1912, it established a permanent committee on municipal and state issues as well as a clearinghouse for information for party members serving in public office. That committee recommended to members that they propose programs of municipal ownership, home rule, public health, and other social legislation as well as city planning. The program that the St. Louis comrades had constructed was clearly in alignment with party sentiment. Indeed, overviews of Socialist Party municipal efforts demonstrate a consensus despite the decentralized nature of the programming. Socialists in both large cities and small towns promised their citizens that they would seek the municipalization of local services, the legitimization of workers' interests, the expansion of social and public services to workers and their neighborhoods, increased regulation of business, and equitable taxation policies.[21]

The St. Louis socialists worked in tandem with the Missouri State Socialist Party. In 1914, as an example, they promoted the state platform which echoed their own planks on homerule, unemployment relief and insurance, public employment bureaus and public works jobs, and the eight-hour day. They also endorsed the state party's additional planks, which included proportional representation, abolition of the State Senate, the Governor's veto and the recall, prohibition of contract system public projects and convict labor, prevention of police strikebreaking activities, and a graduated income tax. Candidates for state-wide offices were feted with a banquet prepared by the German- and English-language Socialist women's groups and nominated in a convention that year in St. Louis. As delegates to state conventions, St. Louis socialists participated in the formulation of the policies of the state party. As an example, that year a major agenda item was a right-to-work state constitutional amendment. The Missourians agreed to promote it, emulating the socialist state legislators in adjacent Kansas who had introduced such a measure. The amendment sought to guarantee jobs for all Missourians, with the state required to establish farms, factories, or public works projects as necessary to insure full employment. Party members were instructed by State Secretary Vierling to obtain signatures on petitions on behalf of the proposed amendment in hopes of securing it by a state-wide initiative.[22]

The general policies of the St. Louis socialists placed them very securely in the dominant reformist wing of the Socialist Party of America. Theirs was a step-at-a-time path of educating and legislating their way toward modifications of the capitalist system. They were not swayed by the argument within the national party, offered by the more ideologically revolutionary faction, that reform measures might undermine worker interest in a full and revolutionary transformation of the system. Nor were they impressed by the leftists' condemnation of campaigns for public office as self-serving. The St. Louis comrades' emphasis on the propaganda value inherent in such campaigns led to a firm belief in the possibility of electoral victories. Within the St. Louis branch ideological arguments did not rage between reformists and revolutionists as it did in New York and elsewhere, at least in the years before the Bolshevik Revolution. A reformist consensus existed, shared by long-time leaders such as Gottlieb Hoehn and newcomers to the St. Louis party such as Kate and Frank O'Hare, no matter what other differences they may have had as individuals. The St. Louis party also cooperated amicably with other municipal and state parties that shared their commitment to running candidates for local government, and they swapped organizers and speakers. For example, State Senator Winfield R. Gaylord of Wisconsin spent the summer months in St. Louis in 1911 as an organizer sent from the electorally successful Milwaukee Social Democratic party, and *St. Louis Labor* routinely publicized the Milwaukee socialist scene.[23]

Virtually the only times the St. Louisans did battle with revolutionaries were at conventions of the national party and in the pages of newspapers. However, one such major controversy occurred—the details of which are somewhat obscure—among the St. Louis membership in the pre-war years. Charges were pressed against the party office-holders that they had violated policy on candidate selection for state party officials. The National Executive Committee called for new elections under its supervision, but a referendum to that effect was defeated. *St. Louis Labor*, the mouthpiece of those who had always run the St. Louis party, cited the principle of local autonomy and fumed that "outsiders" could have no role in settling the dispute. The editor even grumbled about the meddling of "direct actionists" locally. Over the next six months the division was at least formally healed and unity restored. A new charter was issued by the national office for St. Louis, another by the Missouri State party, new elections held, and the party's local hierarchy was restructured. But the same handful of members—Hoehn, Brandt, Kaemmerer, and Pauls—continued to dominate the St. Louis party thereafter.[24]

At national conventions St. Louis socialists lined up with the party majority on controversial issues. On an issue that tore the party apart in 1912, the St. Louis representatives voted for an anti-IWW measure that provided for the expulsion of a party member who advocated the use of sabotage. After a bitter debate, the constitutional amendment passed 191 to 90, with the St. Louis delegates endorsing it (see Chapter 6). But occasionally the pattern altered, for example, in regard to a policy on immigration (see Chapter 1). In this case the St. Louis delegation was split, with Hoehn for restrictionism and O'Hare opposed.[25]

During Senator Gaylord's lengthy stay in St. Louis in 1911 he predicted that socialists of the Mound City would continue to expand their membership and increase their votes, and would follow their Milwaukee comrades into office. He told an audience that St. Louis would be "the second city of the first class to go socialist." Milwaukee stood as a model to the socialists of St. Louis and elsewhere. In St. Louis the socialists between 1900 and World War One nominated candidates for virtually every local and state campaign. Socialists ran for mayor, the bicameral city council (usually fielding nominees in all but one "silk stocking" ward out of the city's twenty-eight), the Board of Education, railroad and warehouse commissioner, auditor, governor, the state legislature, and for seats in the U.S. House of Representatives and the Senate.[26]

As the years went by, the socialists campaigned with increasingly intensive efforts to win public attention to their platforms, eventually blanketing the city with their message. Indeed, it was incumbent upon them to do so; they had to rely entirely on their own resources because the local major dailies, for example, the nationally respected *Post-Dispatch*, rarely reported on socialist campaigns and even failed to include socialist totals in its printed election tabulations. The St. Louis comrades, however, had an advantage that many other socialist parties in the same situation lacked. The socialists had both their English-language and German-language weeklies. In addition to *St. Louis Labor* and *Arbeiter Zeitung*, they tried to establish a county-wide newspaper in 1912. That same year they borrowed directly from their Milwaukee comrades and issued an election campaign broadside called *Voice of the People*. It was published in the several weeks leading up to every primary and general election, perhaps five or six separate issues for a campaign, and the party hoped it might be possible to transform it into a monthly for circulation in Missouri and the adjacent states. The entire rank-and-file was invited to participate in its distribution, and it was hand-delivered throughout the city via a battalion of volunteers called—as in Milwaukee—the "Bundle Brigade." During the 1912 Presidential campaign about one-half million issues of *Voice of the People* were distributed, and about 300,000 issues were circulated in the course of the non-Presidential election campaign of 1914.[27]

Eugene V. Debs saw his presidential vote totals dramatically increase in both St. Louis and Missouri as the local socialists widened their own propaganda outreach. In 1908 Debs won 4,901 votes in St. Louis; four years later he more than doubled that with a total of 9,159 votes. That vote gain was quite impressive, as it was in the state of Missouri, where Debs won 15,431 votes in 1908 and 28,466 in 1912. It was no doubt helpful that Debs himself appeared in St. Louis a few days before the 1912 election, drawing a huge crowd to Turner Hall, where the standing room only audience spilled over and massed in the street. His running mate, Emil Seidel, former mayor of Milwaukee, also spoke in the city a few days earlier.[28]

In local races the party's best showing occurred in 1911. In the municipal election that spring the party drew about 4,000 more voters to its banner than it had in several races in November 1910. Hoehn, Pauls, and Kaemmerer each averaged about 11,000 votes in their respective races for the city council, as did Dr. Emil Simon, who was elected to the Board of Education. In each of several wards, those where German workers resided in heavy numbers—the 8th, 9th, 10th, 11th, 12th and 27th—about a thousand voted the socialist ticket. Hoehn might have won his race in the twelfth ward except for the strong likelihood that his ballots were undercounted. The party did not formally challenge the outcome, however, because its leaders believed that they had even more clearly been cheated out of a victory in the tenth ward where Brandt had run. He was credited with a total of 1,475 votes, losing to the Republican incumbent, George Eigel, an attorney, by twenty votes. While the socialists were delighted at coming in ahead of the Democratic candidate—"the handwriting is on the wall," the editor of *St. Louis Labor* chortled—they proceeded to challenge the validity of the election. In November, 1911, a rematch was held to fill the vacant seat on the council. Eigel won again with 19,382 votes to Brandt's 16,050, with the Democrat again third with 14,695. This time the party accepted the outcome and chose to celebrate the fact that their vote had grown, doubling in a year in that ward.[29]

In 1912 Hoehn ran for Congress in the Tenth Congressional district, which included South St. Louis, the county, and some city wards. His 1,705 votes in the primary surpassed the 724 total in 1910 and 691 in 1908, which earlier socialist races had gleaned. In the general election Hoehn won 7,154 votes. Brandt, the candidate in 1914, won 5,162 in his race for Congress. The overall prospects for the St. Louis Party were indeed promising, so that it was entirely possible that Gaylord's prediction of victory would come to fruition in the near future.[30]

The St. Louis socialists sought to represent the needs of working-class neighborhoods. For example, they joined with the unions and middle-class reformers—especially the Wednesday Club, composed of philanthropic-minded women (called by Roger Baldwin, then a professor of sociology at Washington University, the "swankiest" woman's club in town)—in a "playground movement" to provide open space in the inner city. Between 1903 and 1909 the coalition succeeded in establishing more than a dozen new parks and playgrounds. Dr. Emil Simon, the socialist member of the Board of Education, successfully proposed a program of hot lunches in the schools in both black and white working-class districts. The party also promoted opening up the schools after hours to community groups, to which the Board of Education agreed. On an issue of the widest general interest, the socialists were among the many heavily Germanic groups who fought vociferously against the introduction of prohibition.

A very significant local matter that the party promoted was construction of a free bridge to connect St. Louis with Illinois. The issue dragged on for years and, in fact, outlived the socialists. It was clearly a working-class issue in that the existing toll bridge meant that soft coal brought over from southern Illinois mines was priced artifically high. The construction of a free bridge became a rallying cry throughout the poorer neighborhoods, and was promoted by the socialists and by the Central Trades and Labor Union. A bridge bond was passed in 1906 but construction was never authorized. By 1910 the St. Louis Civic League, led by Baldwin, took up the issue again as symbolic of the thwarting of the people's will. In 1912 socialist and labor representatives joined with Baldwin and other groups in a new Civic Federation and succeeded in 1914 in passing another bond measure. Four years later a free bridge was built, but it was limited to vehicle traffic. The issue of free freight still remained unresolved over the next generation despite two more referendums on behalf of free freight.[31]

An even more major battle, if less protracted, occurred over the issue of charter revision. The socialists came to strenuously oppose a measure in 1911 to revise the city charter. At first they worked with a civic coalition on behalf of charter revision, promoting incorporation into the charter of the initiative, recall and referendum, which the party had favored since its inception. Hoehn accepted a nomination to the Joint Charter Revision Committee but was not elected. The eventual charter proposal, as discussed by historian James Primm, was shaped to institutionalize business domination of government, since it strengthened the mayor's office and replaced a bicameral legislature with one body and therefore fewer elected officials. Moreover, the document lacked the three direct democracy measures. Socialists, labor, and middle-class reformers such as Baldwin attacked the proposal as an oligarchic plot. Maintaining that the revision would disenfranchise the working people of the city, the Socialist Party opposed the measure and celebrated when it was defeated in a landslide, 65,046 to 24,891. *St. Louis Labor* exulted that the vote was a "great victory for the people."

When the idea of charter revision was revived three years later, the party again geared up to oppose it, arguing once again that it would diminish the political power of the working people of St. Louis. This time the socialists chose not to cooperate in any way with the charter revision campaign, but they circulated an advertisement in favor of adopting the three measures of direct legislation. The new charter proposal in fact incorporated those measures, but it also reduced the number of elective offices in favor of a unicameral legislative body and a system of at-large representation. When it passed in June 1914, the central wards found their political strength much reduced. The wards where the socialists were strongest voted against revision, but the proponents of the new charter prevailed.[32]

Clearly, the socialists often found it to their advantage to work in tandem with progressive, civic-minded groups when their interests converged. On many occasions they cooperated with numbers of them against local monopolistic forces or political corruption. In the first decade of the twentieth century the "Missouri Idea," which has been characterized by historian David Thelan as the popular restraint of business and political forces, was publicized by the national media. Following a citywide streetcar strike and boycott of the monopolistic St. Louis Transit Company in 1900, the public remained agitated over reduced services and dangers to public health and safety. Democrat Joseph W. Folk became Circuit Attorney following his defense of the workers, and in 1904, after successfully prosecuting many officials for corruption, and incidentally awakening journalist Lincoln Steffens to the scope of illegal ties between politics and business, he became Governor of Missouri. In that office he campaigned statewide against bribery, corruption, and partisanship and in favor of direct democracy. His administration was a leading component in the antitrust movement nationally. By the time of the next administration, led by Folk's Republican Attorney General Herbert S. Hadley, reform-minded officials and civic leaders shifted their emphasis toward reliance on experts and regulations, with greater stress on non partisanship, and away from representative democracy. At that point the progressives abandoned what had made possible cooperative efforts with the socialists. The latter, with their basic faith in empowerment of the average voter, that is, of working-class neighborhoods, found their paths diverging.[33]

Indeed, it had been possible for the socialists to cooperate with middle-class reformers only on a specific number of issues, such as exploitative transit companies, the need for parks in poor neighborhoods, or the injustice of tolls on the necessities of life. Their long-range goals, of course, were totally distinct. The socialists continued to look toward the eventual replacement of the capitalist system of production and distribution with a collectivist one, while progressives of various stripes favored a capitalist system in which small entrepreneurs could function in a marketplace that was not skewed against them. The socialists accepted the fact of increasingly large corporate enterprises, and expected that one day the people would control them, while some progressives wanted the government to regulate the giants of industry and others wished to break them down into their component parts. Mutually desired immediate goals did allow collaboration between socialists and progressives until progressive-minded reformers embraced structural changes in municipal government which limited representation, and the coalition collapsed.

In 1914, when the new charter took effect and modified the local political system, not only was the informal coalition disrupted but the death knell of the socialist movement was sounded. The introduction of the principle of at-large representation to the city council undermined the decision-making power of the neighborhoods. Such a measure reflected a municipal trend nationally, decreasing grassroots political influence through a variety of structural reforms in city government, which were often hailed in the name of efficiency. In St. Louis the innovation minimized the political strength of the socialists and perpetuated a pattern of non-socialist office-holders. The socialists never again made a serious bid for public office.

Both external and internal factors need to be considered in seeking an explanation for the socialists' inability to become more electorally successful in St. Louis. The socialists could not overcome manipulation of the political system against their interests: for example, in 1902 during five weeks of the fall election campaign, a Missouri Supreme Court decision temporarily stripped them of the use of the name "socialist" on the ballot, causing endless confusion. But beyond those types of machinations that socialists faced almost everywhere, it seems clear that a cap on party growth can be recognized as early as 1912. The socialists peaked in their popularity in 1911–12, as seen in several strong races for the city council. The stark fact remains that they never elected anyone to the council, and the undercounting of their votes in one race or another, while connoting explicit violation of the electoral system, is not a sufficient explanation. While socialists faced the same challenges in other municipalities and yet elected whole slates to city and county positions, including mayors, the St. Louis socialists at best made very modest showings. They elected a member to the Board of Education, where they were able to shape policy, but otherwise their only influence in public policy rested on alliances with civic-minded groups on behalf of sometimes relatively minor social issues.[34]

Probably a key reason for the socialist inability to play a larger municipal role prior to charter revision was the party's lack of a nationally known figure. They had no one person whose name and activities brought immediate attention to the socialist banner, who could win elections and shape the local party in his own image. They did have a major party figure for a half-dozen years between 1911 and 1917 when Kate Richards O'Hare lived in St. Louis. However, she was always treated as an outsider by the local leadership. She was summoned on occasions when a speaker with name recognition was needed and they nominated her for public office twice, but the party did not welcome her fully or use her renown as outreach to new constituencies.

Leadership fell to a small number of men whose profiles were all of a piece. They were almost entirely first or second generation German-American skilled working men. Thus the party could most easily appeal to that particular segment of the electorate. Had the party showcased a diversified slate of leaders with whom native-born Americans and recent immigrants from a variety of backgrounds, women as well as men, could identify, it might have been successful in attracting more of a following. Unlike New York socialists, who nominated black candidates in Harlem, or Milwaukee socialists, who systematically sought out Polish candidates, the St. Louis comrades confined themselves to their original ethnic base. Moreover, they did not use the potential of their women members or systematically seek to organize more women. Instead they continued to offer a narrow profile to the public, which might or might not choose to join what seemed to be a Germanic workingman's club. Thus, while the St. Louis party on the surface seemed to run its campaigns, offer platforms, and issue propaganda in as systematic and comprehensive a manner as their comrades elsewhere, it nevertheless bore self-imposed limitations. German workers were a shrinking proportion of the population, with possibly a diminshing interest in socialist ideology. The party never burst through what was clearly a ceiling on its potential for both internal and external reasons.[35]

Moreover, the labor alliance itself, which was a cornerstone of the Socialist Party, was less stable than it appeared to be. No official of the CTLU or State Federation could run on the Socialist ticket because of local labor's official nonpartisan position, and therefore the more influential and important labor leaders who were socialists by inclination could not represent the party. Further, the fragile and impermanent nature of that alliance would be revealed in the next few years when the stresses of World War One weakened and disrupted the coaliton. Then in the first postwar year, when the Socialist Party of America was on the defensive in the face of the Red Scare and the emergence of the communist movement, it virtually collapsed. Its St. Louis branch reflected that same experience, as it first struggled to prove its patriotism and then was abandoned by some of its members and charged with a lack of revolutionary fervor. While those events will not be traced in these pages, the St. Louis Socialist Party's history ended in the tumult of World War One and the postwar aftermath. The party's promise was never realized.[36]

Lastly, defining issues which assisted socialists to gain municipal offices elsewhere did not have that result in St. Louis. In Milwaukee, for example, the obvious corruption of the local Republican and Democratic parties helped lead the voters to opt for the entire socialist ticket in 1910. In

St. Louis, however, in both older parties the presence of progressive politicians, most notably Joseph Folk, apparently convinced the voters that they did not need to turn to a minor party. In Minneapolis the socialist Thomas Van Lear was swept into the mayor's office in 1916 on the basis of two basic issues which fully polarized the city: a fierce open shop struggle and intractable utilities companies that created a hospitable environment for a socialist option. The two possible defining moments that might have brought victory to the St. Louis socialists simply were not realized. The potential of charter revision for a socialist triumph fizzled, for example, when the socialists and civic-minded middle-class reformers split on a key measure. The other major issue which the socialists might have ridden into office was that of a toll-free bridge, but while it had strong appeal to lower-income St. Louisans, the middle class did not find it to be of crucial enough importance to turn away from traditional political allegiances to the free bridge's leading advocate, the Socialist Party. The stark choices that elsewhere brought socialist victory were absent in St. Louis.[37]

NOTES

1. *Fourteenth Census of the United States: Population* vol. 1, 1920. *Number and Distribution of Inhabitants* (Washington, DC, 1921), 320.

2. Margaret LoPiccolo Sullivan, *Hyphenism in St. Louis, 1880–1921* (New York: Garland Publishing, 1990), vii, 21 [quotation]; Gary Ross Mormino, *Immigrants on the Hill: Italian Americans in St. Louis, 1882–1982* (Urbana: University of Illinois Press, 1986), 17; James Neal Primm, *Lion in the Valley: St. Louis, Missouri* (Boulder, CO: Pruett Publishing, 1981), 345; David Thelen, *Paths of Resistance: Tradition and Democracy in Industrializing Missouri* (New York: Oxford University Press, 1986), 137; Audrey Louise Olson, "St. Louis Germans, 1850–1920: The Nature of an Immigrant Community and its Relation to the Assimilation Process" (Ph.D. diss., University of Kansas, 1970), 110. See also Merle Fainsod, "The Influence of Racial and National Groups in St. Louis Politics (1908–28)" (Ph.D. diss., Washington University, 1929).

3. Sullivan, vii, 9, 37–46; Primm, 370, 357, 458. As late as 1914 the state of Missouri was home to more than 300,000 first- and second-generation German Americans. See William E. Parrish, Charles T. Jones, Jr., and Lawrence O. Christensen, *Missouri: The Heart of the Nation*, 2nd edition (Arlington Heights, IL: Harlan Davidson, 1992), 277.

4. Gary M. Fink, *Labor's Search for Order: The Political Behavior of the Missouri Labor Movement, 1890–1940* (Columbia: University of Missouri Press, 1973), 25–27; Edwin James Forsythe, "The St. Louis Central Trades and Labor Union, 1887–1945" (Ph.D. diss., University of Missouri, 1956), 42–48, 69–71; Sally M. Miller, *From Prairie to Prison: The Life of Social Activist Kate Richards O'Hare* (Columbia: University of Missouri Press, 1993), 83.

5. Fink, 52–53, 25, 9, 4; Forsythe, 46–48; "Rueben Terell Wood," in Gary M. Fink, *Biographical Dictionary of American Labor leaders* (Westport, CT: Greenwood Press, 1974), 382–83.

6. Obituary, *St. Louis Post-Dispatch*, April 9, 1951, 30; G.A. Hoehn to Mr. English, March 4, 1945, Folder 8, Gottlieb A. Hoehn Papers, Western Historical Manuscript Collection, University of Missouri-Columbia. This folder contains a five-

page autobiographical sketch by Hoehn. See also folder 2, which contains another autobiographical sketch written in 1935. Also see Hartmut Keil, "A Profile of Editors of the German-American Radical Press, 1850–1910," in *The German-American Radical Press: The Shaping of a Left Political Culture, 1850–1940*, eds. Elliott Shore, Ken Fones-Wolf, and James P. Danky (Urbana: University of Illinois Press, 1992), 21–23.

7. Obituary, *St. Louis Post-Dispatch*, June 23, 1942, 41; Socialist Party of St. Louis, Missouri Collection, Box 1, Folder 3, Western Historical Manuscript Collection, University of Missouri-St. Louis. This contains a slim number of party files but they offer glimpses of Brandt, as do the Hoehn Papers at Columbia, Missouri. Brandt's career can also be traced through the pages of *St. Louis Labor*, which often reprinted his talks to party faithful and his campaign speeches. As an example, see *St. Louis Labor*, November 23, 1912.

8. Missouri State Federation of Labor, *Proceedings of the 21st Annual Convention*, September 16–19, 1912, 38–39, 60–61; Missouri State Federation of Labor, *Proceedings of the 23rd Annual Convention*, September 14–18, 1914, 92–93, 192; *St. Louis Labor*, April 15, 1911, June 15, 1912; VIIe Congrès Socialiste International Rendu à Stuttgart du 16 au 24 août 1907. *Compte Rendu Analytique*, 5.

9. Information on Pauls is limited, as it is for most of these individuals. See as an example of a column of his, *St. Louis Labor*, January 17, 1914. Socialist Party of America Collection, Missouri Party Papers, Reel 99 of Microfilm Edition.

10. Socialist Party of America Collection, Missouri Party Papers, Reel 99 of Microfilm Edition.

11. *St. Louis Labor*, January 1, 1909.

12. Folder 51, Box 6, Western Historical Manuscript Collection, University of Missouri–St. Louis; Socialist Party of America Collection, Reel 99 of Microfilm Edition.

13. See, for example, *St. Louis Labor*, January 2, 1909; *Missouri Socialist*, No. 91, October 25, 1902.

14. See, for examples of party activities and events, *St. Louis Labor* issues of February 5, 1910, February 25, 1911, May 2, 1914, and August 22, 1914. The best way to trace party activity on the grassroots level is through a time-consuming reading of a run of issues of *St. Louis Labor*. Archival holdings are simply inadequate. The quotation on solid workingmen's wards compared to slum wards appears in *St. Louis Labor*, July 23, 1910.

15. *St. Louis Labor*, March 28, 1914, February 5, 1910, June 4, 1910; *Socialist Woman* (also *Progressive Woman*, and finally, *The Coming Nation*), November 1908, No. 16, 2: July 1907, No. 2, 3. A check of issues of *Labor* in 1909 will provide a sample of women's columns. Issues of November 13, 1909, December 25, 1909, January 1, 1910, and January 8, 1910, cover a visit to St. Louis by Lena Morrow Lewis.

16. Socialist Party, *Official Bulletin*, IX (February 1913), No. 5, 4. In 1909 the Missouri Socialist Party reported that the St. Louis party had one woman's committee; it was more likely two or even three. *Socialist Woman*, October 1909, No. 29.

17. Ella Reeve Bloor, *We Are Many: An Autobiography by Ella Reeve Bloor* (New York: International Publishers, 1940), 140–41; letters from Kathleen Brown, University of Washington doctoral student, Seattle, Washington, October 26, 1993, January 3, 1994.

18. Miller, 85–86, 90–91, 104–11; idem, "Kate Richards O'Hare: Progression toward Feminism," *Kansas History* 7 (Winter 1984–1985), 263–79; *Missouri Socialist*, No. 58, March 1, 1902.

19. *Fourteenth Census of Population, 1920* (Washington, DC, 1921), vol. 3, 590; *Missouri Socialist*, October 5, 1901, November 23, 1901; *St. Louis Labor*, April 9, 1910, July 9, 1910; Carl D. Thompson to State Secretaries, and replies, May 1913, Socialist Party of America Collection, Duke University; James Weinstein, *The Decline of Social-*

*ism in America, 1912–1925* (New York: Monthly Review Press, 1967), 63–74; Lawrence O. Christensen, "Race Relations in St. Louis, 1865–1916," *Missouri Historical Review* 78 (January 1984), 125–36; Primm, 435–39; Thelen, 139–45. The Socialist Party partial records on race do not include any St. Louis references, but two locals in rural Missouri reported to a National Office survey that they had no black members.

20. For announcements of some of the major speakers, see *St. Louis Labor* issues of July 24, 1909, September 4, 1909, June 11, 1910, August 27, 1910, February 25, 1911, December 9, 1911, May 4, 1912, February 14, 1914, and May 16, 1914, among others.

21. *St. Louis Labor*, May 2, 1914, March 7, 1914, February 4, 1911; "Report of Committee on Municipal and State Programs," Appendix K of the Socialist Party, *Proceedings of the 1912 National Convention*, 214–17. See also Richard W. Judd, *Socialist Cities: Municipal Politics and the Grass Roots of American Socialism* (Albany: State University of New York Press, 1989).

22. *St. Louis Labor*, August 29, 1914, March 7, 1914, May 9, 1914; Socialist Party, *Party Builder*, No. 58, December 13, 1913, 2; Socialist Party of America Collection, State Party Records, Reels 96 and 99, microfilm edition. *St. Louis Labor* lists Hoehn and Phil Wagner, editor of the *National Rip-Saw*, as St. Louis delegates to the state party convention in 1912. See issue of May 11, 1912. The State Federation of Labor and the CTLU endorsed the right-to-work constitutional amendment.

23. *St. Louis Labor*, June 24, 1911, July 8, 1911.

24. *Missouri Socialist*, No. 1, January 5, 1901, No. 15, April 13, 1901; *St. Louis Labor*, May 15, 1909, June 19, 1909, August 20, 1910, November 12, 1910, November 26, 1910, December 3, 1910, July 15, 1911, August 19, 1911, December 30, 1911, and March 9, 1912.

25. See, for example, Socialist Party, *Proceedings of the 1908 National Convention of the Socialist Party*, 107–08; Miller, *From Prairie to Prison*, 99; *International Socialist Review*, XII, 826; *St. Louis Labor*, February 10, 1912, June 8, 1912. The St. Louis socialists had voted in a referendum against holding a national congress in 1910 on the grounds that it might be a "talkfest" that would invite "mischief" by leftists, as reported in *Labor* on May 28, 1910. In a similar vein, the newspaper had rejoiced on February 19, 1910, when the Old Guard of Victor Berger, Morris Hillquit, and their allies were reelected to the National Executive Committee, and noted that no "mouth revolutionists" had been elected.

26. *St. Louis Labor*, August 5, 1911. The several meager archival collections that touch on the St. Louis Socialist Party do not include election slates or tallies. For municipal returns, an interested reader must consult the pages of *St. Louis Labor*; as indicated in the text, the St. Louis metropolitan dailies tended not to report the socialist vote. For the result of state races, the State of Missouri *Official Manual* must be consulted.

27. *St. Louis Labor*, June 22, 1912, January 13, 1912, September 19, 1914, November 2, 1912, November 7, 1914.

28. Ibid., November 9, 1912, November 2, 1912; State of Missouri, *Official Manual*, 1911–12, 1913–14.

29. *St. Louis Labor* April 8, 1911, April 15, 1911, May 6, 1911, July 1, 1911, September 30, 1911, October 7, 1911, November 18, 1911.

30. Ibid., August 17, 1912, August 24, 1912; State of Missouri *Official Manual*, 1913–14, 1915–16.

31. Peggy Lamson, *Roger Baldwin: Founder of the ACLU* (Boston: Houghton Mifflin, 1976), 59; Primm, 421–25; *St. Louis Labor*, October 14, 1911, November 11, 1911, October 3, 1914. Dr. Simon, who had earlier lost a race for coroner, had won election to the Board of Education because of Republican support. The Republicans wanted to defeat the Democratic "good government" candidate, so they endorsed Simon. He also had the support of the German-American Alliance, which described him as a "good citizen." See *St. Louis Labor*, November 9, 1909.

32. *St. Louis Labor*, September 16, 1911, June 13, 1914, June 20, 1914, May 16, 1914, May 30, 1914, May 9, 1914; Primm, 417–34; Fink, 34–37; Forythe, 74–75. Years later, Roger Baldwin was reported to have stated that the passage of charter revision represented a pinnacle of democracy. Lamson, 48.

33. Thelan, 220–33, 257–63; Primm, 380–81, 393.

34. *Missouri Socialist*, No. 90, October 18, 1902.

35. Primm, 441.

36. Socialist Party of St. Louis Collection, Box 1, Folder 3, Western–Historical Manuscript Collection, University of Missouri-St. Louis. This may be the only extent record of minutes on a monthly basis that highlight the 1919 schism of the Socialist Party of America on a local level.

37. Marvin Wachman, *The History of the Social Democratic Party of Milwaukee, 1897–1910* (Urbana: University of Illinois Press, 1945); David Paul Nord, "Hothouse Socialism: Minneapolis, 1910–1925," in *Socialism in the Heartland: The Midwestern Experience, 1900–1925*, ed. Donald T. Critchlow (Notre Dame, Indiana: University of Notre Dame Press, 1986), 133–66.

PART IV
GENDER

# 5 Women in the Party Bureaucracy

## Subservient Functionaries

In recent years, the bibliography on women and socialism has begun to grow. Studies on the Socialist party of America have appeared focusing on the era of World War I, the party's most expansive period. Biographical articles on women organizers and intellectuals have provided additional data but have not fully illuminated basic questions about the role of women in radical politics, or that is, radical politics and woman's "place." This essay is an institutional study of the Socialist party and its women members, their role in its power structure, their views on policy, their activities, and their priorities.[1]

The Socialist party of America at its founding convention in 1901 included in its platform a commitment to "equal civil and political rights for men and women." Indeed, following the position taken in the late nineteenth century by European socialism, the party was virtually obligated to support such a position. Moreover, influential socialists abroad, such as August Bebel of the German Social Democratic party, Paul Lafargue of the French socialists and the son-in-law of Marx, and Frederich Engels himself, had acknowledged the exploitation of women in a special guise and had written on behalf of sexual equality.

Women were perhaps one-tenth of the membership of the Socialist party, and played a visible role in its internal affairs. In national conventions between 1904 and 1912, women were conspicuous, serving on subcommittees, leading floor fights, and lobbying for resolutions. Unlike the dominant political parties where women were almost never convention delegates (from 0 to under 1 percent in these years), the socialists had relatively large female contingents. In 1904, 6 percent of the delegates were women, in 1908 10 percent, and in 1912, again 10 percent.[2]

Women served the party as organizers, propagandists, pamphleteers, and candidates for public office. In 1912, the party sent sixty speakers throughout North America on a lyceum circuit, and over one-fifth of these were women. Party journalists were women almost as often as men, with copy editors and staff people tending to be women. Autonomous women's socialist study groups, organized in most of the states and also in Ontario, Manitoba, Alberta, and British Columbia, coordinated their programs and their lobbying around party initiatives. Women party members raised funds for strike benefits and campaign expenses, distributed propaganda, served as poll watchers, established and taught in socialist Sunday schools and, in general, built bridges to nonsocialist women and women's organizations. In 1908, responding to the possibility of an autonomous national organization of socialist women, the party convention established a Woman's National Committee as a clearinghouse and focus for women's party activities. A salaried woman national organizer was assigned specifically to seek out women for membership, while each state organization and every local was urged to utilize women organizers and to form a woman's committee. The Woman's National Committee raised funds, commissioned leaflets, and otherwise sought to increase party strength by appealing to women's interests and needs.[3]

However, party treatment of the so-called Woman Question and of women members often seemed perfunctory, more lip service than genuine commitment. The platform demand of 1901 for equal rights was virtually a dead letter. The platform plank of 1904 supporting equal suffrage for men and women seemed an absentminded acknowledgment. No literature was commissioned for women in these early years, no organizers assigned. It was not until the convention of 1908 when women delegates forcefully acted as a special interest group that the party pledged an active campaign for unrestricted and equal suffrage.[4]

Through those first half-dozen years prior to the appearance of a cohesive woman's bloc, the Socialist party had expended no energy in organizing women or appealing to their needs. As a leading male socialist, John Spargo complained, that not only did the party fail to seek out women, but it often held its meetings in the locker-room atmosphere of neighborhood saloons. Such locations were clearly unattractive to women who might often be circumspect about venturing into politics. When women joined the party on their own initiative, no effort was made to fit proceedings into a framework understandable to political novices. Moreover, propaganda and arguments were always expressed in terms of the male identity, concerns, and life style. No campaign was initiated to reach women in their dual capacities as wage workers by day and housewives by night, nor was any real attempt made to penetrate the ignorance in which it was believed organized religion had trapped women. Women's role in the party, some women noted, was to be no more than cake bakers and tea pourers. "Women are tired of being 'included',"one wrote,"but not really recognized." As to party politics, women could be seen, possibly, but not heard in the locals.[5]

In addition to such institutional sins of omission, male party leaders informally revealed strong reservations about women activists. When a woman was first elected in 1909 to the party executive, Victor Berger, a dominant force in the party right wing, commented to a colleague, Morris Hillquit, that having a woman on the National Executive Committee was " . . . by no means necessary for a political party at this stage of the game and under the present conditions." In 1913 when Kate Richards O'Hare was elected as a representative to the International Socialist Bureau in Brussels, the same two leaders feared that she would make the Socialist party look ridiculous abroad. Berger as a congressman fulfilled his obligation to introduce a bill for woman suffrage, only to find such efforts suspect. A woman's socialist group complained that the two socialists elected to Congress, Berger of Milwaukee and Meyer London of the lower East Side, minimized the suffrage issue, and Florence Kelley of the Henry Street Settlement House and a sometime socialist, questioned the sincerity of their commitment to protective legislation for women. To reassure doubters, male party leaders emphasized the pioneering commitment oᶠ socialists everywhere to woman suffrage, but some admitted a belief that votes for women would delay the advent of socialism since women were presumed to be dominated by reactionary priests and ministers.[6]

Patronizing of women was rampant in the party. A leading journal, the *International Socialist Review*, described women delegates as "On all questions . . . acquit[ting] themselves nobly." The socialist press was also capable of referring to one woman convention delegate as having "her feathers all ruffled", and Eugene V. Debs, the party's perennial candidate for the presidency, generously commented on the value of women speakers who always attracted a crowd.[7]

In short, women were not taken seriously by a political party theoretically committed to equality. " . . . how bitter is our disappointment," one woman wrote, "whenever we come to look upon matters as they really are." Women were not welcome in the party's power structure. They were clustered in the lower levels of the party hierarchy, far from positions of authority. Women members were relegated to precinct work and thus were effectively segregated from responsibility. At best, women played roles at conventions, although even there resentments surfaced over all-male state delegations. The National Office of the party and its National Executive Committee (N.E.C.), the decision-making body between conventions, were masculine provinces. Even the day-to -day decisions on fiscal matters, policy determinations, and organizational campaigns were prerogatives of the professional functionaries and the most prominent party politicians. With women effectively barred from this segment of the party arena, a pattern of institutional discrimination prevailed; only upon occasion were women allowed other than marginal roles. Prejudicial attitudes and institutional arrangements meant that hers were party bazaars but not party power.[8]

The identity of the women activists was remarkably homogeneous. The background of most of these women was middle class and native American. In fact, the pattern was predominantly bourgeois WASP. Of two dozen women who served on the Woman's National Committee, three-fourths were American born, perhaps reflecting the fact that the socialist movement itself had shrugged off its nineteenth-century domination by European immigrants. Among seventeen other women featured in cover stories by the only national woman's socialist monthly, the same percentage prevailed. Among these forty-one prominent women socialists, only four could claim working-class backgrounds: Rose Pastor Stokes, Kate Richards O'Hare, Elizabeth Gurley Flynn, and Theresa Malkiel. The typical profile was of a college-educated woman, often a teacher, many with formative experiences in evangelical or suffrage movements.[9] These women were relatively youthful, in their thirties and forties, with only an occasional older activist who had participated in abolitionist struggles. A few were offspring of activist mothers. Most of these women were married, usually to men who were also socialists. In instances where couples shared a party prominence—Algie and May Wood Simons, J. G. Phelps and Rose Pastor Stokes, Victor and Meta Berger—the wife generally worked in the shadow of the husband's more important position. But whether married, divorced, or single, most appeared to live independent lives which were not male dominated.[10]

Geographically, an overwhelming proportion of these women came from the rural Middle West and the Far West, with a few hailing from the South. Illustrative of that pattern, more than 50 percent of women convention delegates from 1904 to 1912 represented areas west of the Mississippi River, and 25 percent the Great Lakes. Most of the autonomous women's socialist organizations except for a number headquartered in New York, were established in the western half of the continent. This pattern may be explained by the fact that many western women had won the franchise a generation earlier, and therefore the political process was not alien to them. Thus, socialist women helped underline the party's own western tilt.[11]

In 1908, soon after the establishment of the Woman's National Committee (W.N.C.), a Woman's General Correspondent was appointed, and her office became the keystone of a vertical organization which extended increasingly deep and independent roots. A distinct separatism that almost no one wanted developed. While all W.N.C. decisions had to be endorsed by the party's executive and while the committee lacked budgetary authority, nevertheless its network spread throughout the country. An office of Woman's State Correspondent was also established at this time, to serve as liaison among local, state, and national woman's committees. This office, set up immediately in four midwestern and western states, was always held by women, although not so legislated, and was closely tied to a woman's state committee. In the next eighteen months ten additional states (two-thirds west of the Mississippi River) established the same offices. When other states did not follow suit, the W.N.C., after some prodding, considered submitting its own nominations for the unfilled posts, an action sure to be perceived as a threat to local autonomy. However, by 1915 such an edifice for women's activities existed in thirty-seven states.[12]

On the local level, wide discrepancies existed in practice. Party policy provided that each local organize a woman's committee, but in some locals apparently the only action was the posting of a "Ladies Invited" sign. By 1911 the woman's committees were said to have been established in 69 percent of reporting locals, but this fact was based on a questionnaire to which only 7 percent of the locals responded. Regional differences were pronounced. The Mississippi State Correspondent reported that she found that southern notions of woman's "place" and of male chivalry adversely affected party efforts toward organizing women, while the New Mexico State Correspondent reported that her state's poverty and sparse population hindered organizational drives. But the California State Correspondent wrote that 13 percent of her state's membership was female, and the New York State Correspondent estimated 10 percent. Throughout the country areas of party strength were often reflected in an expanding women's sphere, while party weaknesses were usually paralleled by a low level of such activity.[13]

However, data indicates that there was greater willingness in certain areas than others to include women in the regular party apparatus. Women still served infrequently on the National Committee, showing a small percentage growth (never more than six women, with fluctuations from 1910 to 1914 of 3.5 percent to 8.5 percent), and seldom were they elected by eastern states, despite the fact that a state like New York had many prominent women members. The all-important N.E.C., to which five to seven mem-

AMERICAN RIVER COLLEGE LIBRARY

bers were elected annually between 1901 and 1917, had only a total of three women. All three were exceedingly prominent party organizers: Lena Morrow Lewis, elected in 1909; Kate Richards O'Hare in 1911; and Anna A. Maley in 1916. Among state secretaries, women held a maximum of 16 percent of the positions. The official delegates to the International were almost entirely male in 1904 and 1907, but in 1910 three of the party's eight mandated delegates to the Congress of the Second International at Copenhagen were women, and in 1913, as mentioned above, O'Hare was elected as one of the few women ever to sit on the International Socialist Bureau in Brussels.

Ad hoc party committees tended to be exclusively male. The only type of position for which the Socialist party turned regularly to women nominees was in the field of education. In 1909 Milwaukee elected the first socialist woman to a public post in the United States when the party ran Meta Berger for the Milwaukee School Board, a position she held for over two decades. The party's National Education Committee in 1913 was chaired by May Wood Simons, and consisted of three women and four men. In 1908, the socialists named 13 women among its 271 candidates in state races (4.7 percent), and of that number, 8 were candidates for Superintendencies of Public Instruction or for Regents of State Universities. In 1910, of 255 candidates for state level public offices 16 were women (6.2 percent), half of whom ran for educational posts.[14]

Clearly, then, woman's sphere was carefully defined; in effect the party had made room for women in a hierarchy of their own. Their socialist activity was confined to their own structure, reported in their own separate newspaper columns, and it was their energy alone that would determine how widely their sector of the party might grow. The Woman's National Committee developed a "Plan for Work in Socialist Locals" which established guidelines for attracting women to membership. The plan was based on the stated assumption of "the need to make distinct efforts to reach women . . . ." Separate woman's locals were officially eschewed in favor of mixed locals, although a few women favored separatism temporarily in order to establish a relaxed environment in which to raise consciousness. But woman's committees were elected by locals from their entire membership, and each chose a correspondent to maintain contact with other woman's committees. The committees distributed party publications, promoted specific issues, sought out new members, and sponsored entertainments and social events. Increasingly, emphasis was placed upon combining serious study with social events or traditional woman's activities such as sewing bees in order to attract potential converts.[15]

After a few years, the W.N.C.'s Plan for Work became quite refined. The pioneering day of general organizing had ended, as one woman declared, and organizers had to respond to varieties of life styles among women. The woman's committees, now called Local Committees on Propaganda among Women in order to minimize implications of auxiliary functions, were to be integrated into the general work of the locals, sharing responsibilities on all issues. The members were to canvas house-to-house, in shops, and wherever women congregated. Special distributions and demonstrations occurred on the annual Woman's Day, May Day, the Fourth of July, and Labor Day. The W.N.C. published monthly programs for the guidance of local committees and routinely sent appropriate articles to the labor and socialist press. The local committees formed strike subcommittees and suffrage campaign groups. In some large cities, a Central Woman's Committee, composed of delegates from each ward branch, was organized, and inner-city socialist locals were provided with special guidelines to transcend the suspicions of tenement women. The W.N.C. also offered suggestions for reaching women on farms and in prairie hamlets, emphasizing the ways in which the party could serve a poignant human need by alleviating the loneliness of such isolated women.[16]

The W.N.C. issued approximately two dozen leaflets of interest to women. The leaflets appealed to women in their various working capacities and dealt with issues such as suffrage, social problems, socialism and the home, the boy scout movement, and the cost of living, the most widely distributed leaflet. The party executive, bearing veto power over publications, occasionally requested revisions for stylistic reasons and sometimes for matters of substance. One leaflet was criticized for using the expression, "the sex struggle."[17]

Each year the W.N.C. focused on a few specific lines of activity. In 1913, for example, the emphasis was on promoting suffrage, winning new members, and cooperating with immigrant women's organizations. Depending on the thrust, the W.N.C. tried to route organizers on various issues and in specific regions of the country. It considered placing organizers in an area for three days instead of the party's usual practice of one-day whirlwind visits, since feeling was widespread that a more comprehensive type of barnstorming was necessary to break through the barriers surrounding women. Organizing methods were modified in favor of meetings in private homes, congenial environments where the uncommitted would feel comfortable. The Woman's National Committee established a Socialist Teachers' Placement Bureau and a Childrens' Strike Fund, and explored the idea of "family dues" instead of the humiliating lower dues for women. It encouraged using women on the party's major committees, on delegations, and as national organizers, filled requests for women speakers, and tried to arrange national tours for European socialist women. Throughout all the W.N.C.'s efforts to involve women in routine party work and to encourage the cooperation of locals, it sought to minimize any suggestion of separatism. Lena Morrow Lewis, arguing unsuccessfully against a national conference of socialist women, cautioned that their work must always illustrate the fact that the Socialist party was not a men's club: "We must never allow our woman's committees or conferences to be the means of eliminating [the] women from the regular party."[18]

The socialist women succeeded in forging an institutional structure in over three dozen states, some of which became vigorous pockets of party activity. However, despite their wide-ranging efforts, while women joined the party, they did not flock to it. Fragmentary evidence clearly indicates a rise in women members. Just prior to the founding of the Woman's National Committee, a survey of 15 percent of the locals suggested that women were 4.9 percent of the membership. In 1912, the general correspondent, Winnie E. Branstetter, estimated—based on returns from only thirty-five locals—that 10 percent of the membership was female. The next year the reports of the state correspondents suggested 15 percent, while in 1915 May Wood Simons guessed that women made up 17 percent of the party. The dimension of the struggle to increase the female contingent can be gleaned from the fact that even membership data by sex remained elusive. The W.N.C. was obviously envious when it noted that the Young People's Socialist League claimed a membership that was one-third female.[19]

The Woman's National Committee sought to develop dialogues with several peer groups external to the party proper: women in the socialist movement overseas, immigrant women, and the bourgeois suffrage movement. The American women who attended the Congress of the Second International in Copenhagen in 1910, Luella Twining, May Wood Simons, and Lena Morrow Lewis, eagerly participated in the Second International Conference of Socialist Women which preceded the Congress. German women had raised the Woman Question years before at the founding of the Second International in 1889, and by 1907 they had won an endorsement of universal suffrage and had organized an international conference of socialist women. American women, an ocean away, could not play a full role, yet the infrequent gatherings were inspirational to them. They enjoyed the collegial environment at the 1910 conference, but nevertheless did not hesitate to oppose Clara Zetkin and other leaders who eschewed reforms such as protective legislation for women. The W.N.C. studied the European women's methods of propaganda and data collection, and created a position of International Correspondent to systematize their contacts. The correspondent, Meta Stern Lilienthal of New York, monitored European publications and translated pertinent articles into English. The W.N.C. regularly sent reports of its work to Zetkin in Germany and to Annie Grundy in London, and saw its own annual Woman's Day adopted by some of the European socialists. In 1914 the W.N.C. elected its own representative to the anticipated Third International Conference of Socialist Women scheduled for August in Vienna prior to the opening of the Congress of the International, and it also prepared a report for presentation there on the woman suffrage movement in the United States.[20]

The W.N.C., whose own membership sometimes included women of European background, was somewhat slow to recognize the potential for socialism among immigrant women, but eventually the committee sought to mine that resource. At the 1912 party convention, Caroline A. Lowe, a midwesterner, pleaded for funding for translators so that W.N.C. leaflets could reach the foreign-speaking. In 1913 the W.N.C. tried to forge links with the occasional woman serving on the executives of the party's foreign-language federations and with their few woman's branches. The federations, clearly male in leadership and, among certain nationalities, in membership as well, were asked by the W.N.C. to translate its woman's publications into their own language. Translations appeared in Finnish, Slovak, Polish, Bohemian, Hungarian, German, and Yiddish, with only the South Slavic and the Italian Federations lacking leaflets. The W.N.C. debated whether perhaps a "cultural problem" existed which might preclude verbatim translations into Eastern European languages and considered preparing a "simpler" literature for immigrant working-class women. A new leaflet was issued for such women on the importance of naturalization.[21]

A subcommittee was established to formalize a link between the W.N.C. and the party's foreign-language federation women. This move made feasible a survey of ethnic women's attitudes and situations. The survey, limited to women members of the foreign-language federations, showed that the Finnish Federation led all wings of the party; with its family-based party activities, one-third of its membership was female. The Scandinavian and German Federations were 15 percent women, the Bohemian, Polish, and Jewish were 10 percent female, and the South Slav and Italian—immigrant groups in which men often came without their families—only 1 percent female. Valuable data was assembled on the occupational status of women by ethnic group, putting the W.N.C. in a position to make knowledgeable appeals to each language group.[22]

The Woman's National Committee maintained an ambivalent relationship with the woman's suffrage movement. The W.N.C. found it necessary to justify any collaboration with the National American Woman's Suffrage Association because both the Second International and the Socialist party opposed cooperation with middle-class suffrage efforts. But the W.N.C. spoke of capturing and radicalizing the suffrage movement; it maintained that its propaganda was always based on class consciousness, emphasizing that the ballot was only one means toward the goal of social transformation. Despite the fact that the Socialist Party never resolved the suffrage issue, the W.N.C. always assisted suffrage campaigns in every municipality and every state, it cooperated with the non-socialist suffragists, and even joined them in testifying before the House Judiciary Committee in its hearings on several woman suffrage bills, one of which had been introduced by Socialist Congressman Berger. The W.N.C. sent observers to the conventions of the N.A.W.S.A. and shared credit with the suffragists when a state enacted woman suffrage.[23]

Most socialist women believed that the suffragists were short-sighted; they reasoned inadequately on the basis of natural, that is, political, rights, while socialist women stressed economic and social questions, and realized that the ballot was not an end in itself. Still, some socialist women considered suffrage a major goal, calling it as important as the demands of labor, while others stressed woman suffrage as a step toward socialism, and a number noted that to delay woman suffrage until the revolution would be as unreasonable as delaying the eight-hour day. To those who argued that women themselves had to energize their cause outside of the socialist movement, party feminists asked if worker propaganda should be set aside until the workers awoke.[24]

The issue crystallized at the party congress in 1910. By then, the Woman's National Committee under Simons had embarked on a sweeping educational campaign to convince women that the suffrage struggle should not be "a pure and simple feminine affair" but, rather, a class-conscious movement. Nonetheless, the debate demonstrated that a large number of women delegates favored cooperation with suffrage groups. An emotional discussion culminated in the defeat of a resolution to support the suffrage movement. Thus party doctrine still sought to restrict suffrage activity to internal efforts, and the Woman's National Committee's main thrust continued to be encouraging every local and state organization to establish a woman's committee which, in turn, would push suffrage. And yet at the next convention, when the feminist movement within the party was still at its height, a delegate questioned whether or not a belief in woman suffrage was necessary to a commitment to socialism.[25]

Aside from the Woman's National Committee and the woman's columns in the various socialist newspapers, socialist activity within the party structure was limited to the party's Information Department. In 1914 this party clearing house contacted the state secretaries of seven states with full or partial woman suffrage, and determined that, despite voiced fears, women voters were not adversely affecting the movement. The department examined the historical experiences of states with woman suffrage and also surveyed the effect of minimum wage laws for women across the country. The efforts of the Information Department, like the W.N.C. itself, were focused on social reforms rather than the theoretical impossibility of emancipation within the capitalist structure.[26]

Socialist state legislators introduced a great number of bills and resolutions which either directly related to women or were thought to appeal to them. In addition to measures on behalf of woman suffrage, legislators introduced bills for women to serve as jurors, for free school lunches and textbooks, child labor legislation and protection for the rights of illegitimate children, minimum wage laws, Mothers' and Widows' Pensions, and various other protective measures such as maximum hours and rest periods. In contrast, the national platform of the Socialist party in 1916 offered women only the equal franchise and the Mothers' pension. Aside from those commitments, the national party apparatus was likely to turn to women only when policy required demonstrations and petitions against militarism, conscription, or war itself. Such appeals to socialist women were issued during the mobilization of American troops on the Mexican border and during the World War. Thus, women were still channeled into innocuous and undemanding areas without real responsibility. As mothers, women could always be counted on to provide antimilitary troops.[27]

But in several of the states and in various locales, the socialist woman's movement was growing into an energetic and imaginative, expansive focus for party activity. Based on their earlier socialization, many socialist women sought to tap segments of what could be termed a woman's network. Many turned to lyceums and chatauquas to interest women who might be intimidated by direct socialist approaches. In California, for example, a socialist chatauqua was held in 1909. Elsewhere in the West, women sponsored party booths at state and county fairs; they pioneered weekly or monthly party suppers in Pennsylvania, Washington, D.C., and elsewhere; and they arranged for entertainments and speakers as they caravaned out to workers in lonely mining camps in Kansas. Various approaches were used in order to transform public schools into community centers so that party activities could encompass the entire family. Plays were presented during strikes here and there to raise funds and to lift morale.

Monthly reports of the state correspondents recorded new party members, listed sympathizers, and informed the general correspondent of the names of local women organizers and speakers. Newly organized woman's committees sometimes revived an entire area. In Nevada in the summer of 1913, for example, ten new locals were 50 percent female in membership. In Utah, it was reported, women of the Mormon faith who were hesitant to join the party, nevertheless participated in party activities. Women even held state-wide socialist conferences in New York, Massachusetts, and Kansas. The woman's effort, thus, was developing grassroots and a responsiveness to local conditions and emerging needs. The socialist woman's movement, in but not of the party through its separate bureaucracy, was succeeding in minimizing isolation, providing role models and opportunities for leadership, stimulating awareness and organization, and apparently spreading socialism.[28]

In regard to policy, most socialist women accepted the revisionist and gradualist direction of the party. With a few exceptions, socialist women by their votes, statements, and writings supported the reformist wing of the party which controlled the bureaucracy and policy. But while most of the women activists agreed with mainstream party thinking, their distance from party responsibilities granted them some independence in policy formulation,[29] including the paramount issues of these years which revolved around the party's relationship with organized labor. In the winter of 1909–1910 a party crisis erupted stemming from failure to attract large numbers of working people. Eventually all party leaders polled by the *International Socialist Review* disavowed the idea of forming a separate labor party. Not one of the two dozen polled was a woman as only candidates for the National Executive Committee were interviewed, and thus women played no part in discussion.[30]

The Wobblies, too radical a group for the tastes of most party officials, enjoyed the support of some women socialists. A woman organizer, Ida Crouch-Hazlett of Montana, argued unsuccessfully against party discouragement of any evidence of worker solidarity. When the Industrial Workers of the World (IWW) led so-called free speech fights on the west coast, using civil disobedience to publicize the closing of street corners to their soapbox speakers, Kate Sadler of Washington and Marguerite Prevey of Ohio joined a minority effort to force the party to give moral support to the Wobblies' struggle. In 1912, the party in convention amended its constitution to make an endorsement of sabotage, considered an IWW tactic, grounds for expulsion from the Socialist Party. Prevey argued that such a move could only assist capitalists in the protection of private property. Women delegates divided over the amendment, fifteen supporting it and nine opposing. As a post-script, the IWW leader, Big Bill Haywood, was soon manipulated out of the party and recalled from the N.E.C. in an extraordinary procedure. Thirteen of the three-dozen activists writing to condemn the railroading tactics were women.[31]

Another issue concerned a party compromise on the subject of im-migration restriction. Despite its avowed internationalism, the Socialist party did not wish to contravene the restrictionist policy of the American Federa-tion of Labor (A.F. of L.). Socialist women, however, had little difficulty sup-porting internationalist principles. They tended not to be linked to the A.F. of L. as were many of their male counterparts, and thus some women freely acknowledged that exclusion was a pseudo-issue, merely a bone thrown to satisfy West Coast trade unionists. Josephine R. Cole, a California journal-ist, argued that labor had not reached an anti-immigrant consensus, and she maintained that the Socialist party had to assume the lead in uniting all races [sic] against capitalism. A Washington State woman, however, at the 1910 party congress, vilified Chinese workers. While such remarks were not ex-traordinary, one woman, a Finnish delegate from Minnesota, cited the ab-surdity of the pluralistic United States excluding nationality groups, and took the unusual step of forthrightly denigrating A.F. of L. restrictionism on the grounds of its minority status in the labor movement. But as in various party debates, the voices of the women members tended to be muted, at best. Since they were absent from policy-making positions, intraparty controversies lay in the male domain. Women activists were left to "woman's issues," that is, issues that fell "naturally" to their "place."[32]

Women's concerns as reflected in their writings and speeches related especially to family fragmentation and social problems under capitalism. Not only did the male-dominated party generally reserve these issues for women members, but the life experiences of these women shaped them toward such concerns which then were reinforced by the party. A consensus among so-cialist women appeared to exist over some issues: the importance of pro-gressive education and the evils of child labor, the capitalist foundation of alcoholism, divorce, and white slavery. Marriage itself was likened to pros-titution because some women had to sell their bodies for economic security. On many matters, however, socialist women disagreed. Most stressed the equality of the sexes while a few implied female superiority. A majority ap-peared to support birth control as a necessary factor in the emancipation of human beings, while a minority—perhaps influenced by Clara Zetkin—

viewed increasing numbers of workers' children as assets in the class struggle. Most socialist women welcomed protective legislation for working women, but a vocal handful considered it patronizing and empty reformism. As to the future of the family, a common view held that socialism would emancipate wives from domestic drudgery; under the socialist system, readily available appliances would simplify household chores. But a few stressed the importance of women having an opportunity to be individuals, in addition to being mothers and wives, and theorized that perhaps marriage would become a relic of the capitalist past. Viewing marriage as an economic institution, some suggested that the independence inherent in the new system would drastically alter the marital relationship. Often on such basic questions a Marxist-feminist split was evident. The most radical women in terms of Marxist ideology tended to lack a feminist consciousness.[33]

On the fundamental issue, the Woman Question itself, the division among socialist women was searing. They never reached a solid consensus on the emancipation of women as a legitimate issue for the Socialist party. Those who opposed the Woman Question as an issue maintained that the socialization of property was the only means to insure economic independence for all and, therefore, overt concern for a specific group would simply waste energy. The struggle to raise class consciousness must be waged without regard to sex or color. It was argued that even a direct attack on beliefs in female inferiority would be a tactical error, resulting in a monolithic alliance of men against women. In contrast, the avowedly feminist position emphasized that the unique political and economic tyranny to which women were subject required a special campaign within the class struggle. Women, especially working women, were not only oppressed by capitalism but were also oppressed as the proletariat of the family, as Engels had noted. Many socialist feminists wrote of the double enslavement of women—bearing the burden of class and sex—and the need for double emancipation. Women's economic exploitation was more complex than that of workingmen, as a realistic appraisal of conditions would indicate.[34]

Ironically, many vigorous arguments on behalf of the Woman Question were home-centered, focusing on women's special biological nature and their greater spirituality and sensitivity, and thus were ultimately traditionalist in their thrust. American women were advised by socialist women to join the party because of their unique concerns as mothers, and they "should throw . . . [the] strength of maternal altruism into the only cause that can give equal opportunity for children of the human race." Modern women, editorialized the *Socialist Woman*, have to be taught that socialism is the only way to solve the increasing problems of the family and the home. While often socialist women objected to the view that socialism would permit women to be home full time without social responsibility, nevertheless a consistent theme placed the emancipated woman in that setting. Women party leaders were often praised as model homemakers, examples that socialism would not destroy domesticity. And, indeed, their pride as homemakers and their marital life styles, other than the not uncommon use of the hyphenated name, demonstrated little that set them apart from their bourgeois counterparts. As one woman wrote, "The genuine good old standards need never be lost in gaining the genuine goal of new freedom . . ."[35]

The vision of socialist women was neither cohesive, incisive, nor innovative. Those who saw women's liberation as a distinct part of the class struggle often did not transcend traditional role assignments and family structure. They, like most sexist male comrades, ultimately viewed the sexes and the family according to standards which the male-dominated institutions of western society had shaped. One socialist feminist might argue that society must be organized so that women, like men, were seen as bearing potential beyond the reproductive. Another might stress that marriage must mean more for women than the termination of their personal aspirations. But no one designed a new family structure to facilitate full female liberation. A basic social transformation was never conceptualized.[36]

The Woman's National Committee, after six years of intense activity, was undercut by forces in the party that either considered the Woman Question irrelevant trimmings or a divisive threat. Thus, in 1914, work on behalf of the socialist woman's movement halted without the resolution of the internal tensions or the further development of programs then maturing. But, logically, if there were no real Woman Question, there was no need for a woman's sector. The aftermath of the national campaign of 1912 witnessed party retrenchment due to membership slippage, a type of leveling off of activity familiar to all political parties following elections. The National Executive Committee embarked on a cost-cutting crusade, involving the cancellation of meetings, publications, and any efforts thought to be unessential. Accordingly, the N.E.C. "withdrew all support from the W.N.C."

The W.N.C. could no longer publish leaflets, field organizers, effect policy decisions, or even maintain its correspondence. No money was budgeted for W.N.C. operations and its meetings were discouraged. Some of the women concluded bitterly that totally eliminating possibly flawed machinery clearly demonstrated that women's organized activities were no more than ornamental to the male hierarchy. May Wood Simons, the dominant figure in the establishment of the Woman's National Committee and the only person to have served on it since its founding, resigned in protest. In 1914 the National Committee discussed the abolition of the W.N.C., and in 1915 such a motion was passed and sustained in referendum. With that stroke of a pen, as it were, the entire structure in which the socialist woman's movement was concentrated dissolved. In the aftermath, a number of women spontaneously demonstrated against the dissolution of their party machinery, while a few women registered their approval, arguing that mechanism had served to shunt them off to a corner of the party. Most of the protesters emphasized that women would again be invisible in the party and might once more work outside it. A few affirmative action resolutions by men and women were submitted in favor of proportional representation for women on major committees in lieu of a special hierarchy. As a probably not unconnected development, a woman did win election to the N.E.C. for the first time in four years.[37]

In the subsequent years of war and strife, culminating in the party schism of 1919, women resumed the peripheral role they had played earlier, as some had predicted. Only a few of the "exceptional" continued to be prominent, and women made up nearly 6 percent (a loss of 4 percent) of the delegates to the Emergency Convention of 1917 at the start of war intervention. Such an unimpressive figure, as well as the infrequency with which women members were nominated for public office, suggests as little visibility as before. Wartime resolutions for reestablishing a woman's sector were tabled.[38]

The unwanted party-within-a-party which had provided the movement with new sources of energy was ironically snuffed out arbitrarily in the midst of its most dynamic and vital period, just as the Socialist party itself was to be cut down in World War I by forces external to it. No evidence exists to prove a thesis that the woman's movement within the party peaked in 1912 and then declined.[39] Rather, that movement continued to sink roots and to establish an increasingly comprehensive network which, however, was handicapped by its lack of autonomy and by the constant need to fight a rearguard action to convince both men and women of the seriousness and the legitimacy of its effort. In the final analysis, the woman's movement proved a fragile structure because of the lack of a powerful base in the national bureaucracy. Tensions and ambivalence destroyed the separate and parallel movement.

## NOTES

1. See, for example, "Women and Socialism," in James Weinstein, *The Decline of Socialism in America, 1912–1925* (New York: Monthly Review Press, 1967), 53–63. He does not systematically explore the extent of female integration into the party structure and, moreover, takes individuals' statements and party pronouncements con-

cerning women's rights at face value. Also see Ira Kipnis, *The American Socialist Movement, 1897–1912* (New York: Monthly Review Press, 1972), 260–65, for the only historical consideration of this question prior to the mid-1960s.

2. Edgard Milhaud, "Socialist Propaganda Among Women in Germany," *International Socialist Review* 1 (May 1901), 713–18; Paul Lafargue, "The Woman Question," ibid. 5 (March 1905), 547–59. See lists of delegates, Socialist Party, *Proceedings of the 1904 National Convention* (Chicago: Socialist Party, 1904), 16; S.P., *Proceedings . . . 1908*, 16–18; S.P., *Proceedings . . . 1912*, 83–85, 204–08.

3. For a general overview of women's socialist activities, see *Socialist Woman* 1907–1913 (renamed *Progressive Woman* and then *Coming Nation*; each name change was symbolic of a search for wider support). Arthur Brooks Baker, "Be a Party Builder," *International Socialist Review* 13 (September 1912), 259–62; *Socialist Woman* 2 (August 1908), 16; *Socialist Woman* 3 (September 1909), 15; *Socialist Woman* 2 (April 1909), 8; Socialist Party, *Proceedings . . . 1904*, 326; S.P., *Proceedings . . . 1908*, 10–11; S.P., *Proceedings . . . 1912*, 205–06; "Plan of Work for Women in Socialist Locals," Woman's National Committee, Socialist Party, 1913. For the autonomous socialist woman's clubs, see Bruce Dancis, "Socialism and Women in the United States, 1900–1917," *Socialist Revolution* 6 (January–March 1976), 109–10.

4. Socialist Party, *Proceedings . . . 1912*, 204. See, for example, the instructions of Oklahoma Assistant State Secretary Winnie E. Branstetter that all speakers work for woman suffrage, in *Socialist Woman* 1 (February 1908), 5.

5. John Spargo, "Woman and the Socialist Movement," *International Socialist Review* 8 (February 1908), 449–55; Theresa Malkiel, "Where Do We Stand on the Woman Question?," ibid. 10 (August 1909), 159–62; Lida Parce, "The Relation of Socialism to the Woman Question," ibid. 10 (November 1909), 442; Josephine Conger-Kaneko, "Are the Interests of Men and Women Identical? A Suggestion to the National Convention," *Socialist Woman* 1 (May 1908), 5. Those women arguing for separate locals actually favored mixed locals but thought they were feasible only where the men were responsive to women's needs and where the women were sufficiently enlightened. Separate locals, never effected, were expected to raise women's consciousness, educate them, and give them the confidence for an active role in mixed locals. But such views led to the necessity of a public denial by the head of the Woman's National Committee that a separate women's organization was their goal. See Josephine Conger-Kaneko, "Separate Organizations," *Socialist Woman* 1 (April 1908), 5; "Socialist Women Hold Meetings During Convention Week," ibid. 2 (June 1908), 9–10; Theresa Malkiel, "Some Impressions of the New York State Women's Conference," ibid. 2 (August 1908), 12–13; May Wood Simons, "Origin and Purpose of the Woman's Committee," ibid. 5 (July 1911), 6; Josephine Conger-Kaneko, "Why the Movement Has a Woman's Paper," ibid. 5 (July 1911), 15.

6. Spargo, "Women and the Socialist Movement," p. 450; Parce, "The Relation of Socialism," 442. See also Victor Berger to Morris Hillquit, February 13, 1910, Morris Hillquit Collection, State Historical Society of Wisconsin; Morris Hillquit to Victor Berger, October 16, 1913; Berger to Hillquit, October 23, 1913; Berger to William James Ghent, November 13, 1911; Bronx Socialist Women's Society to Berger, March 8, 1915; Florence Kelley to Berger, May 15, 1911; and also Berger note, July 1912, Socialist Party Collection, Milwaukee County Historical Society; Josephine R. Cole, "The International and Woman Suffrage," *Socialist Woman* 1 (November 1907), 3. Mary White Ovington, a socialist more active in the National Association for the Advancement of Colored People than in the Socialist Party, echoed these concerns, and noted that many writings by socialists featured "not a word . . . on woman and her disabilities, . . ."; Mary White Ovington, "Socialism and the Feminist Movement," *New Review* 2 (March 1914), 114–15. John Spargo and John Work seemed to be the only male party leaders to have believed genuinely in sexual equality. John Work argued for a fuller recognition of women

within the party in his "The Party Machinery," *Socialist Woman* 5 (July 1911), 10. One male state secretary maintained that perhaps only 10 percent of the men in the party actually believed in sexual equality, and he said that the Woman's National Committee ought to make the elevation of men's consciousness a top priority. See *Party Builder*, August 9, 1913, 5.

7. Editorial, "Sparks from the Convention," *International Socialist Review* 10 (June 1910), 1127–29; Henry C. Slobodin, "The National Socialist Convention of 1912," ibid. 12 (June 1912), 824; Eugene V. Debs, "Women Needed in Campaign," *Socialist Woman* 2 (August 1908), 4.

8. Malkiel, "Where Do We Stand?," 161. On the manifestation of oligarchic tendencies in the bureaucracy of a radical political party, see Carl Schorske, *German Social Democracy, 1905–1917: the Development of the Great Schism* (Cambridge, MA: Harvard University Press, 1955), 116–45.

9. See the monthly profiles in the *Socialist Woman*, 1907–1909. This composite is based on that important primary documentation, a crucial source since the *American Labor's Who's Who* (1925), the best source for biographies of radicals, lists very few women. Flynn, of course, was closely associated with the IWW rather than the Socialist Party. There are few collections of the correspondence of these women; the papers of only those women whose husbands' letters have been saved tend to be extant.

10. Ages are deduced from internal evidence in the monthly biographies. The women biographers in *Socialist Woman* politely omitted the birthdates of their subjects. While Rose Pastor Stokes was more famous than her husband, he rather than she served on the National Executive Committee.

11. See list of delegates, as cited in note 2, for the geographic breakdown.

12. Socialist Party, *Official Bulletin* 4 (June 1908), 1; ibid. 5 (May 1909), 1; ibid. 6 (May 1910), 4; ibid. 7 (October 1910), 1; ibid. 8 (August 1911), 5; *Party Builder*, January 23, 1914, 5. Two women of the Plains States, Caroline A. Lowe of Kansas and Winnie E. Branstetter of Oklahoma, served as the general correspondent.

13. Prizes were given to locals for attracting women members as part of the campaign of the Woman's National Committee, but whatever its efforts or a state's conditions, an individual official could discourage women from joining the party. Socialist Party, *Official Bulletin* 5 (June 1909), 4; ibid. 7 (October 1910), 1; ibid. 7 (December 1910), 2; ibid. 9 (February 1913), 2; *Party Builder*, October 2, 1912, 2; October 16, 1912, 2; October 23, 1912, 2; October 30, 1912, 2; January 25, 1913, 2; July 12, 1913, 4; August 9, 1913, 5; August 23, 1913, 5.

14. For representative National Committee membership data, see Socialist Party, *Official Bulletin* 6 (January 1910), 4; ibid. 8 (August 1912), 8; *Party Builder*, March 7, 1914, 5. The Woman's Department Report in S.P. *Proceedings of the 1912 National Convention*, 204–05, provides information on convention delegations. For other data, see S.P. *Official Bulletin* 5 (July 1909), 4; ibid. 5 (September 1908), 1; ibid. 7 (September 1910), 3.

15. A letter to the editor summarized these views by stating that unfortunately a special appeal to women was necessary due to their capitalist-induced conservatism. See *Socialist Woman* 1 (July 1907), 8, and also "Grace D. Brewer," (a biographical study), ibid. 1 (January 1908), 2; Josephine Conger-Kaneko, "Separate Organizations," ibid. 1 (April 1908), 5; Ida Crouch-Hazlett, "Women's Organizations," ibid. 2 (September 1908), 11. One woman argued that any desire for separate locals was an unfortunate indication of social norms; see Mila Tupper Maynard, "Woman Suffrage as Observed by a Socialist," *International Socialist Review* 5 (January 1905). W.N.C., "Plan of Work for Women in Socialist Locals," Chicago, 1913; *Party Builder*, August 28, 1912, 3; May 31, 1913, 2; September 13, 1913, 5; September 20, 1913, 5; March 7, 1914, 5. Informal talks on the cost of living and on shoddy consumer goods were considered especially good openers when approaching potential women members. *Party Builder*, December 25, 1912, 2.

16. S.P., *Official Bulletin* 7 (October 1910), 1; ibid. 8 (June 1912), 3, 4; *Party Builder*, October 30, 1912, 2; November 20, 1912, 2; December 25, 1912, 2; March 26, 1913, 2; July 19, 1913, 4; October 18, 1913, 5; February 14, 1914, 5; March 7, 1914, 5.

17. Copies of the various Woman's National Committee leaflets can be found in the files of the Socialist Party, National Office Papers, Duke University. A discussion on possible leaflet topics can be traced in the *Minutes of the Woman's National Committee* meeting of May 20, 1910, which appears in S.P. *Official Bulletin* 6 (May 1910), 4. See also ibid. 5 (November 1908), 2, and ibid. 5 (August 1909): 3, and *Party Builder*, May 10, 1914, 5.

18. Winnie E. Branstetter, "Woman's National Committee Enters a New Field of Activity," May 28, 1913, Socialist Party, National Office Files, Duke University; S.P., *Official Bulletin* 4 (May 1908), 2; ibid. 5 (May 1909), 2; ibid. 7 (August 1911), 5; ibid. 8 (November 1911), 2; ibid. 8 (March 1912), 2; ibid. 8 (June 1912), 4; *Party Builder*, May 31, 1913, 2; July 19, 1913, 4; July 26, 1913, 5; November 15, 1913, 5. The independent *Socialist Woman* editorialized on the need to elect a woman or several women to the party executive, arguing that women knew best their own condition. See *Socialist Woman* 1 (January 1908), 6. The *International Socialist Review* editorialized in the same vein in its issue of January 1909 (vol. 9, 535).

19. A 1908 survey of the membership showed that of 325 women members responding, 177 were housewives; one-third were in the 30–45 age bracket, with the rest evenly divided between younger and older women. S.P., *Official Bulletin* 5 (April 1909), 2; ibid. 8 (June 1912), 4; Socialist Party, *Proceedings* of the 1912 National Convention, 205; *Party Builder*, May 31, 1913, 3–4; May 16, 1914, 5; *American Socialist*, January 1915, 4.

20. S.P., *Official Bulletin* 4 (May 1908), 2, ibid. 6 (August 1910), 5, ibid. 8 (July 1912), 4; ibid. 9 (October 1912), 8; *Party Builder*, May 31, 1913, 2; January 10, 1914, 5; March 14, 1914, 5; June 6, 1914, 3; "From the International Congress," *Socialist Woman* 4 (October 1910), 2–3. See also, Second International Conference of Socialist Women, *Program*, 1910, Copenhagen (bound with *Report* of the Socialist Party Delegation to the International Socialist Congress, 1910, at International Institute of Social History, Amsterdam) and Socialist Labor Party, *Report* of the Socialist Women of Greater New York to the International Socialist Congress, 1910, Copenhagen.

21. Socialist Party, *Proceedings* . . . 1912, 88, 207; *Party Builder*, October 11, 1913, 5; S.P., *Official Bulletin* 8 (September–October 1911), 3; ibid. 6 (May 1910), 4; ibid. 8 (September 1912), 7. The issues of *Party Builder* in 1913 and 1914 provide a good overview of the W.N.C.'s growing relationship with the foreign-language contingent. Apparently the first W.N.C. formal consideration of immigrant women occurred in 1911. See S.P., *Official Bulletin* 8 (July 1911), 1.

22. Contradictory data exist on the percentage of women in the foreign-language federations; the percentages used in the text seem the most reasonable (an unlikely listing of the Hungarian federation as 20 percent female was dismissed as suspect). Centers of activity for foreign-speaking socialist women were clearly New York City, Chicago, and some Finnish-dominated rural areas. *Party Builder*, May 31, 1913, 3–4; July 5, 1913, 5; November 1, 1913, 4; February 7, 1914, 3; February 21, 1914, 5; May 23, 1914, 5; S.P., *Official Bulletin* 7 (August 1911), 5; ibid 8 (June 1912), 4.

23. Corinne S. Brown, "Votes for Women," *Socialist Woman* 1 (February 1908), 4, criticizes the International's 1907 position at Stuttgart against collaboration with the suffrage movement. The Socialist party debate on this point is summarized in "Sparks from the Convention," *International Socialist Review* 9 (June 1910), 1126–27. See also Ida Crouch-Hazlett, "The Socialist Movement and Woman Suffrage," *Socialist Woman* 2 (June 1908), 5. A letter from M. J. Scanlon to Winnie E. Branstetter, Carson City, Nevada, February 22, 1915, indicates that the Nevada state suffrage movement credited local socialist help for its triumph at the polls the previous No-

vember. See letter in S.P., National Office Files, Duke University. S.P., *Official Bulletin* 6 (April 1910), 2; ibid. 8 (November 1911), 7; ibid. 8 (April 1912), 4; ibid. 8 (May 1912), 3; ibid. 9 (December 1912), 1; *Party Builder,* May 31, 1913, 2.

24. Cole, "The International and Woman Suffrage," 1, 3; Lena Morrow Lewis, "Woman Suffragists and Woman Suffragists," *Socialist Woman* 1 (February 1908), 3; Brown, "Votes for Women," 4; Winnie E. Branstetter, "Socialist Party Should Make a More Active Propaganda for Female Suffrage," ibid., 5; Anna A. Maley, "The Suffrage and Freedom," ibid., 10; Crouch-Hazlett, "The Socialist Movement," 5; "First State Conference of Woman's Socialist Union of California," ibid. 3 (June 1909), 9; "Women at the Convention," *International Socialist Review* 7 (June 1908), 782; Parce, "The Relation of Socialism," 443.

25. "Open Letter to Socialists from Woman's National Committee," *Socialist Woman* 3 (September 1909), 15–16; May Wood Simons, "Aims and Purposes of Women's [sic] Committee," ibid. 3 (October 1909), 2; E.C.U., "The Suffrage Question and the Congress," ibid. 4 (June 1910), 5; "Sparks from the Convention," 1126–27; Socialist Party, *Proceedings* of the 1912 National Convention, 119; Ira Kipnis, *The American Socialist Movement,* 264. E.C.U. was no doubt the party theoretician, Ernest Untermann.

26. See the records of the Information Department of the Socialist Party in the S.P. National Office Files, 1914–1915, Duke University, for correspondence with party officials in states with woman suffrage, for a study of minimum wage laws and for surveys of states' suffrage patterns.

27. Ethelwyn Mills, ed., *Legislative Program of the Socialist Party: Record of the Work of the Socialist Representatives in State Legislatures, 1899–1913* (Chicago: Socialist Party, 1914), 13–14, 18, 20, 24, 25–26, 33, 38–39; "Massachusetts Socialist Bills," January 15, 1913, listed in Information Department Files in S.P. National Office Files, Duke University; George W. Downing to Winnie E. Branstetter, Sacramento, February 21, 1915, S.P. National Office Files, Duke University; *Official Bulletin* 8 (January 1912), 3; ibid. 8 (June 1912), 4; *Party Builder,* May 2, 1914, 2; *American Socialist,* September 5, 1914, 3; "Socialist Party Platform," in S.P., *Socialist Handbook* (Chicago: Socialist Party, 1916). As late as fall 1914, May Wood Simons argued that it was necessary to prod socialist state legislators to introduce woman suffrage bills. See *American Socialist,* January 2, 1915, 4.

28. See, for example, S.P. Grand Rapids, "Suggestion for Social Center Work," S.P. National Office Files, Duke University; "News of Organizations," *Socialist Woman* 3 (September 1909), 13, 15; "Conference of Socialist Woman's Committees of Kansas," ibid. (July 1909), 9; *Party Builder,* July 12, 1913, 4; August 23, 1913, 1, 5; September 6, 1913, 4; November 11, 1913, 4; January 7, 1914, 5; March 7, 1914, 5. S.P., *Official Bulletin* 4 (June 1908), 1; ibid. 9 (March-April 1913), 2. For examples of the extensiveness of the reports of the state correspondents, see S.P., *Official Bulletin* 9 (January 1913), 2.

29. Examples of women leaders' endorsements of reformism are Mila Tupper Maynard, "The Socialist Program," *Socialist Woman* 3 (October 1909), 12; "Hurrah for Milwaukee," ibid. 4 (May 1910), 8; S.P., *Proceedings* of the 1904 National Convention, 244–63. For an overview on party policy, see Sally M. Miller, *Victor Berger and the Promise of Constructive Socialism, 1910–1920* (Westport, CT: Greenwood Press, 1973), 6–14.

30. See *International Socialist Review* 10 (January 1910), 594–606.

31. Ida Crouch-Hazlett, "The Other Side," *International Socialist Review* 5 (March 1905), 86–91; Slobodin, "The National Socialist Convention of 1912," 817, 825–27; for a list of Haywood supporters, see ibid., 13, 623; Socialist Party, *Proceedings* of the 1912 National Convention, 61–62, 70–71, 135–37, 127.

32. S.P., *Proceedings* of the 1908 National Convention, 114–15, 120; Josephine Conger-Kaneko, "Notes on the National Congress," *Socialist Woman* 3 (June 1910), 4–5. S.P., *Proceedings* of the 1910 National Congress, 121, 140.

33. "Rose Pastor Stokes," *Socialist Woman* 1 (October 1907), 2; Robin E. Dunbar, "Girls and Bourgeois Philosophy," ibid. 5; May Walden, "True Home Under Socialism," ibid. 1 (January 1908), 5; "Party Politics and Prostitution," ibid. 1 (February 1908), 2; Mary S. Oppenheimer, "Is It a Handicap?" ibid. 2 (October 1908), 13–14; Josephine Conger-Kaneko, editorial, ibid. 4 (October 1910), 12; William J. Robinson, "The Birth Strike," *International Socialist Review* 14 (January 1914), 404–06; Caroline Nelson, "The Control of Child Bearing," ibid. 14 (March 1914), 547–48.

34. S.P., *Proceedings* of the 1908 National Convention, 302–05; Charles Kerr, "Socialist National Convention," *International Socialist Review* 8 (June 1908), 736–37; Malkiel, "Where do we stand?" ibid. 159–61; "News and Views," ibid. 9 (February 1909), 630; 'Hebe,' "Message to Socialist Party Convention," *Socialist Woman* 1 (May 1908), 3; "The National Convention on the Woman Question," ibid. 2 (June 1908), 3–4; "Women's Socialist League of Chicago Meeting," ibid. 2 (June 1908), 10.

35. Georgia Kotsch, "The Mother's Future," *International Socialist Review* 10 (June 1910), 1099; Spargo, "Woman and the Socialist Movement," 453; Elizabeth H. Thomas, "Why Women Should Be Socialists," *Socialist Woman* 1 (June 1907), 2; Mila Tupper Maynard, "Our Women Delegates to the International—May Wood Simons," ibid. 4 (August 1910), 10; "May Wood Simons," ibid. 1 (June 1907), 3; Lena Morrow Lewis, "Letter," ibid. 4 (October 1910), 3.

36. Grace C. Brown, "Why Women Should Organize," *Socialist Woman* 1 (July 1907), 2; Lida Parce, "What is the Woman Question," ibid. 2 (March 1909), 3–5.

37. See the weekly issues of *American Socialist* from January 1915 to September 1915, especially the letters to the editor, for discussion of the dissolution of the Woman's Department. Sophia Salkova of Cincinnati angrily wrote that the party pattern showed that women were seen as "the rear end of the movement." Replying to the comment by a sympathetic John Work that the loss of the Woman's Department reflected an attempt at a unifying effort, she said that by the same logic the foreign-language federations should be abandoned. See *American Socialist*, September 25, 1915, p.3. For the decision of the Social Democratic Party in Germany to provide proportional representation for women members on its various executive bodies, see Werner Thönnessen, *The Emancipation of Women: The Rise and Decline of the Women's Movement in German Social Democracy*, 1863–1933 (London: Pluto Press, 1969), 129.

38. Kate Richards O'Hare and Kate Sadler played possibly the most significant roles at the Emergency Convention where the party hammered out its antiwar position, as suggested in a summary of the proceedings of the secret sessions of the Committee on War and Militarism. See S.P., *Emergency Convention, Minutes* (summary of), Fifth Day, April 11, 1917, n.p., Second Day, April 8, 1917, 16; S.P., National Executive Committee-State Secretaries, *Minutes* of the Joint Conference, August 1918, 256–59. At the assembling of what turned out to be the schismatic convention, August 30, 1919, ten of 137 (or 7.2 percent) of the uncontested delegates were women. See list in S.P. National Office File, Duke University.

39. This position is argued in Mari Jo Buhle, "Women and the Socialist Party," *Radical America* 4 (February 1970), 51; Dancis, "Socialism and women in the United States," 126–30.

# 6 A Voice of the Party Left

## The Intellectual Odyssey of Mary E. Marcy

Among the many propagandists and publicists for the dynamic early twentieth century American socialist movement, columnist and editor Mary Edna Marcy was one of the most influential. While she did not attain the widespread and lasting fame of some of her flamboyant and even swashbuckling colleagues, such as Upton Sinclair, Jack London, Floyd Dell, John Reed, and Max Eastman, Marcy's monthly editorials, columns, and features were more omnipresent and arguably more integrated into ongoing discussions within the party and in the evolution of policy debate than were many of those individuals' writings. Joining the Socialist Party in 1903, Marcy chose not to participate directly in official activities as a candidate for party committees or public offices or as a convention delegate. Instead her role was that of a commentator, a gadfly and a critic, seeking to persuade others through her writings in the *International Socialist Review*, one of the most significant and widely read radical American periodicals of the first two decades of this century. Dismissed by some party leaders as a voice of the "direct action crowd" based at the *Review*, Marcy's relentless and energetic pen found a following among party faithful.

Mary Edna Tobias was born in 1877 in Belleville, Illinois, near East St. Louis. Relatively few details are known of her life, and she left behind no autobiography or collection of personal papers. It is clear that she was orphaned at an early age but managed to complete high school while working at clerical jobs. She supported her younger siblings, Inez and Roscoe, and became a stenographer.[1]

In 1896, while working in Chicago, she was fired for wearing a William Jennings Bryan campaign button in the office despite warnings. Her principled stance was somehow made known to Clarence Darrow, who obtained a secretarial position for her on the staff of William Rainey Harper, the first president of the University of Chicago. Her three-year tenure on that campus opened intellectual vistas for her. As an employee Tobias was able to enroll in university classes without paying tuition; she studied literature and philosophy, taking courses from John Dewey, with whom she developed a close friendship. After three years at the university, she met and married journalist Leslie H. Marcy in 1901, and they moved to Kansas City, Missouri.[2]

In 1902 Mary Marcy accepted a secretarial job at a meat-packing company, and her three years in that position familiarized her with the methods and practices of the industry and led to her debut in the world of socialist publishing. She wrote a muckraking series, "Letters of a Pork-Packer's Stenographer," four sections of which appeared in *International Socialist Review* between August, 1904, and January, 1905. This was just before the appearance of Upton Sinclair's commissioned articles on the same subject, which were published in the widely-read socialist newspaper, *The Appeal to Reason* and became his 1906 best-seller, *The Jungle*.[3] Marcy's series focused on the cutthroat practices of meatpackers rather than on the dangers of their adulterated products to consumers. The series dramatized issues such as dangerous working conditions, the plight of working women and children, and inadequate wages for employees. The framework of the series was the growth of the power of the trusts which, she argued, used mechanization to reap higher and higher profits with no concomitant gain for the work force. The series bore all the hallmarks of her writing style over the next eighteen years. Her articles were chatty, clear, and succinct, and they addressed readers directly as fellow members of the working class. The series also led to a subpoena for Marcy to testify before a grand jury in Chicago investigating the "beef trust" and, additionally, resulted in her employer firing her and seeking to have her dismissed from her next job.

Marcy was then hired by the Associated Charities of Kansas City. Like many other young women of her generation, she was attracted to so-called uplift work. Many daughters of the middle class participated in the evolving helping professions—working with the destitute, alcoholics, prostitutes, and other vulnerable groups; such work often engaged young women for at least an interlude in their lives before they settled into marriages. At a time when those fields were in transition to becoming professionalized, volunteers participated in various types of settlement and social work endeavors, from which they would later be excluded by the professionally trained. Marcy's position was somewhat unique, however, in two ways. First, she was already married and, second, she was not a middle-class woman indulging her curiosity about and sympathy for the downtrodden but rather a working-class woman herself, which gave her a strong sense of identification with people in need. Based on her perspective, she quickly found herself at odds with procedures of the Associated Charities, which required full investigation of applicants prior to their eligibility for assistance, and Marcy worked to have the stipulations reordered. Her experiences at the Associated Charities resulted in a publication. A booklet, *Out of the Dump: A Story of Organized Charity*, was published after it appeared serialized that year (1908) in the *International Socialist Review*. In this work Marcy didactically dramatized the plight of the poor in need of concrete assistance rather than of lectures on morality; she wrote of unsanitary hovels and slums, disease and death, unemployment and family desertion. While organized charity singled out the worthy poor, she wrote, people were dying of poverty.[4]

Marcy's writings proved to be popular with readers of the *International Socialist Review*, and its publisher, Charles H. Kerr, invited her, and later her husband Leslie Marcy, to join the staff. For the next decade and a half Mary Marcy was the major writer, editor and bookkeeper as well as manager of the catalog of the Kerr Publishing Company. She and Charles H. Kerr had met a few years earlier and, in fact, had had an intimate, somewhat brief, relationship as early as 1904, which may have been a factor in Kerr's divorce from the socialist author and organizer, May Walden, that year. He had organized the Charles H. Kerr Publishing Company two decades earlier in 1886 in Chicago as a radically-oriented religious publishing house. Gradually, the religious bent had disappeared in favor of purely radical publications, including a series of booklets of socialist tracts, English translations of contemporary European socialist writings, and the first English-language publication of the three volumes of *Capital* by Karl Marx.[5]

By 1908, when Mary Marcy joined the staff, the *International Socialist Review* had undergone far-reaching changes. In its initial issues in 1900 the *Review* had emphasized lengthy theoretical discourses on Marxism, as promoted by its in-house intellectual and managing editor, Algie Martin Simons, former student of Richard Ely, influential professor of economics at the University of Wisconsin. Simons also tried to deal with the American environment from a Marxist perspective in his own writings in the monthly and in a series of separate pamphlets published by Kerr. Articles were aimed at those already familiar with Marxism rather than the ideologically uninitiated. By the time that Marcy was offered a staff position on the *Review*, Simons had departed for work on *Chicago Daily Socialist*, *Coming Nation*, and other papers, and the periodical had begun to feature short, pithy and breezy, well illustrated pieces that might easily hold the attention of relatively unlettered workers. Marcy's own direct, instructional style fit the new format and approach. She further refined the *Review's* efforts to reach out to its audience on its own terms, and subscriptions increased from 6,000 in 1908 to 40,000 by 1911.[6]

Once at the periodical Marcy found herself embroiled in party factionalism. The *Review* was usually in conflict with the right-wing leadership of the Socialist Party, led by Victor L. Berger of Milwaukee and Morris Hillquit of New York City. It increasingly attacked the general reformist direction advocated by the party leadership and the party's support for the craft-oriented American Federation of Labor. The periodical leaned toward industrial unionism over trade unionism and toward direct action rather than political action.[7] While Simons in the middle of his tenure as editor had attended the founding convention of the Industrial Workers of the World in 1905 and then quickly dropped his support of the Wobblies, Kerr and the periodical sustained that support.[8] Moreover, the editorial board and staff came to include Wobbly leaders Big Bill Haywood and Ralph Chaplin.[9] Thus, Marcy climbed aboard a vehicle which stood to the left in party disputes and, as all evidence suggests, she felt quite comfortable there.[10]

Mary Marcy became secretary of the Kerr Publishing Company and managing editor of the *Review*, attaining increasing managerial and editorial responsibilities from Kerr as the years passed. Through her writings it seems clear that the primary task she assumed was the reduction of the essence of Marxist writings to a set of basic ideas that could be clearly understood and persuasively presented to her readers. Marcy turned out a series of eight articles in 1910 and 1911 called "Beginners' Course in Socialism and the Economics of Karl Marx," which explained the surplus theory of value in terms of workers' own life experiences. The Kerr Company then published those articles in the form of a booklet entitled *Shop Talks on Economics*; over the following decade it was issued in various editions and translated into a number of languages, selling over two million copies. Marcy also published supplementary articles in the *Review* from time to time that sought to explicate further Marx's writings in *Capital*; these articles sometimes concluded with an assignment for her readers of a chapter or two from Marx himself.[11]

Marcy tended to construct her theoretical essays as a series of brief chapters, each of which was followed by a quiz so that a reader could study the chapters or articles as in a school workbook. She explained to her readers that the ability to perform work was "the one commodity you have," addressing them in her trademark one-on-one style. The one element common to all commodities, she wrote, was the labor that went into producing them, and the value of a commodity was determined by the "social labor-time" it represented (Marcy, *Shop Talks on Economics,* p. 10). As an example, she explained that while workers could be paid in accord with their output, instead they received values based merely on what was necessary for their basic subsistence.[12] Graphically pinpointing that lesson in another short piece, she wrote that workers were the geese that lay the eggs of profits which they never realize.[13] Employers, she elaborated, always retained the surplus value of products, which by rights belonged to those who produced those products. Where workers successfully achieved a raise in wages, they then received more of the value of the product at the expense of the capitalist, who then enjoyed less of the surplus value. Properly, she argued, workers ought to own the entire product they produced. Capitalists did not merit any reward because capital by itself was incapable of producing anything.[14] The reason that workers did not receive all of what they produced was that they had failed to organize themselves as a class. Once they did so, then the issue would be transformed from the current one of higher wages to that of the abolition of the wage system itself.

Workers had become slaves, Marcy told her readers, because of the system of private ownership. All the major nations forced indigenous peoples to labor for invading newcomers ". . . upon the land that had once been theirs, in order to earn money to pay RENT." Laws were made to protect the land grabbers. Workers had to obtain jobs to pay rent, and in those jobs they forked over the things they made. "And the government stands by to say that these things shall continue to be, to send armies and militias to murder the workers who arise to claim the coal they have dug, the railroads they have built and run, to claim the food they have produced or the clothing they have made."[15]

It was imperative, Marcy wrote, that workers, rather than capitalists control the supply of labor. In order to do so, she recommended that workers expand the way in which they defined themselves to include the unemployed. Rather than ignoring them or fearing them as job competitors and potential scabs, the employed needed to cooperate with the unemployed. Employers, she emphasized, are "absolutely *dependent* on the *unemployed to keep down wages*" and to insure the weakness of the working class. But should those with jobs and those without work coalesce, the pendulum would begin to swing against capitalist control. Such broad worker cooperation could lead to job sharing, she wrote in a suggestion unique for her time, which would strengthen labor's ability to control its own supply.

We must stand by the unemployed in order to have them stand by us. When one of the shops closes down, let the men in the other shops unite to share with their out-of-work comrades. . . . If the men and women *on the jobs* would support their unemployed comrades for one month with the understanding that nobody should go to work for less than the prevailing rate of wages—those on the job would be in a position to *dictate new terms* to their employers. They could demand shorter hours—which would give work to some of those who were unemployed. Or they could enforce a five-work-day week and force the bosses to employ those who were out of work the other day.

Such a united front strategy, Marcy wrote, could be the beginning of the end of the existing system in which capitalists enjoyed the profits of the workers' labor (*ISR* 15, 157–59).[16]

Beyond that new approach to self-definition, all workers must view the class struggle in which labor and capital were pitted against each other as broadly as possible. That struggle to control surplus value must be seen in light of the fact that all institutions of capitalist society—the media, the schools, organized religion and every other organization—were on the side of the capitalist in the ongoing struggle over the control of economic institutions. They all reinforced each other in their support of the capitalist system. In fact, everything had to be viewed as part of the class struggle so that the struggle itself becomes "our yardstick for measuring any activity."[17]

Marcy urged her readers to become socialists and to join the party. She asked rhetorically: "Why is the Socialist party different from the Republican and Democratic parties? And why should workingmen and women join the Socialist party . . .?" She explained that while the politicians of "the old parties" made promises to the workers, pledged to eliminate graft, vowed to lower prices and establish equitable taxes, the laws they passed were always in the interest of the employing class. "They have failed you upon every possible occasion," she told the workers. In contrast, the socialist program was crafted in the interests of the workers; it was issued by a party of working men and women, and it had representatives in public office whose measures sought "to lighten the burdens of the workers by reform legislation, such as shortening the hours of labor." However, she went on to emphasize that reform measures were not the "real business" of socialism. While a Republican or a Democrat might support a shorter work day, the goal of socialism went beyond amelioration of harsh working conditions to abolition of the wage system. Socialism, she wrote, meant ownership of the factories by the workers (*ISR* 13, 157).[18] Once workers understood the meaning of socialism, Marcy maintained that they would flock to the Socialist

Party as "the only hope . . . for the working class" (*ISR* 12, 106–07). In fact, she was quite optimistic that a "world-wide revolt" that would usher in socialism was imminent. Socialism would make workers their own masters, no longer needing to beg for a job and forever after able to enjoy the full fruits of their labor (*ISR* 12, 261–65).[19]

Marcy actually viewed the Socialist Party with some ambivalence. Given her critical stance toward its dominant reformist faction, her endorsements of the Socialist Party were often supplemented by warnings that it must not fail to pursue the ultimate goal of socialism. "There are some socialists," she wrote, "who think that Socialism is only the action of the workers on election day to elect representatives to Congress or to the Legislature. This is only a very small part of the Socialist and Revolutionary working class movement." Moreover, government in its support of the capitalist system could at any time move to disenfranchise the workers. Therefore the party must remember that the essence of the socialist program was the struggle to abolish the wage system (*ISR*, 15, 701).[20]

At the time that Marcy issued these warnings, the Socialist Party was at the pinnacle of its electoral strength.[21] One of its most spectacular municipal victories occurred in Milwaukee in the spring of 1910 (see chapter 3). In April it won a sweeping victory in city and county elections. [22] The socialist press enthusiastically celebrated the Milwaukee victory as a harbinger of great triumphs, with, however, a few discordant voices. Marcy, as befitted her ideological perspective, gave the Milwaukeeans a mixed review. Writing in the *Review* the month of the election, Marcy rejoiced that the "twelfth largest city in the United States has elected a socialist mayor, a socialist city council, in fact has placed the entire city administration in the hands of members of the Socialist Party." Further, she was delighted that the new mayor was a worker who lived in a simple "frame cottage on one of Milwaukee's unfashionable streets (*ISR* 10, 991)." Yet she felt it was incumbent to sound a cautionary note. Electoral politics could achieve only so much, and clearly a socialist administration in one city could not abolish capitalism. The socialists in office were in a position to improve working conditions and to prohibit police violence against workers. But those socialists needed to remind themselves constantly that their greatest responsibility was to support workers in their ongoing actions in the class struggle. Marcy's position was reinforced in the pages of the *Review* a few months later by an article from the pen of Gene Debs, which declared that some socialists had become merely vote chasers. And Marcy herself proposed a requirement that those elected to office sign undated resignations to insure that they did not easily violate party policies.[23]

Further, Marcy criticized Socialists in public office who announced that they served all their constituents, not only socialists. She admonished unnamed office-holders that they could not serve two masters simultaneously, and declared that each benefit accruing to one class was inevitably at the expense of the other class. A public official who tried to represent everyone, she said, revealed ignorance of the basics of Marxist teachings. Such intentions were so opposed to socialist ideology that, she wrote, "we will not permit avowed Socialists whom we elect to office to SERVE US and OUR CLASS to promise to serve our enemy, the Capitalist Class. We put men in office to do all in their power, by any and every means FOR the WORKING CLASS. Every man who refuses to so serve us is a traitor to the Cause he is supposed to represent (*ISR*, 12, 151)." Such an individual would be a proven "political trimmer and compromiser," and would never be trusted again. There would be no place in the party for him. Marcy was inviting expulsion from the party, an implicit message clearly understood by the readers of the *ISR*.[24]

Ironically, it was one of Marcy's most admired comrades who became the object of such party action for ideological positions claimed by the dominant faction to be in conflict with policy. Big Bill Haywood of the Wobblies was elected to the National Executive Committee of the Socialist Party in December, 1911. Normally he and those who shaped party policy maintained a distant and antagonistic relationship with each other. Party leaders such as Berger, Hillquit, Robert Hunter, a wealthy journalist, and Adolph Germer, an organizer for the United Mine Workers, feared that party links to the flamboyant Wobblies would label the socialists as violent. They sought to avoid any association with the IWW, to the extent of torpedoing proposed official party support for ongoing Wobbly "free speech" fights over the right to speak on street corners in western cities. Furthermore, in order to avoid endorsing the IWW organizing principle of industrial unionism, the party's National Congress in 1910 voted that the form of labor organization was a matter for the workers themselves to decide rather than the party. Dividing the two organizations was the Wobbly emphasis on direct action, its stress on the economic over the political struggle, and its acceptance of anarcho-syndicalism. The IWW wanted to control the means of production and distribution through industrial unions and to abolish the state once that change occurred. An additional barrier between the two organizations was the Socialist Party's support, however unenthusiastically, for the American Federation of Labor. Their rare cooperation, in the instance of the Lawrence millworkers' strike in 1912 (to be discussed below), was the subject of an article in the *International Socialist Review*, which celebrated industrial unionist direct action in combination with political action.[25]

Haywood was ideologically in the minority during his term on the National Executive Committee when he proposed that the party encourage industrial unionism and use of the general strike. He was clearly out of tune with the dominant faction, which earlier had adopted an amendment to the party constitution to expel those opposed to political action. In 1912 a new clause was added to the constitution prohibiting a party member from advocating a crime, sabotage, or other methods of violence. Thereafter, in an extraordinary recall measure that was at variance with party procedures, Haywood was removed from the executive committee for advising tactics of direct action and sabotage. There is no record indicating that Haywood had specifically condemned political action, nor had he publicly advocated the use of violence. During the recall campaign Marcy, who herself believed that strikes were by definition battles, published excerpts from Haywood's writings in the *Review* to exonerate him but did not succeed in preventing the recall. It passed by more than a two to one margin. While she nevertheless remained in the party and urged others to do so, this event seemed to have hardened Marcy's contempt for the reformists and intensified her commitment to the party left, especially those identified with direct action.[26]

Marcy favored industrial unions from the start of her career as a columnist. She always urged workers to join the Socialist Party and industrial unions in order to push the class struggle on both the political and economic fronts. The Socialist Party, however, continued to support the A.F. of L. in an effort to bore from within and convert it to socialism, although many of its leaders were privately critical of its craft or trade union principles. Marcy's positions were more straightforward and less hypocritical.

Marcy had absolutely no patience with the A.F. of L., and she believed that "[T]he skilled trade union group is least revolutionary among the workers . . . and are least aggressive in conduct for improving the conditions of the whole working class." Her articles consistently advised workers that they needed to proceed to what she described as the maturer form of unionization, the industrial union, for its greater potential in the class struggle. "The larger our organization, the stronger we will be," she wrote. Workers united throughout their industry could control that industry; they could simply stop working for a few days, and by so doing exert sufficient pressure to shorten the work day and raise wages, and, more importantly, gain control of conditions on the job. "Let one working man fold his arms and cease to labor and the world moves on about him; but let a hundred thousand . . . or ten thousand . . . and see what would happen!" She stressed that a more inclusive unionism leading toward organizing the whole working class could result in workers' control of the system. She wrote, "All things are possible to us through industrial organization" (*ISR* 16, 142–43).[27]

In the article "The Power of the Railroad Boys" she pointed out, as an example, the untapped strength of transportation workers. Their strategic importance was crucial to a nation's well-being, and accordingly, transportation workers were potential revolutionists. At will, they could stop the movement of food and other necessities. They could also prevent arms intended for use against workers from reaching their destination. She told a tale in which "two railroad boys" from Indiana dropped into the office of the *Review*. They reported handling ammunition that was en route to Rockefeller holdings in Colorado, perhaps "to kill off more Ludlow men, women, and children," she wrote, in a reference to the massacre of miners' families the previous year by the Colorado National Guard. The shipment never reached its destination. One day, she predicted, such ammunition would be intercepted and sent to "OUR SIDE in any labor war." She added that it would be better to eschew violence ("the best method of fighting the boss is with organization instead of with GUNS"), and rather, unite and work for "ONE BIG working class union" (*ISR* 15, 670).[28]

Marcy described a few examples of successful localized strikes, such as a streetcar strike in 1916 in Chicago where each worker walked off the job at the same moment. "The elevated trains were stopped and all of the surface lines were tied up," she noted, and the middle class as well as the workers saw graphically how powerful were two unions that had learned to act together. Multiplying that coordination would lead to fundamental changes in the system (*ISR* 16, 179).[29]

Marcy held in contempt those unionists and socialists who continually measured advances and setbacks by looking to actions of legislatures and the judiciary. Their laws and decisions were, she wrote, only pieces of paper. Unionists who declared that the well-known Danbury Hatters case of 1908, or the joint decision in 1917 in the Bache-Denman Coal Company of Arkansas case and the Pennsylvania Mining Co. case that made unions liable for damages, "threaten the existence of the entire trade union movement" were quite shortsighted. The United Mine Workers had concluded that any strike could bankrupt a union because of such legal implications. Marcy acknowledged that in fact a strike was an effort to damage, and therefore, one might say, to sabotage the property interests of employers. She wrote that "Every intelligent striker hopes for victory *thru the destruction of property interests*. It is by stopping production, and, therefore, stopping *profits* that all strikers hope to attain victory. They hope to bring employers to the point where they prefer to yield a part rather than to lose *all*" (*ISR* 17, 226–27).

Marcy agreed that an isolated union might be bankrupted by adverse court decisions, but she quoted Haywood to the effect that a union should never even have a sizeable treasury. It should spend its funds on revolutionary class literature and on organizing additional workers. And if a union seemed helpless when confronted by court decisions, an obvious way to fight back existed. The unions had, she said, "forged their own chains," when they acted alone, stood alone, and signed contracts alone. It was a given to her that the courts and the laws were against the workers and for the owners. But the workers had the means to confront their united opposition through worker unity. That would be what she called the "Court of Last Appeal (*ISR* 17, 227)."[30]

Her various writings pointing to the possibility of "One Big Union" and to the use of the general strike demonstrate that Marcy's direct actionist views remained very much in line with policies of the IWW. Her commitment had not weakened after Haywood's ouster from the party executive and the subsequent dropoff of numbers of IWW members in the party. While she had not become a member of the Wobblies, she showed unbending confidence that direct action was the correct path for the working class. Her writings during World War One, as discussed below, reflect a more nuanced but even bolder perspective on the potential of direct action.

Marcy wrote a number of articles in which she discussed technological developments in various industries, such as cement and automobiles. She turned these brief discussions of industrial developments into lessons on the way in which technological advancement continued to undermine the demand for skilled work. For example, in the automobile industry when Henry Ford opened his plant in Michigan in 1903, car manufacturing was in its infancy, and at Ford and the many other competing car manufacturers skilled workers were in great demand. Wages were high, and operations were often idiosyncratic and eclectic. But as years passed standardization and specialization quickly became the norms, and the incessant modernization of equipment eliminated the necessity of manual skills. In short order, wages declined, and the unskilled came to dominate the work force. Thus within less than fifteen years of the establishment of Ford, Marcy was able to recognize and analyze the sophisticated rationalization of the automobile industry to the detriment of its workers. She warned that those skilled workers still employed in the industry would certainly lose their positions in time, or as she stated, "the good old days for the skilled worker and the mechanical expert are over in the automobile industry (*ISR* 15, 411–12)." Accordingly, it was incumbent to reach the non-unionized unskilled and get them "organize[d] into One Big Union." Anticipating by two decades the rise of the CIO, she pleaded for auto workers to propagandize among one another in favor of joining together in industrial unions.[31]

Marcy provided coverage and publicity in the pages of the *Review* for major strikes of the pre-war era, such as the Lawrence Mill Workers strike of 1912 and the New York Garment Workers strike of 1913. She had already written on company towns and their domination of all aspects of the lives of the workers, and noted that even when "model" conditions were touted, any benefits of such company-owned towns accrued to the bosses.[32] Lawrence was an early Massachusetts mill town where perhaps one-half of the population of 85,000 was employed at the American Woolen Company and at smaller textile mills. Whereas decades before American-born farmers' daughters made up the nucleus of the workforce, by 1912 the women of a variety of European groups as well as French Canadians dominated mill labor. Despite their disparate languages and culture, they came together that year and struck over short pay envelopes following a state-mandated reduction of the work week from fifty-six to fifty-four hours. These non-unionized workers were supported by their community institutions and led by a spontaneous grassroots leadership, who arose and turned to the Wobblies for help. Haywood himself came to Lawrence in the second week of the strike, and addressed the workers. An article by Marcy quoted approvingly from his speech to them:

> My dream in life is to see all workers united in one big union. You should carry this idea into effect because without it you will be forced back into the mills and have even worse conditions, not only in the textile works, but all workers [*sic*]. It behooves you to stick together and fight this present strike to a finish . . . . Do not let them divide you by sex, color, creed or nationality . . . . The only way to win is to unite.(*ISR* 12, 538)

Marcy applauded the efforts of Haywood, Elizabeth Gurley Flynn, Joseph J. Ettor, and Arturo Giovanitti of the IWW for the organizational strength, education, and funds they provided for the cause, and she quoted Haywood's remark that it was immaterial whether or not a legislative investigation of conditions at the mills occurred. She also saluted a direct-action tactic the Wobblies adopted from European strikers of sending some of the children of Lawrence to safe havens in New York, which won wide media publicity for them.

The over twenty-three thousand strikers were triumphant after eight weeks. Mary Marcy described the strike in great detail in a ten-page article, one of the lengthiest to appear under her byline in the *Review*. The Lawrence strike was to her an example of how worker solidarity, once unleashed, built on its own energy, "bringing with it a sense of [workers'] power." A fighting instinct, she believed, was always present in the workers, needing only a spark to be ignited. Lawrence clearly was an instance of how a strike, no matter how unlikely its chance of success might appear, was in itself an energizing and positive phenomenon, and in this instance it led to a revolt. Marcy concluded that "class solidarity has sounded throughout the land. . . . An injury to one worker is an injury to all workers. We cannot save ourselves without freeing the whole working class (*ISR* 16, 433–34).[33]

The next year, 1913, Marcy offered coverage of another large extended strike. Thousands of garment workers on the Lower East Side of New York struck for almost a month over generally abominable conditions. Marcy's tone was enthusiastic, emphasizing hopeful signs such as garment workers in Rochester pledging to strike in sympathy if their employers sought to produce clothing for the struck firms. Marcy saw indications of a recognition that workers could not win isolated strikes. She welcomed one unionist's call for a general strike in every branch of the needle and garment industry. But when Abe Cahan, the publisher of the influential *Jewish Daily Forward*, urged workers to carry an A. F. of L. card in one pocket and a Socialist Party card in another, she dismissed his words as a confusing appeal for craft division and class organization simultaneously. She commented pointedly, "This is very different from the calls of the Industrialists, all of whom insist upon a CLASS UNION card on the industrial field and a Socialist party card to represent their class interests upon the political field." She welcomed the ardent support which the New York Socialists were providing to the strikers, and guardedly cautioned: "We hope they will not neglect the greatest opportunity of their lives to teach class unionism as well as class political action. . . . we should point out that strikes are only a part of the great class struggle and that if the workers would only unite in one great working class union and one great proletarian socialist party they could forever banish exploitation and the wages system" (*ISR* 13, 586). Marcy noted that the New York strike, in contrast to Lawrence, was from the top down, with the union leaders calling the strike and controlling it. In her opinion a more constructive approach was to permit the strikers "to have the deciding voice in their own affairs; in teaching them self-reliance and class solidarity." But at least the strike represented direct action and was teaching workers how to conduct their own struggle, and it brought out "the class character of all existing social institutions . . . and the necessity of revolutionary class unionism" (*ISR* 13, 588). In the end, however, Marcy was disappointed. While the strike was successful, the issue of wage increases was referred to the garment industry's Board of Arbitration. Furthermore, a Board of Grievance was to be established to determine outstanding issues, during which time neither strikes nor lock-outs could occur. In Marcy's view, this hamstringing of the workers was a costly error.[34]

Marcy gave some of her attention to the situation of working farmers in at least two published pieces. The Socialist Party itself struggled sporadically with developing an appropriate policy for attracting farmers to its banner. The issue of the collectivization of private property was an ambivalent one for many American socialists. A policy which supported private ownership of land would contradict socialist principles, but if the party opposed private holdings, clearly it might undermine the possibility of attracting any agrarian support, or at least some members so argued. A platform demand calling for collective ownership of all land very briefly served as party policy in 1908 but was defeated in a national referendum.

Most of the party leadership, in fact, had no serious interest in any group other than the male urban proletariat, but a few of the leaders at least believed it was mandatory that the party develop a farmers' plank or program. In 1902 A.M. Simons wrote *The American Farmer*, published by Kerr, in which he analyzed the ways in which farmers might benefit from socialism. He believed that small farmers were—potentially—revolutionary proletarians. The exploitation they experienced endowed them with views similar to radical urban workers, and they might in fact lead a proletarian revolution. Victor Berger, perhaps influenced by the fact that the German Social Democrats, to whom he often looked for guidance, had established a farm program, argued in 1908 that most farmers were toilers, even if self-employed, and were caught up in the vise of the class struggle. Agricultural concentration was not developing at the same rate as industrial concentration, and thus individual small farmers were not disappearing, despite Marxist predictions. Finally in 1912 the Socialist Party adopted its farmers' program in which it sidestepped the issue of collectivization in favor of taxation on land not in cultivation, tying land titles to actual use and occupancy. It also stated that the means of transportation, storage and machinery upon which farmers depended must be socially owned and democratically managed.[35]

Marcy's writings addressed to farmers appeared four years later, and she did not shrink from the endorsement of a collective approach to agriculture. Claiming a great grandfather as a farmer who was able to produce almost all life's necessities, she discussed modern economic circumstances in which farmers had to purchase much of what they required at high prices while earning for their products less than their social value. She sympathized with small farmers who had to confront the competitive marketplace, monopolists, and middlemen. But she explicitly dismissed those small owners who worked beside hired help whose products they appropriated, and she attacked buyers' associations that became so powerful that their charges squeezed out individual farmers from the market. To the individual working farmer, Marcy explained that the goal of the socialists was to see that all workers, including farmers, had access to the means of production and distribution and to the full value of their product. Under socialism, land ownership would become a minor issue. No one would care "to own land so long as he possessed an opportunity to produce and to exchange his product(s) at their value" (*How the Farmer Can Get His*, 25–28). People would be compensated equally and fairly according to their labor rather than the product; whether they worked on fertile or infertile land, whether they had a good year or one in which a natural disaster destroyed the crop would in no way determine the value of their labor. In such an industrial democracy, Marcy wrote, "[t]he whole wheat product would represent *all* the necessary social labor expended in producing it, . . . [and] hours spent by [those] . . . whose labors have proved fruitless will . . . be included in the total number of hours spent in farm production by all the workers" (*ISR* 16, 561).

Thus farmers as a whole would be insured against crop failures and other calamities; in addition, they would be freed of farm drudgery, which modern machinery would abolish for all farm workers. Further, they would enjoy the results of their work collectively. Whether or not Marcy's ideas convinced any farmer to throw in his lot with the Socialist Party cannot be determined, but it may be said that she was more forthright than virtually any of her party comrades on a farmers' program. Her writings always reflected her ideological commitments, and nowhere was that more clearly shown than on this question.[36]

An issue that took a great deal more of the party's attention than a farmer's program was its position on the Woman Question (see chapter 5). The basic party view was that the contemporary so-called Woman Question was subsumed in the Labor or Social Question. The expected transformation from capitalism to a socialist system would solve all existing inequities, including those faced specifically by women. But some party members, most but not all of whom were women, believed that the party must address existing inequities marking women's lives and seek appropriate reforms, including female suffrage. Women socialists themselves, however, were divided on this issue, and so while some goaded the party into allowing them to establish a woman's sector to attract women to the party and to deal with issues of seeming concern to them, other women opposed that policy as counter-productive in the class struggle. The pages of the *International Socialist Review*, particularly between 1907, when the issue of a Woman's National Committee was seriously raised, and 1915 when the committee was dissolved, were filled with articles on both sides of the argument. Marcy herself, who would have commissioned at least some of those features, spent little time on the Woman Question in her own writings and wrote virtually nothing on behalf of the struggle for female suffrage. No doubt she endorsed a June, 1910 unsigned piece in the *Review* which cautioned against the party being drawn to "a sex movement" and approved the party position condemning collaboration with suffrage societies. The party "was not to go rainbow chasing after the Belmont and Morgan suffragettes" but confine itself to "a class demand" for the enfranchisement of working women (*ISR* 10, 1126–27).

As a socialist who consistently played down reform activities while encouraging direct action on the economic battlefield, it is not surprising that the Woman Question did not have much attraction for Marcy. As a woman, however, Marcy demonstrated a certain sensibility in her writings on labor issues that few of her male comrades did. For example, she frequently addressed herself to "workingmen and workingwomen," which was rare in socialist writings, so she was acutely conscious of the fact that women were a component of the proletariat. Nevertheless, an examination of the body of her writings demonstrates that the bulk of her work was addressed to the plight of male workers with women typically dealt with as wives who shopped for groceries on husbands' inadequate wages. As Marcy depicted the situation in one article, "you are going around with the same old, skimpy pay envelope in your pocket trying to keep clothes on your back and feed yourself and the wife and kiddies" (Marcy, *The Right to Strike*, 5).[37]

A few of her writings focused on the plight of working class women under industrial capitalism. Her first ambitious article on the subject appeared in the *Review*, and was thereafter reprinted as a booklet entitled "100 Years Ago." (See Documents, pp. 241–48.) The second was published in 1918 as a lengthy booklet co-authored with her brother, R.B. Tobias, entitled, *Women as Sex Vendors: Why Women Are Conservative (Being a View of the Economic Status of Women)*. The first essay assessed the conditions of women in modern society and was twice the length of her usual three-page articles. Marcy wrote of traditional "woman's work," of the myriad of chores which homemakers of the previous century had performed, and she described how so many of those tasks—whether yarn-spinning, fire-building, water-carrying or soap-making—had disappeared from the home.

"Gone are the candle-making seasons," she wrote, and the need to put aside blocks of time for other traditional chores. Economic change had destroyed the old way of life, and daily took away additional tasks from what had been virtually self-sufficient industrial units. "The home of today has become the shell of the home of yesterday," she told her readers, and the housewife must now sell her labor power. The inventions that might have lessened a woman's labor did not do so as the mill and factory encroached upon the home without liberating its inhabitants. She blamed capitalism for undermining the home, scattering its residents to jobs far and near, and providing them with neither independence nor security. But she advised her readers of the solution to their plight:

> Whether or not you are one of the fast decreasing numbers of house-wives today, or whether you are a wage slave directly exploited in the factories, mills or department stores, your home broken up in capi-talist society of today, Socialism is a message of hope for your hus-band, your father, your children as well as for yourself. . . . The So-cialist party is the one party in the world today that represents the working class. It offers to every woman equal political and economic rights to those accorded men. (ISR 12, 842–43)

Marcy advised women in the work force to join an industrial union as well as the Socialist Party, just as she encouraged men. So while hers was not a leading socialist voice addressed to women, she was able to sympathize with their situation, explain its changing contours, and recommend socialism as their path too.[38]

In a case study that focused on some of the same themes, two years later she wrote on the canning industry, describing specific advances inher-ent to the age of specialization taking "[a]nother slice" out of a woman's traditional sphere." These mechanical advances meant further industrial progress, one more domestic industry replaced, and women increasingly wage-earners rather than home-makers. Marcy could not but applaud the mechanical advances, she admitted, but argued that such progress ought to be for the benefit of the human race rather than of only the capitalists.[39]

However, in Marcy's longer work on the subject of women, written in collaboration with her brother, she seems somewhat harsher in her view of modern women, perhaps influenced by the arguments of Roscoe Tobias. In Women as Sex Vendors, the writers explained that the reason women were not involved in world affairs, particularly absent in the vanguard of move-ments for social change, was that they were "the owners of a commodity vitally necessary to the health and well-being of men" (Tobias and Marcy, p. 9), which resulted in their occupying an advantageous place in society through economic support and "legal favoritism." Accordingly, most women did not tend to oppose a social system that accorded them an advantage. Women bartered their sex, they were competed for and, as a result, most aspired only to beauty. The authors repeated Friedrich Engels' view of how the coming of the institution of private property had led to enforced monogamy for women. They argued that especially women with children were conservative, trying to insure that "their wares [are] attractive and . . . [by] binding the male by habits and associations that hold him and induce him to continue to pay" (Tobias and Marcy, p. 22). All women were potential parasites, akin to the leisure class, they maintained. Like the petty bourgeoisie, women in contrast with men did not prepare themselves for honest work. Meanwhile, industrial society, anxious to protect women for the sake of a future labor supply, gradually developed social legislation for women. In only lightly qualified generalizations, the authors surprisingly obscured the scope of the class struggle for women by sweeping statements about women who were or hoped to be supported extravagantly and by exaggerated notions of women's legal and cultural advantages.

The authors stated that: "If a wife deserts her husband and her children, the law does not make her a criminal; . . . No matter what the offense of the woman, custom and public opinion demand that every 'decent' man permit his wife to accuse him on 'just grounds' and to secure the divorce and call on the law to force him to pay her alimony . . . . No matter what the provocation, legally or sentimentally, any woman may kill almost any man" (Tobias and Marcy, p. 51). The laws today, Tobias and Marcy summarized, protect the owners of property and the economically powerful, and because women own a commodity which men buy and barter, modern legislation protects women at the expense of men. "That there are no women hoboes in the civilized world today is incontestable proof of the superiority of the economic status of woman over man" (Tobias and Marcy, p. 53).

They argued that women were not by nature inferior to men or more lacking in morality but that they had been subject to different social and economic conditioning. The authors refrained from predicting detailed future patterns in sexual and social relations, but they noted that social institutions always evolved, and that relations would be shaped by the coming socialist society where men would have no occasion to buy the surrender of women, and women would have no occasion to give themselves to men other than for love.[40]

A few other writings by Marcy referred specifically to women. In one piece attributed to her she urged efforts on behalf of family planning. Marcy wrote one somewhat lengthy work on social and sexual relations that focused on women. A play called "A Free Union: A One Act Comedy of 'Free Love'" examined the "New Woman" of the early twentieth century. It was a didactic work in which she focused on four young bohemians who claimed to live in accord with a philosophy of free love. One of the women challenges her lover to admit that he believes that a woman's place is in the home, while she declares that she feels no obligation to handle the housework since she is neither his wife nor his servant. "I'm a free woman," she proclaims, and she is not fazed when he threatens to leave. However, jealousy causes her to back down, disowning the idea of each of them being free to come and go. This slight play reinforces Marcy's earlier view of women as parasites, in this instance including those of a cultural elite.[41]

Two other specific groups were the subject of attention in party debate and in the pages of the *International Socialist Review*, African Americans and immigrants (see chapter 1). Marcy herself did not contribute explicitly to the debates, and in the case of African Americans most of the discussions occurred prior to her joining the staff of the periodical. While she commissioned some of the articles for the *Review*, she did not herself focus on either of these matters. However, it is clear from the broad sweep of her writings that her belief in the Social Question as the fundamental issue in society meant that no special attention needed to be assigned to the transitional problems that hampered African Americans under the current economic system. The attainment of a socialist society would mean that blacks as workers would be emancipated along with the rest of the working class. In regard to immigration restrictions, it is clear that Marcy did not favor restricting certain nationality groups from entering the United States. She was in tune with an unsigned staff assessment of the 1910 National Congress of the Socialist Party, which celebrated two speeches as "splendid arguments against Asiatic exclusion."[42]

In an article on an unrelated matter, she made perhaps her most explicit statement on peoples of color and the class struggle:

> On the Western coast the capitalists are telling the wage-workers that the Japanese and Chinese are their enemies; that if the Japanese and Hindus were prevented from coming into America there would be more jobs and higher wages for the American workingmen . . . . In the South there are many socialist workingmen who refuse to unite with their colored proletarian comrades. The capitalists there tell them in their papers that if there were fewer colored men competing for jobs, there

would be better conditions and higher wages for the white wage slaves. WE DO NOT REALIZE THAT THE HINDUS, the NEGROES the JAPANESE and CHINESE WORKINGMEN are our exploited comrades and that our common enemy is CAPITALISM.[43]

Marcy, unlike some other socialist comrades such as Morris Hillquit and Kate Richards O'Hare, did not often challenge organized religion, and she never debated members of the clergy in public forums. But she did make it a point to invite all workers regardless of their spiritual allegiances to convert to socialism. In her only lengthy consideration of the subject, in a booklet entitled *Why Catholic Workers Should be Socialists*, she wrote that socialism had no opinion on matters of faith and took issue only with exploitative religious institutions. A future socialist society, she maintained, would no more legislate on religious matters than it would interfere in other personal aspects of life. She excoriated Roman Catholicism for failing to support its working-class faithful, and she criticized the opposition of priests to socialism as based either on ignorance or on misinterpretation.[44]

Marcy published a handful of pieces which focused on imperialism. For example, she wrote an article on the Kaiser's Germany having gained control of Turkey without dispatching invading armies and subjugating that empire by force. German financiers and business interests had simply captured its economy, she informed her readers. They gained control over natural resources, railroad rights of way, and vast tracts of land, and also supplied Turkey's military needs in her Balkan wars, resulting in great debts. At the same time, in another article, she reported on how the British were enlarging their dominion over parts of Africa. In fact, a planned railroad intended to cut a swath through the continent from the Cape of Good Hope to the Mediterranean was certain to result in the opening up of what Marcy called "the last continent" with "no more frontiers to conquer." While she noted that the indigenous peoples and animals were being shunted aside, she did not bemoan the effects on the environment but, rather, emphasized how those changes promoted a positive transformation of the economic system. "It will mean the modernization of Africa and the ultimate rise of Socialism on the dark continent," she predicted (*ISR* 13, 416).[45] In the same vein, Marcy wrote a few articles on modernization in China. She applauded the fact that new methods of production were certain to bring on socialism, and she celebrated the emergence of a revolutionary socialist hero, Sun Yat Sen. She cautioned that while "many are the predictions of a revolution in the Celestial Empire in the near future," it would take time. "The initial steps of the introduction of machine production are usually followed by an era of prosperity to the majority of the people. It is only when competition grows keen and trustification sets in that a really revolutionary army of the working class arises that will usher in the new day of economic freedom (*ISR* 10, 691)." Concerning the process of economic imperialism, she called her readers' attention to the "moral campaigns" proclaimed by rich nations to "protect" native peoples. "We are frankly skeptical when we find [white] men spending money to protect the lives and limbs of unknown, distant black natives out of sheer goodness of heart." It typically resulted in the planting of their flag "'For God and Country.' This usually means something like Rockefeller and Guggenheim" (*ISR* 13, 466). Exploring the example of a rubber company in Peru, Marcy elaborated on the pattern of labor exploitation that inevitably occurred:

> Where land is free, food abundant, shelter available and clothing still a matter of ornament, men and women are practically free economically. It is the private ownership of land, food, clothing and houses that makes slaves of the non-owners. They are forced to work for wages to get money to buy these necessities. Everywhere we find that capitalism on invading 'uncivilized' lands, either grabs up the land and other natural resources, so that the natives are forced to find jobs in order to live, or the 'civilized' intruders command the 'heathen' by physical violence. (*ISR* 13, 468)[46]

The moral sophistry of the press and the priests in these matters, she argued, had become so transparent that ulterior motives were becoming clear to everyone. Overall, in her treatment of imperialism, Marcy's was not a distinctive voice. Her views represented what must be termed the basic perspective of pre-war socialists on imperialism, with minimum differences between party factions.[47]

Marcy wrote numerous features and columns on a wide variety of miscellaneous topics, all of which she placed within a socialist frame of reference. She wrote children's stories that were suitable readings for the Socialist Sunday Schools that the party organized in a few cities. Marcy's two children's series were entitled, respectively, *Stories of the Cave People* and *Rhymes of Early Jungle Folk*. They drew on some of the writings of Engels and the anthropologist Lewis Henry Morgan, with whose work Engels was familiar, to trace the evolution of human societies in language understandable to elementary school children. The idea of evolution as an on-going phenomenon was used to demonstrate that the current social system was transitory and would be replaced by a more mature and cooperative system.[48]

Marcy wrote a few parables and sardonic tales, especially early in her writing career, such as "William the Faithful," which described a dutiful hard working son and his worthless brother, and it drove home the point that the virtue of hard work was not necessarily rewarded. "A Felicitan Fair" dramatized labor's exploitation in terms of a curse of plenty in which workers could not buy all the goods they produced so their masters decided there would be no more work until all products were sold. "Skinny's Turkey Dinner" offered a tale of a working class family who received a free Thanksgiving turkey only to find that meatpackers had supplied spoiled fowl.[49]

Marcy's writings sometimes appeared without her byline or under pseudonyms, particularly after 1915. Her pen seems clearly to have been wielded on articles under names such as Jack or James Morton, Jack Phillips, John Randolph, Max Roemer, and in one instance, Edna Tobias, in that case making use of her middle and maiden names. She also sometimes was responsible for unattributed editorials. Both the content and the style of capitalization in these writings suggest the work of Marcy herself. An example of the former is a discussion of the "fighting instinct" in an essay by Max Roemer, a subject to which she under her own byline had devoted a feature piece earlier. The reason that some of her writings appeared under other names or anonymously may only be conjectured. It might have seemed reasonable to avoid having the monthly issues of the *Review* so much the work of one writer. It might also have been thought that writings by male authors might be taken more seriously than a woman's, but this is not likely since Marcy was well established by then as the *Review's* lead writer and editor.[50]

In June 1914, Marcy wrote a column on the subject of war which eerily forecast a main theme of her writings over the next four years. Commenting on skirmishes on the Mexican border during which American soldiers entered that country, she asked caustically, "Shouldn't Hearst and John D. lead the troops?" (*ISR* 14, 730) She emphasized that Mexican and North American workers had no quarrel with one another. Sounding a common socialist thesis, she wrote that workers had no country, and then reversed the concept and suggested that the capitalist was the only foreigner.[51]

Marcy's world began to change in the summer of 1914, never to be restored. For the next four years her attention was riveted on world war and its revolutionary potential. Relatively few of her writings were henceforth devoted to month-to-month criticisms of American capitalism's internal developments as they had been prior to the war. In the course of those years Marcy would come to a decision to leave the Socialist Party for the organization with which she had always been so much more in accord.

Marcy's early comments on the war in Europe were straightforward Marxist ideology; similar to her previous writings on war and on imperialism, her views would probably not be challenged by any of her Socialist Party comrades. She wrote of the profit system as "the cause of all wars today," with capitalists constantly seeking additional markets and investment possibilities. She declared that:

> . . . this is the cause of all capitalist wars. The capitalists in Germany, in America, in England, France, Italy and Belgium—all want to seize, or to hold, territory . . . They want to have an army and navy in order to protect these foreign investments—from the armies and navies of the capitalist government[s] of other countries . . . Wars are caused by the competition of various national capitalist groups (*ISR* 18, 28–29).

Such warfare was of no benefit to the workers, she maintained. The results of that competition might bring profits to the capitalists but the workers would only bear the costs. Therefore they had no interest in fighting for their nation. In fact, she asked:

> Mr. Workingman, what has your native land done for you that you should fight for her flag, her glory or her power? . . . "Your" country has protection only for the powerful, the rich, the idle; she has no care for those who are hungry, cold and sick. The flag of "your" nation is borne by the troops sent into districts where the hosts of poverty congregate, to drive them from the sight of the wealthy (*ISR* 15, 177).

Workers of all countries faced the same situation, Marcy wrote. None of them had a country, and consequently, she concluded "There is only one flag worth fighting for and that is the red flag, which means universal brotherhood of the workers of the world in their fight to abolish the profit system" (*ISR* 15, 178).[52]

Marcy, like many other American socialists, was aghast to witness most European socialists supporting their nations at war, encouraging the workers to join the armed forces, and voting for war appropriation measures. Such a posture contradicted pre-war policies of the Second International, and it was, ironically, left to the reformist-dominated Socialist Party of America to represent orthodox Marxist principles on militarism and war. Indeed, American socialists, except for those who broke with the party, remained ideologically consistent in their opposition to the war, which they condemned as imperialistic. In this unique instance Marcy's was a voice of her party as a whole rather than of a particular faction when she wrote in 1915: "We want NO army, NO navy, not one cent expended in the implements of warfare . . . . Workingmen of all countries have no fight against each other."[53]

That first year of the war she analyzed what had gone wrong when the majority of the German Social Democrats, whose party had been seen as the very essence of international socialism, had sent their young men off to kill. She tried to deduce what American socialists might learn from the Europeans' disastrous experience. She noted that the German socialists had led the way at an International Socialist Congress in Copenhagen in 1910 in stifling consideration of any practical measures for preventing war. "Here we find," she wrote, "the largest body of Socialists in the world, the strongest numerically, permitting its elected delegates to evade the question of WHAT TO DO in a world crisis" (*ISR* 15, 245).

While a few delegates from various countries at the Congress had proposed the use of the general strike as a weapon to prevent war—including American delegate Big Bill Haywood—they did not win support for that proposal and it was tabled. Marcy urged American socialists to agree on a specific tactic to prevent American intervention in the war, although she nevertheless predicted U.S. participation. The party's opposition to war in general was too vague, Marcy argued, and indeed reflected the prewar stance of the European socialist parties. "We must," she wrote, "avoid the mistakes of our European comrades. . . . We must go on record for a General Strike in time of war" (*ISR*, 15, 246). It was absolutely mandatory that socialist strength be measured by concrete positions and achievements rather than by votes in elections, she concluded, with pointed criticisms of both the German socialists and her party comrades.[54]

Continuing to analyze the German failure, she attacked the discipline and obedience to the principle of majority rule which that electorally successful party represented. The dependence on elected leaders by the German workers and their lack of spontaneous actions were reflected in their willingness to enter the armed forces. She condemned a labor movement that repressed freedom of expression and so-called premature or wildcat strikes. A rank-and-file that had training only in obedience rather than openness to spontaneous rebellious activities could not be prepared for revolutionary actions when the moment presented itself, she concluded. American socialists should encourage initiative and rebellion by the workers at all times, and in the event that the war might promote revolutionary trends, workers must be ready to seize the initiative.[55]

Marcy was more certain than ever by the time of President Woodrow Wilson's preparedness campaign in 1916 that genuine socialist activity was unrelated to office-holding or publishing newspapers. Influenced by radical leaders of the European socialist parties, such as Karl Liebknecht, she pointed out to her readers that socialist officials could always be expelled from public offices by their governments and dissident media could be intimidated or repressed. Therefore what was needed was "mass action" by workers as the only form of self-expression and of democracy available to them. She applauded the idea of industrial strikes, which could be developed into political or class strikes wherever possible. Conversely, she repudiated some of her comrades who marched in preparedness parades, as did socialist Mayor Daniel Hoan of Milwaukee, or endorsed the idea of national service, as did Victor Berger. They were, she charged, traitors to the working class. The Socialist Party's 1916 platform endorsed the concepts of mass action and the general strike to prevent war, as she reminded her comrades, and thus American workers at last were being encouraged to develop their own initiatives, weapons, and tactics.[56]

When the German resumption of submarine warfare in early 1917 made war imminent for the United States, Marcy announced that workers had no reason to respond to that German military initiative, however much the American press ranted in "hypocritical horror." Workers, owning no ships or cargoes nor having the money to book passage across the seas, had no personal interest in taking up arms. But they needed to be alert for the possibility of government moves toward conscription. She told American workers that they had the power to prevent such a measure by walking off the job, going home and "*stop[ing] the wheels of all industry*, until all danger of *universal military service being made into a law is passed* [*sic*], and until the thought of war is impossible" (*ISR* 17, 520–21).[57]

Within less than a month of Marcy's recommendation the United States Congress declared war on Germany in April, 1917, and later that spring established a selective service system. By then Marcy had developed a much more elaborate analysis of the efficacy of the general strike than she had held in the pre-war period. The idea of a general strike to bring down the government and its war machine became the central theme of her writings. Like some European socialists, including most visibly Vladimir Lenin, she was convinced that the world war offered the opportunity to destroy capitalism and establish socialism. By May, 1917, she observed that the warring nations had unloosed a force beyond their control as the various belligerents modified capitalist institutions in order to proceed more efficiently with the war effort, and production and distribution had become "social and national in scope." The collapse of the Czarist government in Russia pointed toward the decline of the old order, perhaps in Germany next, and then everywhere else. The task of "the advanced guard," of the working class, she wrote, was now to fight explicitly on behalf of the workers. She declared that, "We are not pacifists. We believe in *war*, but war upon the enemy of our own class—Capitalism!" (*ISR* 17, 522).[58]

Marcy believed that the war should not be viewed apart from the class struggle. They were, in fact, identical. It was possible that the current war might be succeeded by other major wars, and the workers might thereby have the opportunity for world-wide revolution. Moreover, the revolutionary upheavals in Russia were very encouraging to her. In the final analysis, she argued, it was "Their War and Our Revolution" (Marcy in Rosemont, p. 41).[59]

She returned to an earlier sub-theme of the need for One Big Union as proposed by the Wobblies so that workers could exert their utmost economic power. She pointed out that German Left Wing socialists were urging miners and railroad workers to cease work in order to force the government to accept a peace without conquest, and that in Russia workers earlier had gone on strike in key industries to demand the end of private profit. Sounding a confident note, she wrote that "the industrial unionists, the socialists and the militant trade unionists are gradually coming closer together, gradually realizing that they must organize on the job, as industries and as a class, and thru the use of the economic power of the workers, make possible the glad day when Labor shall come at last into its own."[60]

Marcy's early postwar writings continued to emphasize the value of the general strike amid predictions that the contradictions within capitalism would lead to its collapse. But she could not help but be less confident. She surveyed the domestic scene, and doubted that veterans would receive available land for low payments. In one of her angriest writings, she worried about the starving unemployed, bemoaned the American "exceptionalism" which meant the United States alone of modern economies did not offer unemployment compensation, and endorsed the concept of shorter shifts so everyone might work. Predicting some of the themes of the 1920s in industrial relations, she denigrated the concept of profit-sharing. She saw it as a means of isolating workers from one another while tying them to their employers. She also attacked the concept of shop committees through which workers could present their grievances, that is, company unions, and she pointed out that such committees would function at the expense of bona fide unions. She was alarmed about the possibility of the right to strike being outlawed. While doubting that such legislation would be passed, she accurately guessed that injunctions might be used by whim to contain individual strikes.[61]

Marcy's comments on the postwar world were limited. Changed circumstances—for her and the world of the left—silenced her. Wartime government censorship and repression had destroyed the *International Socialist Review* which ceased publication in February 1918. Its records were confiscated and the Kerr Publishing Company itself just managed to survive.[62] Additionally, Mary and Leslie Marcy's home was invaded by government agents who ransacked their files. At the same time the Socialist Party began to unravel, given the pressures from governmental surveillance as well as arrests and indictments of many of the leaders, and increased factionalism over the party's relationship to the new Russian government. Mary Marcy broke with her party, and—in a move which could have been foreseen—officially joined the Wobblies, mass numbers of whom were experiencing indictments under the Sedition Act. Nevertheless she advised her comrades to refrain from factional disputes. In 1919 she circulated a letter among delegates to three rival conventions, the Socialist Party, the Communist Party, and the Communist Labor Party, all convening simultaneously in Chicago. She told them that "we are all so close together that we ought to present a solid front to the capitalist enemy, [and] we might then develop a movement in this country that would actually move and grow" (Marcy quoted in Carney, p. 10).[63]

The Marcys had mortgaged their home in Bowmanville, Illinois twice in those years on behalf of indicted IWW officials. The second time they helped Bill Haywood, with whom Mary especially had been quite close, raise funds. When Haywood jumped bail in March 1921, fleeing to the Soviet Union, the Marcys lost their home. Mary Marcy had always faced health problems, and the emotional strains of the war and postwar crisis of the left clearly destroyed her defenses. By December 8, 1922, she apparently was worn out. Still writing articles and handling her managerial responsibilities at the Kerr Publishing Company toward the very end, she gave up and drank a pesticide mix.[64]

Marcy's most extensive last words appeared in the IWW publication, *Industrial Solidarity*, the month of her death. She wrote that the Wobblies pointed to the only path for the working class. Agreeing that the word communist might be used, she looked to a society in which all able men and women would work at necessary labor, and would produce great plenty which would meet all their needs and hopes. Implicit was her belief that politics had no necessary role in that future order, for the workers by themselves would fashion their own salvation. Despite the existence of the Soviet Union, Marcy had come to believe that the American industrial proletariat was the most advanced—as a product of a highly developed capitalist economy—and therefore potentially the most class conscious. She believed that the proletariat would find its way without what she called "professional jobholders."[65]

That voice which had reflected the various issues of the American left in an extraordinarily tumultuous period was now stilled.

NOTES

1. Jack Carney, *Mary Marcy* (Chicago: Charles H. Kerr, 1922), 3. While May 8, 1877 has been accepted as Marcy's date of birth, the St. Clair, Illinois, County Clerk reported on September 14, 1993 that no record of the birth of a Mary Edna Tobias could be found between 1877 and 1881. Socialist Party Organizer Lena Morrow Lewis referred to the "direct action crowd" in a letter to May Walden Kerr, May 9 (1914?), May Walden Kerr Collection, Box 3, Newberry Library, Chicago.

2. Carney, 3–4; see Allen M. Ruff, "'We Called Each Other Comrade!' Charles Kerr and the Charles H. Kerr and Company, Publishers, 1886–1928" (Ph.D. diss., University of Wisconsin, 1987); Allen Ruff, "Mary Edna Marcy," *Encyclopedia of the American Left*, eds. Mari Jo Buhle, Paul Buhle, and Dan Georgakas (New York: Garland Publishing, 1990), 451. Years later Marcy quoted John Dewey in one of her articles in support of a political position. She referred to his view that the ". . . highest type of man can adapt to a new environment." Mary E. Marcy, "The I.W.W. Convention," *Liberator* 2 (July 1919), 11.

3. Elliott Shore, *Talkin' Socialism: J.A. Wayland and the Role of the Press in American Radicalism, 1890–1912* (Lawrence: University Press of Kansas, 1988), 168; Louise Wade, "The Problem with Classroom Use of Upton Sinclair's *The Jungle*," *American Studies* 32 (Fall 1991), 79–80, 92–96.

4. Carney, 5; Peggy Pascoe, *Relations of Rescue: The Search for Female Moral Authority in the American West, 1874–1939* (New York: Oxford University Press, 1990), 40–46.

5. See May Walden Kerr's note of May 1, 1904, Chicago, which implicates Marcy in the collapse of the Kerrs' marriage, found in The Charles H. Kerr Company Archives, Box 37, Newberry Library, Chicago; Ruff, "We Called," 255–56. The Newberry Library is the repository of the Charles H. Kerr Publishing Company papers. However, the large collection contains business and contractual details more than substantive correspondence.

6. Ruff, "'We Called ,'" 237–41; William A. Glaser, "Algie Martin Simons and Marxism in America," *Mississippi Valley Historical Review* 41 (December 1954), 419–34. See also Kent Kreuter and Gretchen Kreuter, *An American Dissenter: The Life of A.M. Simons* (Lexington: University of Kentucky Press, 1969). Simons, like Marcy, early in his career had written a study of the meatpacking industry, *Packingtown*, published in 1899. One anthology has appeared of Marcy's writings: see Frederick Giffen, ed., *The Tongue of Angels: The Mary Marcy Reader* (Selinsgrove, PA: Susquehanna University Press, 1989).

7. Ruff, "*International Socialist Review*," in Buhle, Buhle, and Georgakas, 374; Herbert G. Gutman, "*The International Socialist Review*," in Joseph R. Conlin, *The American Radical Press, 1880–1960*, I (Westport, CT: Greenwood Press, 1974), 82–86.

8. David A. Shannon, *The Socialist Party of America: A History* (New York: Macmillan, 1955), 19.

9. Ruff, "*International Socialist Review*," 374.

10. Standard histories of the Socialist Party of America include Shannon, cited above; Howard H. Quint, *The Forging of American Socialism: Origins of the Modern Movement* (Columbia: University of South Carolina Press, 1953); and Ira Kipnis, *The American Socialist Movement, 1897–1912* (New York: Columbia University Press, 1952). Biographies of the major leaders include Nicholas Salvatore, *Eugene V. Debs: Citizen and Socialist* (Urbana: University of Illinois Press, 1982); Sally M. Miller, *Victor Berger and the Promise of Constructive Socialism, 1910–1920*, (Westport CT: Greenwood Press, 1973); and Norma Fain Pratt, *Morris Hillquit: A Political History of an American Jewish Socialist* (Westport CT: Greenwood Press, 1979).

11. Mary E. Marcy, *Shop Talks on Economics* (Chicago: Charles H. Kerr, 1911). See also her "Economic Determinism," *Industrial Pioneer* 1 (September 1921), 9–10.

12 Marcy, *Shop Talk*, 10–12, 53–57.

13. Mary E. Marcy, "The Goose and the Golden Egg," *International Socialist Review* 16 (February 1916), 494–95. The *Review* will hereafter be referred to as ISR.

14. Mary E. Marcy, *Industrial Autocracy* (Chicago: Charles H. Kerr, 1919), 23.

15. Mary E. Marcy, "Your Great Adventure," *ISR* 16 (July 1915), 44–46.

16. Mary E. Marcy, "Organize with the Unemployed: A New Way to Fight," *ISR* 15 (September 1914), 157–59; idem, "What You Have to Sell," *ISR* 16 (September 1915), 141–43.

17. Mary E. Marcy, "The Class Struggle," *ISR*, 16 (October 1915), 206–08.

18. Mary E. Marcy, "Why the Socialist Party is Different," *ISR* 13 (August 1912), 157; idem, "The Near Socialist," *ISR* 11 (October 1910), 215–16.

19. Mary E. Marcy, "Are You a Socialist?" *ISR* 12 (August 1911), 106–07; idem, "The World-Wide Revolt," *ISR* 12 (November 1911), 261–65.

20. Mary E. Marcy, "Why You Should Be a Socialist," *ISR*, 15 (May 1915), 700–02.

21. The best secondary source for electoral party data and lists of its publications is James Weinstein, *The Decline of Socialism in America, 1912–1925* (New York: Monthly Review Press, 1967), 116–17, 85, 94–102.

22. For Milwaukee city and county election results, a useful compilation is Sarah C. Ettenheim, ed., *How Milwaukee Voted, 1848–1969* (Milwaukee: Institute of Government Affairs, University of Wisconsin–Milwaukee, 1970), 124.

23. Mary E. Marcy, "The Milwaukee Victory," *ISR* 10 (May 1910), 991–92; Eugene V. Debs, "Danger Ahead," *ISR* 11 (January 1911), 413–14; Edna Tobias, "How to Help Yourself," *ISR* 14 (September 1913), 161. Marcy's proposal for undated resignations on file signed by socialists elected to public office soon became party policy.

24. Mary E. Marcy, "Can A Socialist Serve 'All the People'?" *ISR* 12 (September 1911), 150–51.

25. Socialist Party, *Official Bulletin*, May 1912, June, 1912; Socialist Party, *Proceedings of the National Convention, 1912* (Chicago: Socialist Party, 1912), 60–63; Vincent St. John, *The I.W.W.: Its History, Structure and Methods*, rev. ed. (Chicago: Industrial Workers of the World, 1919), 3–4; Paul F. Brissenden, *The Industrial Workers of the World: A Study in American Syndicalism* (New York: Columbia University Press, 1919), 62–63; Leslie H. Marcy and Frederick Sumner Boyd, "One Big Union Wins," *ISR* 12 (April 1912), 627–29.

26. "The Motion to Recall Haywood," *ISR* 13 (February 1913), 625; Socialist Party, *Official Bulletin*, March 1, 1913; Mary E. Marcy, "Ladylike Men," *Solidarity* 18 (December 1909), n.p.

27. Mary E. Marcy, "What You Have to Sell," *ISR* 16 (September 1915), 141–43.

28. Mary E. Marcy, "The Power of the Railroad Boys." *ISR* 15 (May 1915), 669–71.

29. Mary E. Marcy, "Direct Action," *ISR* 16 (September 1915), 179–80.

30. Mary E. Marcy, "Hamstringing the Unions," *ISR* 17 (October 1916), 226–

27. In Mary E. Marcy, "They Belong Inside," *ISR* 17 (December 1916), 146–48, she recounts how workers in Norway were defeated when labor arbitration was established, thus duping that nation's proletariat.

31. Mary E. Marcy, "Auto Car Making," *ISR* 15 (January 1915), 406–12.

32. Mary E. Marcy, "A Strike in the 'Model Village'," *ISR* 10 (May 1910), 699–701

33. Mary E. Marcy, "The Battle for Bread at Lawrence," *ISR* 12 (March 1912), 533–43; idem, "The Fighting Instinct," *ISR* 16 (January 1916), 433–34; Sally M. Miller, *The Radical Immigrant, 1820–1920* (Boston: Twayne Publishers, 1974), 109–11; Donald B. Cole, *Immigrant City: Lawrence, Massachusetts* (Chapel Hill: University of North Carolina Press, 1963), 68–75, 120–21, 179, 193; Brissenden, 290.

34. Mary E. Marcy, "The New York Garment Workers," *ISR* 13, (February 1913), 583–88. In "The White Flag Agreement Brigade" in *ISR* 13 (February 1913), 760–62, Marcy excoriated her fellow socialists as traitors for endorsing the garment industry agreement and also one in a West Virginia mining industry upheaval.

35. A.M. Simons, *The American Farmer* (Chicago: Charles H. Kerr, 1902); Socialist Party, *Proceedings of the 1908 National Convention* (Chicago: Socialist Party, 1908), 15; Farmers Committee Report, Appendix D, Socialist Party, *Proceedings of the 1912 National Convention.*

36. Mary E. Marcy, *How the Farmer Can Get His* (Chicago: Charles H. Kerr, 1916), 25–28; idem, "How the Farmer is Exploited," *ISR* 16 (March 1916), 559–61.

37. "Sparks from the National Convention," *ISR* 10 (June 1910), 1126–27; Mary E. Marcy, *The Right to Strike* (Chicago: Charles H. Kerr, n.d.), 5. Internal evidence suggests that the latter item may have been published in 1921. Marcy downplayed the election of the first woman to the party executive, and emphasized instead that an efficient party organizer, Lena Morrow Lewis, had won a seat on the N.E.C. Mary E. Marcy, "Efficiency the Test," *New York Call*, May 8, 1910.

38. Mary E. Marcy, "100 Years Ago," *ISR* 12 (June 1912), 837–43. This feature was reprinted as a booklet later that year by Kerr under the title *Breaking Up the Home.*

39. Mary E. Marcy, "The Advancement of the Canning System," *ISR* 14 (December 1913), 351–55.

40. R.B. Tobias and Mary E. Marcy, *Women as Sex Vendors, or Why Women are Conservative (Being a View of the Economic Status of Women)* (Chicago: Charles H. Kerr, 1918), 9–10, 12–13, 20, 22, 37, 47, 48, 51, 53, 58.

41. James Morton, "Fewer and Better Children," *ISR* 15 (November 1914), 302–03; Mary E. Marcy, *A Free Union: A One Act Comedy of Free Love* (Chicago: Charles H. Kerr, 1921).

42. "Sparks from the National Convention," 1,128. In one postwar essay in an era of racial turmoil, Marcy addressed the issue of black workers, and urged that workers not allow themselves to be divided by race. Mary E. Marcy, "Our Real Enemy," in Harrison George, ed., *Chicago Race Riots* (Chicago: Great Western Publishing Co., 1919), 4–6.

43. Mary E. Marcy, "The Boys on the Grand Trunk," *ISR* 11 (October 1910), 162.

44. Mary E. Marcy, *Why Catholic Workers Should be Socialists* (Chicago: Charles H. Kerr, 1914), 3, 11, 21–22, 24.

45. Mary E. Marcy, "The Germans in Turkey, *ISR* 13 (June 1913), 871–74; idem, "Through the Jungle by Rail," *ISR* 13 (November 1912), 415–16.

46. Mary E. Marcy, "The Awakening of China," *ISR*, 10 (January 1910), 632–35; idem, "Progress in China, *ISR* 10 (February 1910), 689–91; idem, "Changing China," *ISR* 13 (January 1913), 528–32; idem, "China and Standard Oil," *ISR* 14 (April 1914), 594–96; idem, "Morals in Rubber," *ISR* 13 (December 1912), 466–69.

47. Mary E. Marcy, "Morals in Rubber," 466. For an analysis of variations among socialist views on imperialism, with some equating westernization and mod-

ernization with the introduction of "civilization," see Julius Braunthal, *History of the International, 1864–1914* (New York: Frederick A. Praeger, 1967), 318.

48. Mary E. Marcy, *Stories of the Cave People* (Chicago: Charles H. Kerr, 1917); idem, *Rhymes of Early Jungle Folk* (Chicago: Charles H. Kerr, 1922).

49. Mary E. Marcy, "William the Faithful," *ISR* 7 (March 1907), 557–58; idem, "A Felicitan Fair," *ISR* 6 (June 1906), 729–30; idem, "Skinny's Turkey Dinner, *ISR* 10 (November 1909), 385–91. "A Felicitan Fair" was later republished posthumously as "The Barbo Fair," *The Industrial Pioneer* 1 (May 1923), 5–6.

50. Max Roemer, "Carrying Things," *ISR* 16 (February 1916), 488–90. The author wishes to thank Franklin Rosemont, current publisher of Kerr Publishing Company and authority on the *International Socialist Review* for suggesting this line of reasoning.

51. Mary E. Marcy, "Whose War is This?" *ISR*, 14 (June 1914), 729–31.

52. Mary E. Marcy, "The Cause of War," *ISR* 18 (July 1917), 28–29; idem, "The Real Fatherland," *ISR* 15 (September 1914), 177–79.

53. Mary E. Marcy, "Where We Stand on War," *ISR* 15 (March 1915), 561.

54. Mary E. Marcy, "Socialist Unpreparedness in Germany," *ISR* 15 (October 1914), 245–47; see also Mary E. Marcy, "When We Go to War," in *You Have No Country! Workers' Struggle Against War*, ed. Franklin Rosemont (Chicago: Charles H. Kerr, 1984), 34–37. Marcy erroneously dated the Copenhagen Congress as having been held in 1912 (see *ISR* 15, 245).

55. Mary E. Marcy, "Better Any Kind of Action than Inert Theory," *ISR* 15 (February 1915), 495–96.

56. Mary E. Marcy, "Mass Action: Where Do We Stand?" *ISR* 17 (December 1916), 367–69.

57. Mary E. Marcy, "Killed Without Warning by the Capitalist Class," *ISR*, 17 (March 1917), 519–22.

58. Mary E. Marcy, "Killed Without Warning . . .," 522; idem, "Our Gains in War," *ISR*, 17 (May 1917), 650–52; idem, "We Must Fight It Out," *ISR* 15 (April 1915), 627–28.

59. Mary E. Marcy, "The Class Struggle Disguised," *ISR* 17 (June 1917), 751–52; idem, "The Time to Strike is Now," *ISR* 16 (June 1916), 752–53; idem, "Their War and Our Revolution," in Rosemont, 41–42; Mary E. Marcy to Eugene V. Debs, March 6, 1918, Chicago, Eugene V. Debs Papers, Cunningham Memorial Library, Indiana State University, Terre Haute, Indiana.

60. Mary E. Marcy, "Economic Power," *ISR* 18 (February 1918), 405.

61. Mary E. Marcy, *Industrial Autocracy* (Chicago: Charles H. Kerr, 1919), 43–44, 51: idem, *The Right to Strike* (Chicago: Charles H. Kerr, n.d). This was probably published in 1921. Idem, "Open the Shops and Factories," *Industrial Pioneer* 1 (June 1921), 19–21; idem, *Open the Factories* (Chicago: Charles H. Kerr, 1921), 6–7, 26, 28.

62. Marcy and Kerr put together a labor "scrapbook" as an occasional publication to replace the *Review*. See Mary E. Marcy to Eugene V. Debs, February 18, 1918, Chicago, Eugene V. Debs Papers, Cunningham Memorial Library, Indiana State University, Terre Haute, Indiana; Ruff, "We Called . . .," 508–09.

63. Carney, 9–10. Carney erroneously dates the conventions as 1917, when they were held in early September 1919.

64. Carney, 12; Katharine Kerr Moore to May Walden Kerr, December 13, 1922, December 29, 1922, Box 4, May Walden Kerr Collection, Newberry Library, Chicago.

65. Mary E. Marcy, "Only One Way," *Industrial Solidarity*, December 23, 1922, 6.

# 7 THE SOCIALIST PARTY AND THE AFRICAN-AMERICAN

PARTY DEBATES

THE NEGRO RESOLUTION
*International Socialist Review*
5 (January 1905): 392–93

Whereas, the negroes of the United States, because of their long training in slavery and but recent emancipation therefrom, occupy a peculiar position in the working class and in society at large;

Whereas, The capitalist class seeks to preserve this peculiar condition, and to foster and increase color prejudice and race hatred between the white worker and the black, so as to make their social and economic interests to appear to be separate and antagonistic, in order that the workers of both races may thereby be more easily and completely exploited;

Whereas, Both the old political parties and educational and religious institutions alike betray the negro in his present helpless struggle against disfranchisement and violence, in order to receive the economic favors of the capitalist class. Be it, therefore,

Resolved, That we, the Socialists of America, in national convention assembled, do hereby assure him of the fellowship of the workers who suffer from the lawlessness and exploitation of capital in every nation or tribe of the world. Be it further

Resolved, That we declare to the negro worker the identity of his interests and struggles with the interests and struggles of the workers of all lands, without regard to race or color or sectional lines; that the causes which have made him the victim of social and political inequality are the effects of the long exploitation of his labor power; that all social and race prejudices spring from the ancient economic causes which still endure, to the misery of the whole human family, that the only line of division which exists in fact is that between the producers and the owners of the world—between capitalism and labor. And be it further

Resolved, That we, the American Socialist Party, invite the negro to membership and fellowship with us in the world movement for economic emancipation by which equal liberty and opportunity shall be secured to every man and fraternity become the order of the world.

## The Negro Problem
A.M. Simons
*International Socialist Review*
2 (October 1901): 204–11

A series of events running through several years and leading up to a climax within the last few months have served to bring the "negro question" prominently before the public. The succession of terrible outrages committed in the Southern states—the burning and torturing of defenseless negroes, often innocent, and always without form of trial—have attracted universal attention. The horrible barbarities accompanying these scenes—the slow roasting alive of human beings, the tearing to pieces of the still quivering bodies and the distribution of portions of them among the mob as "souvenirs"—all this bore witness to the fact that capitalism had developed within itself a body of demons more ferocious than African head-hunters or prehistoric savages.

Perhaps the feature of these horrors that impressed the ordinary observer trained to capitalist methods of thought was that throughout the portion of the country in which these ghastly orgies took place the so-called "respectable" or bourgeois element of society, who are supposed to be the especial conservators of "morality" and "law and order," apologized for, excused or openly encouraged such acts. Still further, at the same time that these outrages were being inflicted upon a helpless people these same bourgeois pillars of society were conspiring to take away their only means of legal defense—the ballot. Apparently more remarkable still, although the votes thus destroyed were almost wholly Republican, that party made no emphatic or significant protest against such action. On the contrary, the last few weeks have been the beginning of a series of outbreaks against the negroes in Northern cities, that for unreasoning, brutal violence rival those that have gained so much notoriety for the Southern states. New York, Brooklyn, and Akron, Ohio, have been the seats of "race riots" as ferocious as those of the South, and it was apparently only the lack of opportunity that prevented the perpetration of equally hideous barbarities. Here, too, the "authorities" and "respectable citizens" lent open sympathy, if not active assistance, to the perpetrators of the outrages. In New York city it was especially noted that the police often lent assistance in the beating of the helpless negroes.

These are the phenomena with which we are confronted. It now remains to find an explanation. To do this it will be necessary to pass hastily in review the various phases that the "negro problem" has assumed in American history.

During the pre-revolutionary period those who sought to live upon the labor of others found themselves confronted with the problem which always arises in a new country where natural opportunities are not yet wholly monopolized by a possessing, employing class. Such opportunities being open to all and capable of utilization with simple individually-owned tools, everyone can secure the full product of his labor in this crude form of production, and there is no class whose members are compelled to sell themselves to the owning class in order to live. This is the situation at present in the S. African diamond fields, and the Philippine Islands. In all of these cases it was found necessary to introduce some form of chattel slavery until the natural opportunities could be sufficiently monopolized to make it impossible for anyone possessing nothing but his labor power to exist without selling himself into wage-slavery.

In America all attempts to reduce the Indians to slavery having failed, recourse was had to Europe and white "indentured servants" and negro slaves were imported. Owing to a variety of circumstances, such as the long Winters, an increasingly intensive system of agriculture, a more concentrated population, hemmed in by natural features and hostile Indian tribes, and the growth of a trading class, there soon arose in the North a body of men who were compelled to sell themselves into wage-slavery while at the same time life ownership of the slave became unprofitable.

Under these circumstances chattel slavery became "immoral" and the New England Puritans "freed their slaves," and thus avoided the burden of their support at unprofitable periods of the year, while they well knew that monopolized opportunities would keep them close at hand eager to sell themselves for a limited period when needed. This left the highly moral New Englander free to organize "abolition" societies and carry New England rum to the Gold coast with which to buy the "black ivory" so much in demand in the Southern states.

With the settling up of the great West the two systems came into conflict, and, the Northern capitalist being in the ascendant in Congress, cut off one source of supply to the slave market by forbidding the further importation of chattel slaves. At the same time he began in every possible way to encourage the importation of wage-slaves for the Northern labor market.

. . . At the close of the Civil War, when the victory was won the conquerors wished to revel in the spoils of the conquered and complete the humiliation of their fallen foe. As instruments to that purpose they chose the former chattel slaves, and through a series of constitutional amendments gave them full political equality with their late owners. With the mock morality that has ever marked all the dealings with the helpless negro since the time he was brought from Africa to "enjoy the blessings of a Christian civilization" this was nominally done for the protection of the former chattel slaves. But precious little good it has done him up to the present time, and when he does show some signs of using it for his own good it is promptly taken away.

In the "reconstruction period" immediately following the war the negro was but the helpless tool of the horde of Northern "carpet-baggers" who rode upon his back through the prostrate defenseless South to a career of plunder and pillage that had scarce been equaled since the days of Alaric or Atilla. And this period, when the helpless blacks were but mute tools in the hands of a new and more unscrupulous set of masters, is known in history by the bitterly ironical name of the "period of negro domination."

With the passage of time the South too began to be capitalistic and the interests of the ruling classes of the two sections, North and South, became the same. Both desired submissive wage-slaves. The troops were withdrawn from the South by President Hayes and the Southern employers were left to treat their black wage-slaves as they chose. Steps were at once taken to disenfranchise the negroes. At first this was accomplished by the clumsy methods of intimidation and fraud. These were the days of the Ku Klux Klan, the "tissue ballot" and the "shot-gun campaign."

But shortly after this great industrial changes began to take place in the South. The great superiority of wage over chattel slavery from the point of view of the employer began to make itself felt. Factories of all kinds sprang up throughout the South.

. . . when slaves are bidding against one another in the labor market for a job they are much more docile, and profitable to the slave owner than when masters are bidding against each other to secure possession of the slaves. They will work harder to fit themselves for their masters' work and are no expense to him save when actually engaged in production. At first only white laborers were used in the new Southern industries. The "poor whites" and "crackers" who fought so valiantly from '61 to '65, that their rich neighbors might have the right to own black laborers for life, are now pouring into the cities to fight each other for the chance to sell their own bodies and brains for such periods as they can make themselves profitable to their buyers. Unorganized, composed mostly of women and children, helpless, untrained to resistance, with a low standard of life in a semi-tropical climate, wages are soon forced down to the subsistence point, hours lengthened to the limit of endurance, and abuses of all kinds multiplied until the terrible horrors of the early days of the English factory system are almost duplicated to-day in many a Georgia, Alabama or Mississippi cotton factory.

But the black can live even cheaper than the white, and so another phase is given to the "negro question."

. . . Lured on by the will-o'-the-wisp hope of economic advance that has for these many years sufficed to lure the white worker into the swamps of capitalism, the negro is crowding into Tuskegee, Berea, Hampton, and a host of other "colleges" and "training schools," where he is fitted to better serve the purposes of his new capitalist masters.

These developments have for the first time made the negro an essential element of the capitalist system. The "negro question" has completed its evolution into the "labor problem." This at once made itself felt in two directions. Of one of these, the introduction of the developed factory system into the South, we have already spoken. The other was the use of the negro by Northern capitalists to break the resistance of organized labor. At Pana, Virden and the Chicago Packing Houses, and at various other points, strikes of organized white labor have been followed by the wholesale importation of negro "scabs." Their presence added the fury of race prejudice to the natural hatred of union and non-union men and was the occasion of bloody race riots.

. . . it will not be very long before the negroes, who are now meeting the same problems, bearing the same burdens and groaning beneath the same form of slavery as their white fellow toilers, will begin to realize the fact of the solidarity of interests which unites the workers of the world. The history of the world has shown that no difference of race, religion, color or politics is able to maintain itself permanently against the terrible leveling influence of capitalism. Hence the time cannot be far away when the white and black laborers of the United States will join hands in their unions to resist economic tyranny (indeed, the process is already well advanced), and there are even signs that the time may be closer than we think when the fact of the common economic interests will find expression in common political action and a joint protest against the entire capitalist system.

Under these circumstances every material interest of the ruling class both North and South pointed to one course of action—the excitation of race hatred, followed by disenfranchisement of the negro before he could intelligently protest. Hence the open encouragement or silent approval of negro lynchings, burnings and torturings, the quiet acquiescence by the "authorities" in negro riots in Northern cities, and, most significant of all, the general acceptance of wholesale disenfranchisement of the black laborers . . .

THE NEGRO PROBLEM
Charles H. Vail
*International Socialist Review*
1 (February 1901): 464–70

To many the negro problem was forever solved when the shackles were struck from the four millions of the colored race. This act was thought to fulfill the theory embodied in the Declaration of Independence,—that all men were created free and equal. The emancipation of the negro from chattel slavery—an act necessary to modern capitalist industry—was, from the standpoint of economic progress, a great step in advance, but instead of solving the negro problem it merely changed its aspect. The negro was emancipated from chattel slavery, only to be plunged into wage slavery. This change merely altered the relation in which the negro stood to his master.

The ultimate cause that led to the Northern revolt against the chattel system was its unprofitableness. As soon as industry passed from the individual and manufacturing period into modern mechanical industry, it became unprofitable to own workers as chattels. The change at the North caused New England morality to revolt against the chattel system and inaugurate in its place wage slavery. The new order was exceedingly profitable to the capitalist class and enabled the Northern masters, when the crisis came, to conquer the South and force it to accept capitalism and the wage system. The rapid invasion of the South by capitalism after the civil war,—the industrial revolution which supplanted the crude tools by mighty machines,—completely overturned previous relations and gave rise to a new negro problem which was none other than the modern problem of labor.

At first the Southern masters looked upon the loss of their slaves as a severe blow, but they soon began to see, what the North had long since known, that the ownership of land and capital meant the virtual ownership of those who must have access to those instruments or starve. The negro had been freed, but as this freedom did not include freedom of access to the means of livelihood he was still as dependent as ever. Being unable to employ himself he was compelled to seek employment, or the use of land upon which to live, at the hands of the very class from whom he had been liberated. In either case he was only able to retain barely enough of the product to keep body and soul together. The competition among the newly-emancipated for an opportunity to secure a livelihood was so great that their labor could be bought for a mere existence wage. The negro labor had become a commodity, and like all commodities its price was determined by its cost of production. The cost of producing labor-power is the cost of the laborer's keep. The master class were able to secure the necessary labor-power to carry on their industries for merely a subsistence wage—for no more than it cost them when they owned the negroes as chattels.

The wage slave spends his own subsistence wage, which, under the chattel system, the owner was obliged to spend for him. The chattel method was fully as desirable to keep him in good condition. The wage slave-owner, however, does not particularly care whether his wage slave lives or dies, for he has no money invested in him and there are thusands [*sic*] of others to take his place. Surely wage slavery is an improvement upon the old method of property in human beings. It saves the useless expense of owning workers as chattels, which necessitates caring for them and involves loss in case of death. The results of slavery are secured by simply owning the means of production. The new system, with its revolution of industry, gives to the masters, without expense, an industrial reserve army who can only secure employment through their grace. This secures to the master class cheap labor, for laborers, both white and black, having nothing but their labor-power to sell and thus being unable to employ themselves, must compete with each other for an opportunity to earn a livelihood.

In the days of chattel slavery capitalist production on a large scale was impossible, because it was unprofitable for the master to keep more slaves than he could profitably use all the time. He could not afford a reserve army, for he must feed and care for his workers whether he could use them or not. This difficulty is overcome by the wage system. The conditions and even the name of slavery have changed, but the fact remains untouched. Indeed, slavery is not yet abolished. So long as the laborer is deprived of property in the instruments of production, so long as his labor-power is a commodity which he is obliged to sell to another, he is not a *free being*, be he white or black. He is simply a slave to a master and from morning until night is as much a bondsman as any negro ever was below Mason and Dixon's line before the war. Slaves are cheaper now and do more work than at any time in the world's history. The same principle of subjection that ruled in the chattel system rules in the wage system.

Let us inquire here, of what does slavery consist? It consists in the compulsory using of men for the benefit of the user. One who is forced to yield to another a part of the product of his toil is a slave, no matter where he resides or what may be the color of his skin. This was the condition of the negro before the war and it is his condition to-day, and not only his condition but the condition of *all* propertyless workers. That the workman can to-day change his master does not alter the fact. The negro was a slave, not because of a certain master, but because he must yield a part of the wealth he produced to a master. Today he may desert one master, but he must look up another or starve, and this necessity constitutes his continued slavery. Under the old system he was sure of a master and consequently his livelihood. One of the greatest curses of modern slavery is the fear of the slave that he will lose his position of servitude. Many a negro wage slave, and white as well, would gladly exchange their freedom to leave their master, for a guarantee that their master would not discharge them.

The loss of the security of existence is the fearful price which the negro has been obliged to pay for his so-called liberty. The insecurity of the wage worker is the greatest curse of the present system. Closely connected with this is the dependence which inheres in the wage system. The wage worker is absolutely dependent for his daily bread upon the favor or whim of his master. Indeed, the wage earner is a wage slave. The intensity of this slavery depends upon the amount of time which the workers are compelled to work gratuitously for others. Under present conditions they must work the greater portion of their time for some one else. It is thus that the wage-earning class is a slave to the employing class. Workingmen may change their master, but they are still at the mercy of the master class. The choice of a wage slave is between work and starvation. The whip of hunger is all sufficient to drive the wage slave to his task.

The worker today, then, is a slave, bound by the pressure of economic wants to compulsory servitude to idle capitalist masters. He is obliged to sell his liberties in exchange for the means of subsistence. He is under the greatest tyranny of which it is possible to conceive,—the tyranny of want. By this lash men are driven to work long hours and in unwholesome occupations, and to live in tenement rookeries in our city slums that for vileness would surpass the slave quarters of old. The man who has no work or is compelled to submit to wages dictated by a corporation, and is at the beck and call of a master for ten hours a day, has not much personal liberty to brag of over his prototype—the chattel slave. A man thus conditioned is far from free. John Stuart Mill said that "the majority of laborers have as little choice of occupation or freedom of locomotion, are practically as dependent on fixed rules and on the will of others, as they could be in any system short of actual slavery." This is the condition into which the negro was "liberated." It is quite evident that he has not yet secured anything worthy to be called *freedom*—he is still in need of emancipation.

The changed conditions which transformed the negro into a wage slave, identifies the negro problem with the labor problem as a whole, the solution of which is the abolition of wage slavery and the emancipation of both black and white from the servitude of capitalist masters. This can only be accomplished by collective ownership of the means of production and distribution. Socialism is the only remedy,—it is the only escape from personal or class rule. It would put an end to economic despotism and establish popular self-government in the industrial realm. Economic democracy is a corollary of political democracy. We want every person engaged in industry, whether male or female, white or black, to have a voice in making the rules under which they must work. Under socialism the workers would elect their own directors, regulate their hours of work and determine the conditions under which production would be carried on. We may be sure that when this power is vested in the producing class, the factories will be arranged according to convenience and beauty, and all disagreeable smells, vapor, smoke, etc., eliminated, the buildings well lighted, heated and ventilated, and every precaution taken against accidents. In other words, under socialism the laborers would have absolute freedom in the economic sphere in place of the present absolute servitude. Socialists emphasize the need of this economic freedom, for it is the basis of all freedom. Intellectual and moral freedom is practically nullified to-day through the absence of economic liberty . . .

But it may be said that although socialism would emancipate the negro from economic servitude, it would not completely solve the negro problem unless its advent would destroy race prejudices. This is precisely what socialism would do. Of course, it would not accomplish it all at once, but race prejudices cannot exist with true enlightenment. Socialism would educate and enlighten the race. It would secure to the laborers, whether black or white, the full opportunities for the education of their children. Socialism would not only demand that all children be educated, but it would make compulsory education effective by removing the incentive to deprive children of instruction. Today thousands of children, white and black are robbed of the bright days of childhood simply because employers can make money out of them. The income of the parents being insufficient to keep them in school, they are withdrawn from the school and sent to the factory. It does but little good to pass laws prohibiting child labor so long as it is beneficial to both parents and capitalists; they will conspire in some way to evade the law. The lack of learning, then, is not the fault of our schools but of our economic system which deprives the poor of the opportunity of utilizing them. Socialism would secure to all children this opportunity by giving to the head of the family sufficient income so that his children would not be obliged to become bread-winners. Socialism would not only secure to the child an education but it would secure to the adult ample leisure for the cultivation of those tastes which his training has awakened. These blessings would not be confined to the white race; socialism recognizes no class nor race distinction. It draws no line of exclusion. Under socialism the negro will enjoy, equally with the whites, the advantages and opportunities for culture and refinement. In this higher education we may be sure race prejudices will be obliterated.

Not only will universal enlightenment destroy this low prejudice but abolition of competition will aid in working the same result. The struggle between the black and white to sell themselves in the auction of the new slave market has, in many quarters, engendered bitter race feeling, and that they might bid the fiercer against each other the masters have fanned this prejudice into hate. In other sections, as in the coal mines and railroad camps, the blacks have been used by the masters as a club to beat down striking whites. This antagonism will cease under socialism, and with it the hatred which springs from all class conflicts. It will even disappear under the present system just in proportion as workingmen recognize the solidarity of human labor. Socialism emphasizes the fact that the interests of all laborers are identical regardless of race or sex. In this common class interest race distinctions are forgotten. If this is true of socialists to-day, how much more will it be true when humanity is lifted to the higher plane where the economic interests of all are identical.

Socialism, then is the only solution of the negro problem. It offers to this much-wronged race the joys and privileges of an emancipated humanity. It proposes to make him joint owners with his white neighbor in the nation's capital, and to secure him equal opportunity for the attainment of wealth and progress. Socialism will secure to him the enjoyment of the inalienable rights of all men to life, liberty, and the pursuit of happiness. Today, in common with all wage slaves, he is deprived, by an economic system of inequality, of the privilege of exercising such rights. In the new economic environment where the negro will enjoy equality of opportunity, he will take on a new development.

The new hope for the colored race is in socialism, that system of society that gives to every individual, without regard to race, color or sex, an equal opportunity to develop the best within him. In such a society an individual's social position will be determined by the use he makes of his opportunities—by what he becomes.

Socialism, then is the only hope for the negro and for humanity. To realize this ideal is the mission of the working class. Modern production is wiping out all distinctions of race and color and dividing society into two classes—the laborers and the capitalists. The interests of these two classes are diametrically opposed, and the time has come for the black and the white to join hands at the ballot box against the common enemy—capitalism.

The Socialist party is the only political organization that has anything to offer the colored race. The Republican and Democrat parties are both parties of capitalism and could not help the negro if they would and would not if they could. There is absolutely no choice between these two parties so far as the rights of labor are concerned. They both represent the interests of the capitalist class and their sham battles are for the purpose of dividing the laborers into various factions lest they unite to secure their freedom.

The experience of the negro since the civil war has proven that the colored race will never secure equal opportunities so long as the present system exists. They were given the ballot by the Republican party, because that party wished to use them as a tool against the Democrats. The white laborer was originally endowed with the franchise for precisely the same motives. When the mercantile class wished to wipe out the last thread of landed aristocracy they gave the ballot to the workers and used them as a weapon to accomplish that end. The laborers have been continually deceived and intimidated into doing the master's bidding every since. The negro, perhaps, has been the most deceived of any branch of the working class. He has been taught that he is the special ward of the Republican party, and he has turned in the midst of the barbaric outrages committed by Southern fanatics and asked his supposed friends for help, but his appeals have fallen on deaf ears. The recent disfranchisement of the negro in the South is but an indication of what capitalists will soon try to do with all the workers regardless of color and regardless of location. The conditions of forty or fifty years ago have changed. The capitalist class of the North and the South have now joined hands as the owners of wage slaves, and while the Democrat party represents the interests of the small capitalist, the interests of both are opposed to the laborer.

May the negro wage slave become awakened to his own interests, the interests of the class of which he is a member, and cast his ballot for the only party that stands for human emancipation-the Socialist party. When socialism supplants capitalism the negro problem will be forever solved.

INTERNATIONAL SOCIALIST BUREAU
Manifesto condemning the Lynching of Black Americans, Brussels, November 22, 1903, in Georges Haupt, ed. Bureau Socialiste Internationale, I, *Comptes rendus des réunions Manifestes et circulaires* (Paris: Mouton & Co., 1979, pp. 91–92 (translated by Kathelen Johnson).

To the workers in all countries!

The Socialist Parties of France, Argentina, and the United States have called the attention of the International Socialist Committee [*sic*] to the rapid multiplication of cases of lynching in North America.

In 1902 there were 103 lynchings in one single state. The federal government's investigation of this has revealed in the states of the South a state of affairs reminiscent of the horrors of slavery: the Negro is working under the regime of the whip and the stick; sometimes he is beaten to death by the blows. In order to prevent him from escaping and fleeing this daily martyrdom, he is required to work naked. He's imprisoned, shot, the women are massacred, the homes of children and men of the Black race are burned, they are burned alive, thanks to the apathy or with the encouragement of the authorities and at the instigation of the owners.

In the ranks of the American Socialist democracy, one is not without worry for the future; the bloody conflicts threaten to explode from one day to the next; the violent reprisals are to be feared. The existence of nine million Negroes is threatened. One whole human race is refused the right to life.

The United States republic declared the emancipation of the Negroes forty years ago, and yet slavery still exists.

In olden days the Negro, purchased from those who stole men, represented capital: he was defended by the owners because he was their property.

Nowadays he no longer represents the same value in their eyes, but he is, in the hands of the capitalist, a weapon against organized white workers.

Capitalism, which is endeavoring everywhere to supplant the work of men with that of women and children, has instigated racial rivalries in the states in the North, in New York, Brooklyn, Akron, Ohio, and elsewhere.

Formerly, the question could have been a racial problem. Since the states in the South have become industrialized, there are no longer distinctions to be made between the North and the South. *The question has become a labor problem.*

The Negro is, in the hands of capitalism, a means of breaking up the labor union and Socialist organization of workers in the states in the North. The strikes by white workers have failed because of the importation of masses of Black scabs.

Besides, the surge of Socialist democracy is rising in the United States; it menaces the plutocracy. Consequently, capitalism is looking for a counter-irritant in a racial war.

This will not be!

Capitalism makes no distinction at all, when it comes to living off the work of others: the interest of the working class is to unite all its members, no matter what differences of race or religion there may be, in order to be assured of its complete emancipation.

Servitude is neither white, nor yellow, nor black; it is proletarian. The revolt against capitalist exploitation should be one [unified whole].

The interest of the working class demands the unity of all workers, without distinction between races, and it requires an energetic protest by Socialist democracy against the abominable acts which are committed daily in the United States.

THE NEGRO IN THE CLASS STRUGGLE
Eugene V. Debs
*International Socialist Review*
4 (November 1903): 257–60

It so happens that I write upon the negro question, in compliance with the request of the editor of the *International Socialist Review*, in the state of Louisiana, where the race prejudice is as strong and the feeling against the "nigger" as bitter and relentless as when Lincoln's proclamation of emancipation lashed the waning confederacy into fury and incited the final and desperate attempts to burst the bonds that held the southern states in the federal union. Indeed, so thoroughly is the south permeated with the malign spirit of race hatred that even socialists are to be found, and by no means rarely, who either share directly in the race hostility against the negro, or avoid the issue, or apologize for the social obliteration of the color line in the class struggle.

The white man in the south declares that "the nigger is all right in his place"; that is, as menial, servant and slave. If he dare hold hope that some day may bring deliverance; if in his brain the thought of freedom dawns and in his heart the aspiration to rise above the animal plane and propensities of his sires, he must be made to realize that notwithstanding the white man is civilized (?) the black man is a "nigger" still and must so remain as long as planets wheel in space.

But while the white man is considerate enough to tolerate the negro "in his place," the remotest suggestion at social recognition arouses all the pent up wrath of his Anglo-Saxon civilization; and my observation is that the less real ground there is for such indignant assertion of self-superiority, the more passionately it is proclaimed.

At Yoakum, Texas, a few days ago, leaving the depot with two grips in my hands, I passed four or five bearers of the white man's burden perched on a railing and decorating their environment with tobacco juice. One of them, addressing me, said: "There's a nigger that'll carry your grips." A second one added: "That's what he's here for," and the third chimed in the "That's right, by God." Here was a savory bouquet of white superiority. One glance was sufficient to satisfy me that they represented all there is of justification for the implacable hatred of the negro race. They were ignorant, lazy, unclean, totally void of ambition, themselves the foul product of the capitalist system and held in lowest contempt by the master class, yet esteeming themselves immeasurably above the cleanest, most intelligent and self-respecting negro, having by reflex absorbed the "nigger" hatred of their masters.

As a matter of fact the industrial supremacy of the south before the war would not have been possible without the negro, and the south of today would totally collapse without his labor. Cotton culture has been and is the great staple and it will not be denied of the southern states the greatest in the world is due in large measure to the genius of the negroes charged with its cultivation.

The whole world is under obligation to the negro, and that the white heel is still upon the black neck is simply proof that the world is not yet civilized.

The history of the negro in the United States is a history of crime without a parallel.

Why should the white man hate him? Because he stole him from his native land and for two centuries and a half robbed him of the fruit of his labor, kept him in beastly ignorance and subjected him to the brutal domination of the lash? Because, he tore the black child from the breast of its mother and ravished the black man's daughter before her father's eyes?

There are thousands of negroes who bear testimony in their whitening skins that men who so furiously resent the suggestion of "social equality" are far less sensitive in respect to the sexual equality of the races.

But of all the senseless agitation in the capitalist society, that in respect to "social equality" takes the palm. The very instant it is mentioned the old aristocratic plantation owner's shrill cry about the "buck nigger" marrying the "fair young daughter" of his master is heard from the tomb and echoed and re-echoed across the spaces and repeated by the "white trash" in proud vindication of their social superiority.

Social equality, forsooth! Is the black man pressing his claims for social recognition upon his white burden bearer? Is there any reason why he should? Is the white man's social recognition of his own white brother such as to excite the negro's ambition to covet the noble prize? Has the negro any greater desire, or is there any reason why he should have, for social intercourse with the white man than the white man has for social relations with the negro? This phase of the negro question is pure fraud and serves to mask the real issue, which is not *social equality*, BUT ECONOMIC FREEDOM.

There never was any social inferiority that was not the shrivelled fruit of economic inequality.

The negro, given economic freedom, will not ask the white man any social favors; and the burning question of "social equality" will disappear like mist before the sunrise.

I have said and say again that, properly speaking, there is no negro question outside of the labor question—the working class struggle. Our position as socialists and as a party is perfectly plain. We have simply to say: "The class struggle is colorless." The capitalists, white, black and other shades, are on one side and the workers, white, black and all other colors, on the other side.

When Marx said: "Workingmen of all countries unite," he gave concrete expression to the socialist philosophy of the class struggle; unlike the framers of the declaration of independence who announced that "all men are created equal" and then basely repudiated their own doctrine, Marx issued the call to all the workers of the globe, regardless of race, sex, creed or any other condition whatsoever.

As a socialist party we receive the negro and all other races upon absolutely equal terms. We are the party of the working class, the whole working class, and we will not suffer ourselves to be divided by any specious appeal to race prejudice; and if we should be coaxed or driven from the straight road we will be lost in the wilderness and ought to perish there, for we shall no longer be a socialist party.

Let the capitalist press and capitalist "public opinion" indulge themselves in alternate flatter and abuse of the negro; we as socialists will receive him in our party, treat him in our counsels and stand by him all around the same as if his skin were white instead of black; and this we do, not from any considerations of sentiment, but because it accords with the philosophy of socialism, the genius of the class struggle, and is eternally right and bound to triumph in the end.

With the "nigger" question, the "race war" from the capitalist viewpoint we have nothing to do. In capitalism the negro question is a grave one and will grow more threatening as the contradictions and complications of capitalist society multiply, but this need not worry us. Let them settle the negro question in their way, if they can. We have nothing to do with it, for that is their fight. We have simply to open the eyes of as many negroes as we can and bring them into the socialist movement to do battle for emancipation from wage slavery, and when the working class have [*sic*] triumphed in the class struggle and stand forth economic as well as political free men, the race problem will forever disappear.

Socialists should with pride proclaim their sympathy with and fealty to the black race, and if any there be who hesitate to avow themselves in the face of ignorant and unreasoning prejudice, they lack the true spirit of the slavery-destroying revolutionary movement.

The voice of socialism must be as inspiring music to the ears of those in bondage, especially the weak black brethren, doubly enslaved, who are bowed to the earth and groan in despair beneath the burden of the centuries. For myself, my heart goes to the negro and I make no apology to any white man for it. In fact, when I see the poor, brutalized, outraged black victim, I feel a burning sense of guilt for his intellectual poverty and moral debasement that makes me blush for the unspeakable crimes committed by my own race.

In closing, permit me to express the hope that the next convention may repeal the resolutions on the negro question. The negro does not need them and they serve to increase rather than diminish the necessity for explanation.

We have nothing special to offer the negro, and we cannot make separate appeals to all the races.

The Socialist party is the party of the working class, regardless of color—the working class of the whole world.

NEGRO LOCALS
Eraste Vidrine
*International Socialist Review*
5 (January 1905): 389–92

So far as I am informed, every local in the State of Louisiana is composed exclusively of white members, excepting one at the little town of Lutcher which, as I understand, is composed exclusively of negroes. The facts thus far obtaining, considered in connection with well known conditions and sentiments in this section, make it clear to my mind that every local hereafter organized in this State will be composed, in the first instance, exclusively of white members. Concerning the composition of the membership elsewhere, I am not informed, but have every reason to believe that what is true of Louisiana will be found applicable to every other State south of Mason and Dixon's line. The question therefore naturally presents itself: shall the negroes be taken into the same locals with the whites, or shall they be required or permitted to organize into separate locals?

That the negroes should be organized as fast and as far as possible, is the universal conviction and the universal desire. Every one appreciates how suicidal it would be for the Party to ignore entirely the presence of eight million men, women, and children in our midst. From a military standpoint alone, if from no other, every one feels the importance, in our own self-interest, of obtaining the good will and co-operation of eight million people. Nor is there any lack among the Southern comrades of that fine sense of justice and those broad principles of humanity which animate the true socialist in every spot on the globe.

Still the matter is not without its difficulties. The stand taken by the National Committee in at first refusing a charter to the Party of Louisiana, on account of a plank in its original platform calling for a separation of the races, has left the impression, in this locality at least, that the organization of the negroes into separate locals would be discountenanced by the National Party; notwithstanding the fact that there is no constitutional prohibition against separate locals, and that every State Party is given the power under the National Constitution to regulate its membership in any manner not inconsistent with that organic instrument. But at the same time, there is a formidable sentiment among the comrades, particularly those of the gentler sex, against the idea of having negro members in the locals to which they belong.

I have had occasion to discuss the question with many of the New Orleans comrades, some of the most active among whom are of the fairer sex, and I have found them full of declamation against racial discrimination; but I have yet to meet any one who is outspoken in favor of soliciting the membership of negroes into his or her local, and the fact remains that in the State organization, which is now two years old, the negroes are conspicuous almost entirely by their absence.

That the sentiment against the commingling of the two races in the same locals is not a mere southern prejudice, is seen from the fact that every little town in the State which has been built up of recent years largely by immigrants from the North, has a separate quarter for the negro race. That it is not confined exclusively to the white comrades, is seen from the fact that the black comrades are not any more active in seeking membership into white locals, than the white comrades are inactive in soliciting the membership of black comrades. An instance illustrating one phase of this sentiment is furnished by the fact that when Comrade Goebel, National Organizer, went to Lutcher some time ago, for the purpose of delivering a lecture before the local at that point, composed as aforesaid exclusively of negroes, he was asked by the members not to deliver his lecture, lest it should injure the cause by identifying it too closely in the minds of the natives with the idea of social equality and fraternization between the races. But aside from the outside effect of promiscuous locals, which is not without its danger to the comrades, there is, as previously stated, a dominating sentiment within the ranks of the faithful themselves, both white and black, which is sufficient to exclude them from participation in the same locals; and, in the meantime, the negroes remain unorganized, untrained and to a large extent uneducated.

I am not one of those who take the view that the organization of separate locals must necessarily violate the national constitution or that it is essentially opposed to the socialist philosophy. But in view of the general character of constitutional provisions, and the still more general character of philosophical principles, I believe it would be wise to have some specific declaration from a national source, on this question. Hence I suggest for consideration the idea of what might be called "optional" locals: by which I mean that, in those localities where there is a large negro element, the black comrades should be allowed, at their discretion, to organize themselves into separate locals or sub-locals. This would not obviate the commingling of the races in a representative capacity, but it would remove the necessity of having them in the same locals or sub-locals.

I might say that of late there seems to be a growing disposition on the part of some among the comrades, to cut the gordian knot which the question apparently presents to their mind, by what must be considered as an underhand [sic] or surreptitious organization of separate locals; the members assuming that this is the only course by which they can escape from falling into the Scylla of promiscuous locals on one side, and the Charybdis of the national discountenance expected for an open party declaration on the other side. But there is something so cowardly in such a proceeding; it is so repugnant to every principle of common honesty and so hypocritical in character; that as a remedy for the situation it must, in my estimation, be considered worse than the disease. Besides serving as an apple of discord among the comrades themselves, it must place a powerful weapon in the hands of our opponents, and tend to alienate instead of conciliating or drawing the black comrades into the movement. Besides, I do not see how the National Party could consistently with its self-respect, allow itself to connive at such a proceeding should it involve a violation of the national constitution.

But, on the other hand, I consider separate locals as the only method by which the black comrades can be assimilated into the movement, to any considerable extent in the South.

I believe a national attempt to coerce the admission of negroes into white locals would result in a disastrous failure. In the first place, I do not believe the black comrades themselves could be prevailed upon to obtrude their presence into unwelcome locals. And in the second place if they made the attempt, I believe they would be black-balled; but if they were not black-balled, I believe their admission into white locals would tend to weaken and stunt if not even to disrupt the movement entirely among the white element in many localities.

I have no doubt that official sanction for the creation of separate locals would be hailed by the comrades of both races with a feeling of welcome and relief; and that it would greatly facilitate and accelerate the organization of the negroes by directing it along the line of least resistance.

Such a step need not carry violence to any of those necessary regulations of a territorial or other character without which it would not be possible to carry on the proceedings of the Party. And instead of denying any rights to the negroes, it would in fact be securing to them the exercise of a right from which they are now largely debarred by the sentiment hereinabove considered.

If we are going to have negro locals, it may be asked, why, then, not also have Jewish locals, Italian locals, German locals, or locals for all the different races of this country? And in answer to this objection, I can only repeat why not? Why should we not have Italian locals, for instance?

In some quarters of our big cities, the population is composed almost entirely of Italians who do not understand and cannot speak [the] English language. Is there not something unjust in expecting such people to become members of the regular locals without being able to participate in the deliberations or to vote intelligently on the questions that come up for consideration? Is it not evidently to the interest of the movement that such people should be encouraged to join the party by the creation of locals in which the official proceedings would be carried on in a language which they can speak and understand? Would not this be the shortest, quickest and most efficacious method of securing those equal political and economic rights for which the Socialist Republic stands? And can there be anything repugnant to the true tactics of the party or the principles of the Socialist Philosophy in anything which will hasten the advent of Socialism itself?

In New Orleans, we have an Italian local holding a charter, not from the National Party of the United States or the State Party of Louisiana, but from the Socialist Party of Italy. Many of its members are citizens, but as they do not understand the English language, they prefer to have their own "academic" local, rather than constitute but so many figureheads in the English speaking locals; and, therefore they do not take any active part in the internal affairs of the movement of this country. I believe such locals should be taken into our own movement.

Now, if the obstacle of language may properly be removed by the creation of special locals, why not also the obstacle of color or race, or any other obstacle which can be removed better by exceptional than by the regular locals?

That fatal economism or economic determinism which we are told levels down all racial barriers, has it thrown down the barriers between the Gentile and Jewish races? The Jewish race contributes its share to the economic rulers and the proletariat of every country; it forms a component part of every nation in the civilized world, and furnishes as many national types as there are different nations; yet it preserves and maintains its racial integrity everywhere . . .

May it not be, therefore, that the economic advantages and political rights of the negroes could be secured to them better by a method which would tend to preserve or maintain their integrity as a race, than otherwise?

Be that as it may, there is no doubt that so far as the organization of the party is concerned, the creation of optional locals for the negroes would be conducive to the advancement of the movement, by securing to them a means of exercising their right to participate in the party, from which they are now deprived, and as such I should like to have it specifically sanctioned by a national expression.

SOCIALISM AND THE NEGRO
E.F. Andrews
*International Socialist Review*
5 (March 1905) 524–26

. . . Socialism is primarily an economic and industrial movement, the object of which is to secure to every man, white and black alike, economic justice and equality in the full enjoyment of the product of his labor. It has no direct concern with questions of social equality, whether between individuals or races. If I object to associating with a person because he has blue eyes or red hair, I may be acting foolishly, but nobody has the right to compel me to do otherwise so long as I accord my blue-eyed or red-headed brother the economic justice that Socialism claims for him. Similarly, if I object to consorting with a man because he has a black skin or a red skin or a dirty skin, nobody has a right to coerce me, so long as I leave him in undisturbed possession of the fruits of his labor. And by parity of reasoning, it seems to me that any interpretation of the national constitution of the Socialist Party which would make it infringe upon the right of every individual to choose his own company, by making a mixture of the races in the locals obligatory, would be as unsocialistic in principle as it would be disastrous in effect to the interests of the party in the South.

Socialism has made headway slowly in the Southern States, not because our people are lacking in intelligence to appreciate its claims, but because of the prevalence of conditions which have forced the whites into an iron-bound political solidarity that left no room for independent initiative and held it fast in blind allegiance to the only party which seemed to offer aid in a situation of peril so imminent as to thrust economic and industrial questions into the background. But the collapse of the old Democratic fetish in the last election has cleared the way for other gods. The farmers, left helpless by the downfall of their old political Baal, and their precious panacea of "restricting production" having worked itself out to the logical absurdity of making themselves rich by burning their cotton, are running hither and thither, vainly inquiring "What shall we do to be saved?" Socialism alone can point out to them the true way of political salvation. There never was such an opportunity offered to any party for the success of its propaganda as is opened to the Socialist Party to the South today, and it would be the height of political folly to choose such a moment for flaunting the red rag of "social equality" in its face; for nothing is more certain than that neither Socialism nor any other philosophy will ever make headway at the South which seems to carry with it the menace of a repetition of our terrible reconstruction experiences.

It is difficult for a Southerner to discuss the social phase of the race question intelligibly with our Northern comrades, on account of the difference in the point of view. When a Northern man talks about the negro, he too often means Booker Washington, or some other distinguished member of the race, who is perhaps the only negro that he knows anything about. When a Southerner talks on the same subject, he means some eight millions of more or less civilized people, belonging to a race in a stage of evolution so far removed from our own that for aught we can see at present, assimilation must be impossible for an indefinite period. Now, it would seem but reasonable to suppose that people who have lived in actual contact with eight million negroes all their lives are better qualified by experience to establish the social relations of the races on a satisfactory working basis, than those of our comrades whose ideas are influenced by what they have heard about some few exceptional negroes. It would be just as reasonable to attempt to measure the average white man by the standard of Shakespeare or Victor Hugo. It is not a question here of dealing with a few picked individuals of either race, but with the rank and file of several millions of ordinary human beings in widely different stages of evolution, and the feeling that induces two races so distinct to seek separate social relations is not a mere local or transient prejudice, but a biological fact as old as the first dawn of life. "Each to its kind," is a law of nature so rigidly adhered to throughout the whole scale of animate existence that it must have served some useful purpose in the scheme of evolution, and we have no reason to infer that it can be violated by us with impunity.

This social cleavage along the lines of ethnical cleavage is not necessarily an expression of antagonism or contempt on the part of the dominant race towards the people so segregated. The Jews, for instance, the most gifted race the world has ever known, are today, even in civilized countries, living in a state of more or less complete segregation from their gentile neighbors, and yet, whatever stupid and wicked prejudices may have led to this separation in the first place, no one will claim that there is, in any civilized community deserving the name, any vestige of ill-will between the two peoples. The Jew regards the descendants of his mediaeval [sic] persecutors without bitterness, and certainly no modern man in his senses, least of all a Socialist, would dream of looking down on a race that has given to the world three such names as Moses, Jesus and Karl Marx. Such being the case, we may regard the sentiment that still keeps Jew and Gentile two separate groups in civilized America, as an inherited survival from the ages of superstition. Now, if a purely psychological impression of this kind, which we know to have been artificially acquired within historic times, can be so persistent that generations have not been able to efface it, how can we expect to extinguish at will that inveterate biological law of like to like which nature herself has interposed between widely differing races, and without which the evolution of life as we now know it, would have been impossible?

The moral of all this is that the Socialist Party keep itself free from unnecessary complications with the race question and all other side issues that do not immediately concern it. Its duty to the negro is to insist that he gets full economic justice. If he prove as efficient a laborer as the white man, he will get under Socialism, the same reward; if he prefers to be idle and inefficient, he will get precisely the same treatment as the idle and inefficient of the white or any other race. But his social status is not a proper subject for legislation any more than it would be to legislate you or me, or our friends Tom, Dick, and Harry, into the society of the Astors and Vanderbilts by an act of congress—a step that would prove as little acceptable to you and me, no doubt, as to the Vanderbilts and Astors themselves. Matters of this kind can be settled only by the free will of the parties concerned, and so the question of mixed or separate organizations for locals of different races should be left entirely to the option of the locals themselves. If a community in Wisconsin or Massachusetts desires to have a mixed local of whites and blacks, that is their affair; and if a community in Alabama or Louisiana prefers to have mixed locals, that also is their affair; and if a community, in Alabama or Louisiana prefers to have separate locals, that also is their affair, and nobody has a right to coerce them. If the national constitution should be held to take any other ground than this, it must be frankly admitted that the effect upon the prospects of Socialism in the South would be disastrous. As one who has long been working for the cause in this section, I will state that I have met with more opposition on this one point than all others. There is a fear—in many cases, a settled belief, that the Socialist Party stands committed to a repetition of the Republican blunders that have proved so fatal in the past, and it would greatly strengthen the hands of Southern workers if the National organization would convey some explicit assurance that it will not commit itself to anything so contrary to the principles of Socialism as would be an attempt to coerce the people of any race or section in matters that should be left to the social conveniences of the communities concerned.

## African-American Socialist Views

### Socialist of the Path
W.E.B. Du Bois
*The Horizon*
1 (February 1907): 7

I am a Socialist-of-the-Path. I do not believe in the complete socialization of the means of production—the entire abolition of private property in capital—but the Path of Progress and common sense certainly leads to a far greater ownership of the public wealth for the public good than is now the case. I do not believe that the government can carry on private business as well as private concerns, but I do believe that most of the human business called private is no more private than God's blue sky, and that we are approaching a time when railroads, coal mines and many factories can and ought to be run by the public for the public. This is the way, as I see it, that the path leads and I follow it gladly and hopefully.

NEGRO AND SOCIALISM
W.E.B. Du Bois
*The Horizon*
1 (February 1907): 7–8

In the socialistic trend thus indicated lies the one great hope of the Negro American. We have been thrown by strange historic reasons into the hands of the capitalists hitherto. We have been objects of dole and charity, and despised accordingly. We have been made tools of oppression against the workingman's cause—the puppets and playthings of the idle rich. Fools! We must awake! Not in a renaissance among ourselves of the evils of Get and Grab—not in private hoarding, squeezing and cheating, lies our salvation, but rather in that larger ideal of human brotherhood, equality of opportunity and work not for wealth but for Weal—here lies our shining goal. This goal the Socialists with all their extravagance and occasional foolishness have more stoutly followed than any other class and thus far we must follow them. Our natural friends are not the rich but the poor, not the great but the masses, not the employers but the employees. Our good is not wealth, power, oppression and snobbishness, but helpfulness, efficiency, service and self-respect. Watch the Socialists. We may not follow them and agree with them in all things. I certainly do not. But in trend and ideal they are the salt of this present earth.

HOW AND WHY I BECAME A SOCIALIST
Rev. Geo. W. Slater, Jr.
*Chicago Daily Socialist*
September 8, 1908

Having been asked to write an article each week for the Chicago Daily Socialist pertaining to the subject of "Socialism and the Negro Race," and as I have espoused the principles of Socialism just lately, I think it will be both interesting and profitable that in my first article I should relate "How and why I became a Socialist."

Now, it is obvious to me that the reason why I had not espoused the Socialist cause heretofore was due on the one hand to ignorance of its principles, purposes and methods, and also due on the other hand to prejudice which had been engendered by cunning innuendoes and prevalent falsehood disseminated by its detractors. It is all so plain to me now. What a lesson I have learned. How consistent and wise it is to "prove all things" before passing judgment.

Now, for my experience which prepared me for Socialism. Last winter, when my parishioners had little work and little money and the prices of food were exorbitant, I contrived a co-operative scheme whereby I could furnish them food very near the wholesale price.

Before a salesman for a certain wholesale house in this city I laid my plans.

He told me that my plans were feasible and that I could get the goods. He also said that I could save the people at least 25 or 30 per cent on their gross purchases.

At once, I put a young man to soliciting orders. After I had sent in my order I got a letter from the salesman asking me to call immediately. I complied, whereupon he said that he was sorry to inform me that the management of the firm had refused to permit him to fill my order because I was not a bona-fide retail dealer, that I was not buying to sell again at a profit. He said that I must have a store and sell over a counter.

I admitted that I was not seeking profit, but that I was endeavoring to help a large number of poor consumers, and that my plan calculated to get the goods to the people as directly as possible from the wholesale house or the producers, thus cutting out the middleman's profit and the added expense of rehandling.

Upon these grounds I insisted that he should sell me the goods. Then I was plainly told the wholesale people had an understanding with the retail dealers that would make such a business transaction with me a direct violation of that agreement. And further, I was told that if they sold me the goods for the purpose for which I wanted them that the retail dealers would boycott them.

To this I replied, "Is it true that there is an understanding between the wholesale and retail dealers, whereby the poor consumer is compelled to pay more than is necessary for the necessities of life!" The salesman replied by saying, "Mr. Slater, if I had my way I would sell them to you, but I am under orders."

Chagrined and indignant I returned and told my people of the turn of affairs. But I said in my heart and also before the public that such a situation and such agreements were unjust and in the face of such hard times, positively wicked, and that I would find a way out of and break up such a situation.

To carry out my determination I began to inquire about President Roosevelt's "trust busters," as they are called; but I soon found that the trusts were busting the busters.

Several other plans were suggested to me, but I found that they were inadequate. The more I studied the more I saw the direful conditions of the poor people.

About four weeks ago I saw, at the corner of Thirtieth and State streets, a colored man speaking to a very attentive audience. When I drew near I learned that it was Mr. G. Woodby [sic], a national Socialist organizer, whom I had chanced to meet on a north-bound Halsted street car one Monday morning last May, during the Socialist National Presidential convention.

To Mr. Woodby [sic] I listened very attentively. Two or three times afterwards I made it convenient to hear him. I bought several books on the subject of Socialism and read them eagerly. The more I read the more I was entranced with the purity, simplicity and justice of the principles, purposes and methods of Socialism. I saw that tenets of Socialism were the solution of my problem; the ethics of Jesus in economic action; the solution of the poverty question with its attendant evils; the making possible of a practical brotherhood; the solution of the more serious phases of the so-called race problem.

When the facts were made plain to me I at once espoused its cause, brought it before my people, and threw open my church for a Socialist meeting every Tuesday night at 2965 Dearborn street.

THE NEW EMANCIPATION
G.W. Woodbey
*Chicago Daily Socialist*
January 18, 1909

In 1776 the work of the agitators of this country culminated in the issuing of that revolutionary document, known as the declaration of independence, declaring their emancipation from Great Britain and sounding the final death-knell of the so-called divine right of kings, and declared that "All just governments derive their power from the consent of the governed."

The idea then expressed was not that the people might govern themselves, but only that no one should assume to do it without their consent. But, nevertheless, it had in it the seeds of further revolution. Among English speaking people the idea may be traced back to the days of King John in

1215, when the barons forced him from the magna charta. While this was not the work of the masses of poor, yet it served in after ages to put hope into them for better things, as the work of forcing the king could not be done without the aid of the poor class who served these same barons.

Jefferson never dreamed of the broad construction that we Socialists are now putting upon his declaration, "All men are born equal, and are endowed by their Creator with certain inalienable rights, among which is life, liberty and the pursuit of happiness." This notion of equality, while it may at times have been a drawback by satisfying the individual citizen with poor conditions, yet on the other hand it may be now turned to good account as the working man is waking up to the fact that a great deal of the boasted rights which he thought he was secure in have either gone glimmering or else he never really possessed what belongs to him. So the average Socialist sees in it not only political but economic equality.

This work of the fathers was not the work of a day, but required hard work and bitter agitation which caused the revolutionary agitator of that time to be hated then as now as a common enemy of society.

Many of the revolutionists of a hundred years ago were born aristocrats, having little or no sympathy with the poor workers: but they could not accomplish their purpose without them so that now what they said and did will help us in our work.

The present exploiter of the working people can see the sacredness of the revolution of a hundred years ago, but like their Tory ancestry they hang, shoot and imprison the revolutionist of today, who would go on to complete the work begun in the past.

But after all we know that with few exceptions the owners of everything in all ages have stood on the side where they thought their material interest lay.

But in spite of those who would block the wheels of progress the agitator of a right cause is bound to succeed in the end.

We have progressed from an autocracy or government of one man to one that limits the power vested in that one man, by lodging it in the hands of the people. This representative form of government might just as well be called a limited monarchy as a republic and both of them are open to the danger of being turned into a plutocracy or government of the rich, such as we now have in this country, leaving us only the shadow of a government representing the people. Thus it has come about that the men now in congress represent the holding[s] of the rich rather than the masses of the people. What else is meant by a business administration such as Taft is expected to give us? How much business has the working man?

But so long as we recognize the right of the individual to own what the public must use, he must control government in order to protect his holdings.

The next great revolutionary document was Lincoln's emancipation proclamation, issued September 22, 1862, to take effect January 11, 1863. This proclamation, like that of the declaration of independence was the culmination of a fierce agitation which raged for more than a half century, and has not inaptly been styled "the romance of American history."

In this case the slaveholders, like the capitalist, were compelled to control the powers of government in order to protect what they deemed their rights, and slavery died when they could no longer do that.

The slave power, like that of the capitalist, was a gradual growth on the western hemisphere from the time when the Spanish landed the first slaves from Africa in 1517 down to the time when the abolition agitation overturned the whole thing. It would be useless to recount the many horrors through which the negro slaves passed in their capture on the slave coast, in their passage to this country—the bull whip, the slave pen and the auction block—because it is too much like the policeman's club, the lockout and the bullpens from which white and black workers are now suffering. This however, together with the feudal system, shows that the negro was not enslaved because he was a negro, but because it was supposed that more profit could be made out of his labor. For attempting to overthrow the slave system Lincoln and Lovejoy were shot, John Brown was hung, while Garrison, Philips and Fred Douglas were mobbed.

But the workers of all colors now find themselves in need of another emancipation, from a condition of wage slavery which as completely robs them of the hundreds of millions of wealth produced by their labor as did chattel slavery. The agitation is now going on for the new emancipation, and the agitators are equally hated and despised.

Many of the negroes who are just now beginning to wake up to the fact that there is something wrong, are yet under the impression that the accumulation of wealth in the hands of a few negroes will solve this problem, and that, too, notwithstanding the fact that a few white men have all the wealth and the rest of their brothers are getting poorer every day.

Give the negro along with others the full product of his labor by wrenching the industries out of the hands of the capitalist and putting them into the hands of the workers and what is known as the race problem will be settled forever. Socialism is only another one of those great world movements which is coming to bless mankind. The Socialist party is simply the instrument for bringing it about, and the negro and all other races, regardless of former conditions are invited into its folds.

## Socialism and the Negro Problem
W. E. Burghardt Du Bois
*The New Review*
1 (February 1, 1913): 138–41

One might divide those interested in Socialism in two distinct camps: On the one hand those far-sighted thinkers who are seeking to determine from the facts of modern industrial organization just what the outcome is going to be; on the other hand, those who suffer from the present industrial situation and who are anxious that, whatever the broad outcome may be, at any rate the present suffering which they know so well shall be stopped. It is this second class of social thinkers who are interested particularly in the Negro problem. They are saying that the plight of ten million human beings in the United States, predominantly of the working class, is so evil that it calls for much attention in any program of future social reform. This paper, however, is addressed not to this class, but rather to the class of theoretical Socialists; and its thesis is: In the Negro problem as it presents itself in the United States, theoretical Socialism of the twentieth century meets a critical dilemma.

There is no doubt as to the alternatives presented. On the one hand, here are 90 million white people who in their extraordinary development present a peculiar field for the application of Socialistic principles; but on the whole, these people are demanding to-day that just as under capitalistic organization the Negro has been the excluded (i. e., exploited) class, so, too, any Socialistic program shall also exclude the ten million. Many Socialists have acquiesced in this program. No recent convention of Socialists has dared to face fairly the Negro problem and make a straightforward declaration that they regard Negroes as men in the same sense that other persons are. The utmost that the party has been able to do is not to rescind the declaration of an earlier convention. The general attitude of thinking members of the party has been this: We must not turn aside from the great objects of Socialism to take up this issue of the American Negro; let the question wait; when the objects of Socialism are achieved, this problem will be settled along with other problems.

That there is a logical flaw here, no one can deny. Can the problem of any group of ten million be properly considered as "aside" from any program of Socialism? Can the objects of Socialism be achieved so long as the

Negro is neglected? Can any great human problem "wait"? If Socialism is going to settle the American problem of race prejudice without direct attack along these lines by Socialists, why is it necessary for Socialists to fight along other lines? Indeed, there is a kind of fatalistic attitude on the part of certain transcendental Socialists, which often assumes that the whole battle of Socialism is coming by a kind of evolution in which active individual effort on their part is hardly necessary.

As a matter of fact, the Socialists face in the problem of the American Negro this question: Can a minority of any group or country be left out of the Socialistic problem? It is, of course, agreed that a majority could not be left out. Socialists usually put great stress on the fact that the laboring class form a majority of all nations and nevertheless are unjustly treated in the distribution of wealth. Suppose, however, that this unjust distribution affected only a minority, and that only a tenth of the American nation were working under unjust economic conditions: Could a Socialistic program be carried out which acquiesced in this condition? Many American Socialists seem silently to assume that this would be possible. To put it concretely, they are going to get rid of the private control of capital and they are going to divide up the social income among these 90 million in accordance with some rule of reason, rather than in the present haphazard way: But at the same time, they are going to permit the continued exploitation of these ten million workers. So far as these ten million workers are concerned, there is to be no active effort to secure for them a voice in the Social Democracy, or an adequate share in the social income. The idea is that ultimately when the 90 millions come to their own, they will voluntarily share with ten million serfs.

Does the history of the world justify us in expecting any such outcome? Frankly, I do not believe it does. The program is that of industrial aristocracy which the world has always tried; the only difference being that such Socialists are trying to include in the inner circle a much larger number than have ever been included before. Socialistic as this program may be called, it is not real Social Democracy. The essence of Social Democracy is that there shall be no excluded or exploited classes in the Socialistic state; that there shall be no man or woman so poor, ignorant or black as to not count one. Is this simply a far off ideal, or is it a possible program? I have come to believe that the test of any great movement toward social reform is the Excluded Class. Who is it that Reform does *not* propose to benefit? If you are saving dying babies, whose babies are you going to let die? If you are feeding the hungry, what folk are you (regretfully, perhaps, but none the less truly) going to let starve? If you are making a juster division of wealth, what people are you going to permit at present to remain in poverty? If you are giving all men votes (not only in the "political" but also in the economic world), what class of people are you going to allow to remain disfranchised?

More than that, assuming that if you did exclude Negroes temporarily from the growing Socialistic state, the ensuing uplift of humanity would in the end repair the temporary damage, the present question is, *can* you exclude the Negro and push Socialism forward? Every tenth man in the United States is of acknowledged Negro descent; if you take those in gainful occupations, one out of every seven Americans is colored; and if you take laborers and workingmen in the ordinary acceptation of the term, one out of every five is colored. The problem is then to lift four-fifths of a group on the backs of the other fifth. Even if the submerged fifth were "dull driven cattle," this program of Socialistic opportunism would not be easy. But when the program is proposed in the face of a group growing in intelligence and social power and a group made suspicious and bitter by analogous action on the part of trade unionists, what is anti-Negro Socialism doing but handing to its enemies the powerful weapon of four and one-half million men who will find it not simply to their interest, but a sacred duty to underbid the labor market, vote against labor legislation, and fight to keep their fellow laborers down. Is it not significant that Negro soldiers in the army are healthier and desert less than whites?

Nor is this all: what becomes of Socialism when it engages in such a fight for human downfall? Whither are gone its lofty aspiration and high resolve—its songs and comradeship?

The Negro Problem then is the greatest test of the American Socialist. Shall American Socialism strive to train for its Socialistic state ten million serfs who will serve or be exploited by that state, or shall it strive to incorporate them immediately into that body politic? Theoretically, of course, all Socialists, with few exceptions, would wish the latter program. But it happens that in the United States there is a strong local opinion in the South which violently opposes any program of any kind of reform that recognizes the Negro as a man. So strong is this body of opinion that you have in the South a most extraordinary development. The whole radical movement there represented by men like Blease and Vardaman and Tillman and Jeff. Davis and attracting such demagogues as Hoke Smith, includes in its program of radical reform a most bitter and reactionary hatred of the Negro. The average modern Socialist can scarcely grasp the extent of this hatred; even murder and torture of human beings holds a prominent place in its philosophy; the defilement of colored women is its joke, and justice toward colored men will not be listened to. The only basis on which one can even approach these people with a plea for the barest tolerance of colored folk, is that the murder and mistreatment of colored men may possibly hurt white men. Consequently the Socialist party finds itself in this predicament: if it acquiesces in race hatred, it has a chance to turn the tremendous power of Southern white radicalism toward its own party; if it does not do this, it becomes a "party of the Negro," with its growth South and North decidedly checked. There are signs that the Socialist leaders are going to accept the chance of getting hold of the radical South whatever its cost. This paper is written to ask such leaders: After you have gotten the radical South and paid the price which they demand, will the result be Socialism?

## THE NEGRO PARTY
*The Crisis*
12 (October 16, 1916): 268–69

There is for the future one and only one effective political move for colored voters. We have long foreseen it, but we have sought to avoid it. It is a move of segregation, it "hyphenates" us, it separates us from our fellow Americans; but self-defense knows no nice hesitations. The American Negro must either vote as a unit or continue to be politically emasculated as at present.

Miss Inez Milholland, in a recent address, outlined with singular clearness and force a Negro Party on the lines of the recently formed Woman's Party. Mr. R.R. Church, Jr., of Tennessee, and certain leading colored men in New Jersey, Ohio and elsewhere have unconsciously and effectively followed her advice.

The situation is this: At present the Democratic party can maintain its ascendency [*sic*] only by the help of the Solid South. The Solid South is built on the hate and fear of Negroes; consequently it can never, as a party, effectively bid for the Negro vote. The Republican party is the party of wealth and big business and, as such, is the natural enemy of the humble working people who compose the mass of Negroes. Between these two great parties, as parties there is little to choose.

On the other hand, parties are represented by individual candidates. Negroes can have choice in the naming of these candidates and they can vote for or against them. Their only effective method in the future is to organize in every congressional district as a Negro Party to endorse those candidates, Republican, Democratic, Socialist, or what-not, whose promises and past performances give greatest hope for the remedying of the wrongs done the Negro race. If no candidate fills this bill they should nominate a candidate of their own and give that candidate their solid vote. This policy effectively and consistently carried out throughout the United States, North and South, by colored voters who refuse the bribe of petty office and money, would make the Negro vote one of the most powerful and effective of the group votes in the United States.

This is the program which we must follow. We may hesitate and argue about it, but if we are a sensible, reasonable people we will come to it and the quicker the better.

## An African-American Socialist Newspaper: *The Messenger*

### Some Reasons Why Negroes Should Vote the Socialist Ticket
*The Messenger*
November 1917

1. Because the Socialist Party is the Party of the workingman.

2. Because 90 per cent of Negroes are working people.

3. Because the Socialist Party advocates the abolition of high rents by taxing land to its full value.

4. Because the Negroes of New York suffer more than any other people from high rents on account of being segregated and being compelled to live in a special part of the city.

5. Because the Socialist Party advocates the establishment of city markets to sell meat, milk, butter, eggs and vegetables at wholesale prices.

6. Because this market will be run for service and not for profits: it will cut down the present high cost of living.

7. Because the Negroes are the first and hardest hit victims of the high cost of living on account of the starvation wages which they receive.

8. Because the Socialist Party advocates the ownership and operation of the subway, elevated and surface car lines, the electric gas and telephone companies.

9. Because this will cheapen the price of gas, electric light, telephone service and transportation.

10. (a)  In Cleveland, Ohio, the city-owned car lines charge only 3 cents for car fare.

    (b)  In most European cities, gas, electric light, telephone service and transportation cost much less than in American cities because they are owned and operated by the cities.

    (c)  Just as the Post Office, which is run for the benefit of the people and not for the benefit of a few rich individuals, carries your letter for 2 cents instead of 5 cents, which was the case when private companies carried the mails, so will you get cheaper light and transportation when the city owns these public utilities and operates them for service and not for profits.

11.     Because the Negro young man and young woman of education will be eligible to compete in civil service examinations for positions as clerks, bookkeepers in the offices, ticket sellers and ticket choppers in the subway and elevated stations, conductors and motormen on the subway, elevated and surface car lines, gas and electric light meter inspectors, collectors, etc., in these city-owned enterprises.

12.     Because this will open up large avenues of employment for Negroes where they will receive more wages, perform more healthful work and have more leisure.

* * *     All Negroes must ride to work.

Negroes must use gas to light their houses.

Negroes must use gas to cook their food.

Negroes must use the telephone to telephone the doctors.

Hence they must be cheap in order that you may be able to use them when you have to.

13.     Because the Socialist Party advocates more and better schools for the children.

14.     Because this will enable the Negro child to get a better education.

15.     Because the Socialist Party advocates free books free food and free clothing for school children.

16.     Because this will enable poor negro families to keep their children in school.

17.     Because the Socialist Party advocates more playgrounds for children.

18.     Because this will prevent negro children who on account of the lack of playgrounds play in the street from being run over and maimed and killed by automobiles.

19.     Because the Socialist Party advocates more efficient police system, which will use more brains than billies.

20.     Because this protects negroes from ruthless assaults by policemen.

21.     Because the Socialist Party advocates equal industrial and political opportunity to all men and women regardless of race, creed or color.

22.     Because the Socialist Party advocates the abolition of our present wage system which overworks and underpays and destroys our bodies and our minds.

23.     Because the Socialist Party is the party of economic and political justice.

24.    Because the Socialist Party will win.

25.    Because the Socialist Party is for peace.

## WHO SHALL PAY FOR THE WAR
*The Messenger*
November 1917

Who shall pay for the war? This is the question every man and woman called upon to fight; to sacrifice in any way for the prosecution of the war, should ask. But the question should not stay there. The next question should be; who profits from the war? For obviously, those who profit from the war ought to pay for it. But these questions must be followed with a third question, viz: How can profits be made out of the war? The answer to the question is: by selling to the government those things which are needed to keep the war going; for instance, food and clothing for soldiers, steel for battleships, submarines, aeroplanes, coal for transports, etc. money to lend to the government.

Now, Mr. Common-man, do you own any of these things? If you don't, then you cannot profit from the war.

Then you ought to see to it that the government confiscates all profits made out of this war to carry on this war. Let the government take 100 per cent and peace will come.

## WORKMEN'S COUNCIL
*The Messenger*
November 1917

We welcome the formation of the Workmen's Council as one of the most timely and most needed, agencies in the industrial field . Its purpose is to democratize the labor forces in the country; to take them from under the ruthless and reactionary heels of the American Federation of Labor. The Workmen's Council ought to live long since it has a noble, valuable and laudable mission to perform in revivifying, consolidating and mobilizing the powers of labor for labor's final and complete emancipation.

The Workmen's Council must steer clear of the shoals of race prejudice upon which the American Federation of Labor, led by Mr. Gompers, has foundered.

Its primary tenet must be to help all labor without regard to race, creed or color. It is growing. It will win. All hail to the Workmen's Council!

## The Socialist Victory
*The Messenger*
January 1918

The Socialist Party won a great victory in New York City on the 6th of November. It elected eleven assemblymen, seven aldermen and a city court judge. Not only that, the Socialist Party increased its vote 400 per cent.

The trend of socialism is nationwide. Such increases took place all over the country. Chicago polled 34 per cent of the vote for the Socialist Party, and the Democratic and Republican parties there were saved from humiliating defeat only through their combination or fusion against the Socialist Party. Similar successes were registered in Ohio,—Cincinnati, Cleveland, Dayton, Toledo—Massachusetts, Pennsylvania and New Jersey.

The New York Negroes gave 25 per cent of their vote to the Socialists—a thing which gives the Negro the greatest political respect and honor he has ever attained. It stamps him as thinking and not blindly following the eagle—the emblem of the old hypocritical and lying Republican party.

Congratulations to the New Negro who votes the Socialist ticket. We want 50 per cent of the vote next time.

## Socialism The Negroes' Hope
W.A. Domingo
*The Messenger*
July 1919

It is a regrettable and disconcerting anomaly that, despite their situation as the economic, political and social door mat of the world, Negroes do not embrace the philosophy of socialism, and in greater numbers than they now do. It is an anomaly because it is reasonable to expect those who are lowest down to be the ones who would most quickly comprehend the need for a change in their status and welcome any doctrine which holds forth any hope of human elevation. In matters of religion they respond and react logically and naturally enough, for to them, the religion of Christ, the lowly Nazarene, brings definite assurance of surcease from earthly pains and the hope of celestial readjustment of mundane equalities. Their acceptance of the Christian religion with its present day emphasis upon an after-life enjoyment of the good things denied them on the earth is conclusive proof of their dissatisfaction with their present lot, and is an earnest of their susceptibility to Socialism, which intends to do for human beings what Christianity promises to do for them in less material regions.

That they and all oppressed dark peoples will be the greatest beneficiaries in a socialist world has not been sufficiently emphasized by Socialist propaganda among Negroes.

Perhaps this is not clearly understood, but a little examination of the facts will prove this to be the case.

Throughout the world Negroes occupy a position of absolute inferiority to the white race. This is true whether they are black Frenchmen, black Englishmen, black Belgians or black Americans.

As between themselves and the masses of white proletarians their lives are more circumscribed, their ambitions more limited and their opportunities for the enjoyment of liberty and happiness more restricted. White workingmen of England who are Socialists are immeasurably the political and social superiors of the average Negro in the West Indies or Africa; white workingmen of France, who are Socialists are unquestionably the political and social superiors of Senegalese and Madagascan Negroes; white workingmen of the United States who are Socialists are indisputably the social and political superiors of the millions of Negroes below the Mason and Dixon line; yet despite their relative and absolute superiority these white workers are fighting for a world freed from oppression and exploitation, whilst Negroes who are oppressed cling to past and present economic ideals with the desperation of a drowning man.

Socialism as an economic doctrine is merely the pure Christianity preached by Jesus, and practiced by the early Christians adapted to the more complex conditions of modern life. It makes no distinction as to race, nationality or creed, but like Jesus it says "Come unto me all ye who are weary and heavy laden and I will give you rest." It is to procure that rest that millions of oppressed peoples are flocking to the scarlet banner of international Socialism.

So far, although having greater need for its equalizing principles than white workingmen, Negroes have been slow to realize what has already dawned upon nearly every other oppressed people: That Socialism is their only hope.

The 384,000,000 natives of India groaning under the exploitation of the handful of English manufacturers, merchants and officials who profit out of their labor are turning from Lloyd George and the capitalistic Liberal Party to Robert Smillie, the Socialist and the Independent Labor Party. The 4,000,000 Irish who suffer national strangulation at the hands of British industrialists and militarists have turned to the Socialists of England for relief besides becoming Socialists themselves. The Egyptians who are of Negro admixture being convinced that their only hope for freedom from

British exploitation is in international Socialism are uniting forces with British Socialists and organized labor. In fact, every oppressed group of the world is today turning from Clemenceau, Lloyd George and Wilson to the citadel of Socialism, Moscow. In this they are all in advance of Western Negroes with the exception of little groups in the United States and a relatively well-organized group in the Island of Trinidad, British West Indies.

Because of ignorant and unscrupulous leadership, Negroes are influenced to give their support to those institutions which oppress them, but if they would only do a little independent thinking without the aid of preacher, politician or press they would quickly realize that the very men like Thomas Dixon, author of "The Clansman," Senators Hoke Smith of Georgia and Overman of North Carolina, who are fighting Socialism or as they maliciously call it Bolshevism, are the same men who exhaust every unfair means to villify [sic], oppress and oppose Negroes. If anything should commend Socialism to Negroes, nothing can do so more eloquently than the attitude and opinions of its most influential opponents toward people who are not white.

On the other hand, the foremost exponents of Socialism in Europe and America are characterized by the broadness of their vision towards all oppressed humanity. It was the Socialist Vendervelde of Belgium, who protested against the Congo atrocities practiced upon Negroes; it was the late Keir Hardie and Philip Snowdon of England, who condemned British rule in Egypt; and in the United States it was the Socialist, Eugene V. Debs, who refused to speak in Southern halls from which Negroes were excluded. Today, it is the revolutionary Socialist, Lenin, who analyzed the infamous League of Nations and exposed its true character; it is he as leader of the Communist Congress at Moscow, who sent out the proclamation: "Slaves of the colonies in Africa and Asia! The hour of proletarian dictatorship in Europe will be the hour of your release!"

NEGRO WORKERS: THE A.F. OF L. OR I.W.W.
*The Messenger*
July 1919

The giant, Labor, in all the world is awakening. Labor is slowly but surely beginning to realize that the fabric of civilization rests upon its shoulders. Only ignorance stands between labor and economic freedom. Ignorance is the mother of race prejudice, and prejudice still haunts the trail of labor. White and black workingmen, in the South, still fight over race prejudice, while the rich white plutocrats pick the pockets of both. The official American labor organization—the American Federation of Labor is criminally negligent and recreant to its duty, in either ignoring or opposing Negro workers.

Not only does it ignore Negro workers; however, as a rule it also ignores the unskilled worker and the women.

The American Federation of Labor, is essentially a craft or trades' union organization. The Negro is mostly an unskilled laborer. His interests lie with that group, which neither discriminates against workers on account of color, or on account of being unskilled.

There is but one question, which, more than any other, presses upon the mind of the worker today, regardless of whether he be of one race or another of one color or another—the question of how he can improve his conditions, raise his wages, shorten his hours of labor and gain something more of freedom from his master—the owners of the industry wherein he labors.

To the black race, who, but recently, with the assistance of the white men of the northern states broke their chains of bondage and ended chattel slavery, a prospect of further freedom, of REAL FREEDOM, should be most appealing.

For it is a fact that the Negro worker is no better off under the freedom he has gained than the slavery from which he has escaped. As chattel slaves we were the property of our masters, and, as a piece of valuable property, our masters were considerate of us and careful of our health and welfare. Today, as wage-earners, the boss may work us to death, at the hardest and most hazardous labor, at the longest hours, at the lowest pay; we may quietly starve when out of work and the boss loses nothing by it and has no interest in us. To him the worker is but a machine for producing profits, and when you, as a slave who sells himself to the master on the installment plan, become old, or broken in health or strength, or should you be killed while at work the master merely gets another wage slave on the same terms.

We who have worked in the South know that conditions in lumber and turpentine camps, in the fields of cane, cotton and tobacco, in the mills and mines of Dixie, are such that workers suffer a more miserable existence than ever prevailed among the chattel slaves before the great Civil War. Thousands of us have come and are coming northward, crossing the Mason and Dixon line seeking better conditions. As wage slaves we have run away from the masters in the South, but to become the wage slaves of the masters of the North. In the north we find that the hardest work and the poorest pay is our portion. We are driven while on the job and the high cost of living offsets any higher pay we might receive.

The white wage-worker is little, if any, better off. He is a slave the same as we are, and like us he is regarded by the boss only as a means of making profits. The working class as a whole, grows poorer and more miserable year by year, while the employing class, who do not work at all, enjoy wealth and luxury beyond the dreams of titled lords and kings.

As you are both wage-workers, you have a common interest in improving conditions of the wage-working class. Understanding this, the employing class seeks to engender race hatred between the two. He sets the black worker against the white worker and the white worker against the black, and keeps both divided and enslaved. Our change from chattel slaves to wage slaves has benefitted no one but the masters of industry. They have used us as wage slaves to beat down the wages of the white wage slaves, and by a continual talk of "race problems," "negro questions," "segregation," etc., make an artificial race hatred and division by poisoning the minds of both whites and blacks in an effort to stop any movement of labor that threatens the dividends of the industrial kings. Race prejudice has no place in a labor organization. As Abraham Lincoln has said, "The strongest bond that should bind man to man in human society is that between the working people of all races and all nations."

The only problem then, which the colored worker should consider, as a worker, is the problem of organizing with other working men in the labor organization that best expresses the interests of the whole working class against the slavery and oppression of the whole capitalist class. Such an organization is the I.W.W., the INDUSTRIAL WORKERS OF THE WORLD, the only labor union that has never, IN THEORY OR PRACTICE, since its beginning twelve years ago, barred the workers of any race or nation from membership. The following has stood as a principle of the I.W.W., embodied in its official constitution since its formation in 1905.

"By-Laws-Article 1. Section 1. No working man or woman shall be excluded from membership in Unions because of creed or color."

If you are a wage-worker you are welcome in the I.W.W. halls, no matter what your color. By this you may see that the I.W.W. is not a white man's union, not a black man's union, not a red or yellow man's union, but a WORKING MAN'S UNION. ALL OF THE WORKING CLASS IN ONE BIG UNION.

In the I.W.W. all wage-workers meet on common ground. No matter what language you may speak, whether you were born in Europe, in Asia or in any other part of the world, you will find a welcome as a fellow worker. In the harvest fields, where the I.W.W. controls, last summer saw white men, black men and Japanese working together as union men and raising the pay of all who gathered the grains. In the great strikes which the I.W.W. has conducted at Lawrence, Mass. in the woolen mills, in the iron mine [sic] of Minnesota and elsewhere, the I.W.W. has brought the workers of many races, colors and tongues together in victorious battles for a better life.

Not only does the I.W.W. differ from all organizations in regard to admission of all races, but there is a fundamental difference in form of organization from all other labor unions. You have seen other labor unions organized on craft or trade lines. Craft unionism means that any small section of any industry has a labor union separate from all other sections that cannot act in any concerted movement of labor because of this craft separation. For example, in the railroad industry there are the engineers' union, the conductors' union, the brakemen's union and many others on the road in the shops and yards.

Each union acts for itself and usually has time agreements with the companies for a term of years, each agreement ending at a different time than the others. When one craft union goes on strike at the end of the time agreement, the other craft unions keep at work and by remaining on the job act as scabs and strikebreakers in defeating their fellow workers of the craft on strike.

Thus in 1911 the men in the shops of the Harriman lines went on strike and the trainmen, who belonged to different craft unions, remained at work: the train crews took cars from and delivered cars to the strikebreakers in the shops because they were organized separately and had separate time agreements with the companies. The strike was lost because the railroad workers were organized wrong. The I.W.W. has INDUSTRIAL UNIONISM, which means that all crafts in any industry are organized together and act together. Had the I.W.W been in the place of the craft unions on the Harriman lines in 1911, all workers could have gone out together, not a wheel would have turned, not a train would have moved until the companies would have come to terms with the shopmen. For the I.W.W. makes no TIME AGREEMENTS with any employer and makes AN INJURY TO ONE AN INJURY TO ALL. The I.W.W. always leaves its members free to strike when they see an opportunity to better themselves or support their fellow workers.

The foundation of the I.W.W. is INDUSTRIAL UNIONISM. ALL workers in any division of any industry are organized into an INDUSTRIAL UNION OF ALL the workers in the ENTIRE INDUSTRY; these INDUSTRIAL UNIONS in turn are organized into INDUSTRIAL DEPARTMENTS of connecting, or kindred industries, while all are brought together in THE GENERAL ORGANIZATION OF THE INDUSTRIAL WORKERS OF THE WORLD—ONE BIG UNION OF ALL THE WORKING CLASS OF THE WORLD. No one but actual wage workers may join. The working class cannot depend upon anyone but itself to free it from wage slavery. "He who would be free, himself must strike the blow."

When the I.W.W., through this form of INDUSTRIAL UNIONISM, has become powerful enough, it will institute an INDUSTRIAL COMMONWEALTH; it will end slavery and oppression forever and in its place will be a world of workers, by the workers and for the workers; a world where there will be no poverty and want among those who feed and clothe and house the world; a world where the words "master" and "slave" shall be forgotten; a world where peace and happiness shall reign and where the children of men shall live as brothers in a world-wide INDUSTRIAL DEMOCRACY. . . .

## WHY NEGROES SHOULD JOIN THE I.W.W.
*The Messenger*
July 1919

The I.W.W. is the only labor organization in the United States which draws no race or color line. It deals chiefly, too, with unskilled labor and most Negroes are unskilled laborers. They stand on the principle of industrial unionism, which would necessarily include in its organization any Negroes in an industry. For instance, the Brotherhood of Railway Trainmen has in its organization, the conductors, firemen, engineers and switchmen. Negroes are not permitted to join, notwithstanding the fact that there are 149,000 Negroes engaged in the transportation work. The I.W.W. would include those 149,000 Negroes, who have the power, by stopping their work, to tie up the railroads as completely as the Big Four Brotherhood could. If the Negroes stopped loading the cars, repairing the tracks and producing the materials which are necessary for transportation, the engineers would have nothing to carry, but the Big Four Brotherhoods are so highly American that they are shot through with race prejudice which blinds them to their enlightened self interest.

There is another reason why Negroes should join the I.W.W. The Negro must engage in direct action. He is forced to do this by the government. When the whites speak of direct action, they are told to use their political power. But with the Negro it is different. He has no political power. Three-fourths of the Negroes in the United States are disfranchised. Over two million Negro men pay taxes but cannot vote. Therefore, the only recourse the Negro has is industrial action, and since he must combine with those forces which draw no line against him, it is simply logical for him to throw his lot with the Industrial Workers of the World. Nor do the Negroes need to bother about the abuse heaped on the I.W.W. Most of it is lies, told by their opponents, just as the opponents of the Negroes lie about them. Again it needs to be noted that most of the forces opposed to the I.W.W.

are also opposed to Negroes. John Sharp Williams, Vardaman, Hoke Smith, Thomas Dixon, D.W. Griffith, who produced the Birth of a Nation—and practically all the anti-Negro group, are opposed to the I.W.W. Now, as a general proposition and principle, if we found John Sharp Williams, Vardaman, Hoke Smith, Thomas Dixon and D.W. Griffith opposed to anything, we should be inclined to accept it on its face without an examination. And Negroes cannot afford to allow those Southern bourbons and race prejudiced crackers, together with their hand picked Negro leaders, to choose for them the organizations in which they shall go. The editors of the MESSENGER have made a thorough study of the economic and social problems in the United States. We know the history of labor organizations. We know their record on the race question. We have compared them carefully. We know that the American Federation of Labor is a machine for the propagation of race prejudice. We, therefore, urge the Negroes to join their international brothers, The Industrial Workers of the World, the I.W.W.

PSYCHOLOGY WILL WIN THIS WAR
Chandler Owen
*The Messenger*
July 1918

. . . . I maintain that since the Socialist party is supported financially by working men and women and since its platform is a demand for the abolition of this class struggle between the employer and the worker by taking over and democratically managing the sources and machinery of wealth production and exchange, to be operated for social service and not for private profits: and, further, since the Socialist party has always both in the United States and Europe, opposed all forms of race prejudice, that the Negro should no longer look upon voting the Republican ticket, as accepting the lesser of two evils; but that it is politically, economically, historically and socially logical and sound for him to reject both evils, the Republican and Democratic parties and select a positive good—Socialism.

The Negro like every other class should support that party which represents his chief interests. Who could imagine a brewer or saloonkeeper supporting the Prohibition party?

It's like an undertaker seeking the adoption of a law, if possible, to abolish death.

Such is not less ludicrous, however, than that of a Negro, living in virtual poverty, children without education, wife driven to the kitchen or the wash-tub; continually dispossessed on account of high rents; eating poor food on account of the high cost of food, working 10, 12 and 14 hours a day, and sometimes compelled to become sycophant and clownish for a favor, a "tip," supporting the party of Rockefeller, the party of his employer, whose chief interests are to overwork and underpay him. Let us abolish these contradictions and support our logical party—the Socialist party.

## WHY NEGROES SHOULD BE SOCIALISTS
*The Messenger*
October 1919

*The Negro and Labor*

First—Because the Socialist Party represents the workingman and 99 and $^9/_{10}$ per cent. of Negroes are working people.

(a) It can represent the working people because their dimes and quarters support it, they own and control it. Every measure, every policy, is referred to the members of the Socialist Party—they rule.

(b) This is not true of the Republican and Democratic parties; Rockefeller, Morgan, Armour . . . own and control them because they are large contributors to the campaign funds. And whoever finances the party, owns the party, whoever owns the party, controls the party, and whoever controls the party will use it for his own interest.

That is WHY YOU, MR. NEGRO workingman, cannot expect the Republican and Democratic parties, which are owned by big employers of labor, to demand more wages, shorter hours, and better working conditions—the chief needs of all Negroes.

*The Socialist Party Would Abolish Wage-Slavery*

Second—Because the Socialist Party would abolish wage-slavery. Today you work for wages. With wages you get food, clothing, and shelter. Without these things you cannot live. Hence, when wages are low, life is low. And wages are low because private men own the social tool with which you work. They desire to make profits. In order to make large profits they must pay low wages. This is simple. In other words they give you your life on an installment plan, in the form of enough wages per week to keep you barely alive. Your wages may be high but the cost of living is also high. A dollar today buys less than a half dollar bought years ago.

Think of it. You, your wife, and sometimes your children toil, toil, toil and for what? Cheap food, cheap clothing, cheap housing. Nothing more than an animal's existence you get. When death comes, it is but a relief from suffering, anxiety, failure, shame, poverty. Socialism will abolish this.

WHY NEGROES SHOULD BE SOCIALISTS
*The Messenger*
December 1919

*Education and the Negro*

Knowledge is power. Yes, that's true. But knowledge comes from study, and you cannot study, unless you have leisure; but during leisure you must have food, clothing and shelter, and, in order to have these necessities, you have got to have the means with which to get them. In short, you must have more than a mere workingman has.

Less than 2 per cent of the children in the Grammar Schools graduate from the high schools and a smaller percentage of those in the high schools reach the colleges. 21 per cent of the school children in New York City go to school daily, hungry. HOW HARMFUL! This condition is typical of school children throughout the country.

Your girls and boys are driven from the homes and schools into the factories, mills and mines to be ground up into dollars and dividends. There are 2,500,000 children who ought to be in schools, who are at work to help the father whose wages are low. Your children are growing up illiterate to be the preys and dupes of crooks and social vultures. A lack of education makes them hewers of wood and drawers of water— they are mere human machines that work, until worn out, and, like any other machine, goes to the human junk shop—the hospital, a human wreck.

The Republican and Democratic Parties cannot, nor do they desire to educate the youth of the nation. Because they serve the interests of big employers of labor, such as Shonts of the subway, Armour of the meat packing industry, and "OILY" Rockefeller, etc., who desire to exploit labor by paying labor low wages.

Capital can only rob labor when labor is unorganized, and labor will remain unorganized as long as it remains ignorant.

Nobody but a fool will allow a man or group of men to take away what he produces.

THE SOCIALIST would give the school children free food, free clothing and free doctor's care.

Are you opposed to this, Mr. Negro Voter?

A hungry child cannot study. A child shivering for the lack of clothes cannot study. Ponder these vital things and vote for more education for your children by voting the SOCIALIST TICKET; by becoming an ardent advocate of socialism.

And remember, that no Negro representative whom you might elect can do you any material good, who is elected on a Republican or Democratic ticket. No Republican or Democratic administration has objected to the low education given in the public schools of the south to Negroes.

The white people are nearly as ignorant as the black and yet, almost all government officials are white. It is not a question of race. The Republican and Democratic Government officials are not interested in educating the children of the masses, white or black.

Employers of labor want to exploit any kind of labor, white or black, man or woman, adult or child. Thus the officials, whom their campaign contributions elect, are compelled to do their bidding by opposing legislation calculated to create a more intelligent and consequently discontented workingclass.

*Poverty and the Negro*

Most Negro families are upon the brink of poverty. They are not striving to live but they are struggling to keep from dying. Poverty strangles and suffocates the mind.

Capitalism or the private ownership of the social tools of production and exchange, is the mother of poverty and poverty is the mother of ignorance, crime, prostitution, race prejudice, etc.

Republicans and Democrats support this system that raises property rights above human rights.

Socialism would abolish poverty and its consequences, by removing the causes of poverty—the profit system.

Socialism would remove Negro workers from the base of the working world.

MR. NEGRO WORKER ARE YOU OPPOSED TO THIS? . . .

IF YOU ARE NOT VOTE THE ENTIRE SOCIALIST TICKET.

# 8 THE SOCIALIST PARTY AND ETHNICITY AND IMMIGRATION

## PARTY DEBATES

### IMMIGRATION IN THE UNITED STATES
Morris Hillquit
*International Socialist Review*
8 (August 1907): 65–75

One of the important questions left undecided by the last International Social [*sic*] Congress was the attitude of Socialism towards immigration. The subject was as novel as it is large, and it found the delegates unprepared to deal with it in an intelligent and satisfactory manner. Of the two resolutions offered, the one drafted by the commission practically declared itself for unrestricted labor migration, while the other proposed by several representatives of Holland, Australia and the United States, voiced the opposition of organized labor to the importation into advanced countries of laborers of backward races, such as Chinese and African coolies. On the suggestion of Keir Hardie, both drafts were finally withdrawn in order to afford the socialist parties opportunity to make a more thorough study of the subject.

The discussion on Labor Immigration will be resumed in the coming Stuttgart Congress, and in conjunction with it the experience of the United States in that domain may play an important part in aiding the delegates to arrive at a proper solution of the problem.

The United States is the country of immigration par excellence, and that not only because, historically speaking, we are a nation of immigrants, but also because immigration has at all times been, and to present days remains, a most potent factor in the growth and development of our country, and in the formation of its industrial and social conditions.

The census of the United States in 1820 showed a total population of 9,638,453; in 1900 that number had risen to 76,303,387. If we consider that during the same period over 19,000,000 immigrants were admitted to the United States, and that the birth rate of immigrants is considerably higher than that of the natives, the conclusion is irresistible that they and their descendants constitute the bulk of the present population of the country.

The majority of "native" citizens to-day can probably not trace their American ancestry to more than two or three generations while the number of foreign born inhabitants in 1905 was between 13,000,000 and 14,000,000.

And the immigration is constantly increasing in volume. During the thirty-year period of 1850–1880, the average number of yearly arrivals vacillated pretty uniformly around a quarter of a million, in the succeeding two decades it rose to almost half a million, per year, and in 1905 the number of immigrants passed the million mark, and in 1906 it was over 1,250,000.

The United States is thus the classic soil of modern immigration, and the study of the sources and causes of that immigration, its effects on the welfare of the country, and particularly the working class of the country, are of more than local interest.

### Sources, Causes and Effects of Immigration

About the middle of the last century, the American immigration recruited itself chiefly from Ireland and Germany. In the decade of 1840 to 1850, nearly one-half of the total immigration was Irish, while one-quarter was German, and in the succeeding decade both nations were almost equally represented, and together constituted about two-thirds of all American immigration, the balance being chiefly made up of emigrants from England, Scotland, France and Sweden. The German, Irish English [sic] and Scandinavian immigration reached the highest point about 1880, but the last twenty-five years show a steady decline in the influx from this countries [sic]. Austro-Hungary, Italy and Russia henceforward supply the bulk of American immigrants. In 1870 all immigrants from the three countries mentioned constituted only one per cent, of the total immigration of the United States, in 1880 they rose to ten per cent, while in the five-years period of 1901 to 1905, two-thirds of all immigrants came from these countries. The number of Italian immigrants for that period was 959,768, that of the Austro-Hungarians 944,239, while Russia furnished 658,735.

The causes of this varying stream of immigration are to be found primarily in the industrial conditions of the countries of Europe as well as in those of the United States. It will be noticed that the American immigration commences to assume very large dimensions around the middle of the last century, i.e., at a time when in the more advanced countries of Europe the capitalist mode of production, with its inevitable blossoms of industrial crisis, unemployment and poverty, had reached a high point of development, while the United States was about entering on its industrial career, and had an abundance of cheap fertile land and other unexploited natural resources. The operation of this economic motive on immigration is clearly shown by the immediate effects of the fluctuating industrial conditions of the country on it. During the Civil War the immigration decreased to less than 90,000 in each of the years 1861 and 1862, in 1865 after the close of the war, it rose again to almost a quarter of a million, and continued increasing until 1873, when it reached the high record of 459,803. But the industrial depression ushered in by that year immediately reflected itself on the immigration which fell from year to year until 1878, when it was reduced to a total of 138,469. The somewhat milder depression of 1894–1898 again witnessed a falling off of almost half of the yearly immigration.

But the economic considerations are not the sole cause of immigration: political motives have also from time to time largely contributed to its growth. The defeat of the revolution in 1848 and the enactment of the Exceptional Laws of 1878 have in each case more than doubled the emigration from Germany; the French risings of 1848 and 1870 had a similar effect, and the political and religious persecutions of the Jews in Russia have resulted in a veritable exodus of the victims to America.

The immigration from these causes represents a natural and spontaneous movement, and must be carefully distinguished from immigration purposely and artificially stimulated.

For a very considerable portion of American immigration is produced by artificial and unscrupulous means, and the worst offenders in this respect are the trans-atlantic steamship companies. The business of steamship travel has increased enormously within the last decades, and more than $125,000,000 is said to be invested in the principal steamship lines. The chief source of profits of the industry is the carrying of steerage passengers. The steerage passengers are the least troublesome and best paying cargo: they are herded together in such numbers that a large ship frequently carries as many as 2000 of them, their food is of the cheapest, and they receive no attendance worth mentioning. It is, therefore, of the most vital interest to the steamship companies to solicit steerage passengers, and since steerage travel is rarely undertaken for pleasure, the traffic can only be supported by emigration. The part of the steamship companies and their agents in inducing emigration is not generally known or appreciated, for the reason that it is in most cases conducted clandestinely on account of the laws of the United States and some other countries prohibiting such practices. It is, however, an open secret that the principal lines maintain hosts of paid agents in all parts of Europe, whose business it is to induce the poor and the ignorant to seek wealth and happiness in the New World by glowing descriptions of the conditions in the United States, its high wages, free land and great opportunities. The Red Star Line formerly had no less than 1500 of such agents, the Anchor Line had 2500, and the Inman Line 3400. All of these are smaller concerns, and each of the other companies probably employ still larger numbers. But in addition to such professional solicitors, the steamship companies know how to press tens of thousands of amateur agents into their service . . . .

And the steamship companies are not the only capitalist concerns to stimulate artificial immigration to the United States. In many large industries, the employers find it to their advantage to import foreign labor; unskilled workingmen are imported in large numbers by mining concerns and by railroad companies engaged in the construction of new roads, on account of the low wages for which they consent to work; and skilled workingmen are generally imported in cases where the American workingmen are on strike, or where their organizations are so strong as to enable them to maintain a high standard of wages. Such skilled laborers from foreign countries are usually brought over under contracts of employment, written or oral.

But with all that the question of immigration had not, up to the latter part of the last century, attained to the dignity of a social problem in the United States. The unoccupied territory was so vast, and the nascent industries grew so rapidly that the powerful flow of immigration was easily absorbed by the new country.

Within the last generation, however, practically all the unappropriated and unreserved land of the country suitable for cultivation was disposed of, the inherent forces of the now fully developed capitalist system of production created the usual "surplus population" of workingmen, and the wisdom of continuing the policy of unrestricted immigration began to be questioned by both employers and employees.

To the employing class, on the whole, the problem was, comparatively speaking, simple. It is in the interest of that class to maintain not only a number of workingmen sufficient for the actual needs of the industries of the nation under existing conditions, but also a certain surplus or reserve army of unemployed in order to keep wages at a low level. Until that point had been reached in our labor population, immigration was encouraged and our good capitalists were exceedingly hospitable to the persecuted and oppressed coming from the different despotic countries of Europe. Our immigration laws were very liberal. But after that critical point had been reached, all further "surplus population" became not only unnecessary, but highly embarrassing. Our ruling classes consequently became more apprehensive of the evil social and moral influence of the foreigners of an inferior grade of civilization, and our laws show a tendency towards increasing strictness in the admission of immigrants.

These considerations apply to the capitalist class on the whole, but, of course, there are still the numerous individual capitalist concerns which have good use for cheap foreign labor, and these continue the wholesale importation of such labor in spite of any and all prohibitive laws.

*Attitude of Organized Labor*

As far as the American workingmen are concerned, only the organized portion of it has expressed definite views on the question, and these views are decidedly in favor of greater restriction of immigration.

Within the last thirty years or more the Order of Knights of Labor and the American Federation of Labor, have repeatedly adopted resolutions demanding such restrictions. Among the favorite demands of these organizations were a physical and educational test, prohibition of importation of contract labor and "assisted" immigration and even the wholesale exclusion of certain races.

Mr. Samuel Gompers presented the problem to the annual convention of that body in 1905, in the following language:

"More than a million immigrants landed on our shores during the years [sic] which ended June 30, 1905. For the greater part of them were men who have entered at once into the competition for work. They are already a part of our American industrial system. A few years hence many of them will be loyal and earnest members of the organization of their crafts, as many thousands who came like them a few years ago are loyal and earnest supporters of the American labor movement to-day.

"But in the meantime their coming places several problems before us. One is the problem of bringing them within the circle of the labor movement. Most of them have known nothing of the principles of unionism in their own country. Hard experience will give them some inkling of the need of united action, but to make them steady and intelligent union men requires our most careful and persistent effort.

"And while the organized labor of this country is struggling with this problem of education and organization, it cannot lose sight of the effect of these immigrants on the old and everpresent problem of maintaining and raising wages and shortening hours. Additional workers, anxious for a chance to labor, is [sic] calculated to diminish the share of the product of labor that goes to the laborer, and to increase the share that goes to the employer. Additional men anxious to work in shop of field or on railroad or in forest have precisely this effect; to enable the owners of land and of monopolies to get more of the product of the laborer's work, and to compel the laborer himself to take up with less.

"It is with no ill-will to our brothers from over the sea that we point out the unfortunate results of their coming. We have only good wishes for them. More than that, their interest is ours.***

"The greatest hindrance to the rapid rise of our million comrades who came in last year is the other millions who are coming after them. The competition of these other millions will hold them down, and in holding them down will hold down the whole body of American workers. We wish nothing but good to such future immigrants. But we hold that we ought not, for their good, as well as our own, to sacrifice the interests of all the workers on this continent and of the generations that are to follow.

"If we and our children are not to be sacrificed, some check must be put upon the constant overstocking of what some are pleased to term 'labor market'. Some check would have to be put upon it even if the competition between those who are here and those who are coming were on equal terms. But it is not equal. The great mass of our present-day immigration is far inferior to the great body of American workers, and for that very reason its competition is the more hurtful. The more ignorant and poorer a man is, the more completely is he at the mercy of an employer. The weaker he is in body or mind, the better can he be used to break down the independence of his fellows. Just as the cheap labor of women and children displaces the labor of men, so the cheap labor of the unenlightened immigrant displaces the labor of Americans who insist upon American wages and conditions.

"Though most concerned in our own interest and welfare, it is not these considerations entirely that prompt us to restrict, limit and regulate future immigration.***

"If the workingmen of foreign countries would more largely remain at home, conditions and circumstances would so develop that they would demand and secure material as well as political and social relief, and make for liberty and justice in their own countries. It is the free and unlimited opportunities for the workmen to leave their homes that perpetuates economic, social and political evils at home.

"Our demand for immigration restriction is as humanitarian for the people of other countries as well as it is wise, just and protective for the people of our own."

This is one of the more enlightened expressions of the pure and simple trade union view on the subject. Many of the strongest trade unions, some of them affiliated with the American Federation of Labor, show far less tolerance towards the immigrant-workingmen of their trades. Their policy is to keep them out of their organizations by exacting unreasonably high initiation fees, and not infrequently requiring a certain length of residence in the country as one of the conditions of their admission. This short-sighted policy is, of course, the exception rather than the rule, and is pursued only in such cases where the trade unions are strong enough to practically control the labor market.

And it must be admitted that the unfriendly attitude of American labor towards immigration is not entirely without foundation, at least as far as the economic aspect of the question is concerned.

The standard life of the American workingmen is above that of the average immigrant laborer.

Thus the average wage of the American agricultural laborer outside of harvest time is estimated at $1.25 to $1.50 a day, while that of the English laborer is about 50 cents, that of the Russian and Austria-Hungarian about 30 cents, and that of the Italian still less. Of course, these figures do not take into account the cost of living of the laborers, which is about three times higher in America than in the countries mentioned, but even with proper allowance for that difference, the foreign laborer still underbids the native workingman, so much so that the latter has been driven out from several entire industries. In the mining regions, for instance, the America workingman was first supplanted by the English and Irish immigrant, who in turn made room for the German, and the latter finally yielded the field to the cheaper labor of the Italian and "Slav."

And the life of these new comers [sic] is, at least in the beginning, very miserable. Herded together in large numbers, they live in small and dirty shanties, are poorly nourished and clad, and compelled to send their children to work at a very tender age. Compulsory education is a dead letter as far as they are concerned. The degradation of this cheap foreign labor finds perhaps its most revolting expression in the development among them of the "padrone" and "sweating" system, both of which had a somewhat demoralizing effect on the American labor market.

It is true that the competition of cheap immigration labor is felt most keenly in the "unskilled" trades, but it would be a mistake to assume that the "skilled" organized workingmen are entirely unaffected by it. The development of machinery has a strong tendency to obliterate the distinction between "skilled" and "unskilled" labor, and in many "skilled" trades the workingmen have long periods of idleness during which they are compelled to eke out their existence by common labor.

Thus it happened that on the question of immigration the apparent interests of organized labor have within the last decades largely coincided with those of the employing classes, and the demands of the former for restriction of further immigration have found rather willing ears in the legislatures of the latter. It is a noteworthy fact that of all the demands made from time to time by organized labor in our country, those relating to restriction of immigration have been most readily granted by our ruling classes. The course of immigration legislation in the United States Congress has within the last thirty years been one of successive restrictions.

The first significant act of Congress in that direction was the Chinese Exclusion Law and the different amendments it passed from 1882–1888. Around 1880 there were more than 100,000 Chinamen in the United States, and the majority of them settled in the State of California. They were engaged in mining, in the work of constructing the Pacific railroads, and fruit growing and farming. Their lack of requirements, cheapness of labor, inability to merge with the American workingmen and to organize, and their strange garb and habits, had early engendered a hostile feeling towards them on the part of the local working population, and when, towards the end of the seventies of the last century, the unprecedented industrial depression in California threw most of the native workingmen out of employment, this hostility was fanned into a blaze of hatred. Chinese labor was made responsible for all existing social and economic evils on the Pacific coast, a strong and turbulent agitation sprang up and culminated in the formation of the Working-men's Party of California with the platform: "The Chinese Must Go!" The two old parties were quick in endorsing the motto, and Congress promptly responded to the general demand of the Californians. At present all Chinese immigrants are excluded from the United States except officials, teachers, students, merchants and travellers for curiosity or pleasure.

Other restrictive measures were adopted by Congress one by one, and to-day the immigration laws of the United States bar the following classes of persons from landing: (1) Idiots, insane persons and epileptics; (2) Persons afflicted with contagious or dangerous diseases; (3) Criminals, polygamists and prostitutes; (4) Paupers, beggars and persons likely to become a charge on the public; (5) Contract laborers and assisted immigrants. The barring of the last mentioned class of immigrants and in some measure also the fourth class, is chiefly due to the agitation of organized labor.

After the assassination of President McKinley by the native American anarchist Czolgosz, Congress passed the notorious law excluding anarchists, defining the term as "persons who believe in or advocate the overthrow by force or violence of the government of the United States or of all government or all forms of law, or the assassination of public officials." Our present laws also prohibit all encouragement and solicitation of immigration on the part of the steamship companies, and impose a head tax of four Dollars on every immigrant.

## The Socialist View

The socialists of the United States have heretofore occupied themselves but little with the question of immigration. The problem has never attained the magnitude of an important political issue which would force the Socialist Part [y] as a political party to define its attitude on it, and the socialist influence on the trade union movement of our country is unfortunately so weak, that the party is not yet called on to act as the theoretical adviser on matters of general interest to organized labor.

As a rule the socialists of the United States do not share the narrower views of pure and simple trade unionism on the question of immigration. From the point of view of the immediate economic welfare of the American workingmen, immigration is certainly not a blessing, but its evil effects are largely exaggerated. The immigrant workingman certainly swells the supply of labor power but to some extent he also helps to increase the demand for it. He is not only a producer, he is also a consumer, and while under the present system he is bound to consume less than he produces, it is still a gross error to overlook his stimulating effect on the industrial growth of the country. The immigrant's low standard of living is also often a temporary rather than a permanent condition. Experience has demonstrated that in most cases the newly arrived workingmen after some time raise their standard of life, assimilate with the American workingmen and join their labor organizations. In fact the organized "American" workingmen to-day are the best proof of that assertion, for in a large, if not in a majority, of cases, they are themselves immigrants or immigrants' children.

And to the extent to which immigration actually is an evil to the working class of the receiving country, it is an evil inseparable from the existing economic system, as inseparable from it as the evils of child labor or woman labor, or the existence of the standing "natural" army of unemployed workingmen in every country with a capitalist development.

The migration of workingmen is caused and regulated largely by economic conditions, it is just as much a part of or industrial order as the movement of the masses from the village to the city and from city to city within every country. Capitalism is international, and the working class of the "civilized" world is its marching army, whose battalions are constantly ordered from town to town, from country to country, from hemisphere to hemisphere according to the exigencies of industrial developments and changes. And just as little as any modern country can withdraw from the international market, just so little can it permanently protect itself by artificial barriers from the natural stream of modern labor migration. It is the inexorable rule of supply and demand that in the last instance determines the volume and direction of migration and all legal enactments opposed to that rule are but temporary and inefficient makeshifts. Should the labor market in the United States fall below that of the European markets, the immigration of European labor will fall off no matter how liberal and attractive our immigration laws may be, and should, on the contrary, a condition arise where our employing classes would need more labor than they can advantageously find in their own country, all restrictive immigration laws will be speedily repealed and foreign laborers will be imported in larger numbers than ever. The efforts of organized labor should, therefore, be directed towards the organization and elevation of their immigrated brethren rather than towards their exclusion.

But if the socialists are thus unable to share all the current views of organized labor on immigration, they can just as little afford to ignore all their views.

The considerations indicated above apply only to immigration naturally and normally produced by existing economic conditions, and we may also add to that class immigration produced by political causes. But an entirely different standard must be applied to the other aspects of immigration mentioned in this article. Immigration artificially stimulated for the benefit of the steamship companies, land agents and similar commercial concerns, is just as pernicious to the workingmen of the country of emigration as to those of the receiving country, and should be discouraged with all means at the command of the socialists and workingmen of all countries. The international importation of workingmen from foreign countries for the purpose of breaking strikes or weakening or destroying labor organizations, is just as obnoxious to socialists as it is to the trade unions, and all measures to check these capitalist practices have the full support of the socialists. And finally the majority of the American socialists side with the trade unions in their demand for the exclusion of workingmen of such races and nations as have as yet not been drawn into the sphere of modern production, and who are incapable of assimilation with the workingmen of the country of their adoption, and of joining the organizations and struggles of their class. This demand is a direct expression of the natural instinct of self-preservation.

Just what races are to be included in this category is a question that can only be decided from time to time with reference to the particular circumstances and conditions of each case. Years ago the Chinese laborers in

California were by common consent declared to be undesirable immigrants, and very recently the same issue was raised in the same state with reference to the Japanese laborers. Whether the claim is justified this time, whether the Japanese workingmen have proved themselves incapable of organizing on American soil and taking part in the struggle of their American brethren is the subject of quite animate discussions in American party and labor circles just now. Personally I am not sufficiently familiar with the question to pass judgment on it.

IMMIGRATION AT STUTTGART
Louis B. Boudin
*International Socialist Review*
8 (February 1908): 489–92

The resolution on Immigration adopted by our last International Congress has called forth a discussion of this subject in our press which could have been more apropos before the Congress, but ought to be welcomed even at this late date. It is unfortunate, however, that the discussion has assumed a somewhat personal character. Our Party's delegates at Stuttgart have been criticized for neglect of duty in not pressing the "American" point of view. It is quite natural that I should be criticized more than any other delegate, and should feel the general criticism more keenly, because I not only "failed and neglected" to press this point of view, but actually opposed it, doing my level best to defeat the resolution proposed by our National Committee. That my position should be criticized was to be expected and I am not surprised to find Comrade Hillquit, the author of the ill-fated resolution, complain of me, although he refrains, in very comrade-like fashion, from openly criticizing me. But there is no mistaking the temper in which the following passage which I quote from Comrade Hillquit's article in The Worker, was written: "When it came to a vote,—says Comrade Hillquit,—we found that on the particular point in issue we could probably count on the support of Australia and South Africa, each represented by one delegate as against almost 900 delegates representing the other twenty-two countries. And what was worse, the American delegation was by no means a unit on our proposed resolution: The Socialist Labor Party had naturally taken the extreme impossibilist view of opposing not only all restrictions of labor immigration, but also all safeguards against the dangers arising from it, and even among the delegates of our own party there were those who were opposed to all restrictions, and refused to be bound by our own resolution on the subject."

I feel therefore in duty bound to inform the comrades of the reasons which actuated me in the course which I adopted at Stuttgart, and incidentally to state just what happened at the Congress, as Comrade Hillquit's article in The Worker leaves much to be desired on these points both in clearness and accuracy. Comrade Hillquit makes a labored attempt to create the impression that the "American" Resolution was not rejected in toto and that the resolution actually adopted was a compromise. What actually happened was quite different: our resolution was rejected in toto "on the particular point in issue," by the overwhelming vote of the other twenty-two countries, and there was no thought of a compromise. Comrade Hillquit makes out the semblance of a compromise by simply misstating the position of the other comrades, including my own, on the subject. Not only that: he even misstates the meaning of our own resolution, although it is his own handiwork and he ought to know it. According to Comrade Hillquit (in the Worker) our resolution is not opposed to "involuntary" or "natural" labor migration, but merely to the "importation" of foreign labor. It follows of necessity that those who were opposed to this resolution must have been in favor of such importation. And Comrade Hillquit is not slow to draw this conclusion: so he states in one place that the "extreme left" at the Congress "stood for absolutely free labor migration without any restriction or even safeguard," (whatever that may mean). And in another: "even among the delegates of our own party, there were those who were opposed to all restrictions." This statement evidently referring to myself. The compromise, according to him, consisted in the congress expressing itself for the exclusion of "contract-labor."

A mere recapitulation of the facts as Comrade Hillquit would have us understand them shows that he must be mistaken somewhere. For, the following very pertinent questions naturally suggest themselves: 1st. How is it possible that at a gathering of socialists there should be even an "extreme left" that should be opposed to the prohibition of the importation of contract-labor? And if by some chance such "enemies of labor" and "reactionaries" smuggled themselves into the Congress and got representation on the Immigration Commission, is it likely that it would have taken the commission two days hard fighting to dispose of them? 2nd. If Comrade Hillquit's statement as to the meaning of our resolution be true, then our resolution was actually adopted. Why, then, does he call it a compromise in one place and a defeat in another? Why does Comrade Hillquit complain that "we were beaten, hopelessly beaten." Why does Comrade Berger accuse Comrade Hillquit of being derelict in his duty, instead of hailing him victor? How account for the deluded ones who intimated that our delegation should have bolted the Congress for adopting our resolution? And how does it all harmonize with the statement that "on the particular point in issue" we knocked up against the solid wall of practically all of the socialists of the rest of the world?

The truth of the matter is as follows: There was no such "extreme left" at Stuttgart that anybody but Comrade Hillquit could see. Certainly there were none among our party's delegates at Stuttgart who were opposed to legislation excluding "imported" immigrants. And there was no compromise at Stuttgart on the immigration question, either, for there was nobody to compromise with except the supporters of our resolution, and they were "hopelessly beaten." The demand for the exclusion of imported contract labor contained in the Stuttgart resolution was not inserted therein as a concession to those in favor of the restriction of immigration, for all those who opposed "restriction" in general were in favor of this particular restriction. There were really no two opinions on the question. This was not the "point in issue," nor any part of it. That lay at another point. Let us see what it was.

Our resolution is drawn in such a way that it not only does violence to all logic, but is extremely treacherous. At first glance it looks innocent enough, and the worst that could be said about it is that it is meaningless. At least one member of our National Executive Committee is known to have been deceived by its innocent-looking meaninglessness into voting for it. How many more members of our National Executive Committee and National Committee were so deceived I have no means of telling. Our European Comrades, however, were not deceived, nor were all our delegates. They detected the "nigger in the woodpile," and that raised the issue between our delegation and the rest of the world, the debate over which lasted in committee for two whole days, and ended in our being "hopelessly beaten." Yes, ignominiously beaten. It was the attempt of our resolution to establish the principle of dividing immigrants along racial lines into "organizable" and "unorganizable," and to lay down as a rule of socialist policy, based on such principle of division, the demand for the exclusion of the so-called "unorganizable races." On this issue our resolution met with the solid opposition of the socialists of the world with the exception of a few trade-unions. And there was no compromise: the resolution is as emphatic on this point as it could possibly be made. Not, however, because our European comrades have no careful regard for the fate of the American workingmen or their indifference to the fortunes of the socialist movement in America. But from a conviction, fully justified, that the principles and demands formulated in our resolution are a snare and a delusion, and cannot possibly result in any permanent good to the working class of this country or of the world. These principles and demands are unsocialistic, that is to say, they are repugnant to the permanent and lasting interests of the workingclass.

That this is so, and that Comrade Hillquit saw it in that light at Stuttgart, is proven by the fact that Comrade Hillquit was finally moved to make a speech in favor of the resolution as adopted by the committee. To be frank about it: I was at first surprised to hear Comrade Hillquit speak in favor of the resolution reported by the committee, particularly in view of the fact that nobody opposed it. But as I stood there listening to his speech I saw the reason for it. Comrade Hillquit saw that the introduction of the resolution sadly damaged the reputation of our movement in the eyes of the socialist world, exposing us to the suspicion of utopianism on the one hand and sordidness of motive and egoism on the other, and he attempted to retrieve what was lost by arguing that we were really not as bad as we were painted, and that there really is not much difference between our resolution and the resolution adopted by the committee. The latter was, of course, no truer when stated at Stuttgart than when it is stated here. But there was an excuse for it at Stuttgart which is absent here, which makes the statement here absolutely indefensible. When Comrade Hillquit made the statement at Stuttgart he was engaged in the laudable effort of rehabilitating us in the opinion of our comrades, and the means adopted were at least harmless. Here, however, the situation is different: There is no reason for hiding the truth. With the better light that Comrade Hillquit has seen at Stuttgart, he ought to be showing the comrades who still abide in darkness the error of their ways, instead of telling them that our resolution was all right, but that we must submit, etc. Of course, Comrade Hillquit is right when he says that as good socialists we have to abide by the decision of the majority. But it is hardly worth while wasting much effort on this subject: there is no danger of our refusing to abide by the decision of the International Congress. But there is danger of some of us retaining our false notions on the subject-matter itself to the great detriment of our movement.

ASIATIC EXCLUSION
Cameron H. King, Jr.
*International Socialist Review*
8 (May 1908): 661–69

The problem of the influx of Asiatic labor into the United States seems to present itself to the Socialist Party in a somewhat different light than it does to other working class organizations. We are, or at least if we ever expect to be a power, we should be a party representative of the working class. Furthermore while we hold fraternal relations with the Socialist Parties of other countries, it is our particular and especial business to develop our own home organization. As scientific Socialists we know the only force which can ever effect the social revolution we hope and work for is the working-class. And we know further that the working class can accomplish that revolution only by a powerful and efficient organization. It cannot be achieved in the face of the skillfully organized forces of Capital by a mere mob. It is to the organized working-class, therefore, that we must look for our strength and support, for the means of our final victory.

The materialist conception of history teaches that it is folly to expect men in the mass to accept beautiful ideals and work for those ideals as against their present material interests. Marx has clearly shown that it is the material interests and economic necessities of men as individuals and classes that dictates their social conduct and political action. Accepting Marx we are driven inexorably to the position that an organization becomes stronger the more accurately it meets the material interests and economic necessities of the people. Indeed it was for this purpose that the materialist conception of history was made a part of the socialist propaganda—to be a lamp unto our feet, a guide in the darkness, that we would not fall into the morass of impractical schemes while pursuing the beautiful but illusory ideals of altruistic utopianism. So the Communist Manifesto says "The Communists fight for the attainment of the immediate aims, the enforcement of the momentary interests of the working-class."

We have then the organized working-class as the means, and its material interests and economic necessities as the force by which alone can be achieved the social revolution. We are further limited that this revolution is to be effected, so far as our efforts extend, within the United States, a definite political and geographical territory.

Viewed merely as a matter of political expediency it is evident that the way to gain the good-will and support of the working man is to aid him to a better condition of life. The sure way to gain his ill-will and hatred is to participate in or advocate the degradation of his standard of life, or to remain neutral while he is sore-pressed by his capitalist enemies. If we are to build up a class-conscious workingman's political party then we must appeal to the material interests of the organized workingmen and encourage the betterment of their conditions as far as we are able. Shall we not say "We, the Socialist Party, as workingmen are resolved to use the ballot for our own benefit; we have organized the Socialist party to advance politically our material interests?" Thus we take the scientific socialist position and face the question of Asiatic exclusion from the standpoint of how it will affect us as workingmen.

It is idle for the idealists in the Socialist Party to prate about our duty to the Japanese workingmen or to preach of "internationalism" and fraternity. My personal experience is that it is the professional and small business men who are animated by these noble ideals, and who can cherish them with some safety as Japanese immigration has not yet seriously threatened their livelihood. With the organized workingmen and the unorganized, unskilled laborers, however, it is a different matter. For them to welcome the intense competition of Asiatic immigration with its low standard of living is to immolate themselves on the altar of international ideals and leave their wives and children go more hungry and ragged than ever. The reply of the workingmen to such a proposition is plain and emphatic. Unanimously in every organization the workingmen of America have declared for the exclusion of Asiatic labor.

In California the exclusion sentiment is so unanimous that all the political parties, depending for power as they all do on popular suffrage, were compelled to subscribe to this demand of Labor for the exclusion of Asiatics. But some Socialists who believe they cannot be truly revolutionary unless they are on the opposite side of the question from everyone else, whose only method of distinguishing the socialist position is to find out what organized labor wants and then take the antagonistic position—these Socialists . . . feel encouraged by the action of the Stuttgart Congress which adopted a long and contradictory resolution expressing the muddled idealism of that body to whom the question was necessarily academic and unrelated to their material interests. Had it been subjected to the touchstone of the economic welfare of the German and French proletarians, there can be little doubt as to the attitude of Bebel and Jaurès. Bebel would have declared as he declared in regard to disarmament. "The culture, education, art, and literature of Germany were the heritage of the race, the property of the proletariat and that to defend them was no false patriotism, no treason to the workingclass." He would have declared that to permit the influx of millions from Asia would be "to put the more advanced nations at the mercy of the more backward ones" and to "adopt such tactics would be fatal to the German Social Democracy." . . . So too would Jaurès have spoken defending at all hazards the standard of life of the French workingman. Neither of these men could maintain their position as leaders of the proletarian party did they not always fight for the betterment of the conditions of their constituents. But the American workers were represented by not a man from the West who knows what Asiatic immigration means, and were misrepresented by delegates better acquainted with Europe than with that portion of the United States lying west of New York City. It is significant that the three countries that have Asiatic immigration are opposed to it, viz., South Africa, Australia, and America. The people that are not opposed to it are just those who have none of it. And of course those socialist residents of the United States who import their opinions ready made from Europe and are incapable of applying the fundamental principles of Socialism to the local facts cannot be independent in this matter from the dictum of our well-meaning European Comrades who did not know what they were talking about.

Three reasons all false are adduced for favoring an open shop, for that is the practical meaning of the anti-exclusionist's argument.

First:—It is asserted that the Japanese standard of living is as high as that of the European immigrants or of the native workingman, hence there can be no competition disastrous to the workers already here.

Let us appeal to the facts!

Hawaii has been open to the unrestricted immigration of the Japanese and may therefor be taken as an illustration of what would happen on the mainland of America were the Asiatic given perfect freedom to come. Bulletin No. 66 of the Bureau of Labor deals with the question statistically. The Capitalist planters had declared that "the success of the plantations is conditioned, not only by cheap labor but also by law-abiding and docile labor. White labor is either too expensive or too unreliable for profitable operation." And on this demand the importation of Asiatics began. In 1884 there were some 116 Japanese in the island, the plantations were being operated by whites, Hawaiians, and Chinese. In 1900 there were 56,000 and now there are probably 60,000 Japanese. The percentage of the total population was 0.14% in 1884 and 36.50% in 1900. In 1905 the Japanese constituted 65% of the employees on the sugar plantations. Most of these were contract laborers, whose condition was little removed from serfdom. The testimony of wage-schedules and of capitalists combines to show that though strikes have occurred the Japanese are far more law-abiding and docile than any other labor . . . .

These figures taken from occupations where white and Japanese laborers are in competition show conclusively that the Japanese are absolutely the worst paid of the whole population, worse even than the Chinese. Not only are their wages worse but their hours of labor are longer. While in some trades a slight advance in wages has been gained in the past decade, in those occupations peculiarly liable to Japanese competition wages have declined. For instance, Field hands received 73c a day in 1900, 64c in 1902, and 63c in 1905. (This is the average including female labor).

First the unskilled laborers, then the skilled labor, then the petty merchants, the little storekeepers feel the disastrous competition of the Japanese. Hawaii is suffering to-day from excessive Orientalization. It is dominated by Japanese standards of living. Take the Building trades. In 1881 one establishment employed 41 white carpenters and 7 helpers; 17 more than the seven largest establishments employed in 1905. One establishment employed 6 bricklayers in 1881 and only three were employed by the 7 biggest concerns in 1905. It is not because building has ceased but because the Japanese with their lower wages and longer hours have displaced the whites. The effect on the merchants is evident. They have fewer customers, and these have slenderer purses; and as the Japanese enter business they become rivals.

The standard of living would be debased were the whites compelled to stay on the islands. Fortunately for them California is not as yet inundated by the flood of Asiatic immigration and still offers good wages and fair employment as things go. It costs a white man $40 month to live in Hawaii. The Portuguese however manage to exist on $15 to $20. But the Japanese saves money on $10 a month.

But Hawaii is only a half-way station. They are coming into the mainland at the rate of more than 2500 a month and in increasing numbers. Unskilled labor has felt this competition for some time being compelled to relinquish job after job to the low standard of living it could not endure. The unskilled laborers are largely unorganized and voiceless. But as the tide rises it is reaching the skilled laborers and the small merchants. These are neither unorganized nor voiceless, and viewing the menace to their livelihood they loudly demand protection of their material interests. This menace is not due to the superior skill of the Japanese but entirely to their inferior standard of subsistence. It was very good of the International Congress to declare that it was the "duty of organized workingmen to protect themselves against the lowering of their standard of life which frequently results from the mass import of unorganized workers." But Necessity had already taught us that duty. When "the Congress next sees no proper solution of these difficulties in the exclusion of definite races from immigration" we are obliged to inquire what is meant by "proper." We of the Pacific Coast certainly know that exclusion is an effective solution. In the seventh decade of the nineteenth century the problem arose of the immigration of Chinese laborers. The Republican and Democratic parties failed to give heed to the necessities of the situation and the Workingman's party arose and swept the state with the campaign cry of "The Chinese must go." Then the two old parties woke up and have since realized that to hold the labor vote they must stand for Asiatic exclusion. It is due to this that we are not now inundated by Chinese coolies in California and faced by a social race and labor problem like that of the South.

The second point urged by those who oppose exclusion perhaps had some weight with the Congress in distinguishing between "proper" and improper solutions. It is said by some of our wise economists that the American workingmen might as well meet the competition of imported Japanese labor as the competition of imported Japanese goods or face their competition in the world market. What reasoning arrives at this conclusion it is hard to discover. It involves the theory of the mutual interest of Capitalists and laborers, that wages depend on the price the manufacturer gets for goods produced. But is it really the same to the American workingman to have his wages (the price he sells his labor for) ground down and his job taken from him by a horde of competing Japanese laborers, as it is to have the price of the goods the capitalists put upon the market ground down by the competition of Japanese goods? In the first place the home markets are saved to the American capitalist by protection, and such employment as that may afford is kept to the American laborer. If the reply be made that the influx of Japanese-made goods into the world-market will cause the shutting down of our factories and the disemployment of labor, we can agree. But will the admission of Japanese laborers into America prevent the Japanese capitalists in the world's commodity market, or the competition of American and Japanese laborers in the United States labor market? While low wages, unemployment and hard times may come from either source, we are bound to protect our own interests first. Let us as workingmen stop as much competition in the home labor market as we can and it will be up to the Capitalist to stop competition in what he has to sell in the world market.

Consider the attitude of the workingman in this matter. He looks naturally to the nearest and last-acting cause of his discharge for the key to a remedy. Though he may dimly perceive remoter causes it is the one right at hand that most powerfully impresses him. We can depend on a great deal of discontent from the man who is thrown out of a job. When the cause of his discharge is a wage-worker cheaper in price, different in color, peculiar in manners and alien in speech all the resentment of the discharged workingman will be directed against this "foreign labor," race prejudice will flare up and the bitter hate of a "scab race" will crush out the last semblance of "brotherly love" and "international solidarity." Protestant Yankee against Catholic Irish, Catholic Irish against the "dagoes" all of them against the "sheeny," and on the Pacific Coast the fierce hoodlumism of a Denis Kearny, group-consciousness in the group-struggle to survive! You can not do away with this by preaching Class-consciousness and international solidarity. The material conditions are fatal to those ideals dealing with the question in that way.

On the other hand, what is the result when the proximate cause of the workman's discharge is the closing down of the factory? He sees then not that there is a job there but that a "foreigner" has it; he sees that the job is gone. The capitalists who have been taking exorbitant profits out of his labor and justifying themselves on the ground that they were providing the workers with a job, have broken this arrangement. They no longer provide the worker with a job. Their ability to dispose of the workman's product and get him his wages out of it for which they have been charging their profit—this ability suddenly vanishes. The capitalists are up against it. Their system of doing business has failed. And when the capitalist business system fails to provide him with the means of life all the revolutionary impulse of the discharged workman's sense of injury is turned, not against a fellow-worker, nor used to fan the flames of race hatred, but becomes the power and energy that drives him into an attack on the capitalist system.

We have now an immense amount of unemployment and the discontent is powerfully felt in the increase of the socialist strength. Shall we turn to the workingman who is now taking refuge with us, because the capitalist system has failed to give him the means of life, and say, "We propose to let the Japanese laborers come here in unrestricted numbers, though they work for half or a third of what you do and will undoubtedly displace you in the small amount of work that hard times has left to the toilers of America." If we do say that we should be locked up alongside of Harry Thaw in the Asylum for the Criminally Insane. It seems almost too preposterous to argue!

However it is not to be supposed that Comrade Boudin will be daunted. Japanese cannot become citizens and practice law, attorneys' fees are in no danger. And well may he "laugh at scars who never felt a wound." I mean simply that Comrade Boudin cannot appreciate the gravity of the situation any more than the European Socialists. His material interests being unaffected he can indulge that natural propensity for idealism which flourishes in academic speculation. I will grant him more. Earnestly and sincerely, coming from a country and being of a race that has suffered persecution and race hatred, his nature revolts at the idea of race exclusion. But that does not qualify him to formulate the policy of a political party in America. Nor does he reason logically nor does the International have good grounds for declaring that exclusion is "in conflict with the principles of proletarian solidarity."

International solidarity does not mean international competition. What monstrous twisting of "Workingmen of the World, Unite!" gives us the slogan "Workingmen of the World, Compete!" Is it our duty to invite the Japanese here to take our jobs at half the wage we get? Or in addition to the great task of organizing the polyglot mass of workers already here are we to have thrust upon us the task of amalgamating the Japanese? And for what and by whom? For a mere phrase! By people necessarily unappreciative of the immensity of the task!

I say a "mere phrase" for absolutely no substantial gain can be pointed out from unrestricted immigration. For Japan it would mean the loss of the boldest and most enterprising of her proletariat. These men kept at home would turn their strength to upbuilding the unions and the Socialist party there, economic pressure would so compel them. But by immigration they encounter better conditions and the revolutionary impulse is lost in the opportunities for advancement. As for us our first duty is to ourselves; to make ourselves strong enough to achieve the social revolution here in the United States. The best service we can do the Japanese is just that. And let them settle their own fight at home. The gain in wages of the Japanese immigrants would not mean a gain to the Japanese proletarians who have the work of the Japanese fight for Socialism upon them. To the American worker it would mean the loss of a standard of living gained at great cost. It would mean the diversion of revolutionary energy into race riots.

Internationalism means that we do not believe in the wars of aggression and invasion that have marked the world's history heretofore. If we do not believe in military invasion can we consent any more readily to an economic invasion? Hervé's impassioned declarations that the French workers have nothing to lose by a German invasion and German domination indicates that were there a loss his anti-militarism would be modified. His hold on the French workers is conditioned by their belief that they would be as well off under German capitalists as under the French. But if the Germans came into France with nothing in learning, nothing in culture, nothing in aid of art or science, if they brought only a grievous menace to the standard of life of the French workers, would Hervé still say they should not be opposed or would he be listened to if he did?

In conclusion we may say that the time has come for the Socialist Party to decide what its relations shall be to the working-class. Are we going to bend the knee in worship of the idealistic phrase "The Brotherhood of Many" or are we going to affirm our solidarity with American labor and struggle to prevent the destruction of its hard won standard of life? In short are we to remain idealists out of touch with red-blooded, self-assertive life or are we to take our place in the workingman's struggle for existence, organizing his forces and always fighting for an advance in his means of life. Our feelings of brotherhood toward the Japanese must wait until we have no longer reason to look upon them as an inflowing horde of alien scabs. So long as the fact remains the enmity born of these facts will abide with us.

SOCIALIST PARTY, *Proceedings* OF THE 1908 NATIONAL CONVENTION (Chicago: Socialist Party, 1908), pp. 105–15 (excerpts)

*Immigration*

"The Socialist Party, in convention assembled, declares that the fundamental principle of Socialism is the struggle between the exploiting and exploited classes. The controlling principle of the political Socialist movement is the economic interest of the workers.

"In conformity with this principle the National Convention of the Socialist Party affirms that the working class must protect itself against whatever imperils its economic interests. The mass importation by the capitalist class of foreign workers with lower standard of living that those generally prevailing may in some instances become as serious to the working class of the nation as an armed invasion would be to the nation itself.

"To deny the right of the workers to protect themselves against injury to their interests, caused by the competition of imported foreign laborers whose standards of living are materially lower than their own, is to set a bourgeois Utopian ideal above the class struggle.

"This principle compels us to resolutely oppose all immigration which is subsidized or stimulated by the capitalist class, and all contract labor immigration, as well as to support all attempts of the workers to raise their standards of living. It does not, however, commit the Socialist Party to any attitude upon specific legislation looking to the exclusion of any race or races as such.

"The question of racial differences involved in the agitation for the exclusion of Asiatic immigrants this convention does not feel itself competent to decide upon at this time in the absence of a scientific investigation of the matter.

"Therefore, we recommend that in view of the great importance of this subject to the life of the workers of the nation, a special committee of five members be elected at this convention to carefully study and investigate the whole subject of immigration, in all its aspects, racial no less than economic, to publish from time to time such data as they may gather, and to report to the next convention of the party."

The reading of the resolution was followed with applause.

DEL SPARGO: Mr. Chairman, I move, on behalf of the committee, the adoption of that resolution. (Seconded.)

DEL WOODBY [sic] (Cal.): It is generally supposed that the western people, those living on the Pacific slope, are almost as a unit opposed to Oriental immigration. I am not saying that those living on the western slope oppose them, but where Oriental immigration comes to the western coast it is supposed that the people of the west are in favor of their exclusion. I am in favor of throwing the entire world open to the inhabitants of the world. (Applause.) There are no foreigners, and cannot be unless some person came down from Mars, or Jupiter, or some place. I stand on the declaration of Thomas Paine when he said "The world is my country." (Applause.) It would be a curious state of affairs for immigrants or the descendants of immigrants from Europe themselves to get control of affairs in this country, and then say to the Oriental immigrants that they should not come here. So far as making this a mere matter of race, I disagree decidedly with the committee, that we need any kind of a committee to decide this matter from a scientific standpoint. We know what we think upon the question of race now as well as we would know two years from now or any other time.

And so far as reducing the standard of living is concerned, the standard of living will be reduced anyhow. You know as well as I do that either the laborer will be brought to the job or the job will be taken to the laborer. Understand? We will either have to produce things as cheap as they can be produced upon foreign soil or the means of production will be carried to the Orient and there the thing will be done. The natural tendency of capitalism is to reduce the standard of living; the standard of living will be reduced anyhow.

Now, listen: It seems to me if we take any stand opposed to any sort of immigration that we are simply playing the old pettifogging trick of the Democrats and Republicans, and will gain nothing by it. (Applause.) I believe it is opposed, as I understand, to the principles of international Socialism. I do not pretend to say that the international Socialist organization takes square ground as to what we should say on the question, but to me Socialism is based, if anything, upon the Brotherhood of Man. This stand that we take in opposition to any sort of immigration is opposed to the very spirit of the Brotherhood of Man. I hope, therefore, that all that part of the committee's report which imposes a restriction on immigration will be stricken out by this convention. It ought to be done; in good faith it ought to be done, because, in the first place, the Socialists are organized in Japan; they are getting organized in China; they will soon be operating in every civilized nation on earth. And are the Socialists of this country to say to the Socialists of Germany, or the Socialists of Sweden, Norway, Japan, China, or any other country, that they are not to go anywhere on the face of the earth? It seems to me absurd to take that position. Therefore, I hope and move that any sort of restriction of immigration will be stricken out of the committee's resolution. (Applause.)

DEL MILLER (Colo.): Comrade Chairman, there is another thing that is to be considered in the question of immigration, and that is the class struggle, and that any action on the part of the working class which is in accord with the actions and intentions and interests of the capitalist class is in direct conflict with the interests of the workers. (Applause.) And whenever you take any action that puts your sanction upon the efforts of the manufacturers to bring the hordes of either Europe or Asia to this soil you take your stand for the lowering of civilization. (Applause.)

I want to say to you, my comrades, that brotherhood means something more than a mere mouthing of phrases about that question. There are some limits to be considered. We know the purpose of the mass importation of foreign labor. It is to bring American labor down to the same miserable standard which they occupy. I want to say to you again, on questions of that kind take men of the highest intellectual standard of the working classes of Europe, and they will stay at home to lead the fight in their own country, where they understand the problem and can aid the most in bringing about the brotherhood of man. You and I know that strong, able, intellectual men acquainted with their surroundings at home, among their people, can accomplish vastly more for the uplifting of those people than they can do when they come a few thousand miles away, in a strange country, surrounded by strange conditions and people speaking a strange language.

I want to say to you again, on the question of immigration, that there are biological reasons as well as sociological and economic ones to be considered upon this matter. (Applause.) There has never been a mixture and amalgamation of races that did not end disastrously for those amalgamated. (Applause.) And I want to say to you that it is capitalism that fosters and creates conditions of that kind. People that belong to the same race, unless there are economic reasons for mingling with others, naturally draw those lines pretty closely, and while they may cross those lines in associating and in exchanging ideas, still their life is spent among the people of a common descent. I take it that no mere sentiments or ideals of the present can wipe out the result of centuries of blood and thought and struggle. There are some things along that line that we must consider very carefully. Remember, above all things else, the class struggle lies at the bottom of the Socialist propaganda. It seems to me sometimes that we forget that, in the mouthing of mere sentimental phrases. True, we want also to promote the brotherhood of man. How can we do that? Not by sinking mankind to a common level. The delegate says we will have to take the man to the job or the job will go to the man. I want to tell him he will have to change some of nature's laws before he can take the ore out of the Rocky Mountains to the Chinaman (applause), or before he can bring the coal out of Illinois, out of Pennsylvania, and take it over to the Jap, or to the Greek to dig. It is true that this transporting can be done in some of the phases of manufacturing, in textile operations, etc. But let us look at all questions of this kind calmly and considerately. Above all, we must solve the problems of the people of our own country. This problem comes to us with the most pressing weight, and other men in other countries will meet their problems as best they may. The working class of the world has a common purpose, a common cause, but that does not mean that we shall ignore or neglect these great primal facts. It does not mean at any stage of the game that we shall ever clasp hands with the employer and seek to give our aid to the aims which he seeks to achieve. It is disastrous to the working class whenever that is the result. I think we would do well to appoint a committee upon this question. I am very nearly in complete accord with the report of the Resolutions Committee. Perhaps I would have gone a little bit farther on the question of Asiatic immigration and Asiatic civilization.

DEL HOEHN (Mo.): Comrades, I endorse the first part of the committee's report. I oppose the second part. In the first part of the report the committee states something definite; certain facts are presented. In the second part, in the concluding part of the report, the recommendation is made that no action be taken today, but that we defer final action to four years hence, to our next National Convention. Now, I wish to inform the members of the committee and the delegates on the floor of the convention that the class struggle will not be fought in the co-operative commonwealth in twenty-five or fifty or a hundred years from now, but the class struggle is here today and you will have to fight it today. (Applause.)

. . . Now, as Comrade Miller from Colorado has very properly pointed out, whenever the capitalist class, whenever the American Manufacturers' Association, and the Citizen's Industrial Alliance stand for a certain demand, organized labor and the Socialists of the country ought to be very careful not to fall in line with those corporation representatives. I assure you that nothing would be more welcome today to the American capitalistic corporations than to open the gates on all sides and admit the millions and millions of poor slaves into this country, so that the capitalists could break up every labor union in the country. And I want to say right here, comrades, it would only require about 250,000 Japanese mine workers to be imported in a few months to break up the entire United Mine Workers' Union of America. We as Socialists cannot stand for such a proposition. The Socialist convention, before it adjourns, must take definite action. It has to consider the demand made by the great mass of organized workers. Now, I want to refer to our friend from California. I have noticed that whenever an important question is up our friends from California stand on the class struggle, but unfortunately for our comrades from California, they do not stand on the class struggle, nor do they sit on the class struggle; they are lying on the class struggle, and lying up in the air. (Laughter.) And I want to say to you that the class struggle on the Pacific coast, the class struggle in Los Angeles, and the class struggle in the State of Washington, is going on fiercer than in any part of the United States, and our comrades on the Pacific coast will have to take a little different stand on such an important proposition.

DEL YOUNG (Pa.): Comrade Chairman and comrades, when we go into a skin game we must play the game in accordance with the rules of the game. When we go into the game of capitalism we must play that game in accordance with the rules of capitalism. If we try to inaugurate the great and noble ideas of Socialism in a capitalist community, just as surely as we are in the class struggle we are going to be ground under the wheels of this capitalist juggernaut.

Now, there was a law made before the law of the class struggle, and that was the law of self-preservation. Every workingman in this country is first bound by the law of self-preservation, and if immigration of foreign peoples who are below the standard of living in the United States is allowed to swamp this country with cheap labor from all over the world, just so sure will the standard of living of the workingmen of the United States be reduced. Now, that is not a theory; it is not an opinion; it is a fact. And it is with facts that we have at this time got to grapple. Personally, I would be in favor of absolutely stopping all immigration into this country. (Hisses and manifestations of disapproval.) I think it would be the best thing for the American worker.

(Cries of "Sit down.")

DEL YOUNG: But the report of this committee I take as a most admirable report, and I can only urge with all the power that I have the adoption of that report. And the moment that we take an extreme ground on either side, either for the unlimited influx of labor from foreign countries or for the absolute exclusion of foreign peoples, why, that moment we will come into clash with either the labor interests of this country or the labor interests of outside countries. But our first duty is to the laboring class, the working class of the United States, and not to that of Europe or China, or any other country under the sun. We are here to represent the working class of the United States, and we are bound to do the best we can for the working class of the United States. I strongly urge the adoption of this resolution.

DEL WAGENKNECHT (Wash.): Undoubtedly the hissing that was done here a few minutes ago is a good example of those advocates of brotherly love while the class struggle is going on; a very good example. It proves the statement of my friend, Comrade Young of Pennsylvania, that not only is the first law of life, namely, the law of self-preservation, the main law, the main material law, but when it comes to the preservation of one's personal ideas the self-preservation of his ideas is also a law of human nature, and we do not remember our brotherly love to our fellow men when anybody crosses us in our ideas. (Applause.)

The brotherhood of man is for a future state of society. While my friend from California is talking about the brotherhood of man, thinking about the brotherhood of man, dreaming about the brotherhood of man, the capitalist class is doing something else. (Applause.) The capitalist class don't talk only or think or dream about the brotherhood of man. The capitalist class has its eyes upon the working class. The capitalist class has got its eyes not only upon the working class of America, but also upon the working class of foreign lands. The capitalist class is a class which wishes to preserve not only its ultimate interests, but also its immediate interests, and the capitalist class will preserve its immediate interests by importing not only labor into America, but by exporting its industries to foreign lands. Now, we are not concerned as to whether or not the capitalist will export its industries into foreign lands—but we are confronted with the fact as to whether or not the capitalist class will import foreign labor into the United States right now . . . .

Comrade Young of Pennsylvania and Comrade Miller of Colorado have stated fully the position of those who are in favor of exclusion, and anything more on my part would seem simply to be repetition. But I wanted to make that one point, the fact that the brotherhood of man has no place in a capitalist society in which the class struggle is the main factor . . . .

THE CHAIRMAN: I am not a mind reader.

DEL SMITH (Tex.): About thirty-five years ago, having been born and raised south of this city a few miles, I went down south, married a Mississippi girl, and settled the question between the North and South. And now, if we can harmonize the East and West on this question we will be doing a great thing, and I do not believe if we were to fight two hours over this question we would come any nearer than is to be found in that resolution. I stand for the resolution.

DEL LEWIS (Ill.): Comrade Chairman and fellow delegates, I am in favor of the resolution proposed by the committee. It does not go as far as I would like it to go, but I believe it goes as far as it is possible to carry this convention. The principal argument made in favor of exclusion is that oriental immigration would lower civilization, in the language of Comrade Miller. I have lived some years four years on the Pacific slope, visited all its principal cities and enjoyed the hospitality of most of its jails, and I have come into contact with the orientals in those cities. You cannot get a Chinese cook on the Pacific coast for less than nearly double the wages of a white cook. (Applause.) When you talk to a Chinaman about cooking there is only one phrase he will consent to mention to you, and that is "sleventy dolls month," and he will not work for $69. You can get white cooks in ship loads at $30 or $40 a month. In the city of Bellingham, on the northern part of the Pacific coast, there is the largest salmon cannery in the world, operated by white men. There is only about three months of the year of a season, and they only work about two or three days a week. During that season, when the white wage slaves began to protest that at least during the season they ought to be paid double time, for they were there day and night for two days a week, the employers responded by bringing a shipload of Chinamen from San Francisco to take their places. The Chinamen were shrewd enough to contract that unless they decided to stay they would be shipped back. They came; they worked less than one week, and they issued their manifesto to the employers, and they said: "During the season we are willing to work two days and two nights when the catch is in, and loaf the rest of the week. But, working or loafing from the beginning of the season to the conclusion our wages must be paid for every day, or we go back." (Applause.) And the employers said, "That is a bigger demand than the white men ever made," and they took the Chinamen back to San Francisco.

A DELEGATE: Good for the Chinamen!

DEL LEWIS: As for the Jap, the Japanese workers of southern California, on the railroads applied to the American Federation of Labor for a charter. These men are willing to organize, and once they become familiar with the country they would make better organized workingmen than the white man. (Applause.) No Chinamen ever breaks a contract twice, and very rarely once. These men applying for a charter were refused one by the representatives of organized labor in America—one of the most treasonable acts ever committed in the name of the working class. (Applause.) I have only one minute and a half. I want to tell Comrade Wagenknecht that is only possible in a capitalist society. True, we can not invite all men to unite, because we are divided into classes, but we can invite all the workers of all the world to unite. (Applause.) As for me, on this question class runs deeper than either blood or race (applause), and I say to the Japanese workingman and the Japanese Socialist looking across the Pacific to this convention and asking, shall we include them with our European workingmen and consider them a part of the Socialist international movement, this is my answer: We are exploited with a common exploitation; we are enslaved in a common slavery; and so far as I am concerned, my yellow working wage slaves and comrades, we will stand or fall together. (Applause.)

DEL UNTERMANN (Idaho). I believe in the international solidarity of the working class, and yield to no Socialist on this floor in teaching and practicing such solidarity to the point to which it is possible. But I do not believe in international solidarity to the point of cutting my own throat. So long as this question is discussed merely from the economic point of view, we necessarily come to one set of conclusions; we turn in a circle and get nowhere. Every Socialist writer of any authority has always declared that the Socialist Party considers not merely the economic point of view, but all phases of social life. But when the race question comes into discussion this reasonable declaration is quickly forgotten and the whole debate turns upon the economic factor, without taking the slightest notice of the racial aspect of this question.

This is not only an economic question, but also a race question, and I am not afraid to say so. I believe in the authority of the International Congress, but I do not believe in international dogma. The International Congress is not a church council whose declaration we must accept willingly or unwillingly. I am not going to submit to the mere theoretical declarations of a set of European intellectuals who have never had any actual touch with the race issue. Those comrades who merely consider the economic point of view forget that every argument that can be brought against oriental exclusion from that point of view can also be brought against the immigration of any other race. Only when we take the race issue into consideration along with the economic factors do we get to any satisfactory solution of this question.

I want to ask those comrades who believe in unrestricted immigration of the oriental why they do not demand a vote and homesteads for them? If they demand a vote for the oriental, what will be the consequence for the Socialist Party? Every one familiar with conditions in the southern states knows very well what would be the fate of the Socialist Party if we attempted to organize mixed locals of colored and white people down there. Every one familiar with conditions on the Pacific and in the Rocky Mountain states knows that the same result would follow there if we attempted to organize mixed locals of oriental and whites. The oriental laborers are of no use to us in our political struggle, even if we could organize them and educate them as easily as laborers from other countries. The oriental have no home. They cannot help to fight the political class struggle, and if we demand homesteads for them what will be the result for the white race? How much of the United States are you going to turn over to them? And if they fill them up, how much more and how much more?

I am determined that my race shall not go the way of the Aztec and the Indian. I believe in the brotherhood of man, regardless of races, but I do not believe in extending that brotherhood to the point of eliminating myself voluntarily from the struggle for existence and turning over this country to my brothers of other races. I am determined that my race shall be supreme in this country and in the world. (Applause.)

For this reason I am in favor of the adoption of the report of the committee, and in favor of the appointment of a committee which shall study this question. (Applause.)

DEL BERGER (Wis.): Comrade Chairman and comrades, whatever I may have done, I have not taken up very much of your time so far, and I am not going to take up much of your time. (A voice, "Good.") I am not going to make a long speech. I may not even want five minutes. But we do not want to decide this question on second-hand ideas. The Socialist movement, the International movement, was not founded on second-hand reasons. It does not rest on second-hand reasons. Our basis is materialistic. Our basis is scientific. Let us decide this question as we do every other question, on a scientific and materialistic basis. I will not go over any of the ground that the others have covered. I fully agree with everything that Guy Miller said, and I fully agree with what Comrade Hoehn and some of the others said.

There are about 500,000,000 Chinamen in China. We get now about a million immigrants from Europe. They are of our own race and make-up, in a measure, and yet aren't they lowering the standard of living for the American proletariat? Anybody who tells me that they do not is deceiving himself and he is deceiving us. They do. But we know that in the second generation they will become part of us, that they will become the same as we are. A good many of them become part of us even in the first generation, for they are of the same make-up and they have the same civilization. There is very little difference between the German workingman coming over here and the American workingman. The main difference is in language. A good many of our German comrades know a good deal more than we do; in some respects we may even learn from some of our Russian comrades. (Applause.)

But, comrades, the Asiatic question is entirely different. The Asiatics, while their civilization may be older, while they may be smarter, than the American or European—that is so much more reason—

(Confusion on the convention floor.)

DEL BERGER: Comrades, I have listened to you, and I want you to listen to me. On the contrary, if their adaptability is so much greater and their needs are so much smaller than ours, that is the more reason why we have to defend ourselves. This is a practical question for the working class. China could send over about two million coolies every year and not feel it. They could send over here five millions every year if our capitalists should want them, and China would not miss them. But we would feel it. If you permit them to come over here just for fifteen years at two millions a year you will wipe out our civilization simply by their lower standard of living, by their power to live on a great deal less than you can. There would be a quiet war, but a most terrible war, waged against us—a war of extermination, on economic lines. The white race could not propagate, could not exist in a competition of that kind with the yellow race. That is all I have to say on this.

I want to consider this simply from a working class standpoint, and no other. We are willing to help the Japs in every way; we are willing to help the Chinese in every way. By pulling us down to their level they do not help themselves in any way, but they make us miserable. Your first duty, comrades, is to your class and to your family. Because your neighbor's house is burning, shall you set your own house on fire? No, say I. Defend your own house and then help your neighbor; that is the way . . . .

DEL BERLYN (Ill.): It was sometime ago that I came to this country. I am a foreigner. I remember that in 1850 in the streets of New York I saw riots between the Knownothings and the Wideawakes, between those who were called the dark lantern men, who wanted to keep the foreigners out, and those who were in favor of a larger immigration. The argument on one side was that there were too many people in the country. We had at that time in the United States, according to the census, 31,000,000 people. We were told at that time that the standard of living would be reduced. But since that time the immigrants have come in an ever-increasing flow, but the organization of labor amongst the people has enabled the American workingmen to do something to raise the standard of living, in spite of the immense inflow. That is one side of the question.

But there is another side of the question—that wonderful class struggle that these people talk about and know nothing about. We must keep separate from the capitalists. When the Chinese exclusion act was enacted there was not even a socialist party; don't forget that. I belong to a different race than nine-tenths of you here. I am not only a foreigner by birth, but I am a Jew, so exclude them all—they are no good. Now, let me tell you; we want to keep the class struggle. It is a remarkable thing; the obliviousness of this convention is remarkable in one point. You don't know why the fleet of battleships has been sent to the Pacific. You forget all about that. You forget that both Democrats and Republicans are united on Japanese and Oriental exclusion, and you want us to blow the little whistle and say "Me, too." (Laughter and applause.) Now, I do not think that is the mission of the Socialist party. I believe in the resolution which says that a committee shall be appointed to investigate this matter, and even though we were to get that report inside of two years instead of four years, the exclusion acts will have been passed. There is, with all this talk about immigration, the most efficient exclusion act at work right now. The emigrants exceed the number of immigrants. (Applause.) If you want to exclude them, double up the force of the industrial depression. It is nonsensical to talk about people coming here because they come of their own free will. They utterly ignore the goad of the capitalist whip which sends the proletariat around the world. They ignore it. And then they want to tack on a whole lot of stuff; investigate, and when the next convention comes the exclusion acts will be in full force. We won't elect socialists to the next congress, I am afraid, to affect the standing of the matter, for the unanimity of both capitalist parties on the question will settle the matter, for the coming of the sixteen battering rams that are floating in the Pacific will force them into silence, and we Socialists will proudly say they are doing our work. (Applause.) That is a great class struggle, if you want to chime in with the capitalists and say "Me, too." I have been in this country for sometime. I was here in the days when the abolition question was on, and when the enfranchisement question was up, and I am learning funny lessons. I have learned to look upon all men as equal. You may attempt in this body to make me unlearn it, but you cannot do it. (Applause.) I belong to a despised race. The idea of equality for all men regardless of race can only be accomplished by the Socialist party. (Applause.) But if we permit ourselves to go to work and tack amendments to the proposition of "Workingmen of all countries, unite"—if you tack amendments to that, then tack a clause to the name of the Socialist party, the words "A d—— lie."

DEL ESTER NIEMINEN (Minn.): This question is really a waste of time. We seem to think we have got a Socialist government already. If we Socialists had the management of the United States government, then there would be reason for talking as to whether it would be of any benefit to have the Chinese or not. But now the way it is, you know the capitalists control us and we cannot do anything. If we say we want to exclude Oriental Immigration we cannot do it. If the capitalists want to bring them in, no trade union is strong enough to prevent it. If the capitalists cannot have immigration coming here, if they cannot have Chinamen come here they are going to take out their machinery and move their factories to China. That is what the great trusts are doing today. Even if the different unions become so strong that they cannot make their machinery here, that will make no difference, for the Europeans will then make the machinery. We know that if we try to stop it, if we do pass resolutions that we do not want the Chinaman here or that we do not want the Japanese here, we know that if the capitalists think it is any benefit to them they will bring the Chinaman in.

But the capitalist class today realizes that it is more benefit to have European workingmen here than it is to have Chinese workingmen. Why? The American consumes more than a Chinaman, and the capitalist does not want any one that comes here and works and does not consume something. We undersell the Oriental and crowd them out of employment at home. They come here to seek work, but we good, honest Americans, and even some Socialists, want to starve them. And then we say all men are equal, of whatever color. Soon we will be saying all men are equal but Chinamen. I don't know where the women come in—I mean the Chinese women.

The only way we could reach a solution of this question would be through industrial unionism, and then we would be in danger of losing our dear capitalists, which is awful to think of. Our natural resources won't hold them here.

Another thing, if we do have the Chinaman it is not going to put the workingman out of work. We have found out that the last panic has made more Socialists than anything else, and if all the Japanese came here tomorrow and threw our workingmen out of work, I am sure that they would all be Socialists after a while. (Applause.) We know there are but two ways of making Socialists. The one we put into practice is through the brain. If we don't succeed, the capitalists put the other way into practice, through the stomach.

And here we have been talking like idiots, that we are going to shut out Oriental immigration, just as though we had the reins of government, just as though we controlled the whole country. Let us leave this question go and leave the capitalists do just as they see fit, and let us agitate among the workingmen ourselves. Get them to understand what we mean by Socialism, and after that we will organize the Chinese and let them come. I think it is a benefit. The more we get here the better. It is the capitalists that would prevent them coming out of their own countries, the European countries. You go to any European country, and on their farms who do you see? Nothing but old men, some of them eighty years old. You do not find any young men. All those young men, as soon as they are eighteen or twenty, leave their own country and come to America. If the Japanese would all do that we would all be Socialists in America and we would not have to work as hard as we do now under the capitalist system.

A LETTER FROM DEBS ON IMMIGRATION
Eugene V. Debs
*International Socialist Review*
11 (July 1910): 16–17

Have just read the majority report of the Committee on Immigration. It is utterly unsocialistic, reactionary and in truth outrageous, and I hope you will oppose with all your power. The plea that certain races are to be excluded because of tactical expediency would be entirely consistent in a bourgeois convention of self-seekers, but should have no place in a proletariat gathering under the auspices of an international movement that is calling on the oppressed and exploited workers of all the world to unite for their emancipation . . .

Away with the "tactics" which require the exclusion of the oppressed and suffering slaves who seek these shores with the hope of bettering their wretched condition and are driven back under the cruel lash of expediency by those who call themselves Socialists in the name of a movement whose proud boast it is that it stands uncompromisingly for the oppressed and down-trodden of all the earth. These poor slaves have just as good a right to enter here as even the authors of this report who now seek to exclude them. The only difference is that the latter had the advantage of a little education and had not been so cruelly ground and oppressed, but in point of principle there is no difference, the motive of all being precisely the same, and if the convention which meets in the name of Socialism should discriminate at all it should be in favor of the miserable races who have borne the heaviest burdens and are most nearly crushed to the earth.

Upon this vital proposition I would take my stand against the world and no specious argument of subtle and sophistical defenders of the civic federation unionism, who do not hesitate to sacrifice principle for numbers and jeopardize ultimate success for immediate gain, could move me to turn my back upon the oppressed, brutalized and despairing victims of the old world, who are lured to these shores by some faint glimmer of hope that here their crushing burdens may be lightened, and some star of promise rise in their darkened skies.

The alleged advantages that would come to the Socialist movement because of such heartless exclusion would all be swept away a thousand times by the sacrifice of a cardinal principle of the international socialist movement, for well might the good faith of such a movement be questioned by intelligent workers if it placed itself upon record as barring its doors against the very races most in need of relief, and extinguishing their hope and leaving them in dark despair at the very time their ears were first attuned to the international call and their hearts were beginning to throb responsive to the solidarity of the oppressed of all lands and all climes beneath the skies.

In this attitude there is nothing of maudlin sentimentality, but simply a rigid adherence to the fundamental principles of the International proletarian movement. If Socialism, international, revolutionary Socialism, does not stand staunchly, unflinchingly, and uncompromisingly for the working class and for the exploited and oppressed masses of all lands, then it stands for none and its claim is a false pretense and its profession a delusion and a snare.

Let those desert us who will because we refuse to shut the international door in the faces of their own brethren; we will be none the weaker but all the stronger for their going, for they evidently have no clear conception of the international solidarity, are wholly lacking in the revolutionary spirit, and have no proper place in the Socialist movement while they entertain such aristocratic notions of their own assumed superiority.

Let us stand squarely on our revolutionary, working class principles and make our fight openly and uncompromisingly against all our enemies, adopting no cowardly tactics and holding out no false hopes, and our movement will then inspire the faith, arouse the spirit, and develop the fibre that will prevail against the world.

Yours without compromise,
Eugene V. Debs.

SOCIALIST PARTY, *Proceedings* OF THE 1912 NATIONAL CONVENTION
(Chicago: Socialist Party of America, 1912), p. [*sic*] 209–13
Appendix J

*Reports of the Majority and Minority Committees on Immigration.*

(A) MAJORITY REPORT OF COMMITTEE ON IMMIGRATION.

At the national congress of the Socialist party in 1910, the Committee on Immigration presented a majority report signed by Ernest Untermann, Joshua Wanhope and Victor L. Berger, and a minority report signed by John Spargo.

The majority report declared that the interests of the labor unions and of the Socialist Party of America demanded the enforcement of the existing exclusion laws which keep out the mass immigration or importation of Asiatic laborers.

The minority report declared that the danger from Asiatic labor immigration or importation was more imaginary than real and that, therefore, the Socialist Party should content itself with an emphasis upon the international solidarity of all working people regardless of nationality or race. The minority report did not state whether the Socialist Party should demand the repeal of the existing exclusion laws. When asked during the debate whether he favored the repeal of these laws, Comrade Spargo declined to commit himself to a definite answer.

In the course of the discussion, Comrade Morris Hillquit introduced a substitute for both reports. This substitute evaded the question for or against the existing exclusion laws, merely demanding that the mass of importation of contract laborers from all countries should be combated by the Socialist Party.

An amendment to this substitute, demanding a special emphasis upon the fact that the bulk of the Asiatic immigration was stimulated by the capitalists and for this reason should be excluded, was offered by Comrade Algernon Lee.

After a debate lasting nearly two days, the congress adopted Hillquit's substitute by a vote of 55 against 50.

This close vote induced the congress to recommit the question for further study to a new committee on immigration with instructions to report to the national convention of 1912.

In this new committee the same alignment immediately took place. After a fruitless effort of the chairman to get unanimous action, the majority decided to act by itself and let the minority do the same.

Continued study and the developments on the Pacific Coast during the last two years convinced the majority of this committee more than ever that the existing exclusion laws against Asiatic laborers should be enforced and be amended in such way that they can be more effectively enforced. The details of the necessary amendments should be worked out by our representatives, or by our future representatives, in Congress and submitted for ratification to the Committee on Immigration, which should be made permanent for this purpose.

It does not matter whether Asiatic immigration is voluntary or stimulated by capitalists. There is no room for doubt that the capitalists welcome this immigration, and that its effect upon the economic and political class organizations of the American workers is destructive.

It is true that all foreign labor immigration lowers the standard of living, increases the unemployed problem and supplies the capitalist with uninformed and willing tools of reaction. But of all foreign labor immigration, the Asiatic element, owing to its social and racial peculiarities, is the most difficult to assimilate and mold into a homogeneous and effective revolutionary body. It is all the more dangerous to the most advanced labor organizations of this nation, because it adds to and intensifies the race issue which is already a grave problem in large sections of this country.

In the European countries the labor unions and the Socialist party are not confronted by the task of educating, organizing and uniting vast masses of alien nationalities and races with the main body of the native class-conscious workers. Where alien immigration enters into the European labor problem, it plays but an insignificant role compared to the overwhelming mass of native workers. America is the only country in which the labor unions and the Socialist Party are compelled to face the problem of educating, organizing and uniting not only the native workers but a continually increasing army of foreign nationalities and races who enter this country without any knowledge of the English language, of American traditions, of economic and political conditions. The disappearance of the Western frontier has intensified the difficulties of labor organizations and Socialist propaganda to such a degree that it has become an unavoidable task to decide whether restrictive measures shall or shall not be demanded in the interests of the labor unions and of the Socialist Party. Since the race issue enters most prominently into this problem and has for years been the central point of restrictive legislation, the Socialist Party has been compelled to take notice of it.

Race feeling is not so much a result of social as of biological evolution. It does not change essentially with changes of economic systems. It is deeper than any class feeling and will outlast the capitalist system. It persists even after race prejudice has been outgrown. It exists, not because the capitalists nurse it for economic reasons, but the capitalists rather have an opportunity to nurse it for economic reasons because it exists as a product of biology. It is bound to play a role in the economics of the future society. If it should not assert itself in open warfare under a Socialist form of society, it will nevertheless lead to a rivalry of races for expansion over the globe as a result of the play of natural and sexual selection. We may temper this race feeling by education, but we can never hope to extinguish it altogether. Class-consciousness must be and cannot be wholly unlearned. A few individuals may indulge in the luxury of ignoring race and posing as utterly raceless humanitarians, but whole races never.

Where races struggle for the means of life, racial animosities cannot be avoided. Where working people struggle for jobs, self-preservation enforces its decrees. Economic and political considerations lead to racial fights and to legislation restricting the invasion of the white man's domain by other races.

The Socialist Party cannot avoid this issue. The exclusion of definite races, not on account of race, but for economic and political reasons, has been forced upon the old party statesmen in spite of the bitter opposition of the great capitalists.

Every addition of incompatible race elements to the present societies of nations or races strengthens the hands of the great capitalists against the rising hosts of class-conscious workers. But the race feeling is so strong that even the majority of old party statesmen have not dared to ignore it.

From the point of view of the class-conscious workers it is irrational in the extreme to permit the capitalists to protect their profits by high tariffs against the competition of foreign capital, and at the same time connive at their attempts to extend free trade in the one commodity which the laborer should protect more than any other, his labor power.

It is still more irrational to excuse this self-destructive policy by the slogan of international working class solidarity, for this sentimental solidarity works wholly into the hands of the capitalist class and injures the revolutionary movement of the most advanced workers of this nation, out of ill-considered worship of an Asiatic working class which is as yet steeped in the ideas of a primitive state of undeveloped capitalism.

A proper consideration of working class interests, to which the Socialist Party is pledged by all traditions and by all historical precedent, demands that our representatives in the legislative bodies of this nation should reduce the tariff protection of the capitalists and introduce a tariff, or tax, upon unwholesome competitors of the working class, regardless of whether these competitors are voluntary or subsidized immigrants. Real protection of American labor requires a tariff on labor power and the reduction and gradual abolition of the tariff on capital. Such labor legislation already exists in British Columbia and has proved effective there.

The argument that the menace of Asiatic labor immigration is more imaginary than real overlooks the obvious fact that this menace has been minimized and kept within bounds by the existing exclusion laws, and that it can be eliminated altogether by a strict enforcement and more up-to-date amendment of these laws.

The majority of this committee realize of course, that the development of capitalism in China, India and Japan will necessarily tend to bring the American laborer into competition with the Asiatic laborer, even if the Asiatic does not come to the shores of this country. But the exclusion of the Asiatic from the shores of this country will at least give to the American laborer the advantage of fighting the Asiatic competition at long range and wholly through international commerce, instead of having to struggle with the Asiatic laborer for jobs upon American soil. This will tend to abolish the labor of children and women in American factories, to maintain a national standard of living and to reduce the unemployed problem for adult male workers.

International solidarity between the working people of Asia, Europe and America will be the outcome of international evolution, not of sentimental formulas. So long as the minds of the workers of nations and races are separated by long distances of industrial evolution, the desired solidarity cannot be completely realized, and while it is in process of realization, the demands of immediate self-preservation are more imperative than dreams of ideal solidarity.

The international solidarity of the working class can be most effectively demonstrated, not by mass immigration into each others' countries, but by the international co-operation of strong labor unions and of the national sections of the International Socialist Party.

Socialism proves itself a science to the extent that it enables us to foretell the actual tendencies of future development.

This point of view has been almost wholly overlooked in the discussion and practice of these "immediate" policies which serve as our conscious steps in the direction of Socialism.

In our general propaganda and party organization, we work for the prophesied outcome of capitalist development and shape our actions in harmony with the foreseen probable course which the majority of the citizens will be compelled to adopt during the revolution of the human mind towards a Socialist consciousness.

Not so in discussing and acting upon questions of immediate policy such as the exclusion of Asiatic laborers from the United States. Instead of clearly foretelling the inevitable policy which the majority of the voters of this nation will be compelled to adopt in this particular instance, we are supposed to shape our actions in response to sentimental, utopian or dogmatic arguments dictated by the personal likes or dislikes of a few individuals.

Instead of scientifically foretelling the inevitable logic of events, we are supposed to listen to a logic inspired by the sophistry of the advocates of unrestricted immigration.

Those who affirm the sentimental solidarity of the working classes the world over and at the same time demand a restriction of the stimulated mass importation of contract laborers admit unwillingly that this ideal solidarity is really impossible. And while they thus contradict their own sentimental assertion, they evade the real issue by an exaggerated reverence for a utopian race solidarity.

The common sense Socialist policy under these circumstances is to build up strong national labor unions and strong national Socialist parties in the different countries and work toward more perfect solidarity by an international co-operation of these labor unions and parties. To this end the Socialist Party of America should consider above all the interests of those native and foreign working class citizens whose economic and political class organizations are destined to be the dominant elements in the social revolution of this country.

In the United States this means necessarily the enforcement of the existing exclusion laws against Asiatic laborers, and the amendment of these laws in such a way that the working class of America shall fortify its strategic position in the struggle against the capitalist class.

The majority of this committee are not opposed to the social mingling of races through travel, education and friendly association upon terms of equality. But we are convinced that the mass of the voters, with the growth of socal consciousness, will rather eliminate more and more those warring elements of social development which interfere with an orderly and systematic organization of industrial and political democracy. They will not be anxious to intensify the unemployed problem and the race issue, but will strive to transform the international working class solidarity from a utopian shibboleth into a constructive policy. They will use their collective intelligence to reduce the evils growing out of unemployment and race feeling, until we shall be able to eliminate those evils altogether and strip race feeling at least of its brutalities.

This tendency is so plainly evident to the majority of this committee that we can afford to dispense with appeals to passion. This question will not be solved by a repetition of phrases, but by a conscious and constructive policy which will enforce itself as an inevitable step in the direction of working class solidarity and Socialism the world over.

ERNEST UNTERMANN,

Chairman.

JOSHUA WANHOPE,

J. STITT WILSON,

ROBERT HUNTER.

(B) MINORITY REPORT OF COMMITTEE ON IMMIGRATION.

We, the undersigned propose that this convention endorse the position taken on the question of immigration by the International Congress at Stuttgart.

MEYER LONDON

JOHN SPARGO

LEO LAUKKKI

OUR ASIATIC FELLOWS
Bruce Rogers
*International Socialist Review*
15 (April 1915) 626

The space allowed me here will permit of no more than a syllabus of the case for the Asiatic.

It was when he entered upon business pursuits that the Asiatic became a "yellow peril." From a standpoint of service, excellence and condition of stock, economy of methods, he is the superior merchant and soon takes his place as such, if unhindered. As a competitor he practices a sort of mercantile jiu jitsu that puts the white merchant out for the count.

As a worker he constitutes no peril to white labor, *of himself.* Long under repression, he takes to unionism and Socialism like a duck to water. These are new found privileges to him. He can give us lessons in militancy and solidarity of action. It is only as we exclude and ostracize him that he is any sort of menace.

In the sense of infidelity to his kind there is no such thing as yellow scab. They see to it that scabbing is an avocation in which the mortality rate is total. A yellow strike cannot be broken with yellow labor, and to break a white strike—a rare occurrence—yellow labor must be herded and kept in ignorance of what it is doing. The rule is that a white strike must be broken by white scabs. In the Vancouver traction strike steps were taken to call out other crafts in sympathy. The white carpenters "affiliated" stood upon their agreement and their "craft rights." The yellow carpenters, unaffiliated, came out although excluded and ostracized.

On the Pacific Coast, Japanese workers are slowly crawling their way to job control in those employments wherein they are peculiarly adapted and without reference to the degree of skill required. In domestic service the Japanese drudge has done more to standardize household work than has ever been done. This is uniformly the housewife's experience. She engages a Jap. He agrees to any hours she may name, but when he does what he thinks is enough for the money, he is simply not to be found. Milady is irritated. She storms. She notes that his work so far is exceedingly well done. When he makes his appearance she has decided to keep him until "she can do better." When wash-day comes she shows him the linen, and the soap and the tubs. He takes the clothes and begins carefully to sort and to check them. She knows that he is going to make the same methodical, thoroughgoing job of it, and she departs for a club meeting. Completing his careful count, the Jap calls up the laundry. Milady is irritated again and would fire him if he were about. She frets, but fretting, sees that her house is in order as never before. When Newah comes in the morning she has surrendered and holds him ever after as a treasure.

These are the workers whom the American Federation of Labor excludes from membership, without reference to skill required or developed. Can it be said that in any genuine sense the A.F. of L. seeks the organization of the working class?

And these are the workers whom the Socialist party in America, joining with the capitalist state, seeks to exclude from citizenship. Has the national soil become so sacred to the Socialists? How coyotish then becomes our yelp at capitalism that it deprives us of the right to work and live. What, then, is to become of our legendary "Workers of the World, Unite," etc.?

# 9 THE SOCIALIST PARTY AND GENDER ISSUES

## WRITINGS ON WOMEN AND SOCIETY

100 YEARS AGO
Mary E. Marcy
*International Socialist Review*
12 (June 1912): 837–43

It was not until we knew Grandmother Hopkins, a beautiful old lady of eighty-eight, who had come to make her home with relatives in the city, that we realized what invention and the factory system have done to the old fashioned home. She had grown a little childish but her pain and wonder over the ways of flat dwellers and "roomers" was always accompanied by a flow of words on the good old days and only to hear her was a liberal education on the pioneer days in the Central States.

The switch with which we turned on and off the electric lights, the marvels of the gas range and steam heat would always start her off on reminiscences of the great old fire places and of candle making.

The candle wicks, Grandmother told us, were made of loosely spun hemp, tow or cotton, sometimes even of milkweed. Six or eight long strands of the tow were usually tied to a stick and were dipped into great kettles filled with hot tallow. Later, when the settlers raised bees, wax was often used. Candle making was the work of the women of the household, and the task was an arduous one. The long wicks had to be alternately dipped into the hot tallow or wax and allowed to cool, the candles increasing in thickness with every operation. Feeding the fire alone was a job of no mean proportion. All through the year the women hoarded every ounce of deer suet, moose fat, bear grease and tallow for the time of the annual candle making.

Home made pewter lamps were also used in Grandmother's day. These were mere bowls or cans containing a narrow spout from which hung wicks which, when lighted, gave forth an unpleasant smoke but a glow vastly superior to candle light. Fish and other home made oils were first burned. These were prepared by the women. This was before the day of lamp chimneys.

*Fire*

In the days of the early settlers it was a family catastrophe when the fire went out. But in Grandmother's time flint, steel and tinder were recognized household necessities. In 1827 a patent was granted the inventor of the first matches. These were made of strips of wood dipped in sulphur, and ignited readily. The inventor sold 84 matches for 25 cents, but it was many years before matches came into general use.

Candle making, fire building and light striking are no longer a part of "woman's work." They have been abolished from the home. Gas, steam and electricity are at hand ready to do our bidding. Even the making of matches has become one of the great industries, where thousands of girls and women operating modern machines produce millions of matches in a single day.

The hot and cold water taps were another point of wonder to Grandmother. In her girlhood days water had to be carried sometimes long distances from springs and heated in great pots over the fireplace.

The Pennsylvania Dutch had the first stoves used in America. The first stove was built into the house, three sides being indoors, while the stove had to be fed from the outside. As the men worked out of doors a goodly portion of the time, the fire tending fell to the lot of the women. I doubt not but many of them could wield an ax with any of the men.

As cattle increased, the duties of the dairy grew. There came butter making; and cheese making was an unending care from the time the milk was set over the fire to warm and curdle, through the breaking of the curds into the cheese baskets, through shaping into cheeses and pressing in cheese presses, and placing them on the cheese ladders to be constantly turned and rubbed.

*Soap Making*

Soap making time came in the fall, and meant more work for the housewife. Even the lye had to be manufactured from wood ashes at home. And there were geese to be picked three or four times a year, for everybody slept on feather beds in those days.

I remember one of grandmother's stories of an old time neighbor who burned down a deserted house merely for the sake of the few nails used in its construction. Nails were one of the most valuable of all the commodities in her grandmother's day.

November was the appointed killing time. Of refrigeration there was none and fresh meat lasted only a short time in warm weather. Choice pieces were sometimes preserved in cool springs for a little while but almost all meats had to be promptly pickled and salted away for preservation. Rolliches and head cheeses were made at killing time; lard was tried and tallow saved.

In the winter might be found in the homes of every good housewife, hogsheads of corned beef, barrels of salt pork, tubs of hams being salted in brine, tonnekins of salt fish, firkins of butter, kegs of pigs feet and tubs of souse. And there were head cheeses, strings of sausage, very highly spiced to preserve them, jars of fruit, bins of potatoes, apples, turnips, parsnips and beets.

The kitchen, or living room, was constantly hung with strings of drying apples, onions, rounds of pumpkins and peppers. Sugar was very scarce and its place was taken by pumpkins and very soon by honey, till maple syrup and maple sugar were discovered.

Today some women still preserve the fruit and vegetables for their own families. This is no longer a difficult matter. A telephone message brings the required material from the nearby grocer, also jars to be hermetically sealed. The ingredients are ready to hand, prepared by the thousands of men and women working in huge factories all over the world. Fire is brought up to our very table. We have only to turn it on. But the woman who now does preserving at home is the exception. Little by little the factories have taken up this branch of "woman's work" and it is now much cheaper to buy factory canned goods than to do the work in the home. Perhaps our grandmothers who suffered through the hot summer days over blazing stoves are not sorry to see this branch of home life destroyed by the factory system.

*Spinning and Weaving*

Almost within our fathers' time, every farmer and his sons raised wool and flax. His wife and daughters spun them into yarn and thread. When the flax plants were only three or four inches high they were weeded by the women and children who were compelled to work in their bare feet in order to avoid crushing the young stalks. Unsually men prepared the flax and "broke it," while the girls, working their feet on the treadle, spun the fiber into an even thread. The thread was then wound off into reels or skeins.

These were bleached by being laid in water for four days, the water being constantly changed and the skeins wrung out. Finally they were "bucked," that is, bleached in ashes and hot water for a week or more, after which came a grand rinsing, washing, drying and winding on bobbins for the loom. All this labor in the bleaching process was not by any means the end of the operation.

Steadily wool production increased. The fleeces had to be gone over by the women with care, and all pitched and tarred locks, brands and beltings were cut out. But they were not lost. The cuttings were spun into coarse yarn.

*Dyeing*

The white locks were carefully loosened and separated and tied into net bags to be dyed. Indigo was the favorite blue dye. Cochineal and logwood and madder made beautiful reds. Bark of the red oak or hickory made pretty browns and yellows. The flower of the golden rod when pressed of its juice mixed with indigo and added to alum, made a bright green. Sassafras bark was used to secure a rich brown and orange.

The next process was carding. The wool was first greased with oil, then combed and spun. Later families sent their wool to the mill to be carded by crude machines, while the spinning and weaving was still done at home. This is, we believe, still the prevailing method in Ireland.

The same primitive methods prevailed for a long time in the cotton industry. But the invention of the cotton gin in 1792 soon made necessary the use of machinery to take care of the increased supply of cotton produced by the gin. The spinning jenny and power looms soon appeared. More work, formerly performed in the home, was now done in mills and factories. This meant more "breaking up" of what all our grandmothers'[sic] called home. Cotton cloth was for a time still printed, colored or "stamped" by hand, in the home. Grandmother remembers wearing "beautiful cotton dresses" printed by her mother.

In her home life in colonial days, Alice Morse Earle quotes as follows from a letter written by an American farmer only a little over one hundred years ago:

"At this time my farm gave me and my whole family a good living on the produce of it and left me one year with $150.00, for I never spent more than $10.00 a year for salt, nails and the like. Nothing to eat, drink or wear was bought as my farm provided all."

About the same time Abigail Foote set down her daily work in this wise (Home Life in Colonial Days):

"Fix'd gown for Prude. Mended mother's riding hood. Spun thread. Carded tow. Spun linen. Hatchel'd flax with Hannah. Worked on cheese basket. Spooled a piece. Milked cows. Spun linen. Did 50 knots, Made broom of Guinea wheat straw. Carded two pounds of wool Spun harness twine."

Besides the work of cooking and taking care of the home generally the women of grandmother's time were in charge of the dairying, raising the small stock, combing, carding, spinning, weaving, knitting, sewing, pickling, preserving, salting, soap and candle making. All stockings and mittens were knit at home till 1850, when a patent was granted for wool weaving machines. It was a good many years later that machine weaving became general.

Women made every article of clothing worn by the entire family except sometimes, the shoes. She made bonnets for the girls and hats and caps for the men. She wove the shawls worn by everybody and invented the first straw hat. When there were carpets these too were the work of her hands.

In grandmother's day the home was the industrial unit. Every man, woman and child knew how to produce things for the needs of the family. Nothing was specialized beyond the family. The individual farm was almost sufficient unto itself.

Something has destroyed the home and home life that our grandmothers knew. It is enough that we conjure up a picture of the old ways and compare them to the lives of the flat dwellers, the boarders and roomers of today. More proof is not needed. The old fashioned home has been destroyed, is being further destroyed by the invention of new machinery and the progress of specialized factory production.

From the very first machine carding of fleece was so cheap that farmers were constrained to send this work to be done in the mill. Then came machine spinning and weaving. At every step it became evident that home labor could be performed at such low cost in the mills.

For a long time all the family clothing was still made in the home, where the sewing machine helped to reduce the drudgery of the housewife. And in our own time every article of wearing apparel can be purchased ready made at prices so low that home made clothes have become almost a thing of the past.

Cheapness has battered down the wall of the farmer's prejudice and gradually he has permitted almost every branch of industry to be taken from his home to be done in the mill and factory, while he has set the members of his family to specializing in lines where the pay is better. It was never possible for the seller of home made products to compete with the mill or factory machine commodities for long.

Farm machinery has steadily lessened the work of the men upon the farm. One man can today, by the use of modern machines, accomplish the work that ten men did formerly under the old methods.

But the young men and women have followed their old work into the cities, into the woolen and cotton mills, into the match factories, and packing houses. Many of them no longer have even their meals in their own homes. Great armies of restaurants and cafes have sprung up everywhere,

where people may dine for less than it would cost to cook at home.

Laundries there are too—"breaking up" another branch of the old time "home." With one dozen sheets washed and ironed by machine for 25 cents came the beginning of the end of the old back-breaking wash-tub days. Monday, or "wash day," has lost its old time significance. It is just like any other day.

Gone are the candle-making seasons, the wood splitting times. Of home soap-makers we have none and few of us would even know how to make lye if we had to. Steam heat, electric lights, bakeries, laundries, restaurants, ready-to-wear clothing have destroyed little by little, year by year, the classic institutions of the old time home. Tasks that it took our grandmothers many days in the past are now better done in fewer hours in the factories.

Every day sees new tasks taken from the home and performed in the mills and factories, and every day sees more and more women joining the great army of industrial workers. The home of today has become only the shell of the home of yesterday. Spring house cleaning and sweeping have fallen before the march of the vacuum cleaner. The housewife has been deprived of "woman's work." She is more and more being forced into the class of proletarians. Home owning for the vast majority of people has ceased to exist. Women must find jobs, must sell their labor power—their strength to work, in order to earn a living. The bread and butter problem has given them a new "sphere" in the factory.

They now work beside men in the mills and are forced to compete with them for jobs.

The great inventions that should have lessened woman's labors have benefited her not at all. Stripped of all property, she is in the way of being directly exploited, as her father and brothers are being exploited. In order to earn a living she grinds out profit for some capitalist.

The great factories, and modern machines that perform, with very little expenditure of human labor, the arduous tasks that formerly were hers, do not bring ease or comfort or plenty to her. For these tools, these great machines by which clothes and food and other commodities are produced, are owned by a few men and women who do not operate, or use them.

Because there are always thousands of unemployed men and women seeking for jobs, wages are always driven down to the bare cost of living. For the bosses, the factory and mill owners, always buy labor power or working strength where it is cheapest. All the clothing, the shoes, hats, food, etc., that the workers produce are kept by the factory and mill owners. They should be the property of those who do the work. This is the aim of Socialism. It proposes that the men and women who work shall own the factories, that they shall themselves own the things they make.

The time has come when it is impossible for young men and women to save enough out of their wages to start into business for themselves. Every industry is now controlled by vast aggregations of capital that run up into millions of dollars. It takes great sums of money to buy the necessary machines, to put up modern plants that alone can successfully compete with the great trusts. The time of the poor boy or girl who may become a captain of industry is about past.

The professional fields for men and for women are badly overcrowded and the competition among professional people will bring the remuneration in these fields down to a bare living just as it does in the department stores and sweat shops. A young dentist recently informed us that thousands of boys in America are studying dentistry because there is a demand for them in some of the large foreign cities. Within ten years this field will be overcrowded and dentists will be competing for work till there will be only a scant living in this profession for any of them.

It is too late to go back to Grandmother's way even if we wanted to. There is no more free land. The capitalist system under which we live draws our sons to the cities to earn a living, our daughters into the factories, our husbands into the mines. It sends us into the mills to make cloth.

The capitalist system has broken up the old fashioned home and scattered it to the four corners of the earth for the sake of profits. Our only hope lies in Socialism.

There is no hope for the propertyless young man or woman becoming independent today. There is no one to assure you that you and your husband shall have steady work—that your children shall be able to earn three square meals a day. This is the task of Socialism.

Whether or not you are one of the fast decreasing number of housewives today, or whether you are a wage slave directly exploited in the factories, mills or department stores, your home broken up in capitalist society of today, Socialism is a message of hope for your husband, your father, your children as well as for yourself.

Socialism means that those who work shall eat; that the reaping shall be done by those who sow. It means that every man and woman in the world shall have equal and ample opportunity to work without being robbed of most of his product by a rich boss.

It means that the workers shall collectively own the mines, mills, factories, railroads and land—all the instruments for producing the necessities of life. It means that these men and women shall own the things they produce.

The Socialist party is the one party in the world today that represents the working class. It offers to every woman equal political and economic rights to those accorded men.

If you are a working woman, or the wife of a working man, read the literature of Socialism and join the Socialist party.

Meanwhile, if you are at work in factory, mill or shop, organize in the shop. An industrial union will give every man, woman and child a vote today.

The emancipation of the workers depends on the workers themselves. Write for information on Socialism and the Industrial Union movement.

True Homes Under Socialism
May Walden
*Socialist Woman*
No. 8 (January 1908): 5

The Social Democratic Herald has this panacea to offer for the divorce question: When men are in a position to earn much larger incomes so they can furnish greater comforts to their wives, the friction of home life will be so much lessened that disagreements ending in divorce will be unknown.

This theorist does not seem to see anything but the commercialism of the marriage and divorce question.

He—or she—assumes that a woman will always marry for the sake of a home and the bric-a-brac she can put into it with her monthly allowance, or the fine upholstery with which she may decorate herself. That she may ever occupy a position where she can have a home of her own without depending upon a man to give it to her, is outside the conception of some people. *She will be able to do this when she is economically free.*

Plenty of women, even nowadays, who are earning a comfortable income, keep up a home, but find a husband too great a luxury to indulge in. And as time goes on, and women are freed, politically, economically, and socially, marriage as we know it, will be an unknown institution belonging to the age of women's slavery, and looked upon as a relic of that age.

Socialism has nothing to do with the marriage question; its object is to abolish the system of wage slavery and profits, but it cannot be denied that the establishment of economic independence for everybody will eventually modify the marriage relation.

Our capitalist enemies see this in a dim fashion, and at once declare that "Socialism will break up the home;" that "free love" will prevail, and that society will be in a worse condition than ever before. In assuming this, they show what a very poor opinion they have of women.

When socialism is established, it will be possible for the first time in history for a woman to love a man for himself, and not for the food, clothes, shelter, and amusements he is able to provide for her. For the first time he will be in a position to find out if he is being loved for himself alone. For this reason love will necessarily be put upon a higher plane, for no self-respecting man or woman is willing to admit that love on a purely physical plane is life-lasting, elevating or satisfying.

Every woman will insist upon a mate who is her ideal, temperamentally, intellectually, and ethically. Every man will do the same. Under these conditions people will be much better mated than they are nowadays, and with the absence of friction which comfortable living always gives, there is every reason to suppose that love will be life-lasting.

But if mistakes should occur, why should there be any opprobium [sic] attached to people who rectify them in the safest and quickest way by separation?

Our opponents again tell us, that when the children are cared for by society, when fathers and mothers are no longer held wholly responsible for the welfare and education of their off-spring, that we will have a state of anarchy to which the present cannot be compared. This again implies a low opinion of men and women. I can never be so cynical in my opinion of the human race as to believe that the instincts of father and mother-love will ever die out. From the animals up to the highest and best specimens of the human race, the love for mate and children have been strong and beautiful traits which have prevailed throughout all times.

Instead of taking less thought for these whom we bring into the world we will take more; and we will not lightly thrust away responsibilities which will have more pleasure than annoyance in them.

And all of this will come about through the opportunities, enlightenments, and inspirations of the order of the things we are all working for—the co-operative commonwealth.

## The Law and the White Slaver [EXCERPT]
Kate Richards O'Hare
(St. Louis: The National Rip-Saw Publishing Co., 1911), pp. 28–32

Socialists know . . . that our natural resources and our machinery of production have slipped away from the ownership of the great mass of mankind. A small class owns the means of life: the great mass is dependent upon it for the means of life; and out of this condition has grown not only prostitution, but all the other wrongs, abuses and damnable features of our state of society. The Socialist knows that just as long as the means of life are privately owned by a small class, the oppression and degradation of the masses must continue and grow more unbearable.

We are today facing facts and not theories, and the facts are these: Small groups of organized owners (which for want of a better name we call trusts) are in complete ownership and control of the industries, markets, professions, politics and religious institutions of the whole world. And by this ownership they control food, shelter, clothing, education, enlightenment, body, mind and soul of individual and nation. Either the nation must take over the ownership of these great organized machines of production and distribution, or the trusts will continue to enforce its ownership of nation and individual.

The first great principal [sic] of Socialism is the public ownership of the trusts. But it is not enough for the nation to own the trusts, unless the people can own the nation. We have found, to our sorrow, that our present political machinery will not permit this. Representative government without the power to force our representatives to serve us has proven a delusion and a snare. Socialists see the necessity of certain changes in our fundamental form of government. First the initiative, the right and power of the people to initiate any measures they deem necessary for public welfare; second, the referendum or the right and power of the people to have a deciding voice in legislation and the power to veto harmful measures; third, the right of recall or the power to recall at will the public servant, who after election proves either unsuited to the position, incapable of properly performing his functions or susceptible to corrupting influences; fourth, the right of suffrage for all citizens regardless of sex.

Socialism may be summed up in these simple propositions:

The public ownership of the trusts and public utilities.
The Initiative.
The Referendum.
The Right of Recall.
Universal Suffrage.

The natural result of this would be free and unhampered access to the means of life by the people, the workers alone sharing in the wealth created; the disappearance of the owning class as such; the conversion of its now useless and idle members into useful workers; and, emancipation of the workers from the slavery of the present system. Industrial slavery to the owners of the machine, political slavery to a worn-out and corrupt form of government, and sex slavery in every form would vanish.

This is Socialism, and through it alone can the problem of the social evil ever be solved.

For years the moral have hid their faces, the pious shuddered, and the church trembled every time they heard the word Socialism because they feared that Socialism would bring about an era of "Free Love."

Now, of course, these good people know just about as much about love and freedom as an owl knows of an anthem. They can comprehend neither, but what they think it means is promiscuity and license. Bishop Maguire, of the Catholic Church, has answered this misunderstood idea and I will quote his words:

"Socialists would establish 'Free Love.'

"Our opponents seem to forget that a Socialist state like any other would be but the outward expression of the people who composed it. We would have only that which the people wished. The only meaning to be taken from the assertion of our opponents is that if we had not landlords and capitalists to rob us, we would kick our wives to death, cast our children out of the windows and roam the country like savage beasts, leaving the product of our vice to the state to support. Such are the reasons put forward in favor of retention of landlordism and capitalism. If Socialists wished a state of society in which 'free love' or free lust flourished as the Devil would have it, they would support the present. Ascertain the number of prostitutes known to the police in any city, think of the number of immoral men who maintain such an army, total these and deduct the sum from the adult population. The remainder is that section of the community not known to the police as vicious persons.

"In the course of discussion which took place last year at a Catholic conference, Father Hughes, of Liverpool, told of a girl in that city who was engaged in the drapery trade at 31d or 62 cents a week. She drifted into a life of vice, and when Father Hughes met her she had spent two years thus. He induced her to return to the path of virtue and she then informed him that she had £10,000 worth of jewelry received in presents from her 'admirers' during these two years. The reverend gentleman argued that while girls were offered £15,12 ($65) for two years, honest, virtuous service and £10,000 ($50,000) for the same time spent in a vicious career, we would have this shocking state of society. He might have added that the jewelry was not presented by the working men of Liverpool. The class which deprives the girl of her earnings also robs her of her virtue. Under Socialism the rewards would be reversed and so would the results.

"'Christianity is sufficient to solve the social problem.'

"If that were so we would find least poverty where we found most real Christianity. Ireland should be the happiest country in the world because there are millions of people who believe without doubting, amongst whom the breath of agnosticism has scarcely entered. It is the very poorest country. Why? Because in a community living under the competitive system, one dishonest, unscrupulous man will overcome ninety-nine who conduct their business in the spirit of Christ. The non-Christians will make slaves of the Christians, just as the armed highwayman will subdue a peaceable citizen protected only by a prayer-book. The highwayman is the fitter person according to conditions, so is the non-Christian. It is the conditions which are bad, and for public safety we must change them. Socialism would make robbery of all kinds impossible. When Christianity advises us to be honest, Socialism would compel us to be."

Socialism will give back to women all the freedom and security of the savage fraternal culture and add to it all the advantages of our more civilized life; will make her an equal owner and give her an equal voice in the management of all wealth, that supplied by Nature as well as produced by men's hands. She will have an equal opportunity to have access to the means of life, receive equal returns for her labor, and will thus be enabled to lift herself above the necessity of selling her virtue for bread.

That any woman lives the life of a prostitute because she enjoys it no one with common sense believes. The life is too horrible to contemplate. The sex nature is the most delicate function of life, the most easily disturbed, causes the most intense suffering if abused, and no woman can think (if she thinks at all) that any other woman enjoys receiving the attentions of all comers, at all hours of the day and night, under all condition, and all manner of men, diseased or whole, drunk or sober.

We women know that deep down under the veneer of submission ages of subjection have endowed us with, there is that old savage revolt at forced sex relation. We know that all the primeval savage, all the wild that is hidden somewhere within us is aroused at the slightest show of force in matters pertaining to sex, and can you imagine force less hateful because it is economic force, the force of cold and hunger instead of brute force?

Socialism will shear man of his economic power to force woman to submit either in marriage or prostitution to his sensual desires. A few generations of free women will produce a race free from sensuality, and that old falsehood of the male's greater need of sexual expression and its natural result, a double standard of morals, will cease to carry weight.

## THE NATIONAL CONVENTION AND THE WOMAN'S MOVEMENT
Jessie Molle
*International Socialist Review*
8 (May 1908): 688–90

We are drawing near to a national convention of the Socialist Party when we are to nominate our candidates for president and vice-president, and draw up the national platform. However, this is not all that will be done in this meeting. Resolutions will be introduced pertaining to practically every question of economic interest to the working class. Among these will be resolutions on the attitude of the party toward trade-unions, the negro problem, child labor, and a great many other important subjects.

The problem I which to discuss in this article is the attitude of the Socialist Party toward the woman's movement. It makes very little difference whether we approve of a separate organization of Socialist women or not. We have one—a real, live, revolutionary movement, writing its own literature, managing its own newspapers, planning its own campaign.

It does not have the same name in every state or even in every city. In Philadelphia it is the Socialist Woman's Educational Club, in California, the Woman's Socialist Club; in New York City, Socialist Women of Greater New York. This city is the home also of the Woman's National Progressive League. In Chicago there is the Woman's Socialist League; in St. Louis the Wowan's [*sic*] Socialist Club, while in Kansas City we have the Woman's Progressive League. And so I might go on through all of the states and territories of the nation, naming the cities and towns with their respective clubs.

It is one movement with one mind, one spirit, one thought, one object: "the purpose of stimulating and crystallizing interest among women in economic questions with the view of creating adherents to the principles of Socialism."

How are we men and women of the Socialist Party organization going to act toward this movement? What will our delegates in the National Convention do if they receive a resolution similar to the one presented by the Social Democratic Woman's Society of N. Y., at a meeting at which Mrs. Cobden Sanderson delivered a lecture on "Socialism and Woman?" The part of this resolution that is of special interest to us reads as follows:

"Whereas, The Socialist Party is the political expression of the working class in the United States, be it

"Resolved, By this mass meeting of men and women of New York, that we call upon the National Committee of the Socialist Party to start an energetic fight for equal suffrage for men and women 21 years of age; to put women organizers in the field with same end in view, and to distribute leaflets and literature dealing with this subject."

First, we must realize that this movement is a separate organization composed largely of women who are not members of the Socialist Party. This will prevent us from falling into, what I believe to be, the error that the Missouri State Convention did in 1906. To give the reader a clearer idea of what I mean, I will quote from the report of the proceedings of this meeting as printed in the St. Louis "Labor," Saturday, June 9, 1906 . . . .

"We recommend that special efforts be made to place propaganda literature in all Women's Clubs, Equal Suffrage Socities [sic] and conventions in order that these earnest, enthusiastic and intelligent women may know and understand that the eight short words embodied in the Socialist National Platform—'For the equal suffrage of men and women' cover the whole ground, and express in plain language what the old parties have evaded and juggled with ever since women have demanded equal suffrage." On motion it was adopted.

"We recommend that special attention be given to youths and children, as in a few years the duties of citizenship will fall upon their shoulders. The propaganda work can be interesting, instructive and also a source of income by means of entertainments, literary and debating societies; always selecting subjects pertaining directly toward a better education in the principles of Socialism. To this end we favor the formation of Junior Socialist Leagues to take charge of this work in connection with the regular organization.

"The motion to adopt this recommendation was amended that it be received and, together with the Woman Suffrage recommendation previously adopted, be referred to the Women's Socialist Clubs in the state. Motion was adopted as amended:" Just how the Socialist Party organization can refer any of its business to other organizations not under its jurisdiction, I have never been quite able to understand.

Second, we must realize that these Woman's Clubs cannot do our work. Their work is to sow the seeds of Socialism. They are the "St. John" "crying in the wilderness." In answer to Mrs. Wilshire's "Appeal to Women" in Wilshire's, January, 1907, I closed my letter which was published in the March number of that magazine with the following: "I am very much opposed to forming a separate organization for women. I would be just as much opposed to forming a separate organization for men. Every Socialist should be in the organization. We must work together. To divide our ranks would mean an opening for the enemy. We should always keep in mind the one object, the building up of the Socialist organization.". [sic] However, I see no danger in this woman's movement. The women who are leading it belong to the Socialist Party and well understand the meaning of the words, "Workers of the world unite." They are sowing the seeds and all ready "The harvest truly is great." Will the Socialist Party furnish the "laborers" so "that both he that soweth and he that reapeth may rejoice together?" As a member of both organizations, this question is of the greatest interest to me. I am not asking it of the men or the women but of the party as a whole. We need workers and they should be women with the ability not only of teaching the women what the word Socialism means but also of bringing into the party those who already know its meaning, but who, for one reason or another, stay out. This is a work that the Woman's Movement cannot do.

In conclusion, I suggest that the National Party in its convention take up this matter, and "establish in connection with the party a National Committee of Women to be charged with this special work," as Comrade [John] Spargo suggested. . . I believe the Woman's movement will gladly co-operate with it in furnishing the funds to carry on this movement.

*Proceedings* [EXCERPTS] OF THE 1908 SOCIALIST PARTY CONVENTION,
    "THE WOMAN SUFFRAGE QUESTION"
*International Socialist Review*
8 (June 1908): 735–37

The Committee on the Relation of Women to the Socialist Movement then presented its report by Mila Tupper Maynard, the chairman. She explained that the plank on woman suffrage in the platform already adopted had been drafted by the Women's Committee and that this was the only official declaration thought desirable. She then read the text of the report as follows:

"The national committee of the Socialist party has already provided for a special organizer and lecturer to work for equal civil and political rights in connection with the Socialist propaganda among women, and their organization in the Socialist party.

"This direct effort to secure the suffrage to women increases the party membership and opens up a field of work entirely new in the American Socialist party. That it has with it great possibilities and value for the party, our comrades in Germany, Finland and other countries have abundantly demonstrated.

"The work of organization among women is much broader and

more far-reaching than the mere arrangement of tours for speakers. It should consist of investigation and education among women and children, particularly those in the ranks of labor, in or out of labor unions, and to the publication of books, pamphlets and leaflets, especially adapted to this field of activity.

"To plan such activity requires experience that comes from direct contact with an absorbing interest in the distinct feature of woman's economic and social conditions, and the problem arising therefrom.

"For this reason the committee hereby requests this convention to take definite action on this hitherto neglected question. We ask that it make provision to assist the Socialist women of the party in explaining and stimulating the growing interest in Socialism among women and to aid the women comrades in their efforts to bring the message of Socialism to the children of the proletariat, we recommend the following:

"1st, that a special committee of five be elected to care for and manage the work of organization among women.

"2d, that sufficient funds be supplied by the party to that committee to maintain a woman organizer constantly in the field as already voted.

"3d, that this committee co-operate directly with the national headquarters and be under the supervision of the national party.

"4th, that this committee be elected by this national convention, its members to consist not necessarily of delegates to this convention.

"5th, that all other moneys needed to carry on the work of the woman's committee outside of the maintenance of the special organizers, be raised by the committee.

"6th, that during the campaign of 1908 the women appointed as organizers be employed in states now possessing the franchise."

*Minority Report*

This [above] report was signed by all members of the committee except Laura Payne of Texas, who then presented her minority report as follows:

"The Socialist movement is the political expression of the working class regardless of sex, and its platform and program furnish ample opportunity for propaganda work both by and among men and women when we are ready to take advantage of it. The same blow necessary to strike the chains from the hands of the working man will also strike them from the hands of the working woman.

"Industrial development and the private ownership and control of the means of production and distribution of wealth have forced women and children into the mills and factories, mines, workshops and fields along with the men, dependent for job and wage on the master class. Into that mart of trade they go to sell their labor power, and when for no reason whatever they cannot find a market for it they must seek other means of support. Driven to the last resort, men often become criminals or vagabonds, while women, for food, clothing and shelters, sell themselves and go to recruit the ranks of the fallen.

"Whether it be economic slavery to this extent—or whether it be within the bounds of the possibility of an honorable life—the cause is the same, namely, the private ownership of the means by which they must live.

"It is contended by some that women because of their disfranchisement and because of their economic dependence on men, bear a different relationship to the Socialist movement from that of the men. That is not so. The economic dependence of our men, women and children—whether to a greater or less extent—can be traced to the same cause, which Socialism will alone remove.

"In regard to the ballot in some of our states the men are disfranchised, or practically so, by property qualifications and other requirements for voting, and it seems to this committee that you would just as well waste time in trying to regulate those things as in waging a special suffrage campaign for women.

"There is only one thing, and one only, that will remove these evils and that is Socialism, and the nearest way to it is to concentrate all our efforts—men and women working together side by side in the different states and locals, with an eye single to the main issue, The Class Struggle!

"Therefore, my comrades of this convention, I respectfully submit the following resolution:

"Resolved, that there be a special effort on the part of the speakers and organizers in the Socialist party of America to interest the women and induce them to work in the locals of the respective states, side by side with the men as provided in our platform, and constitution; and be it further

"Resolved, that great care shall be taken not to discriminate between men and women or take any step which would result in a waste of energy and perhaps in a separate woman's movement."

In the discussion which ensued most of the speakers held that it was advisable to carry on a propaganda among women in which should be enlisted the support of those desiring suffrage. Delegate Payne said that most of the work on behalf of women suffrage in various places assumed very much the character of "parlor pink teas." The minority report was rejected by a vote of 35 to 70. The majority report was then adopted and a permanent committee was elected consisting of May Wood Simons, Antoinette Konikow, Marguerite Prevey, Winnie Branstetter and Meta Stein.

AIMS AND PURPOSES OF WOMEN [*SIC*] COMMITTEE
May Wood Simons
*Progressive Woman*
No. 29 (October 1909): 2

At the national convention of the Socialist party held in 1908 a committee on women was elected to formulate a plan for work among women, the work to be carried on directly under the supervision of the Socialist party, its object being to secure women members of the party and emphasize the necessity of obtaining the ballot for women.

. . . Since the close of the convention women, who are already members of the Socialist party in the various locals of the country, have begun active work to accomplish the objects that were put before them by the convention. First, the securing of women members in the Socialist locals; second, the agitation for the franchise for women; third, the work of increasing the usefulness of the Socialist Sunday schools.

The work of securing women members for the party and increasing the attendance of women at the Socialist meetings has been begun systematically in great numbers of the locals.

The function of the national woman's committee is to advise and outline methods by which women may best be interested in Socialism and brought into the Socialist party, and to keep the need of agitation for suffrage for women before the locals.

As an advisory committee it has worked out a plan for work in the locals. It is advised that every local appoint a committee consisting of women who are already members of the local. If no women are at present members, let the secretary of the local act as a committee. Arrange a lecture or entertainment which it is believed would interest women and make an effort to get as many women as possible to be present, wives of Socialist members, teachers, clerks, trade union women, etc.

Secure the addresses of all the women present. Then make it a point to see them within a few days and invite them to attend the Socialist meetings. Have some literature to give them.

Follow this work up and finally urge the women to become members of the local. This method works. It will bring women into the party. It has been tried and when carried on systematically shows results. When a woman member has been secured plan to keep her. Make her feel she is necessary to the local. Give her work to do. Make her a member of the committee. Set her to work to educate and secure more members. If she makes errors in the business meetings help her to correct them.

The national office now maintains a national organizer. As soon as possible every state should put a woman organizer to work and in each state a committee of women acting in conjunction with the state committee of the party should be elected.

The working women of the country are ready to learn of Socialism. If they are not brought in now it is because the locals have not done valuable work that should be done.

Recognizing the fact that a single line of work may tend to occupy the attention to the exclusion of equally important matters, the women carrying on this work emphasize the importance of each woman keeping in the closest touch with her local and the local, state and national organization, and all political issues that may arise and maintain her place as an active member of the Socialist organization. Further, all work being carried on is done in consultation with the party organization and for the purpose of increasing the strength and power of that organization.

## Do You Help Or Do You Hinder?
Anne A. Maley
*Socialist Woman*
No. 5 (October, 1907): 5

How often do we hear the story—"This comrade's wife makes his life a burden because he is in the Socialist movement. She says their friends have deserted them, he is always doing committee work or at a meeting and she has no social life at all."

We women have a long and bitter past to overlive. All the harder must we strive lest we hang as a millstone on the world's rising hope.

Your table is well supplied. Your child studies and plays and sleeps warm. You are well fed, decently clothed, comfortably housed. For you virtue is easy. Yet you know there are bare cupboards. There are children who might be as bright and sweet as yours whose highest joy is the crust picked from the garbage can. There are women, sisters of your blood, whose womanhood is the price of their bread. There are men on the road, men in the cellars, men peeping through prison bars—yea, and men in the river bed, who have been beaten in the fight for a living. And all because the world's industrial life is wrong. All because the masters control our labor. All because a workingman, or a workingwoman, or a working child—or a working babe!—is not regarded by the masters of the bread as a human being but as a thing out of which profits are made.

Your husband in engaged in a movement for the establishment of industrial democracy instead of industrial tyranny. He holds that men and women who work should control the conditions of their labor and this they can do only by owning the tools of the industry. The masters now own these tools and the law protects them in their ownership. The government makes the laws and the political party elects the government. Your husband is helping to build a political party which will elect a government which will make the laws for the protection of the working people—laws which will save the starved child, the debauched woman, and the defeated man. Now do you understand the meaning of his committee work, his attendance at meetings? Now do you understand what the cost would be to the world's miserable if every man gave up his serious work for his wife's pleasure?

O woman, we have been sex-cursed. In the love of one baby we forget the unprotected weaklings of the world. In the care of one home we forget the homeless, we forget the hovel. We think that the husband who shields us should not so much as look beyond our little domestic circle . . . .

Sisters of mine, come, let us leave our past behind us. If we cannot lead the columns in the battle for right, let us be good followers. If we cannot teach our men, we can learn from them, we can cheer their effort, we can give them God-speed. Do not begrudge the dollar that goes to the Socialist work because it means the price of Jane's sash or of John's skates. The world has hosts of children who never know childhood. Arise yourself to the dignity of your place—speak plainly to your boy and girl of the world's wrong and the world's need. The children may be made a force in labor's crusade. Even as mother love may mould the child to selfishness, so may it lead him to high aims; and as the wife of narrow sympathies and mean aspirations may embitter the task of her husband, so may the wife who has caught the "vision splendid," be the courage of his spirit, the strength and glory of his ideal.

SEPARATE ORGANIZATIONS
Josephine Conger-Kaneko
*Socialist Woman*
No. 11 (April 1908): 5

A California comrade wants to know if it would be better if the women joined in the mixed locals and worked with the men, instead of having separate organizations of their own.

In answer to this query I would say that much depends upon the circumstances, both of the women and of the locals. Under favorable condition it no doubt is better to have the men and women work together in every phase of the Socialist movement.

By favorable conditions, I mean a group of women who are advanced sufficiently to be willing to work in the mixed locals, and a group of men who are sympathetic and responsive to those needs of women which lie outside their own. Given these conditions, and the mixed local is ideal.

But the masses of women are so backward, as far as any line of social progress is concerned and especially in the matter of Socialism, that it is difficult to induce them in any appreciable numbers to attend the locals, much less to join them. They need some sort of a preparatory school in which they may train for the more arduous work of the regular branch or local.

In the separate organization the most unsophisticated little woman may soon learn to preside over a meeting, to make motions, and to defend her stand with a little "speech." She has been used to talking and arguing with women all her life; she isn't self-conscious when enacting the business of a meeting before them. After a year or two of this sort of practice she is ready to work with the men. And there is a mighty difference between working *with* the men, and simply sitting in obedient reverence under the shadow of their aggressive power. Women have done this thing all the centuries of their historical lives. If they are willing to continue it, what can one expect from them under the gentle and benign influence of a Socialist regime?

If the terrors and oppressions of the present day are not sufficient to drive them into co-operative activity for their welfare as a class, and as a sex . . . what will they do toward furthering the *public* weal when the Co-operative Commonwealth shall furnish them a home, and a husband who can make enough money to keep them in that home, warm and comfortable, without a great deal of exertion on their part, as some Socialist writers predict will be the case?

There is a very great deal that women need to learn about themselves, about their history, and the traditions of their sex. These things can best be learned, as a rule, in a separate organization, where the mind can be better centered upon the matter in hand. A women's organization with alternate evenings devoted to business matters and to study, is a very good school for the average women seeking after the Socialist interpretation of a life—feminine life, as well as masculine. The members of such an organization *must feel*, however, that their work is as essential to individual and social progress as is the work of any other progressive society. And perhaps a little more so, since women are especially in need of intellectual development to offset the highly emotional development which has been theirs throughout the ages.

These organizations for women are especially essential in those communities where the male members of the local branch are not particularly aggressive in their sympathies with the woman part of the Socialist philosophy. We have known instances where the local was made a sort of man's club—a place where men met and talked and smoked, and split hairs over unimportant technicalities, transacted a little business, talked and smoked some more, and adjourned until the next meeting's program, which consisted of practically the same line of procedure. Sometimes these locals have a series of lectures which are good for the advanced Socialist, but cannot appeal to the mere woman who is seeking for the first steps. To be sure there are always two or three faithful women who will stick with these organizations, and go their lonely way night after night to the meetings. But, if conditions were right, I believe there would not be a Socialist local anywhere that would not have a good attendance of women compared with the percentage of men attendants.

We have to meet these facts, however, and we have to manage, somehow, to get women interested in Socialism. It hasn't been done satisfactorily so far through the mixed local. It remains to be seen what can be done through the separate organizations.

WOMAN AND SOCIALISM
Luella R. Krehbiel
*Socialist Woman*
No. 14 (July 1908): 7

Here are facts that should be stated and stated again until they are indelibly impressed upon the popular mind.

Through all of the world's history it has been possible to measure every civilization by the status of its women. Where women amount to but little men amount to but little more in general summing up.

Woman is more liberal and developed at the present time than ever before, but she is still unrecognized as a political and industrial factor, and we of to-day have but few normal people. Only the truly great are truly normal, and all should be great. Man's greatest mistake was his subjection of woman. Instead of women [*sic*] being subjected she should take the initiative, her individuality should be asserted and her talents developed to their highest capacity that she may transmit them to posterity.

Woman, the mother of the race, is still a subject and we have but few men who are at once "scholars, saints and gentlemen."

The Socialist movement is the first in the world's history that has acknowledged woman's rights as a political and industrial factor—and this movement is divided in its attitude toward the woman question. Some favor separate organizations for women, while others regard this as reactionary. We shall never be a free people until all power of whatever kind is vested in the people instead of a few individuals. The Socialist movement must not be burdened with side issues; it must remain clear cut and revolutionary. It would require almost as much time and money to make suffragists of the people as it would to make Socialists of them and then we should have to start another campaign to teach them how to use the ballot. No mere issue covers its own ground while Socialism covers the ground of all other issues.

We have millions of women in this country who are enduring the tortures of industrial slavery, but they are totally ignorant of any method of liberation. There is a great work that should be done among women by women that cannot be done by men, and this work can be supported and directed by the locals. Our Socialist women should be pushing propaganda among the women just as the men are pushing it among the men.

*We should have a leaflet that briefly expresses the message of Socialism and our women should start a leaflet campaign and not cease until the message of industrial liberation is carried to every sister-slave in the factory, sweatshop, miserable home, or sporting house.* This message should be carried with an expression of love and sympathy that is ever sincere and constant.

What has been done can be done again. I know of several instances where our Socialist women have held propaganda meetings in the different wards of a town. Women who could not have been induced to attend a Socialist local have attended these meetings, becoming students of Socialism and finally joined the locals. I know of several towns where the women prepare the program for every alternate propaganda meeting of their locals. A number of these women are placing children on the programs and thereby arousing an interest among the children.

Some of these organizations are taking up courses of study in history, Socialism and parliamentary law.

These local organizations will interest the women by giving them something to do; they will familiarize the women with official work, and be a most potent factor in spreading socialist sentiment.

I have been very greatly astonished at the work accomplished by several of these organizations, and if we had them in every town we would soon inaugurate the co-operative commonwealth.

## Where Do We Stand on the Woman Question?
Theresa Malkiel
*International Socialist Review*
10 (August 1909): 159–62

Theoretically we Socialists assert the equality of sex and race. We say, "All people are born equal," and accordingly strain all our efforts towards the abolition of the existing social regime. But around the one uppermost problem, like numerous planets around the sun, revolve many smaller problems which, though they will be solved with the solution of the whole, are important enough to be taken up and fought for separately.

The Woman Question is attracting today world-wide attention. The evolution of society has brought woman to the point where she realizes at last her degrading position and vehemently claims redress.

As Socialists we recognize, of course, that the real freedom of woman cannot be achieved before the entire social problem is solved. But we realize at the same time that under a regime of political tyranny the first and most urgent ideal is necessarily the conquest of political liberty. And therefore, our women here, like our disfranchised male comrades abroad, are taking up the fight for universal suffrage.

But there are many Socialists who cry out in fear whenever that subject is viewed from a practical and not only a theoretical point of view. This element, in keeping with its views, demands that we drop the woman question altogether, that it is no concern of ours and that every active participation in the enfranchisement of woman is a crime against scientific socialism.

Another portion of our scientific socialists go a step further and in their great wisdom assert that it is all a mistake, that man and woman are not equal.

Says Enrico Ferri: "Utopian Socialism has bequeathed to us a mental habit, a habit surviving even in the most intelligent disciples of Marxian Socialism, of asserting the existence of certain equalities—the equality of the two sexes, for example—assertions which cannot possibly be maintained." He even censures Bebel for claiming that from the psycho-physical point of view woman is the equal of man.

Then, only as late as last month, comes another of our scientific men and says: "The impulse below intellect is intuition, which is developed further in many animals than in man. And because woman is nearer to the lower forms than man, intuition is more deeply seated in the female race."

Is there greater wisdom in the assertion of a man who says: Woman is nearer to the animal than man, because she is endowed with an extraordinary amount of intuition; then in that of Mr. Roosevelt who says: "Every Socialist must be a free lover, because one or two of the Socialists had rather exciting marital experiences."

Was woman ever given the chance to display fully the strength of her intellectual ability? How could anybody, in view of woman's long subjection, judge her ability or the standard of her intellect? If our scientists would follow closely the history of woman and then note how today, though unprepared, she enters the different sphere of science, literature, music and art, where she holds fully her own with man, they might come to the conclusion that woman belongs rather to the higher plane of animal life.

True enough that there were but few great artists, musicians or scientists among the female of the race, but does not the writer himself state that a prolonged exercise of the brain cells goes to increase their quantity? If woman was able to achieve that much in the limited time of her brain development it goes to show that the quality of her brain cells is as good or even better than that belonging to the members of the opposite sex. In the face of the beastly acts so often characteristic of man, it is simply beyond human understanding how anybody could claim that woman is nearer to the animal, while man remains the supreme being.

With all due respect to our wise men, I think that even they would come to recognize our equality—if we only had the power to enforce it. It may be true that I am expressing myself with too much fervor, but if our male comrades were women they could understand easily how a statement like that goes to exasperate one. I have been always in the habit of speaking my mind freely and cannot see why this subject could not be discussed openly and thoroughly.

It is almost incomprehensible to me how our scientists came to such conclusion [sic]. And I, a plain ordinary mortal, challenge them in the name of my sex to set forth frankly and exhaustively the grounds on which they make these assertions.

My main object, however, in writing this article is to discuss our attitude on the Woman Question. For the workingwoman of today finds herself between two fires—on the one hand she faces the capitalist class, her bitterest enemy: it foresees a far-reaching danger in her emancipation and with all the ability of its money power tries to resist her gradual advent into the civilized world. In her anguish the working-woman turns towards her brothers in the hope to find a strong support in their midst, but she is doomed to be disillusioned, for they discourage her activity and are utterly listless towards the outcome of her struggle.

In the heat of the battle for human freedom the proletarians seem to forget that the woman question is nothing more or less than a question of human rights. That the emancipation of woman means in reality the emancipation of the human being within her. They seem to overlook the fact that it is as much their duty to fight for the workingwoman's political freedom, as it is to her advantage to make common cause with the men of her class in order to bring about the regeneration of society.

What revolution will yet have to take place in the conceptions of men! What change of education, before they will be able to attain the knowledge of a pure human relationship to woman! For every day experience teaches us that even the most progressive of our men are still considering woman as the being who, chained by a thousand fetters of dependency to man-made conditions, broken in spirit and in health by her long degradation and continual maternity, became a weak, thoughtless being that was neither man nor beast. They do not take into consideration that the woman of today has marched forward on the road of evolution.

What grandeur and beauty are contained in the meaning of this sentence in our platform: "There can be no emancipation of humanity without the social independence and equality of sex."

But how bitter is our disappointment whenever we come to look upon matters as they really are—men who take enthusiastically the pledge to abide and follow the party principles and ideals follow their promise to the letter, as far as generalities are concerned, but stop short where the question comes to the practical point of sex equality, an act to which they had earnestly pledged themselves in accepting the Socialist platform.

The bulk of womanhood, that is linked some way or other to the Socialist movement, is kept ignorant of the necessity of its participation in same (as well as of the justice of its political rights), for man is a man for all that and fears that he might suffer by woman's immediate freedom.

To those of us who had the courage and initiative to strike out for ourselves, the path is being covered with more thorns than roses. We are told very often to keep quiet about our rights and await the social millennium. Safe advice, rather, for the men.

The question before us is whether it is really possible that a host of men whose whole life is spent in the fight for human freedom should at the same time turn deliberately a deaf ear to the cry for liberty of one-half of the human race.

It is very humiliating for us Socialist women to be forced to admit this, but the question must be disposed of once for all, for we women cannot possibly build our expectations on the future freedom and at the same time submit calmly to the present oppression.

Among the fifty thousand dues-paying members of our party there are only two thousand women. Or, in other words, one woman member to every twenty-five men. Considering the fact that a number of our women members had entered the Socialist Party on their own accord, we may safely say that out of every thirty men within the party but one was ideal enough to bring in some female member of his family or a friend's into the ranks of the party, while the other twenty-nine preach the ideals of Socialism and the necessity of party alliance everywhere except within the walls of their own homes.

We may bring amendments reducing the dues of the women in our party, we may elect National and Local committees for the purpose of increasing the membership, but we will not achieve any considerable progress until our men will change their views as to woman's scope of activity in the movement. I know my sex and will admit freely that woman still looks to man as the guiding spirit of her life path and it is therefore for him to direct her steps into the party membership where she belongs—side by side with him.

## THE SOCIALIST MOVEMENT AND WOMAN SUFFRAGE
Ida Crouch Hazlett
*Socialist Woman*
No. 13 (June 1908): 5

The American Socialist movement is waking up on the woman question. While the statements of the party have always voiced the International position of sex freedom and expression in every human activity, American Socialists have been remarkably lukewarm in taking any interest in either getting women into the party, organizing them industrially, or bestirring themselves to obtain political expression for women. Within the last year, however, there seems to be a stirring consciousness that women, who constitute one-half of the working class must not only be informed upon the effort of the working class to throw off its chains, but they must be furnished with the weapon to use in that great political contest. In other words, the Socialist party is taking an interest in woman suffrage from a practical, working standpoint.

The chief point in the discussions that are appearing in the Socialist press recently, seems to be as to whether Socialist women should join outside organizations that are working to obtain the ballot for women. "The Socialist Woman" has discussed the matter very ably in its editorial "To Join, or Not to Join?" This editorial refers to the letter issued by Maud Malone, secretary of a woman's suffrage club of New York City, in which she withdraws from the organization because of its unprogressive character, its aversion to working women becoming active in its work, and the evident fear of the extension of the suffrage in the face of rapidly developing Socialistic tendencies.

The writer of this article can most heartily corroborate Miss Malone's statement in regard to the character of organizations formed on other than a Socialist basis. Having been a national organizer for the National [American] Woman Suffrage Association for a number of years, and having participated in all the suffrage State constitutional campaigns from the admission of Colorado with the woman vote, to the last campaign in Oregon a year ago, she feels that she has a reasonable acquaintance with the existing suffrage movement. It is all that Miss Malone states it—composed largely of women seeking selfish publicity and showing a nervous dread of any measure that smacks of sympathy with the fundamental interests of labor. Moreover, working women are not encouraged to enter the organization, and there is a snobbish truckling to the women of influence and social position. If by any chance some working woman, carried forward by her zeal to exercise the normal liberties of a human being, gets into the organization she is expected to remain modestly in the background.

It is the conviction of the writer that the reason the woman suffrage movement in America exhibits such a lamentable lack of vitality is because of the fear of delivering additional political weapons into the hands of the working class.

Such being the situation in regard to active work, it becomes a query in the minds of the Socialists as to how they are to do the most effective work to forward the cause of the woman vote.

In the first place there is no doubt but that extraordinary and persistent efforts should be made by the Socialist party to extend their propaganda among women. The first thing is to get women into the locals, and to spread the Socialist teaching among them by any method that gets results, such as a special national woman's organizer, special State organizers to work among women, special women's committees appointed by locals, and special local clubs of women for propaganda and educational purposes; and to aid the practical work of Socialist locals in communities.

With woman suffrage made one of the special features of all this propaganda a great impetus is thus given to it and disseminated.

It is by belief that these Socialist women would join existing suffrage bodies, and in such numbers as to control them, if possible. If there are no suffrage organizations, or the Socialist women find it difficult to work with those already organized, then they should by all means organize their own, and do vigorous work.

Women must come as an active factor into the demand for the suffrage. Socialists must become aggressive in their support. The fight for the ballot is the first condition to obtain means to facilitate the abolition of economic slavery, and no effort is more worthy the co-operation of every intelligent Socialist.

## ENFRANCHISEMENT OF WOMANHOOD
Eugene V. Debs
*Progressive Woman*
No. 22 (March 1909): 5

Karl Marx declared that the emancipation of the working class must be achieved by the working class itself. The same is true of the enfranchisement of womanhood. The disabilities imposed upon and accepted by woman in the past on account of her sex can be removed only by herself.

The Socialist movement is the first to recognize and proclaim the injustice of sex distinction in reference to the rights, privileges and opportunities of civic and social life, and the Socialist party is the first to pledge itself unqualifiedly to abrogate that relic of barbarism and place woman where she ought to be on an equal plane with man.

There is no need to argue here the question of "woman's sphere" in bourgeois society, it being well understood to be limited by woman's meek submission to the will of her lord and master and by the conventional rules and regulations imposed upon her with or without her consent.

If she be rich she is ordained to be a doll, a plaything, a coquette, spending her time in vain and frivolous, if not harmful and immoral indulgences, wasting her life, dissipating her energies and ending her useless existence in mental childhood, leaving no trace of service to society, and no memory of duties nobly fulfilled to preserve her name.

If she be poor she is doomed to drudgery and is all but a social outcast.

But rich or poor, woman has been and is still treated as the inferior of man in all that is essential to her mental and moral development. She is denied the freedom and opportunity without which she can no more develop the latent qualities of her nature than a flower can bloom without the vitalizing influence of the atmosphere and sunlight.

This is particularly true of the working class woman, who even in her bondage is made to feel the added weight of her sex inferiority and to bear all the odium of being an economic menial, a political nonenty [*sic*] and a social exile.

But happily the days of woman's sex servitude are almost ended. No longer does she tamely acquiesce in her inferiority and degradation. At last she realizes that she has been victimized, that she has been shut out of life's golden opportunities under the hypocritical pretense that she is the "weaker vessel;" and with the growing consciousness of her rightful place in the family, in the state and in society, she is making her influence felt, and in a corresponding degree the horizon of her sphere is expanding.

But even among Socialists there are traces—sadly out of place—of the miserable middle age superstition that woman is but the shadow of man, that she should maintain the deferential attitude of being the beneficiary of a privilege granted, instead of a right conceded, and that her voice should be seldom heard in the party councils, or not at all.

It is true that this sentiment prevails to no great extent in the Socialist party and yet such is the perversity of ancient prejudice that while equality in the abstract is recognized, the true spirit of it is denied in unconscious discrimination.

Here, as elsewhere, the remedy lies with woman herself. She may not in justice to herself or the party acquiesce in any restriction whatsoever, least of all when dictated by a custom born of ignorance and hoary with age. She must insist upon the recognition due her as a human being in the Socialist movement, not merely in the perfunctory sense declared in the law, but in the spirit and essence of its emancipating philosophy.

There are too few women in the Socialist party organization, in proportion to its male members, and far too few who are active in the management and direction of its affairs.

There is no reason why there should not be as many women as men in our locals and in our municipal, state, and national conventions. Nor is there any valid reason why they should not be equally represented in the field as lecturers and organizers and on tickets as candidates.

All that stands in the way is custom, the ignorance implied in the child-like observance of conventional "properties," and this should be battered down with the ruthless iconoclasm the revolutionary spirit has for hoary shams.

Woman loses not one whit of her innate modesty in braving the frowns of fossils, whatever their standing or sex.

In proportion to her numbers woman has a remarkable work to her credit in the Socialist movement. Without her influence and activity the Socialist party would scarcely have an existence. All her zeal and enthusiasm are brought into play, all her patience, persistence and unconquerable fortitude are developed in the struggle for freedom, and she has already proved herself to be a powerful propagandist in the revolutionary movement.

If the Socialist women would realize their ambition to be free and fulfill their manifest destiny they must take their proper places in the movement and demand in all things the consideration due them as equal factors with men in the struggle for emancipation.

REPORT OF THE WOMAN'S DEPARTMENT, APPENDIX I, *Proceedings* OF THE
1912 NATIONAL CONVENTION OF THE SOCIALIST PARTY
(Chicago: Socialist Party, 1912), pp. 204–08

To the Socialist Party National Convention, 1912:

There is nothing more hopeful in the outlook for the Socialist Party than the rapid growth in the number of woman members and the increasing scope of their work in all matters pertaining to its welfare.

Ten years ago the woman's movement in our party was a negligible quantity, existing chiefly in the minds of a few devoted women.

At the birth of the present Socialist Party, which took place at the Unity Convention of 1901, there were eight women who attended as regularly elected delegates.

Their influence was that of individual women and not that of representatives of any special movement of unrest or protest among the women of the working class. Such a movement had not yet had time for formation and we find no mention made in the minutes of the convention of woman's activity in the party organization, or of any need for special propaganda among women. The only mention made of the party's attitude toward women is in the platform which demands "equal civil and political rights for men and women."

Three years later, in the national convention of 1904, the number of women delegates had not increased. California, Oregon, Colorado, Iowa, Wisconsin and Pennsylvania each sent one while Kansas sent two women in a delegation of six.

In the proceedings of this convention, also, we search in vain for any acknowledgment of the special wrongs or needs of the working women, or of the necessity for any particular line of work to reach them with the Socialist message and enlist them in the party organization.

The constitution remained silent upon the organization of women, and the platform simply demanded equal suffrage for men and women.

The Socialist women definitely made their debut in the party organization at the National Convention of 1908. Twenty of them appeared upon the floor of the convention as delegates from fourteen states. Each of the twenty had a decided opinion as to the best way to reach her sisters and bring them into the fold.

From the first day to the last no group in the convention was more active and aggressive than were the women.

During the years from 1904 to 1908 the Socialist party had awakened to the fact that the "woman question" was [sic] a vital, living issue must receive consideration. So, on the afternoon of the first day, the committee on rules recommended that "a committee on women and their relationship to the Socialist Party shall be elected, to consist of nine members," and the committee was duly elected.

The report of this committee recommended that a permanent Woman's National Committee, consisting of five members, be elected to formulate plans for, and to have charge of, the special work of propaganda and organization among women. It also provided that a special woman organizer be kept permanently in the field.

Not only did the convention adopt the above plans for pushing the work among women, but it also enlarged upon the meager platform demand of 1904 by inserting the plank, "Unrestricted and equal suffrage for men and women, and we pledge ourselves to engage in an active campaign in that direction."

The quiet, earnest work of the women pioneers had at least [sic] borne fruit and woman's share in the affairs of the party was now officially recognized. It but remained for her to outline her plan of action and put it into effect.

The Woman's National Committee proceeded to do this in a most efficient manner. A "Plan of Work for Women in Socialist Locals" was prepared and widely circulated.

Special leaflets dealing with many phases of the woman question and the industrial conditions particularly affecting women and children, were published.

By 1910 the special woman's work was so well established that the National Party Congress of that year embodied in the National Constitution provisions for its continuance. An amendment which was included in the report of the Committee on Constitution and adopted by the Congress, provided that a Woman's National Committee, consisting of seven women, be elected in a manner similar to the election of the National Executive Committee and that it have charge of the propaganda and organization among women. It further provided that all plans of the committee concurred in by the National Executive Committee be carried out at the expense of the National Office.

The closing paragraph of the report of the Woman's National Committee contained the recommendation that there be installed a Woman's Department in the National Office and that the manager of this department be one of the regular employees of the office. The report was adopted.

Now, indeed, the women had become a bona fide institution in the party organization. The Woman's National Committee elected a general correspondent to take charge of the Woman's Department and the work among women was established upon a permanent basis.

### GENERAL RESULTS OF 1910–11

Much has been accomplished within the past two years. Many local woman's committees have been organized, hundreds of thousands of leaflets for women have been distributed. Women are serving as secretaries of five states, and of two hundred and seventy locals.

One member of the National Executive Committee, two members of the National Committee and one of the International secretaries are women. Fifteen states have women State Correspondents. Among our best known national lecturers and organizers, eight are women, and over twenty women have come under our notice as doing exceptionally good work on the Socialist platform in a national way.

It is difficult to form an estimate of the results of the special agitation among women that the Socialist Party has been carrying on during the last two years.

We have been unable to get complete information regarding the number of women members of the party or the number of woman's committees, although several times letters have been sent to the local and state secretaries, asking them for this information. A very small per cent of the secretaries complied with the request. It is roughly estimated, however, that the women constitute one-tenth of the entire membership.

About two hundred and fifty circular letters were sent out to locals having active women members, requesting answers to certain questions. Thirty-five replies were received. A summary of the work done by the women in these thirty-five locals shows remarkable activity. But no summary in dollars and cents can measure the actual result of their work. It represents an educational growth that is preparing many thousands of women and young girls to take part intelligently in the class struggle and work side by side with their brothers in winning the emancipation of the working class.

The summary of the reports from these thirty-five committees shows that these locals have a combined membership of 1,677 women.

During the year 1911 these committees have held 850 meetings. This does not account for all the woman's meetings held, even in these thirty-five places. In the New York and Chicago reports, only the largest and most important meetings were recorded. Meetings held by the woman members in the individual branches were not reported for either of these cities.

During the year 1911 and the latter part of 1910, these committees through their own efforts raised nearly $10,000 or, to be exact $9,740.09. This is exclusive of the money they helped to raise in the regular work of the locals: $5,893.96 were raised for strike benefits, $866.50 for campaign funds, $529.49 for the support of the Socialist press, $337.35 for assisting in the furnishing of local headquarters, and $214.93 were spent for special literature for women.

When we realize that $10,000 were raised by the women in only thirty-five out of the five thousand Socialist locals and branches in the United States, we can begin to appreciate that from a financial standpoint, if from no other, it is important to enlist the women in the active work as members of the party.

In ten of these cities—those large enough to require the assistance of the women—they were at the polls serving as watchers and clerks. They also served as registration clerks and, in Los Angeles, went from house to house instructing the women how to vote.

During the Shirtwaist Strike in New York and the Garment Workers' Strike in Chicago, Socialist women addressed their meetings, did picket service, gave benefits and assisted in every way possible.

The women not only fold and stamp the literature, but they go out with the men comrades and distribute it from door to door. They form themselves in squads and sell it at meetings, or distribute it free at the doors of factories and stores. Over 500,000 leaflets, besides thousands of copies of the Progressive Woman, have been distributed in this way.

## SOCIALIST SCHOOLS

When women enter into any movement they take the children with them. Four of our large cities report excellent work being done among the children.

New York has several Socialist schools. Lessons are prepared by May Wood-Simons, Edith C. Breithut and others. The New York schools are experimenting with these lessons and if they are a success they will be published and put into general use through the country for next year's work.

The demand for material for Socialist schools is constantly on the increase. By another year a systematic course of lessons should be ready for use.

Rochester, N.Y., has a school with an average attendance of two hundred pupils. Los Angeles, California, reports a splendid school which they call a Socialist Lyceum.

New Jersey has elected a special school committee, which has prepared a leaflet giving excellent instructions regarding the organization of Socialist schools. This committee is entering upon its work in a thorough manner and good results may be expected.

The New York State Committee on Socialist Schools prepared an outline on "How to Organize Socialist Schools." This has been published by the Woman's National Committee and recommended to be used in locals desiring to reach the children.

### ANTI-BOY SCOUT ORGANIZATION

Bridgeport, Connecticut, has an Anti-Boy Scout organization, with a membership of thirty-nine boys. St. Louis has an organization of boys which they have named the Universal Scouts of Freedom. They are organized by wards, as a part of the work of the ward branches. Through their efforts one corps of Boy Scouts was induced to disband. They also made their influence felt by supporting Union Labor in the stand it took against permitting the Boy Scouts to take part in the parade on the occasion of President Taft's visit to St. Louis.

### WOMAN'S DAY

Woman's Day, February 25th, was observed to a far greater extent than ever before.

Every available speaker was secured by the active locals and the meetings were well advertised.

The White Slave Traffic was the subject chosen for discussion and a special program upon this subject was prepared by the Woman's National Committee.

This program, consisting of songs, recitations and readings, fitted for a full evening's entertainment, was advertised in the weekly and monthly bulletins sent out from our National Office . . .

Glowing reports of the success of the entertainments were sent in by the comrades from many places with the request that similar programs be furnished regularly.

The capitalist papers gave a surprising amount of space to the observance of this day, designating it as the Socialist Woman's Day. In a few instances, more than two columns were given to an account of the celebration.

## EQUAL SUFFRAGE PETITION

In August, 1911, the Woman's National Committee recommended the circulation of a petition for woman suffrage to be presented by Congressman Victor L. Berger, Socialist Representative from Wisconsin. The recommendation was concurred in by the National Executive Committee and the following petition was prepared:

"We, the undersigned citizens of the United States, over twenty-one years of age, hereby request you to submit to the legislatures of the several states for ratification an amendment to the National Constitution which shall enable women to vote in all elections upon the same terms as men."

One hundred thousand copies of this petition have been sent to all of the Socialist locals, thousands of labor organizations, and to every source from which it was believed signatures could be obtained.

Requests for them are still being received. We have sent out the call for all signed petitions to be returned to the National Office and will complete the counting and forward them to Congressman Berger within the next month.

The circulation of this petition has been of great educational value and has afforded one of the best means by which the position of the Socialist Party upon the question of equal suffrage for men and women has been verified.

On January 16, 1912, Congressman Berger introduced in the House of Representatives the . . . Joint Resolution, proposing an amendment to the Constitution of the United States extending the right of suffrage to women. . .

## WOMAN ORGANIZERS

At the opening of the Woman's Department in the National Office, Anna A. Maley was the only National woman organizer sent out by the Woman's National Committee. Comrade Maley is one of the most capable organizers in the Socialist Party. Her work proved of great service to the committee. Later she gave up the work to become the editor of "The Commonwealth."

Florence Wattles and Nellie M. Zeh were selected as organizers for the committee.

Comrade Wattles was assigned to Indiana. As a result of seven weeks' work in this state, two local committees were organized and the woman's movement was given great impetus throughout the state. Much of her work was in unorganized places. She organized many locals, though the movement was too new to form committees of women.

In December, 1911, Comrade Wattles began work in Pennsylvania. During the four months in that state she has organized forty committees and has strengthened not only the work among women, but the general movement as well. The state secretary of Indiana has requested that she be returned to that state for the remainder of the campaign and this has been so arranged.

Comrade Zeh was unable to enter upon the work at that time, but she is now preparing to take it up along special lines in the south.

Mary L. Geffs was authorized to do some special work in Colorado, with encouraging results.

Janet Fenimore, Prudence Stokes Brown and Madge Patton Stephens have been elected by the committee to serve as woman organizers during the coming campaign.

Among the organizers who have carried on the general propaganda work, special credit is due to Mila Tupper Maynard, Theresa Serber Malkiel, Ella Reeve Bloor and John M. Work for their earnest efforts to strengthen the movement among the women. In addition to their regular duties when in the field work, they made a special plea to women to join the party and urged the comrades to elect the woman members of the respective locals into committees to carry on the propaganda among women.

They sent in to the General Correspondent the names of the active women along the route, thereby enabling the General Correspondent to communicate directly with these women and explain the work to be done in their locality.

If all our organizers would adopt this plan the beneficial results upon the organization would soon be felt.

## LITERATURE FOR WOMEN

The Woman's National Committee, through the National Office, has published leaflets upon the following subjects: Boys in the Mines, Boytown Railroad, Boy Scout Movement, Crimes of Capitalism, Work Among Women, Children in Textile Industries, Class War, Elizabeth Cady Stanton on Socialism, Frances E. Willard on Socialism vs. Alcoholism, Literature for Women, Plea to the Club Women, Poverty the Cause of Intemperance, The Teacher and Socialism, To the Working Woman, To Wives of Toilers, Underfed School Children, Why the Professional Woman Should Be a Socialist, Wimmin Ain't Got No Kick, Woman, Comrade and Equal, The Worker and the Machine, Why You Should Be a Socialist, and Woman's Work in Socialist Locals.

Other than these leaflets, the special Socialist literature for women handled by the National Office is exceedingly limited. It consists of the following: Socialism and the Home. Woman and the Social Problem. Women and Socialism. A Woman's Place. and Bebel's "Women and Socialism."

## LITERATURE FOR CHILDREN

There is a growing demand for Socialist literature for children. the supply of this is even more meager than that for women. At present we have nothing on hand that is really applicable to the needs of the average child.

## NEWSPAPER ARTICLES

At the request of the Woman's National Committee, many of our well known comrades contributed short articles upon questions of importance to women. Twenty-three articles were sent out during the year 1911, each going to about 125 papers. If each paper had printed each article, an equivalent of 2,875 articles would have been put in circulation through the work of the Woman's National Committee.

The newspaper propaganda is developing into one of the most important departments of our work. No other woman's organization in the United States—I may say of the world—has such an opportunity to carry its propaganda into working-class homes.

We have at our disposal about four hundred Socialist and other Labor papers that will print upon the average two articles pertaining to women each month. This means an equivalent of 800 articles each month, or 9,600 a year. And the list steadily increases in number.

## NATIONAL TEACHERS' BUREAU

The Socialist Teachers' Bureau is gradually growing in importance as a useful department in the work of the National Office.

It was started in August, 1911, by Comrade Terence Vincent, who conducted it in an able manner. Later it was placed in the hands of the Woman's Department.

The purpose of the Bureau is to enable Socialist teachers to get in touch with Socialist members of School Boards. Also by having a complete list of Socialist teachers on file in the National Office, something in the nature of a loose organization exists which is easy to circularize and to keep in touch with all matters pertaining to their special line of work.

It is useless to apply for assistance in regard to securing either a position or a teacher unless the applicant encloses proof of his paid-up membership in the party. Compliance with this request is a necessary safeguard.

When this proof has been furnished the application is placed on file. All information is considered strictly confidential—only those applicants who have proved their party membership being entitled to it.

A Socialist teacher applying for a position receives a list of the positions open, together with the available information regarding salary and grade. A Socialist school director applying for a teacher receives a list of teachers, stating the positions they are prepared to fill. Then correspondence may be opened between the director and the teacher, and the work of the National Office along this line has been fulfilled.

At the present time we have on hand applications for positions from forty-nine teachers and inquiries regarding the securing of Socialist teachers to fill twenty vacancies.

The National Office does not guarantee positions, nor does it guarantee good faith upon the part of either applicant. It simply helps to bring the teacher and the position together, rendering service free of charge. It does this because of the ever growing demand of school directors for Socialist teachers, and of Socialist teachers for positions in which they can teach unhampered by the prejudice of capitalist-minded school boards

## FOREIGN SPEAKING ORGANIZATIONS

Thus far the Woman's Department has been obliged to concentrate its energies upon the work of reaching the women of the general membership and has found it impossible to conduct special propaganda work among our foreign speaking comrades. The time is now at hand, however, when a start along these lines can be made and preparations are on foot toward this end.

The foreign translator-secretaries have selected the women's leaflets best suited to their purposes and the National Office will publish them in their respective languages.

In the large cities where the Central Woman's Committees are elected to conduct the work of agitation and organization throughout all branches, special effort will be made from this time forth to co-operate with the women in foreign speaking organizations and induce them to send representatives to the Central Woman's Committee.

The Finnish women are doing most excellent work. They have their own weekly paper called "Toveritar," meaning "The Comrades." It consists of eight pages and is well gotten up in every way. Comrade Helen Vitikainen is the editor.

In our Finnish locals the women constitute one-third of the membership and are active in all branches of the work. This no doubt accounts for the fact that the Finnish have one of the most perfect and efficient organizations in the United States. The women are working in the Socialist Party side by side with the men, both of them concentrating their energies upon its work.

The German women comrades of New York City are doing active work. They have organized in separate woman's branches with a total of about 280 members. They also sent a German woman organizer into the field and she formed organizations in Chicago, Syracuse, Rochester and Philadelphia.

The German women raised contributions for the campaign fund and for the Volke-Zeltung, the New York Call and other Socialist papers. They also prepared and distributed Socialist leaflets printed in the German language.

No reports have been received from other nationalities.

### WOMEN'S PERIODICALS

The Progressive Woman is the only Socialist publication for English-speaking women in the United States. It has a circulation of about 12,000.

This paper has made a valiant fight for its life and has received all possible support from the Woman's National Committee. It has been a great help to the committee and has been one of the means through which so much work has been accomplished.

During 1911 programs for use in Socialist locals were prepared by the Committee and published monthly in the Progressive Woman. In other ways it enabled the Woman's National Committee to carry on its work, and it is today the only woman's paper for carrying the Socialist message into English-speaking homes.

During the Mexican revolution, when every effort was being made to fan the military spirit into white heat in the United States, this paper was turned over to the Woman's National Committee and a special anti-military edition was prepared. Over 30,000 copies were placed in circulation . . .

"Toveritar," or "The Woman Comrade." is a Finnish weekly paper for women. It has a circulation of about 5,000 and is doing good educational work among the women of that nationality. Articles sent out by the Womans Department are published in this paper, and in every way it co-operates with the Woman's National Committee . . .

Life and Labor is a monthly magazine appealing especially to women engaged in the industries. It is the official organ of the Woman's Trade Union League and it is deserving of our recommendation and support. We should place it in the hands of all women, especially those who are working in industries that can be organized . . .

The Forerunner is another monthly magazine that is worthy of the attention of the Socialists. It is filled with vital truths presented in a way that appeals to the average woman, whether in the home or out, young or old. Before the reader is aware of it, her ideas have changed from the old conservative viewpoint to the new radical revolutionary position. It is worth while for us to aid in the circulation of The Forerunner . . .

The Young Socialist Magazine is the only Socialist magazine for children in the United States. It contains educational articles and stories tending to teach the children of the working class a correct appreciation of the class struggle. It should be in the hands of every child in the Socialist movement . . .

The editors of all of the above magazines are Socialist.

### NATIONAL AND INTERNATIONAL ACTIVITY

At the present convention twenty-five women were elected regular delegates, which is a fair representation, being about one-tenth of the entire number of delegates.

For the first time the Woman's National Committee of the Socialist Party was represented by a fraternal delegate at the National [sic] Woman's Suffrage Convention, held at Louisville, Ky., on October 17, 1911.

For the first time Socialists took part in the congressional suffrage hearing held in Washington, March 13th. The Socialist Party was represented by three Socialist women. This was due to the fact that we now have a Socialist representative in Congress, and one of the suffrage resolutions before the House was presented by him.

For the first time Socialist women were elected as delegates to the International Socialist Congress, held at Copenhagen in August, 1911 [sic 1910]. Three women delegates from the United States attended this Congress, and one of them was chosen by the United States delegation to serve as its reporter of the proceedings.

### SUMMARY

It has taken but two years for the women to demonstrate the great value of their organized efforts in the work of the Socialist Party. The Socialist Party realizes as never before the absolute necessity of reaching the women with the message of Socialism. The National Executive Committee, the Woman's National Committee and the National Office are sparing no effort in educating them to an understanding of their class interests and in bringing them into the party as dues-paying members, having the same duties and the same responsibilities as the men.

Not only are they educating the women, they are losing no opportunity to teach the men members of the party the senseless futility and the criminal ignorance manifested when one-half of the working class strives to free itself from slavery while leaving the other half in bondage. Women and men, not divided upon a basis of sex, but united upon the basis of working-class solidarity, are a necessary part of the working class program . . .

The question of women and their work in the party is of more importance and should receive more careful consideration by the convention than ever before. The time is ripe for earnest discussion of the woman question. We should go from the convention with clearly defined ideas as to the best plans for educating the women in America to a class-conscious understanding of their needs and of enlisting them for active service in the great army of the working class—the Socialist Party.

Fraternally submitted,

> Meta Berger,
> Winnie E. Branstetter,
> Grace D. Brewer,
> Elaa Carr,
> Lena Morrow Lewis,
> May Wood-Simons,
> Luella Twining.
> Woman's National Committee.
> Caroline A. Lowe,
> General Correspondent

## SOCIALISM AND THE FEMINIST MOVEMENT
Mary White Ovington
*The New Review*
2 (March 1914): 143–47

Socialism and Feminism are the two greatest movements of to-day. The one aims to abolish poverty, the other to destroy servitude among women. Both are world movements. No matter how backward the nation may be that you visit, you will find your revolutionist there preaching that poverty is unnecessary, and that a great organization is working to destroy private capital and to build a co-operative commonwealth. And throughout western civilization, and even in the heart of the Orient, you also find the woman revolutionist telling her enslaved sisters of the effort among women to attain their freedom, to gain the right to live, not according to man's, but according to their own, conception of happiness and right. Ideas fly swiftly about the globe, and we are learning to think on the lines not of family or nation or race but of common interests and common suffering.

But while Socialism and Feminism are world movements they present an immense difference in that Socialism has a well defined policy carried out by a marvelously coherent international organization, while Feminism has an indefinite policy and little organization. The feminist who creeps into the harem and whispers into the ear of the Turkish wife that there are women working to lift the veil from her face cannot at the same time invite her to the feminist local in her nearest precinct. Nor has she any world program by which salvation is to be gained. She is only voicing a discontent with woman's subserviency to man.

Now, the relation of Feminism to Socialism is a matter of profound importance to many women Socialists. They read the party platform demanding that women shall have equal rights with men, they attend the Socialist local and find these rights recognized by their comrades; and this should perhaps assure them that Socialism and Feminism are one. But they are not satisfied. They know that in any big movement certain propaganda is pushed to the foreground, to be striven for without cessation, while certain other [sic] is left behind, only to be considered when more important matters are disposed of. Where, they then ask, does Feminism stand with the Socialist party? Is it forward or is it in a dusky background from which it is rarely brought to light?

In putting this question I realize my incapacity adequately to answer it. This would require a knowledge of both Socialism and Feminism far beyond anything I possess. I can only give a few suggestions that may provoke interest among others more competent to discuss the matter than I.

The feminist movement as we have noted, is difficult of description because it deals with women under all stages of masculine rule; but, broadly speaking, it is a revolt. As Mary S. Oppenheimer tersely put it in the NEW REVIEW, it is "a reaction from the long rule of man and the consequent repression of womankind." The Socialist party in America as elsewhere always recognizes its political aspect when in its platform it demands a universal franchise for men and women alike, and when in its party organization it gives women an equal vote with men. This is a great deal, but the Progressive party has done as much. Is the Socialist party continually carrying on a woman's suffrage propaganda? Is it showing woman's economic condition, the injustices she suffers not only because she is poor but because she is a woman? That is, is it laying emphasis on the aristocracy of sex, on the fact that men to-day are still exercising extraordinary power over one-half the population, and are thus making democracy a farce? Is it doing these things?

Individual Socialists are undoubtedly doing them very often, especially women Socialists. But among many men prominent in America as Socialist writers and party leaders there exists a strange apathy on the woman question. Under Socialism, they assure you, women will have everything, but they are not interested in seeing that she secures her modicum now. They subscribe to the party platform, but they do not think the woman's suffrage plank of vital interest. For instance, at an Intercollegiate Socialist dinner I heard Victor Berger tell where he placed the cause of woman suffrage. He said he was ready to push a woman's suffrage petition, but he regarded securing the vote for women as much less important than securing the old age pension bill which he had then introduced into the House. That is, the democratizing of half the adult population of the country was insignificant compared to providing pensions for old age, the pensions to be given by a capitalist government that would undoubtedly find a way to get the money chiefly from the working class! This is not what I should call ardent championship of woman's rights.

Again, glance through our Socialist writers, and you find an astonishing absence of any expression regarding woman and Socialism. I have lately been reading Allan Benson's admirable little pamphlet, "The Truth About Socialism," but there is not a word in it on woman and her disabilities; and Mr. Benson is but one of many writers of whom this is true.

Perhaps the whole matter may be explained by saying that the majority of the men in the Socialist party recognize no division but the division of class, and no struggle but the class struggle; while many, but by no means all, women Socialists recognize also a woman's struggle, the struggle of a sex for the full development of its powers and for the right to the full use of those powers. And while the woman undoubtedly sees that such development is sadly incomplete for the majority in a capitalistic society, she knows, as the man does not seem to know, that men have gone a long way toward freedom, else the political party of Socialism would not have been born. And she knows too, that the coming of Socialism is not purely material. It does not mean simply a full stomach—that was often attained under chattel slavery—but a full life; and while she looks forward to the Socialist society she desires all the fullness of life that she can get now.

William Englsh [sic] Walling has said that the difference between a conservative and a radical is a difference of time. Both see the wretchedness of conditions and both want a change; but one is willing to wait while the other wants the change now. It is this way with woman and socialism. The

Socialist tells her to work for Socialism and she will then receive all she desires; but the woman intends now to get legal equality with man, the vote, equal pay for equal work, and all the educational privileges open to men. She has no more idea of waiting for Socialism to give her these things than the man has of waiting for the co-operative commonwealth before he enters upon his trade or casts his vote. This is the meaning of the militant suffrage agitation in England. Undoubtedly suffrage will be given to English women in good time, but the militants want it now, and they do not brook waiting with placidity.

The mass of men Socialists, as I have said, recognize no struggle but the class struggle, and thus logically they have no interest in enfranchising any women but those of the working class. Theodore Rothstein, writing in the NEW REVIEW, assures us that women are adequately represented by their fathers and brothers and husbands because these represent their economic rights, and that the Social-Democrat of England favors universal woman's suffrage, "not on general grounds of so-called citizenship, justice and the rest, but because it will add to the political power of the proletariat."

That women are represented by their fathers, their brothers and their husbands is surely gravely open to question. It is only since women have persistently agitated for their rights that the woman of property has been able to control her fortune or the working woman her wage. This, perhaps Comrade Rothstein would say, does not concern the class struggle—the money, whether husband's or wife's, remains in the same class—but it does concern the individual wife. And it is such masculine talk as his that must convince every thoughtful woman of the need of a movement for her release from masculine domination.

But there is a more serious aspect to Comrade Rothstein's reasoning. If as socialists we think of democratic movements simply as means of increasing a class vote, are we not in danger of thinking of them as increasing a party vote, and of refraining from enfranchising those who will not vote with the Socialist party? This is a real question in America where we have the disfranchised Negro. And while the Socialist party is pledged to woman's suffrage, it is quite conceivable that where it has scored a victory it may be lukewarm, if not indifferent, to giving the vote to women even though by so doing the proletarian vote would be increased. It may inquire regarding the character of woman proletarian. Is she not more conservative than the man? Is she not likely to be ruled by the priests? Isn't it better, now at least, to postpone universal suffrage until Socialism is more strongly entrenched in the proletarian mind?

Such reasoning as this seems very dangerous to some of us women who believe in democracy. It is a far-away cry, that of the Declaration of Independence, "that governments derive their just powers from the consent of the governed," but it is one that women are obliged to declare daily. And perhaps the reason men take so little interest in the declaration is that they fought this question out a century ago, and are now in "fresh fields and pastures new." The woman who lives in a country where the franchise has not yet become universal may perhaps obtain it with more ease than the one who lives in America where men have forgotten that there was a time when but few males could vote. A belated movement is the most difficult of movements in which to interest mankind.

I find that my feminist argument has centered about the suffrage movement. But I believe that women for a long time to come, whether they have suffrage or not, will need to be banded together against oppression. They have a work to do in backward countries as educators, as physicians, as preachers of the divine right of revolt. Doubtless socialist women will be in the forefront of the battle, and their Socialism will give them courage for the conflict. But they will also recognize that as women they have their obligation to stand with all other women who are fighting for the destruction of masculine despotism and for the right of womankind.

# 10 BIBLIOGRAPHIC ESSAY

## FURTHER READINGS

Undertaking research on the subject of the history of American socialism in general as well as on specific subtopics means that a student encounters a rich but uneven variety of sources. While some aspects of the topic are unfortunately difficult to research because of limited primary sources, for others adequate materials exist. Due to the attraction of the topic for many scholars over the last thirty years, the history of American radicalism enjoys a plentiful and dynamic bibliography. The discussion which follows can be no more than suggestive.

It is fortunate that a useful if fragmentary body of socialist primary materials has found its way into a number of archival repositories. During World War One, agents of the federal and state governments confiscated and sometimes destroyed runs of newspapers and correspondence as well as other records of a variety of radical organizations and individuals. After the war, the Socialist Party of America decided to discard its remaining papers in the name of economy, and only by a miracle were those records salvaged and purchased by a major archive. Socialist newspapers, as an alternative media, have not tended to be listed in directories, and are often unrecorded and uncollected, with the result sometimes of only incomplete runs ending up in libraries.

Major libraries holding significant materials on the Socialist Party of America include those at Duke University at Durham, North Carolina, the University of Wisconsin at Madison, Stanford University, the University of Chicago, the Newberry Library in Chicago, the Indiana State University at Terre Haute, the State Historical Society of Wisconsin at Madison, and the Tamiment Institute at New York University in New York City. Numerous state historical societies and local university and other libraries contain materials relevant to local and regional socialist history.

The most significant collection for this topic is that of the Socialist Party of America, which is housed at the Perkins Library at Duke University. It is now available on microfilm, and it is found at numerous libraries in that format. The papers and correspondence of Eugene V. Debs are available at Cunningham Memorial Library at Indiana State University in Terre Haute. A three-volume set of the correspondence, *Letters of Eugene V. Debs*, edited by J. Robert Constantine, was published by the University of Illinois Press in 1990. The papers of the two other most significant leaders of the Socialist Party, Victor L. Berger and Morris Hillquit, have been collected by the State Historical Society of Wisconsin. Numerous other repositories contain scatterings of their letters, and in the case of Berger, a large number of his papers have also been collected by the Milwaukee County Historical Society. The papers of other important figures in the history of the party have been collected, while the work of other individuals can only be traced through a laborious search through the collections of others.

Copies of the proceedings of Socialist Party conventions and conferences can be found in some of the major libraries cited above. Many of the newspapers and periodicals connected to the socialist movement may be found, and occasionally as full runs. Those which ought to be consulted include the *Appeal to Reason*, 1895–1918, the *International Socialist Review*, 1900–1918, the Socialist Party's *Official Bulletin*, 1904–1913, its *Party Builder*, 1912–1914, its *American Socialist*, 1914–1917, and the autonomous *The Intercollegiate Socialist Review*, 1913–1920, *The New Review*, 1913–1916, *The Class Struggle*, 1917–1919, *The Revolutionary Age*, 1918–1919, *The Eye Opener*, 1917–1919, *The Masses*, 1913–1917, and *The Liberator*, 1918–1920. Many of these are available in microfilm. For a useful discussion of the role of the radical press, see Joseph R. Conlin's two-volume edited work, *The American Radical Press, 1880–1960* (Westport, CT: Greenwood Press, 1974).

The journal *Labor History* has published several guides to sources on socialist history. They are Gerald Friedberg, "Sources for the Study of Socialism in America, 1901–1919," *Labor History* 6 (Spring 1965), 159–65; Bernard K. Johnpoll, "Manuscript Sources in American Radicalism," *Labor History* 14 (Winter 1973), 92–97; and Clifton Jones, "The Socialist Party of the United States: A Bibliography of Secondary Sources, 1945–1974," *Labor History* 19 (Spring 1978), 253–79. In the same vein, a student must consult the book *American Working Class: A Representative Bibliography*, edited by Maurice F. Neufeld, Daniel J. Leab, and Dorothy Swanson (New York: R.R. Bowker, 1983. In addition, *Labor History* publishes an annual listing of relevant articles which should be consulted. Also indispensable is

*The Encyclopedia of the American Left*, edited by Mari Jo Buhle, Paul Buhle, and Dan Georgakas (New York: Garland Publishing, 1990). Another significant research resource is Solon DeLeon, ed., *American Labor Who's Who* (New York: Hanford Press, 1925).

Some published works, including memoirs, are available by many of the socialists. They include Oscar Ameringer, *If You Don't Weaken* (New York: Henry Holt, 1940); Victor L. Berger, *Broadsides* (Milwaukee: Social-Democratic Publishers, 1912), and *Voice and Pen of Victor L. Berger*, ed. Elizabeth H. Thomas and Meta Berger (Milwaukee: Milwaukee Leader, 1929); William James Ghent, *The Reds Bring Reaction* (Princeton, NJ: Princeton University Press, 1923); William D. Haywood, *Bill Haywood's Book* (New York: International Publisher, 1929); Morris Hillquit, *Loose Leaves from a Busy Life* (New York: Macmillan, 1934), and his *History of Socialism in the United States* (New York: Funk and Wagnalls, 1903); Daniel W. Hoan, *City Government: The Record of the Milwaukee Experiment* (New York: Harcourt, Brace, 1936); Robert Hunter, *Violence and the Labor Movement* (New York: Macmillan, 1914); James H. Maurer, *It Can be Done* (New York: Rand School of Social Science, 1938); Charles Edward Russell, *Bare Hands and Stone Walls: Some Recollections of a Sideline Reformer* (New York: Charles Scribner's Sons, 1933); Upton Sinclair, *Autobiography* (New York: Harcourt, 1962); John Spargo, *Americanism and Social Democracy* (New York: Harper and Bros., 1918); Alexander Trachtenberg, ed., *The American Socialists and the War* (New York: Rand School of Social Science, 1917); Louis Waldman, *Labor Lawyer* (New York: E.P. Dutton, 1944); and William English Walling, *Socialism as it is: A Survey of the World-Wide Revolutionary Movement* (New York, Macmillan, 1912), and his edited, *The Socialists and the War, a Documentary Statement of the Position of the Socialists of all Countries, with Special Reference to their Peace Policy* (New York: Henry Holt, 1915).

Oral history interviews, another important resource, have been preserved with some of the World War One–era socialists through the Oral Research Office at Columbia University, the Bancroft Library at the University of California at Berkeley, and other oral history centers. Both federal and state records can be helpful sources of information. Under the Freedom of Information Act, it is possible to secure papers of or pertaining to some radicals of the past, albeit often with degrees of censorship involved. Nevertheless, records of both the Federal Bureau of Investigation and the Department of Justice are useful on some researach topics.

Secondary works on the Socialist Party in the pre–World War One era have appeared with regularity since the party ceased to flourish, and especially over the last generation. Works that must be consulted in the basic historiography include Donald Egbert and Stow Persons, eds., *Socialism and American Life*, 2 volumes (Princeton, NJ: Princeton University Press, 1952); Ira Kipnis, *The American Socialist Movement, 1897–1912* (New York: Columbia University Press, 1952); Howard H. Quint, *The Forging of American Socialism: Origins of the Modern Movement* (Columbia: University of South Carolina Press, 1953); David A. Shannon, *The Socialist Party of America: A History* (New York: Macmillan, 1955); and James Weinstein, *The Decline of Socialism in America, 1912–1925* (New York: Monthly Review Press, 1967).

Biographies of major figures include Nick Salvatore, *Eugene V. Debs: Citizen and Socialist* (Urbana: University of Illinois Press, 1982); Ray Ginger, *The Bending Cross: A Biography of Eugene Victor Debs* (New Brunswick, NJ: Rutgers University Press, 1949); Sally M. Miller, *Victor Berger and the Promise of Constructive Socialism, 1910–1920* (Westport, Ct: Greenwood Press, 1973); Norma Fain Pratt, *Morris Hillquit: A Political History of an American Jewish Socialist* (Westport, CT: Greenwood Press, 1979); Sally M. Miller, *From Prairie to Prison: The Life of Social Activist Kate Richards O'Hare* (Columbia: University of Missouri Press, 1993); Harry Rogoff, *An East Side Epic: The Life and Work of Meyer London* (New York: Vanguard Press, 1930); Robert A. Rosenstone, *A Romantic Revolutionary: A Biography of John Reed* (New York: Knopf, 1975); Dale Featherling, *Mother Jones: The Miners' Angel* (Carbondale: Southern Illinois University Press, 1974; Linda Atkinson, *Mother Jones, the Most Dangerous Woman in America* (New York: Crown, 1978); and Elliott Shore, *Talkin' Socialism: J.A. Wayland and the Role of the Press in American Radicalism, 1890–1912* (Lawrence: University Press of Kansas, 1988).

Other works that deal with the socialists and the Socialist Party of America before its collapse following World War One include Aileen S. Kraditor, *The Radical Persuasion, 1890–1917: Aspects of the Intellectual History and the Historiography of Three American Radical Organizations* (Baton Rouge: Louisiana State University Press, 1981); Bernard K. Johnpoll with Lillian Johnpoll, *The Impossible Dream: The Rise and Demise of the American Left* (Westport, CT: Greenwood Press, 1981); James R. Green, *Grass-Roots Socialism: Radical Movements in the Southwest, 1895–1943* (Baton Rouge: Louisiana State University Press, 1978); Robert Hyfler, *Prophets of the Left: American Socialist Thought in the Twentieth Century* (Westport, CT: Greenwood Press, 1984); John H.M. Laslett and Seymour Martin Lipsit, eds., *Failure of a Dream? Essays in the History of American Socialism*, second edition (Berkeley: University of California Press, 1984).

Primary research on the history of the so-called Second International can best be carried out at the extraodinarily rich archives of the International Institute of Social History in Amsterdam, the Netherlands. The leading historian of that subject whose several books ought to be studied is the French historian Georges Haupt. See especially his *La Deuxième Internationale, 1889–1914: Etude critique des sources, Essai Bibliographique* (Paris: Mouton, 1964). Works that may be consulted on the history of the International include Julius Braunthal, *History of the International, 1864–1914* (New York: Frederick A. Praeger, 1967); G.D.H. Cole, *A History of Socialist Thought*, 5 volumes (London, England: Macmillan, 1953–60; James Joll, *The Second International* (New York: Harper and Row, 1966); Carl Landauer, *European Socialism: A History of Ideas and Movements from the Industrial Revolution to Hitler's Seizure of Power*, 2 volumes (Berkeley: University of California Press, 1959); Merle Fainsod, *International Socialism and the World War* (Garden City, NY: Doubleday, 1969); and Milorad M. Drachkovitch, ed., *The Revolutionary Internationals, 1864–1943* (Stanford, CA: Stanford University Press, 1968).

The subject of American socialism and the African American still remains a relatively neglected topic. A student should begin research by reading *The Messenger*, which began publication in 1917 by A. Philip Randolph and Chandler Owen as an independent journal of socialist opinion, and later, in 1925, became the organ of the Brotherhood of Sleeping Car Porters. Books and articles that may be consulted include Theodore Kornweibel, Jr., *No Crystal Stair: Black Life and the Messenger* (Westport, CT: Greenwood Press, 1975); R. Laurence Moore, "Flawed Fraternity—American Socialist Response to the Negro, 1901–1912," *Historian* 32 (November 1969), 1–18; H.L. Meredith, "Agrarian Socialism and the Negro in Oklahoma, 1900–1918," *Labor History* 11 (Summer 1970), 277–84; Milton Cantor, ed., *Black Labor in America* (Westport, CT: Negro Universities Press, 1969); Sterling D. Spero and Abram L. Harris, *The Black Worker: The Negro and the Labor Movement* (New York: Columbia University Press, 1931); Philip S. Foner, *Organized Labor and the Black Worker, 1619–1973* (New York: Praeger, 1974); Philip S. Foner, "Peter H. Clark: Pioneer Black Socialist," *Journal of Ethnic Studies* 5 (Fall 1977), 17–35; Philip S. Foner, *American Socialism and Black Americans: From the Age of Jackson to World War II* (Westport, CT: Greenwood Press, 1977); Philip S. Foner and Ronald L. Lewis, eds., *The Black Worker: A Documentary History from Colonial Times to the Present*, volume 5: *The Black Worker from 1900–1919* (Philadelphia, PA: Temple University Press, 1980); Leslie Fishbein, "Dress Rehearsal in Race Relations: Pre-World War I American Radicals and the Black Question,"

*Afro-Americans in New York Life and History* 6 (January 1982), 7–15; Jervis Anderson, *A. Philip Randolph: A Biographical Portrait* (New York: Harcourt, Brace, Jovanovich, 1972); Theodore Vincent, ed., *Voices of a Black Nation: Political Journalism in the Harlem Renaissance* (San Francisco: Ramparts Press, 1973); Manning Marable, "A. Philip Randolph and the Foundations of Black American Socialism," *Radical America* 14 (March–April 1980), 7–29; Manning Marable, *W.E.B. Du Bois: Black Radical Democrat* (Boston: Twayne, 1986); David Levering Lewis , *W.E.B. Du Bois: Biography of a Race, I, 1868–1919* (New York: Henry Holt, 1993); Herbert Aptheker, ed., *The Correspondence of W.E.B. Du Bois*, volume 1 (Amherst: University of Massachusetts Press, 1973); Philip S. Foner, ed., *W.E.B. Du Bois Speaks: Speeches and Addresses, 1890–1919* (New York: International Publishers, 1970); Harry Haywood, *Black Bolshevik: Autobiography of an Afro-American Communist* (Chicago: Liberator, 1978); Wilson Record, *The Negro and the Communist Party* (Chapel Hill: University of North Carolina Press, 1951); Jacqueline Washington-Boulder, "American Socialism: Its Origins, Nature, and Impact on the Black Working Class and the Socio-Economic Development of the United States" (Ph.D. diss., Howard University, 1977); and John W. Van Zanten, "Communist Theory and the American Negro Question," *Review of Politics* 29 (October 1967), 435–56.

An even more neglected subject in the history of American socialism is the connected issue of ethnicity and immigration. An article by Charles Leinenweber is an appropriate starting point for anyone interested in this topic. See his "The American Socialist Party and 'New' Immigrants," *Science and Society* 32 (Winter 1968), 1–25. A student may also consult Gerald Rosenblum, *Immigrant Workers: Their Impact on American Radicalism* (New York: Basic Books, 1973); Sally M. Miller, *The Radical Immigrant, 1820–1920* (Boston: Twayne, 1974); Sally M. Miller, "From Sweatshop Worker to Labor Leader: Theresa Malkiel, a Case Study," *American Jewish History* 68 (December 1978), 189–205; and Sally M. Miller, "Other Socialists: Native-Born and Immigrant Women in the Socialist Party, 1901–1917," *Labor History* 24 (Winter 1983), 84–102.

A number of urban or regional histories of the Socialist Party consider the role of immigrants in the socialist movement. See, as examples, Melvyn Dubofsky, *When Workers Organize: New York City in the Progressive Era* (Amherst: University of Massachusetts Press, 1968); Charles Leinenweber, "The Class and Ethnic Bases of New York City Socialism, 1904–1915," *Labor History* 22 (Winter 1981), 31–56; Marlene Terwilliger, "Jews and Italians and the Socialist Party in New York City, 1901–1917: A Study of Class Ethnicity and Class Consciousness (Ph.D. diss., Union Graduate School, 1978); Paul Buhle, "Italian-American Radicals and Labor in Rhode Island, 1905–1930," *Radical History Review* 17 (Spring 1978), 121–51; Al Gedicks, "Ethnicity, Class Solidarity, and Labor Radicalism among Finnish Immigrants in Michigan Copper Country," *Politics and Society* 7 (1977), 126–56; Jerry W. Calvert, *The Gibralter: Socialism and Labor in Butte, Montana, 1895–1920* (Helena: Montana Historical Society, 1988); Richard W. Judd, *Socialist Cities: Municipal Politics and the Grass Roots of American Socialism* (Albany: State University of New York Press, 1989); and Sally M. Miller, "Milwaukee: Of Ethnicity and Labor," in Bruce M. Stave, ed., *Socialism and the Cities* (Port Washington, NY: Kennikat Press, 1975).

The historiography of the Socialist Party and the role of women is considerably more abundant than it is on the two previous subjects. Anyone interested in this topic should begin by examining the classic Marxist works on the Woman Question, especially Frederick Engels' *The Condition of the Working Class in England* and *The Origin of the Family, Private Property and the State*, and August Bebel's *Woman Under Socialism*. Important writings by women members of the Socialist Party, in addition to those reproduced in this volume, include the two dozen leaflets commissioned by the party's Woman's National Committee, most of which were authored by prominent leaders in the socialist movement. They are available in the Duke University Socialist Party collection, and copies can be found in other libraries as well, such as at the Hoover Institution, Stanford University. Booklets and brochures authored by some of these women on behalf of the socialist movement, such as May Wood Simons's *"Women and the Social Question"* (Chicago: Charles Kerr, 1899) and Mary E. Marcy, *Shop Talks on Economics* (Chicago: Charles H. Kerr, 1911) are available. Some of these individual women have had their correspondence and papers deposited in archives, but few have collections of their own. Exceptions are Lena Morrow Lewis, whose papers are at the Tamiment Institute of New York University, and also Rose Pastor Stokes, some of whose papers rest in collections at Tamiment Institute and at Yale University. More typically, the papers of women leaders that are preserved in archives are located in collections of their husbands' papers. Examples are Kate Richards O'Hare, who has some papers in the Frank P. O'Hare Collection at the Missouri Historical Society in St. Louis, and Meta Berger, whose correspondence may be found in the Victor L. Berger Papers at the State Historical Society of Wisconsin at Madison. The latter repository, however, also houses the joint Algie M. and May Wood Simons Collection. In addition to these significant sources, a researcher would not want to neglect reading through the whole run of the *Socialist Woman*, which was published from 1907 to 1913, undergoing name changes over the years to *The Progressive Woman* and *The Coming Nation*.

Memoirs, biographies or writings of socialist women, in addition to those mentioned earlier, include Ella R. Bloor, *We Are Many: An Autobiography* (New York: International Publishers, 1940); Dorothy Day, *The Long Loneliness* (New York: Harper, 1952); Theresa S. Malkiel, *The Diary of a Shirtwaist Striker*, ed. Françoise Basch (Ithaca, NY: ILR Press, Cornell University, 1990); Josphene Goldmark, *Impatient Crusader: Florence Kelley's Life Story* (Urbana: University of Illinois Press, 1953); Rose Pesotta, *Bread Upon the Waters* (New York: Dodd, Mead, 1945); Arthur Zipper and Pearl Zipper, *Fire and Grace: The Life of Rose Pastor Stokes* (Athens: University of Georgia Press, 1989); Kathleen A. Sharp, " Rose Pastor Stokes: Radical Champion of the American Working Class, 1879–1933" (Ph.D. diss., Duke University, 1979); Mary A. Hill, *Charlotte Perkins Gilman: The Making of a Radical Feminist 1860–1896* (Philadelphia: Temple University Press, 1980); Margaret Sanger, *Autobiography* (New York: Norton, 1938); David Kennedy, *Birth Control in America: The Career of Margaret Sanger* (New Haven, CT: Yale University Press, 1970); Mary White Ovington, *The Walls Came Tumbling Down* (New York: Arno Press, 1969); Helen Keller, *Helen Keller, Her Socialist Years: Writings and Speeches*, Philip S. Foner, ed. (New York: International Press, 1967); Kathryn K. Sklar, *Florence Kelley and the Nation's Work: The Rise of Women's Political Culture, 1830–1900* (New Haven, CT: Yale University Press, 1995); and Crystal Eastman, *Crystal Eastman on Women and Revolution*, Blanche Weisen Cook, ed. (New York: Oxford University Press, 1978). Other prominent women radicals of the era who were not socialists but whose autobiographies might prove to be of interest are Emma Goldman, *Living My Life,* 2 volumes (New York: Knopf, 1931) and Elizabeth Gurley Flynn, *The Rebel Girl: An Autobiography* (New York: International Publishers, 1973).

Only a few of the many books and articles on this subject can be mentioned here. They include Mari Jo Buhle, *Women and American Socialism, 1870–1920* (Urbana: University of Illinois Press, 1981); Sally M. Miller, ed., *Flawed Liberation: Socialism and Feminism* (Westport, CT: Greenwood Press, 1982); Bruce Dancis, "Socialism and Women in the United States, 1900–1917," *Socialist Revolution* 6 (January–March 1976), 81–144; Margaret C. Jones, *Heretics and Hellraisers: Women Contributors to* The Masses, *1911–1917* (Austin: University of Texas Press, 1993); Judith Schwartz, *Radical Feminists of Heterodoxy: Greenwich Village, 1912–1940* (Lebanon, NH: New Victoria Publishers, 1982); D.O. Carrigan, "Forgotten Yankee Marxist [Martha Moore Avery]," *New England Quarterly* 42 (March 1969), 23–

43; Erling N. Sannes, "'Queen of the Lecture Platform': Kate Richards O'Hare and North Dakota Politics," *North Dakota History* 58 (Fall 1991), 2–19; Alice Kessler-Harris, "Organizing the Unorganizable: Three Jewish Women and their Union," *Labor History* 17 (Winter 1976), 5–23; and John Stillito, "Women and the Socialist Party in Utah, 1900–1920," *Utah Historical Quarterly* 49 (Summer 1981), 220–38.

A student of the subject of the Socialist Party and the variables of race, ethnicity and immigration, and gender might profitably peruse related materials on the Industrial Workers of the World and the Communist Party but there has been no attempt here to offer reading suggestions on those topics. Similarly, this bibliographical essay does not repeat any but the most important citations found in the text.

# INDEX

Adler, Victor, 4, 10, 21
Africa, 138
African Americans. *See* Negroes
Alger, Horatio, 42
Amalgamated Clothing Workers Union, 55
American Communist Party. *See* Communist Party
*American Farmer, The*, 132
American Federation of Labor, 4, 14, 35, 39, 53, 66, 76, 109, 122, 126, 127, 131, 187, 191, 195, 203, 204, 240
American Manufacturers' Association, 223
American Woolen Company, 30
Ameringer, Oscar, 7, 58, 81
Amsterdam, Holland, 3, 12
*Appeal to Reason*, 18, 120
*Arbeiter Zeitung. See St. Louis Labor*
Argentina, 10, 12, 164
Arkansas, 6
Armour, Gustave, 196
Associated Charities, 120–21
Atlanta Exposititon, 40
Atlanta Exposition Address, 35
Austria, 10, 12, 13, 50, 533, 65, 200
Austrian Empire. *See* Austria
Austro-Hungarian Empire. *See* Austria
Australia, 199, 209, 215

Bache-Denman Coal Company, 128
Baldwin, Roger, 86, 87, 94n.32
Barnes, J. Mahlon, 11
Basle, Switzerland, 3
Bebel, August, 4, 97, 214
Belgians, 12
Belgium, 12, 141
Benson, Allan, 8, 284
Berger, Meta Schlichting, 56, 57, 100, 102, 282

Berger, Victor L., 7, 14, 15, 22, 35, 36, 37, 38, 53, 57, 58, 59, 65, 67, 72n.31, 72n.32, 93n.25, 99, 100, 106, 122, 126, 132, 143, 210, 228, 229, 234, 276, 284
Berlyn, Barney, 229
Berry, Hope, 79
*Birth of a Nation*, 195
Blease, Coleman, 183
Bloor, Ella Reeve "Mother," 79, 177
Bohn, Frank, 12, 81
Bohemian Americans, 50, 54, 73
Bohemian Socialist Federation, 11, 105
Bolshevik Revolution, 83
Boudin, Louis B., 12, 27n.19, 209–12, 218
Brandt, William, 75–76, 84, 86
Branstetter, Winnie E. 104, 114n.12, 282
Breithut, Edith, 274
Brewer, Grace D., 282
British Columbia, 237
Brotherhood of Railway Trainmen, 194
Brown, Corinne S., 20
Brown, Prudence Stokes, 277
Brussels, 3, 15, 99, 102
Bryan, William Jennings, 119

Cahan, Abe, 131
California, 206, 208. 214, 216. 217, 224, 225
*Capital, Das*, 121
Carr, Ella, 282
Catholic Church. *See* Roman Catholicism
Chaplin, Ralph 122
Charles H. Kerr Publishing Company, 121, 122, 132, 145
*Chicago Arbeiter Zeitung*, 75
*Chicago Daily Socialist*, 7, 28n.32, 121, 176–81

Chicago, Illinois, 51, 75, 121, 128, 188
China, 138, 221, 222, 225, 228, 229, 231, 237
Chinese, 12, 14, 73, 137, 206, 215, 223, 226, 229, 231, 232
Chinese Exclusion Act, 206, 230
Christ. *See* Jesus
Christianity, 188, 252
Church, R.R., 184
Cincinnati, Ohio, 188
Civic Federation (Saint Louis), 87
Clemenceau, Georges, 190
Cleveland Central Labor Council, 14
Cleveland, Ohio, 188
Cole, Josephine R., 109
Colorado, 128
Colorado National Guard, 128
*Coming Nation. See Socialist Woman*
Comintern, 9, 190
Commons, John R., 68
Communist Congress. *See* Comintern
Communist Labor Party, 66, 145
*Communist Manifesto,* 213
Communist Party, 9, 33, 40, 66, 145
Conger-Kaneko, Josephine, 18, 28n.25, 28n.29, 260–62
Congress of Industrial Organizations, 129
Connelly, James, 81
Conzen, Kathleen Neils, 49
Copenhagen, Denmark, 3, 10, 22, 24, 102, 104, 142, 281
Croatian Americans, 73
Crouch-Hazlett, Ida, 108, 267–69
Czechs. *See* Bohemian Americans
Czolgosz, Leon, 206

Danbury Hatters Case, 128
Darrow, Clarence, 119
Davis, Jefferson, 183
Dayton, Ohio, 188
Debs, Eugene V., 6, 7, 14, 42n.1, 48, 81, 85, 99, 125, 165–68, 190, 232–33, 269–71
DeLeon, Daniel, 74
Dell, Floyd, 119
Democratic Party, 39, 55, 75, 90, 124, 163, 184, 188, 196, 197, 216
Detroit, Michigan, 51
*Deutscher Schulverein,* 74
Dewey, John, 120, 146n.2
Dixon, Thomas, 190, 195
Domingo, W.A., 8, 188–90
Douglass, Frederick, 180
Du Bois, W.E.B., 7, 8, 36, 40, 175–76, 181–84

*Dziennik Ludowy,* 77

Earle, Alice Moore, 144
Eastman, Max 119
Eigel, George, 86
Ellison, Ralph, 34
Ely, Richard, 121
Engels, Friedrich, 16, 97, 110, 136, 139
England, 12, 141, 200
Espionage Act, 66
Ettor, Joseph J., 130
Exceptional Laws, 201

Federated Trades Council, 53, 55, 66
Federation of Women's Clubs, 56
Fenimore, Janet, 277
Ferri, Enrico, 264
Fifth Congressional District of Wisconsin, 37, 48, 55
Fink, Gary, 75
Finnish-American Agitation Committee, 19
Finnish Socialist Federation, 11, 105
Florida, 6, 38
Flynn, Elizabeth Gurley, 100, 130
Folk, Joseph W., 88, 91
Foote, Abigail, 244
Ford, Henry, 129
*Forerunner, The,* 281
Fort-Whiteman, Lovett, 40
Fourth Congressional District of Wisconsin, 48
France, 12, 141, 164, 200
*Free Union, A* (Marcy), 137
French Canadians, 130

Garrison, William Lloyd, 180
Gavett, Thomas W., 68n.5
Gaylord, Winfield R., 65, 81, 84
Geffs, Mary L., 277
General Federation of Labor Unions, 81
Georgia, 6, 38
German-American Alliance, 93n.31
German Americans, 48–49, 50, 51, 54, 55, 58, 64, 66, 73, 74, 77, 91n.3
German Empire. *See* Germany
German Left Wing, 144
German Social Democratic Party, 3, 16, 25, 53, 65, 97, 117n.37, 132, 214
German Socialist Federation, 105
Germany, 12, 53, 75, 138, 141, 200, 201, 222
Germer, Adolph, 81, 126
Gilman, Charlotte Perkins, 25
Giovanitti, Arturo, 130
Girard, Kansas, 18

*Gleichheit, Die,* 16, 18, 21, 23
Gobel, George, 11, 170
Goldman, Emma, 43n.13
Gompers, Samuel, 203–04
Great War. *See* World War One
Greek Americans, 50, 223
Griffith, D.W., 195
Grundy, Annie, 105

Hadley, Herbert S., 88
Halling, Daisy, 21
Hardie, Keir, 22, 81, 190, 199
Harlem, New York, 9, 90
Harper, William Rainey, 119
Haupt, Georges, 11
Hauser, Joseph, 76
Hawaii, 215
Hayes, Max S., 14
Hayes, Rutherford B., 156
Haymarket Affair, 20
Haywood, William D. "Big Bill," 21, 109,
    122, 126, 127, 129, 130, 142, 145
Heath, Frederic F., 53, 57
Henry Street Settlement House, 99
Herron, George, 8, 10
Hervé, Gustave, 219
Hillquit, Morris, 10, 11, 12–13, 15, 16, 20,
    40, 93n.25, 99, 122, 126, 138,
    209–12, 234
Hillquit, Vera, 20
Hoan, Daniel Webster, 59, 60, 61, 64, 65,
    66, 71n.27, 71n.29, 81, 143
Hoehn, Gottlieb A., 75, 83, 84, 85, 86, 87,
    223, 228
Holland, 12, 199
Hungarian Americans, 50, 54, 73
Hungarian Socialist Federation, 11
Hunter, Robert, 126, 239

Illinois, 79
Illinois State Federation of Labor, 81
India, 237
Indianapolis, 37
*Industrial Solidarity,* 145
Industrial Workers of the World, 4, 39, 84,
    108–09, 122, 126, 129, 130, 144,
    192–94, 194–95
International Council on the Conditions of
    the Darker Race, 40
*International Socialist Review,* 81, 99, 108,
    119, 121, 122, 125, 126, 127, 128,
    130–31, 124, 137, 140, 145, 153–
    63, 165–75, 199–220, 232–33,
    239–48, 253–58, 264–67
International Socialist Women's Conference,

20–23, 56, 104, 105
International Women's Bureau, 21
International Women's Day, 24, 78
Interparliamentary Commission, 12
Ireland, 200
Irish Americans, 50, 73
Italian Americans, 6, 10, 12, 50, 54, 73, 171
Italian Socialist Federation, 10, 11, 77, 105
Italy, 141, 172, 200

Janssen, John, 61
Japan, 219, 222, 237
Japanese, 12, 14, 137, 215, 216, 217, 223,
    226, 229, 230, 231, 232, 240
Jaurès, Jean, 3, 214
Jefferson, Thomas, 179
Jesus, 174, 178, 188, 189
*Jewish Daily Forward,* 131
Jewish Socialist Federation, 105
Jews, 6, 50, 54, 73, 172, 174, 201, 230
Joint Charter Revision Committee, 87
*Jungle, The,* 120
Jurishitch, M.G., 77
*Justice,* 18

Kaemmerer, Otto, 76, 84, 85
Kaneko, Kiichi, 19
Kansas City, Missouri, 79, 80, 120
Kansas (state), 78, 79, 107, 108
Kautsky, Karl, 21
Kearney, Denis, 217
Kelley, Florence, 99
Kentucky, 38
Kerr, Charles H., 121, 122
Kiel, Henry, 74
King, Clarence H., Jr., 13, 212–19
Kipnis, Ira, 8, 33
Knownothings, 229
Koreans, 14
Kraybill, Luella R. *See* Krehbiel, Luella R.
Krehbiel, Luella R., 79, 262–63
Kreyling, David, 75
Krzycki, Leo, 55
Ku Klux Klan, 41, 157

Labor Day, 82, 103
LaFargue, Paul, 97
Lanfersiek, Walter, 38
Lasch, Christopher, 44n.22
Lassalle, Ferdinand, 82
Laukki, Esther, 14
Laukki, Leo, 239
Lawrence, Massachusetts, 126, 130–31, 193
League of Nations, 40, 190
Lee, Algernon, 13, 234

Legien, Karl, 81
Lenin, Vladimir, 143, 190
Lettish Socialist Federation, 11
Lewis, Arthur Morrow, 81, 226
Lewis, Lena Morrow, 7, 21, 22, 24, 79, 102, 104, 148n.37, 282
Liebknecht, Karl, 143
*Life and Labor,* 280
Lilienthal, Meta Stern, 18, 25, 28n.28, 105
Lincoln, Abraham, 180
Lithuanian Socialist Federation, 11
Lloyd George, David, 189–90
London, Jack, 119
London, Meyer, 38, 99, 239
Lorenzo, A.S., 12
Los Angeles, California, 6
Louisiana, 6, 165, 168, 169
Louisiana State Socialist Party, 6, 168, 169, 172
Lowe, Caroline A., 79, 105, 114n.12, 282
*Lusitania,* 22
Luxemburg, Rosa, 4, 17, 24

McKinley, William, 206
Maley, Anna A., 102, 259–60, 276
Malkiel, Theresa S., 100, 264–67, 277
Malone, Maud, 268
Marcy, Leslie H., 120, 121
Marcy, Mary Edna, 119–46, 146n.1, 241–48
Maryland, 38
Massachusetts, 108, 175, 188
Marx, Karl, 6, 51, 97, 121, 122, 167, 174, 213, 269
Marxism, 3, 47, 52
May Day, 24, 103
Maynard, Mila Tupper, 255, 277
*Messenger,* 9, 39–41, 185–98
Milholland, Inez, 184
Mill, John Stuart, 160
Miller, Guy, 222–28 passim
Mills, Walter T., 81
Milwaukee County Board of Supervisors, 159
Milwaukee Electric Railway and Light Company, 60
Milwaukee Social Democratic Party, 21, 47–72, 84
Milwaukee, Wisconsin, 35, 47–72, 77, 84, 125
Minneapolis, Minnesota, 91
"Missouri Idea," 88
*Missouri Socialist. See Saint Louis Labor*
Missouri State Federation of Labor, 74, 75, 76, 90, 93n.22

Missouri State Socialist Party, 83, 84, 254
Molle, Jessie, 253–55
Montefiore, Dora B., 18, 21
Morgan, J.P., 195
Morton, Jack, 140
Morton, James, 140
Moscow, 190
Moses, 174

*Naprzod,* 55
National American Woman's Suffrage Association, 106, 268, 281
National Association for the Advancement of Colored People, 36, 37, 39
National Negro Committee, 37
*National Rip-Saw,* 80
National Urban League, 51
National Woman's Party, 56
National Women's Trade Union League, 36
Negroes, 5, 6, 33–44, 51, 80–81, 137, 153–98, 285
Nevada, 108
New Jersey, 188
New Left, 33, 42n.2
*New Review,* 181–84, 282–86
*New York Call,* 280
New York (city), 10, 108, 154, 164, 188, 215, 229
Niagara Movement, 35
Nieminen, Ester, 14, 230
Norway, 222

O'Hare, Frank, 80, 83
O'Hare, Kate Richards, 7, 24, 79–80, 81, 83, 84, 89, 100, 102, 117n.38, 138, 249–52
Ohio, 188
Oklahoma, 7, 47, 81
Olson, Frederick I., 71n.28
Oppenheimer, Mary S., 283
*Out of the Dump* (Marcy), 121
Overman, Lee Slater, 190
Ovington, Mary White, 36, 37, 282–86
Owen, Chandler, 8, 39, 40

Paine, Thomas, 14–15, 221
Paris (France), 3, 10
*Parola del Socialista, La,* 77
Pauls, Otto, 76, 84, 85
Payne, Laura, 255
Pennsylvania, 107, 188
Pennsylvania Mining Company, 128
People's Council for Democracy and Peace, 39, 65
People's Council of America. *See* People's

Council for Democracy and Peace

Phillipi, Louis, 75
Phillips, Jack, 140
Phillips, Wendell, 180
Polakowski, Walter, 55
Polish Americans, 10, 49–50, 54, 55, 64, 65, 73
Polonia, 50
Polish Socialist Federation, 105
Pope, L.G., 77
Portuguese Americans, 216
*Post-Dispatch. See Saint Louis Post-Dispatch*
Prevey, Marguerite, 108, 109
Primm, James, 87
Progressive Era, 34, 39, 60, 73
Progressive Party (of 1912), 39, 283
*Progressive Woman. See Socialist Woman*
Putnam, E. Val, 77

Rand School of Social Sciences, 40
Randolph, A. Philip, 8, 39, 40
Randolph, John, 140
Reed, John, 119
Republican Party, 90, 124, 163, 184, 188, 196, 197, 216
*Rhymes of Early Jungle Folk* (Marcy), 139
Rockefeller, John D., 139, 195
Roemer, Max, 140
Rogers, Bruce, 14, 239–40
Roman Catholicism, 58, 138
Roosevelt, Theodore, 39, 178, 265
Rose, David S., 52
Rothstein, Theodore, 285
Romanian Americans, 73
*Rudnicka Strazag,* 77
Russell, Charles Edward, 37, 81
Russia, 40, 144, 145, 146, 200, 201
Russian Americans, 54, 73

Sadler, Kate, 108, 117n.38
Saint Louis, 73–91
Saint Louis Central Trades and Labor Union, 74, 75, 76, 77, 87, 90, 93n.22
Saint Louis Civic League, 87
*Saint Louis Labor,* 74–79 passim, 84, 85, 86, 87, 254
*Saint Louis Post-Dispatch,* 85
Saint Louis Proclamation, 65
Saint Louis Socialist Party, 73, 74–91
Saint Louis Transit Company, 88
Sanderson, Cobden, 253
Scandinavian Socialist Federation, 11, 105
Scotland, 200

Second International, 3, 4, 5, 8–9, 10, 11, 12, 13, 16, 17, 21, 25, 52, 56, 75, 76, 102, 105, 106, 199, 237; Congresses of, 3, 5, 10, 12, 13, 16, 17, 19, 20, 22, 23, 75, 76, 102, 104, 105, 142, 199, 209, 216, 217, 239, 281; Immigration Commission of, 210; Socialist Bureau of, 8, 10, 15, 24, 99, 102
Sedition Act, 145
Seidel, Emil, 57, 59. 61, 71n.29, 81, 85
Serbian Americans, 73
Shannon, David, 53
*Shop Talk on Economics* (Marcy), 122
Simon, Emil, 85, 86, 93n.31
Simons, A.M., 17, 28n.32, 65, 100, 121, 122, 132, 146n.6, 154–57
Simons, May Wood 17, 18, 21, 22, 56, 65, 100, 102, 104, 106, 111, 116n.27, 258–59, 274, 282
Sinclair, Upton, 119
Slater, George W., Jr., 7, 176–78
Slovak Americans, 50
Slovenian Americans, 50, 54
Smillie, Robert, 189
Smith, Hoke, 190, 195
Snowden, Philip, 190
*Social-Democrat* (England), 285
*Social-Democratic Herald,* 53, 56, 72n.31, 248
Social Democratic Party of America, 51
Social Democratic Woman's Society (New York), 253
Social Democracy, 51
Socialist Labor Party, 10, 12, 51, 74, 75, 209
Socialist Party of America: 4–12 passim, 13–16, 17–26 passim, 33, 34, 35, 36, 37–42, 47, 51, 53–54, 65, 66, 74–83, 97, 106, 107, 109, 119, 122, 124–41 passim, 145, 212, 214, 219, 220–32. 234–39, 255–58, 271–82, 283, 285; Children's Strike Fund of, 102; Committee on Immigration of, 232, 234–39; Emergency Convention of, 112, 117n.38; Information Department of, 38, 107; National Committee of, 6, 78, 101, 112, 169, 209, 211, 254, 273; National Congress of, 11, 21, 35, 126, 272; National Convention of 1904, 271; National Convention of 1908, 220–21, 272; National Convention of 1912, 24; National Education Committee of,

56, 102; National Executive Committee of, 7, 11, 17, 21, 74, 80, 84, 99–100, 101, 108, 109, 111, 112, 126, 127, 211, 273, 276, 281; National Office of, 7, 38, 99, 273, 278, 279, 281; Sunday Schools of, 56, 274; Teachers' Placement Bureau of, 103, 278; Unity Convention of (1901), 37, 271; Woman's Department, 271–82; Woman's National Committee of, 17, 18, 21, 23, 25, 56, 78, 98, 100–12, 255–59, 271–82

*Socialist Woman,* 18, 19, 115n.18, 121, 259–64, 267–71, 280

Socialist Women of Greater New York, 253

Socialist Woman's Educational Club (California), 253

Soukup, Franz, 81

South Africa, 13, 209–10, 215

South Carolina, 38

South Slavic Americans, 54, 73

South Slavic Socialist Federation, 11, 105

Spargo, John, 113–14n.6, 221, 234, 239, 255

Soviet Union. *See* Russia

Spies, August, 75

Springfield, Illinois, 36

Stanton, Elizabeth Cady, 277

Stephens, Madge Patton, 277

*Stories of the Cave People* (Marcy), 139

Still, Bayrd, 50

Stokes, J.G. Phelps, 100

Stokes, Rose Pastor, 100

Strunsky, Anna 36

Sun Yat-Sen, 138

Sweden, 12, 200, 222

Syrian Americans, 73

Tennessee, 38

Tenth Congressional District of Missouri, 86

Thaw, Harry, 217

Thelen, David P., 71n.28, 88

Thomas, Elizabeth, 21, 56

Tillman, "Pitchfork" Ben, 183

Tobias, Mary Edna. *See* Marcy, Mary Edna

Tobias, Roscoe B., 134, 135–36

Toledo, Ohio, 188

*Toveritar,* 279, 280

Trotter, Joe William, 69n.10

Twenty-First Assembly District of New York, 40

Twining, Luella, 21, 22, 23 104, 282

Typographical Union, 75

United Cloth Hat and Cap Makers Union, 79

United Garment Workers (Saint Louis), 76

United Mine Workers of Illinois, 81

United Mine Workers Union of America, 38, 126, 128, 224

United States Congress, 206

United States House of Representatives, 21, 37, 38, 42n.1, 48, 53, 66, 76, 79, 85, 106

United States Senate, 80, 85

Universal Negro Improvement Association, 51

Untermann, Ernest, 7, 15, 227, 234, 239

Utah, 108

Van Lear, Thomas, 91

Vardaman, James K., 183. 195

Vierling, Otto, 76–77, 83

Vienna, 23, 105

Villard, Oswald Garrison, 37

Vincent, Terence, 278

Vitikainen, Helen, 279

*Voice of the People,* 85

*Vorwärts (*Wisconsin), 53

Wagenknecht, Alfred, 225, 227

Walden, May, 121, 248–49

Walker, John H., 81

Walling, William English, 36, 37, 284

Wanhope, Joshua, 234, 239

Washington, Booker T., 35, 39, 173

Washington, D.C., 6, 37, 38, 107

Wattles, Florence, 276–77

Wayland, J.A., 18

Weinstein, James, 33

Western Federation of Miners, 21

*Why Catholic Workers Should Be Socialists* (Marcy), 138

Wideawakes, 229

Wikander, Ulla, 20

Willard, Frances E., 277

Williams, John Sharp E., 277

Wilshire, Mrs. Gaylord, 254

*Wilshire's,* 254

Wilson, J. Stitt, 239

Wilson, Woodrow, 8, 39, 190

Wisconsin Loyalty League, 65

Wisconsin State Socialist Party, 57–58, 61, 64

Wisconsin State Teachers Association, 56

Wisconsin Woman Suffrage Association, 56

Wobblies. *See* Industrial Workers of the World

Woman's Day, 22, 24, 103, 105, 275–76

Woman's National Progressive League, Chicago, 253

Woman's Progressive League, Kansas City, 253

Woman's Socialist Club, New York, 253

Woman's Socialist Club, Saint Louis, 253

Woman's Socialist League, Chicago, 253

Woman's Trade Union League, 280

*Women and Economics*, 25

*Women as Sex Vendors* (Tobias and Marcy), 134, 135–36

Women's Christian Temperance Union, 56

*Women's Future*, 25

Wood, Reuben T., 75

Woodbey, George W., 6, 14, 178, 221

Work, John, 113n.6, 117n.37, 277

*Worker*, 209–10

Workingmen's Party (California), 206

World War One, 3, 9, 11, 23, 30, 39, 40, 41, 47, 48, 50, 53, 61, 74, 84, 90, 97, 107, 112, 129

Young People's Socialist League, 79, 82, 104

*Young Socialist Magazine,* 280

Zeh, Nellie M., 276, 277

Zetkin, Clara, 16, 18, 19, 21, 24, 29n.43, 104, 105, 109

American River College Library
4700 College Oak Drive
Sacramento, California  95841